THEY WENT
THATAWAY

THEY WENT THATAWAY

REDEFINING FILM GENRES
A NATIONAL SOCIETY
OF FILM CRITICS
VIDEO GUIDE

Edited by Richard T. Jameson

MERCURY HOUSE
San Francisco

Published in the United States by
Mercury House
San Francisco, California

United States Constitution, First Amendment: Congress shall make no law respecting an establishment of religion, or prohibiting the free exercise thereof; or abridging the freedom of speech, or of the press; or the right of the people peaceably to assemble, and to petition the Government for a redress of grievances.

Cover design: Sharon Smith
Cover illustration: Dan Hubig

Mercury House and colophon are registered trademarks
of Mercury House, Incorporated

Printed on acid-free paper
Manufactured in the United States of America

Library of Congress Cataloging-in-Publication Data
They went thataway : redefining film genres : a National Society of
Film Critics video guide / edited by Richard T. Jameson.
    p.   cm.
Includes index.
ISBN 1–56279–055–2
1. Film genres.   2. Motion pictures—United States—Reviews.   I.
Jameson, Richard T.   II. National Society of Film Critics.
PN1995.T425   1994
791.43'015—dc20   93–15011
                                                                        CIP

5   4   3   2   1

CONTENTS

PREFACE

Genre isn't a word that pops up in every conversation about films—or every review—but the idea is second nature to the movies and our awareness of them. Movies belong to genres much the way people belong to families or ethnic groups. Name one of the classic, bedrock genres—Western, comedy, musical, war film, gangster picture, science fiction, horror—and even the most casual moviegoer will come up with a mental image of it, partly visual, partly conceptual.

It all seems so straightforward. But as I began organizing reviews and articles, a couple of things swiftly became apparent. Some of the most time-honored genres from the first half-century–plus of the American cinema had all but vanished from the modern scene—the musical, for instance, which has been run off by the rock-concert movie and the music video and, perhaps even more decisively, made redundant by the wall-to-wall song accompaniment of nonmusical films. Some genres had undergone significant change—evolved into or been co-opted by more contemporary forms. And others . . . well, that's just it, there *were* others—"genres" that, in some cases, I hadn't even thought to call by name. Women's pictures. Books-into-film. Biopics. Political movies. Baseball movies. Youth movies. Small-town movies. Newspaper movies. Drug movies (psychedelic) and drug movies (nonpsychedelic). Out there in the multiplexes and video stores were new categories of experience, new film galaxies in need of mapping. Maybe, indeed, new genres.

Even before I was inundated by this flood of fresh perspectives, I had resolved that this book would not get nitpicky on the question of what is a genre, what is a subgenre, what is a school, a trend, a style. Life's too short and movies are, even for the most overworked reviewer, too much fun. Distinctions are important but they shouldn't be ironclad. The moviegoer who's comfortable with the conventions can revel in the variations on a theme. Genre works as a taking-off point for directors and viewers alike.

Westerns, for instance, are synonymous with wide-open American spaces traversed by strong, silent horsemen wearing big hats and toting guns, usually sometime between the close of the Civil War and the onset of the twentieth century. Westerns tend to rehearse the same plots (veteran writer Frank Gruber once claimed they numbered only seven) with finite variations and to explore (or just take for granted) the same set of historical, societal, and ethical issues. They may have been made for chickenfeed on the studio backlot with kiddie-matinee stars trading kiddie-matinee dialogue or shot on epic-worthy locations with a literate script and James Stewart or John Wayne in the lead, but "I saw a Western last night" will apply in either case without strain.

Nevertheless, anyone with a modicum of intelligence who has seen more than one Western also knows that the breed is infinitely various in seriousness and quality; that heroes and villains do not all identify themselves by wearing white hats or black hats; and that John Wayne is not always "John Wayne"(check out, for starters, *Stagecoach, Red River, Angel and the Badman, She Wore a Yellow Ribbon, The Searchers, Rio Bravo, The Man Who Shot Liberty Valance*). Two directors as distinctive as Howard Hawks and Anthony Mann can take essentially the same scene written by the same writer, Borden Chase—knifefighting at night with Indians in the underbrush, in *Red River* and *Bend of the River,* respectively—and evoke entirely different dynamics reflecting their particular attitudes to heroism, partnership, and terrain.

Comparable examples could be drawn from any genre. As the moviegoer learns, the more specifically you know a genre, the more you appreciate its continuities and its variety and what both have to do with your satisfaction. Which is to say, the more you get out of movies.

Movies that gave our reviewers a chance to chew on the notion of genre were, therefore, more welcome in this anthology than textbook specimens neatly exemplifying one category. Then, too, I have always been in profound sympathy with the spirit of *Produced and Abandoned,* the debut collaboration of Mercury House and the National Society of Film Critics focusing on worthy films that had somehow fallen through the cracks in the system. In the present book I felt we would accomplish more by calling attention to, say, the satirical science fiction of the little-known *They Live* than by printing one more paean to *E. T.* It's worth noting that many films of the thirties and forties we now take to be supreme classics of their era and genre were critical and box office disappointments on first release.

Speaking of the past, I had hoped that this book would honor the great touchstone films and filmmakers—*Scarface* (1932 version), *Stagecoach, King Kong,* the comedies of Ernst Lubitsch and Preston Sturges, *Double Indemnity, Gunga Din, Laura*—as well as the more contemporary entries in our long-established genres. This proved impractical. Although some of us have become graybeards since taking up Waldo Lydecker's "goosequill dipped in venom," none of us was around to review those films when they first appeared. They—and the irreplaceable talents behind them—are addressed here only indirectly or in overview pieces. (See "Genre Classics," page 347, for a list of key titles.)

I wish, too, that we had the luxury to explore the mutations in American genres when adopted and adapted by foreign film-makers. Certainly the present generation of Hong Kong cinéastes deserves to be represented in any chapter on the aesthetics of the action movie; likewise, the practitioners of the Italian horror film, Gothic black and white or supersaturated Technicolor, in an update of that genre. And the exchange of influences can be fascinating. In France, Julien Duvivier's 1936 gangster picture *Pépé Le Moko* imi-tated characters, compositions, and business in Howard Hawks's *Scarface;* at the turn of the sixties, French New Wave filmmakers and consummate film freaks Jean-Luc Godard and François Truffaut upped the historical and aesthetic ante by imagining characters self-consciously patterning their lives after the iconography and screen destinies of U.S. movie gangsters and film noir characters; a few years later, U.S. screenwriters David Newman and Robert Benton wrote a Depression-outlaw subject for Godard or Truffaut to direct in the States, and even though *Bonnie and Clyde* ended up being directed by an American, Arthur Penn, the New Wavish sensibility stuck—and American cinema would be postmodern forever more. . . . But such cross-pollination must be a subject for another book.

We do get to savor exotic cross-pollination, though. Genre simply doesn't stand still, because the imaginations of the best filmmakers don't. David Cronenberg's 1986 version of *The Fly* is a ferocious and disturbing horror film, and you'll find it filed accordingly in these pages. Yet *The Fly* could also alight in science fiction; it's got a mad scientist, a world-class mutation, a pair of space-age teleporters. But the most audacious generic placement of the movie would go straight to the heart of what's so unexpectedly moving and powerful about it: on top of everything else, *The Fly* is an extraordinary love story, one that takes on virtually metaphysical dimensions as lover watches loved one become someone, some*thing,* else, and the very act of love becomes an act of contamination. A romance for the age of AIDS.

The subtitle of this book reads *Redefining Film Genres,* but what's afoot is less an analytical redefinition by ivory-tower aesthetes than a reinvention in which critics and filmmakers participate mutually. Critics, filmmakers, and now, by all means, readers. *They Went Thataway* isn't the last word on movie genres and genre movies— it's the beginning of a conversation.

That conversation would not be possible without the commitment and cooperation of a great many people. Most obviously, thanks are due to my fellow members of the National Society of Film Critics, who write both for daily newspapers with a space limit of several hundred words per review and for alternative newsmagazines and film journals that permit more room for reflection. The members of the NSFC Book Committee have my undying gratitude: Mike Sragow for suggesting the topic of genres; Sragow, Pete Rainer (NSFC chair), and Jay Carr for strategic advice on the book-editing process and invaluable suggestions for the "Genre Classics" section at the end of the book; and Mike Wilmington for talking genre theory with me and, most of all, for writing an indispensable article on Howard Hawks especially for this volume. *Film Comment* contributing editor Kathleen Murphy read, and offered discerning film comment on, the various introductions. Tom Cucinotta saved me some keyboarding by converting articles from an alien computer mode. On the publishing end, Mercury House rates heartfelt appreciation for its interest in the delightful tradition of bringing out NSFC anthologies; in particular, developmental editor David Peattie and editorial assistant Sarah Malarkey were perceptive and gracious in helping move the present project from castle-in-the-air to workable reality. And back on NSFC ground, I am deeply grateful to Stephen Schiff for having had the foresight to write a scintillating kickoff piece for this book eleven years before the book was ever thought of.

RTJ

INTRODUCTION:
THE REPEATABLE EXPERIENCE

Stephen Schiff

In 1980, a curious event occurred. From all corners of the American film industry, a fanfare arose announcing the return of the Western. There were going to be Westerns in abundance, Westerns of infinite variety and appeal. The stigma that had scarred the genre for years would vanish, and we would all ride the dusty range again. The merchandising prospects were staggering: boots, belts, scarves, ten-gallon hats—maybe even twenty-gallon hats, allowing for inflation. And then along they came, some at a gallop, some limping behind, until 1981 was upon us. *The Long Riders, Tom Horn, Bronco Billy, The Legend of the Lone Ranger, Cattle Annie and Little Britches.* And finally, the biggest of them all, *Heaven's Gate.*

To recite those names is to recall the films' fate. The fact is, American audiences didn't *want* Westerns anymore, and no prodigies of merchandising could change that. A whole genre—perhaps the greatest—had died, and there was nothing anyone in Hollywood could do about it. It wasn't the first time the American film industry had misjudged the public's taste for genres. In the late sixties, for instance, the popularity of *The Sound of Music* and *Mary Poppins* spawned a slew of big-budget musicals—*Star!, Dr. Dolittle, Goodbye Mr. Chips, Paint Your Wagon,* and so forth—that no one wanted to see. But to my knowledge Hollywood had never tried to revive a genre wholesale, out of the ether, the way it did with the

Western. And what it discovered in the process was that the old notions of genre no longer worked. Genre had exploded.

There was a time when the development of genre was relatively predictable. When moviegoing was an American habit, genre films begat genre films. If a movie did well at the box office, the studios churned out more of the same. In fact, the more commercial a national cinema became, the more diverse and profound its genres, which is why the American film industry has produced such an embarrassment of riches: the gangster movie, the Western, the detective movie, the musical, the war movie, the prison movie, the screwball comedy, the weepie, the horror movie, the science fiction movie, the film noir. Genre used to be integral to the studio system: if the studio needed a Western, you got assigned to it and the assigned genre was one of the boundaries you worked within, along with the assigned budget, stars, and script. For a fine director like Howard Hawks or Anthony Mann, directing a genre film was probably a bit like being a blues musician who could wring sublimity out of three chords and a standard 4/4 groove. The director of a Western had certain costumes and settings, character types, and even themes to play with, for those were what the audience expected to see. It was a tiny arena, and a real artist could load a great deal into it.

In fact, there was something almost touching about the thoughtfulness an inspired director could bring to a genre picture (and here is where auteurism and genre criticism mesh). Part of the vast emotional resonance of a film like John Ford's *The Searchers* ('56) or Hawks's *Red River* ('48) comes from the almost tender way the director handles the weary, comfortable tools of the trade—the hats, the six-guns, the brooding Plains. Working within a genre, to the genre's enhancement, brought to the fore a kind of nobility in an artist: a humility, a craftsmanship, a willingness to submit to discipline. The modest adherence to genre belongs to another age, when traditional codes of honor—macho values, patriotic values, even paramilitary values—were fashionable. Men like Hawks and Ford would pooh-pooh the notion that they were *artistes.* They spoke of themselves the way troupers (or troopers) might. There was a job to be done and, by God, they were there to do it.

It's hard to imagine a Francis Coppola or a Paul Schrader talking that way. During the late sixties and early seventies a combination of forces conspired to move Hollywood from the studio era (or, more correctly, the poststudio era) into the Auteur Age. The studios became subsidiaries of conglomerates, and their heads became businessmen, corporate types with law degrees and MBAs. The influence of film criticism—the French variety in particular—catalyzed a certain focus of attention, even within the industry, on the director. And the directors often came from film schools, where they had studied genres and styles historically, and so brought to the movies a new self-consciousness. Like all modernist artists, the directors of the New Hollywood wanted to explode film history, to create ultimates and apotheoses, and to have the last word.

In other arts, modernism meant the systematic demolition of primary forms: tonality in music; representationalism and decoration in art and architecture; narrative, realism, and emotionalism in the novel and the theater. But in the movies, the current of cultural history is always a bit sluggish. The true modernists of film mostly whoosh by outside the mainstream, embellishing movie history but rarely affecting its course. The avant-gardists of film are always easier to discuss with reference to the plastic arts than to what's happening at the movies. The conundrum may be biological. For reasons that probably have to do with how it feels to sit in a darkened room and stare at a pattern of light that passes in front of you just once, movies are inextricably tied to storytelling. In the world of the cinema, the avant-garde is just another genre.

And yet I would argue that the directors of the New Hollywood brought their own modernism to the movies. Instead of attacking primary forms, they took on secondary forms: genres. In *The Wild Bunch* ('69), Sam Peckinpah responded to the Western's fatigue by announcing its death—and then paying a farewell homage to its myths and values. In *Bonnie and Clyde* ('67), Arthur Penn and screenwriters Robert Benton and David Newman turned the gangster genre inside out, transporting it from its urban setting to the countryside (where it united with its cousin, the Western), changing the undercurrent of twisted sexuality into a search for sexual health, exposing the audience's complicity in violence, forging a new, naturalistic language to replace the traditional Runyonesque argot, and transforming the saga of the gangster as a satanic Horatio Alger bent on social dominion into a lament—for the outsider who craves only social acceptance.

After Penn and Peckinpah, the deluge. Directors of the Auteur Age no longer worked *within* the old genres, they worked *on* them. Robert Altman tore into the war movie (*M*A*S*H,* '70), the

Western (*McCabe and Mrs. Miller,* '71), the detective picture (*The Long Goodbye,* '73), the film noir (*Thieves Like Us,* '74), the musical (*Nashville,* '75), and, with much less success, the screwball comedy (*A Wedding,* '77). *Little Big Man, The Missouri Breaks, Bad Company, The Shootist, Jeremiah Johnson, The Great Northfield, Minnesota Raid*—nearly every Western of the seventies was *about* the genre, just as *What's Up, Doc?* and *Paper Moon* were about thirties comedy and movies like *The Late Show* and *The Big Fix* were about the detective movie. In the *Godfather* pictures, Francis Coppola apotheosized the gangster film in a way that proved nearly terminal. In *Blazing Saddles,* Mel Brooks dealt a punishing blow to the Western.

With *Blazing Saddles* ('73) and Woody Allen's early pictures (not to mention the television antics of Carol Burnett and others), the genre spoof became an entrenched form—and a death knell. No one could take, say, the detective genre seriously after it had been turned on its head for so many years. Except perhaps as nostalgia. And one can't call the latter-day versions of *Farewell My Lovely* ('75) or *The Big Sleep* ('78) "true inheritors" of the detective genre, any more than *Body Heat* ('81) or the remake of *The Postman Always Rings Twice* ('81) are true films noirs. It's not a question of whether you like them or not. It's a matter of ontology. When a being is aware of itself, it becomes a different being. And even though *Body Heat* is a very good movie, it's not a true film noir because it's too much *about* the form—as *Double Indemnity* ('44) and *D.O.A.* ('49) and *Out of the Past* ('47) never were and never could be.

As it does always and everywhere, TV took its toll. When the mass audience was regularly exposed to "Bonanza," "Gunsmoke," "Rawhide," "Wagon Train," "The Wild Wild West," and so on, it realized how limited and boring the Western could be. Westerns had been growing increasingly flippant and self-aware since at least the fifties (perhaps the greatest blow to the dignity of the genre was the sight of Dean Martin in cowboy togs). The Clint Eastwood spaghetti Westerns and that gonzo midnight movie *El Topo* ('71) played on the form to make porno-philosophical jokes about violence. And in the year of *The Wild Bunch,* 1969, a much more popular Western, *Butch Cassidy and the Sundance Kid,* used the Western setting in a way that fairly trumpeted its quaintness.

What honor was left the humble oater? Western values had long since gone out of style or been condemned outright. All those savage, ululating Indians rubbed against the grain of racial concern.

The macho-loner ethic died at the hands of feminism and Vietnam. And an era of conspiracy and corruption made us doubt the plain-spoken heroism of Gary Cooper, John Wayne, and Henry Fonda. As the new directors forced us to look at it over and over again, in increasingly harsh light, the Western began to make us uncomfortable. It had become a relic of our innocence.

As the old genres burned, there were stirrings in their ashes. A few new genres, like the disaster movie and the abominable-animal thriller, proliferated, though they were too limited to last. Other genres were vivified by the availability of new technology—the horror movie, for instance, and the science fiction picture. Still others began to use genre as if it were a recombinant nucleic acid to create new forms: the paranoid conspiracy-monster-disaster-buddy picture (*Jaws*, '75), or the religious–sci-fi–fighter-pilot–monster–space fantasy (*Star Wars*, '77).

The recombinant-genre films carry us beyond the self-conscious explosion of forms. A movie like *Star Wars* can give birth to what looks like a new genre (in fact, *Star Wars* is the source of a genre that transcends cinema: the video game), but it doesn't act the way genres act. In *Star Wars*, George Lucas doesn't work within or even on genre—he *plugs in* genre, flashing its proven elements at us as though they were special effects. The genre explorations of the early seventies depended on the audience's awareness of detective movies, Westerns, and monster movies, but the recombinant-genre movies delight in the viewer's ignorance. The audience for *Outland* ('81) doesn't necessarily know from *High Noon,* and the crowds that flock to *Raiders of the Lost Ark* ('81) may never have heard of Lash LaRue or Tailspin Tommy. Parts of old genres replace the nuts and bolts of narrative that used to keep movies running. More and more, genre becomes a secret junkyard.

But maybe one can look at the manipulations of the seventies in another way. Far from strangling the genres, the attention the New Hollywood directors focused on them probably kept them alive because, as far as the audience was concerned, they were dead already. In the studio era, the mass audience didn't care much about whether a director could wrest new beauties from a limited form. What it wanted was a reliable, consistent product—a repeatable experience. To some degree, then as now, star and genre were inextricable: If you went to a Garbo movie, you knew what you were getting. And if you went to a John Wayne movie, it was either a Western or a war picture; and if it were neither (if it were *The*

Barbarian and the Geisha, for instance), then you *didn't* go, and the movie flopped.

In the sixties and seventies, television took over the task of providing repeatable experiences. TV series grabbed old genres and drove them into the ground. In fact, genre scarcely exists now in the eyes of the mass audience. Or, rather, it exists only where it can provide repeatable experiences that aren't available on television: pornography, psycho-killer hack-'em-ups, and space fantasy, which, because it's so technology-intensive, is generally too expensive for the small screen and, moreover, looks terrible there. The "Battlestar Galactica" TV series failed, I suspect, because television made miniatures of spacecraft look exactly like miniatures of spacecraft.

Star vehicles, too, remain a genre form because if you want to see a Burt Reynolds car-chase comedy, you have to go to the movies; Burt doesn't do much TV. Neither does Clint Eastwood or Woody Allen. If you head out to a Jill Clayburgh or Jane Fonda or Richard Pryor–Gene Wilder picture, you know what you'll see. Star is still genre. And when it isn't—when Reynolds makes a *Rough Cut,* or Eastwood a *Bronco Billy,* or Clayburgh a *Luna,* or Fonda a *Rollover*—the audience stays home.

There are those who will argue that genre is *not* ailing, that new genres are being spawned every year. They'll cite the yuppie marital-breakup movie (*An Unmarried Woman, Starting Over, Kramer vs. Kramer, Shoot the Moon*), or perhaps the Broadway weepie (*Tribute, Whose Life Is It Anyway?, On Golden Pond*), or the family-targeted fantasy (*Time Bandits, Clash of the Titans, Dragonslayer, The Great Muppet Caper*). But those aren't genres in the true sense. Perhaps they'd best be called "trends." Trends reflect events, social forces, coincidences. And, all too often, they indicate the dwindling number of subjects deemed safe enough to spend a movie-sized budget on.

But no one turns to his wife and says, "Call the sitter, honey, there's a new yuppie marital-breakup picture at the Bijou." People go to marital-breakup movies because they think they will see something of their lives in them. And that isn't precisely what attracted people to the detective movies or screwball comedies or films noirs. In the heyday of the studio, moviegoers liked genres not because they were relevant or because they were big cultural events or because they were the thing everyone was talking about that week. People went to a genre movie because of its movieness, because they knew it would make them feel happy or sad or just plain entertained in a way that only a certain kind of movie could. The withering of genre may take that direct and simple pleasure away from us. And if it does, the film industry will have lost a piece of its soul.

Film Comment, March–April 1982

POSTSCRIPT: Westerns, of course, don't look quite as passé as they did in 1982—one called *Dances With Wolves* won the Best Picture Oscar in 1991 and another called *Unforgiven* won it in 1993. And, as usual, the success of these two appeared to open the floodgates for a dozen more. Still, *Dances With Wolves* was less a variation on a time-honored genre than a kind of ecological prestige picture—David Lean goes Green. And many of the Westerns being cranked out as a response to the genre's new success seem also to be, as it were, oaters that don't so much perform within the genre as take off from it—black Westerns, feminist Westerns, and so on. *Unforgiven,* on the other hand, was a genuine meta-Western, like *The Wild Bunch* and *McCabe and Mrs. Miller* before it, a masterpiece that examined the Western myth in the light of day, pointed out the holes and failings in it, and then, by cover of one awesome rain-swept night, returned it to its terrible glory. If Hollywood does indeed produce a vital and authentic revival of the genre (and that still doesn't appear likely), *Unforgiven* will be the film to beat.

The gangster film has looked somewhat livelier during the last decade, what with *Prizzi's Honor, GoodFellas, Godfather III, Menace II Society,* and the continuing efforts of Brian DePalma (*Scarface, The Untouchables,* and *Carlito's Way*). All of which makes a certain amount of sense, for the myth of the gangster's inexorable rise is really the American Dream seen in a distorted mirror. Gangster movies are about clawing your way to the top of the urban jungle, so it's not surprising that they suddenly seemed relevant again in the eighties, which were about much the same thing.

A handful of other recombinant genres have emerged as well, but mainly in the secret-junkyard vein. (The most boggling of all, perhaps, are the Teenage Mutant Ninja Turtle films: chopsocky–cartoon–animal–monster–boys'-book–sci-fi–beauty-and-the-beast–buddy fantasies.) The psycho-killer hack-'em-up has combined with the domestic melodrama to create a form I have called the Indoor Psycho movie—films like *The Hand That Rocks the Cradle, Unlawful Entry, Pacific Heights,* and *Single White Female.* And the preteen comedy, which is not so much a recombinant genre as a recycled one (it has its roots in the live-action Disney comedies of the fifties—*The Shaggy Dog* and *The Absent-Minded Professor* and so forth), has emerged as a reliable source of studio income in the wake of *Home Alone.* Unlike adults, who like to see a picture once, or teenagers, who like to go two or three times, preteens like to gobble down their favorite movies five, ten, fifteen times over—hauling their parents with them again and again, and then buying, not renting, the thing in video.

Finally, it's remarkable how out-of-date these reflections look when you get to the part about "star vehicles." The only star I listed who can still command a genre is Clint Eastwood (Burt Reynolds now does almost nothing *but* TV, and the careers of the other stars I mentioned are virtually defunct). Still, the point remains: substitute Arnold Schwarzenegger, Kevin Costner, Tom Cruise, Eddie Murphy, and Sylvester Stallone (but only in an action picture, not in a comedy), and the star vehicle still proves the sort of repeatable experience available only in the movies.

FILM NOIR AND GANGSTER FILMS

ilm noir may be the hottest genre in American filmmaking these days—a strange development when you consider that, until comparatively recently, few Americans knew the term "film noir" at all.

That includes the people who created the breed. The classic period of film noir extended from the early forties into the mid fifties, but no director of that time ever passed a colleague on the studio lot and called, "Hey, baby, I hear they're giving you a film noir to do next." It was French audiences of the late forties, catching up on the half-decade of Hollywood films they had been denied during the war, who noticed a decisive shift in tone from the prewar American cinema: a color shift, a darkening—stylistically and spiritually—manifest in films as otherwise diverse as *Citizen Kane* and *I Wake Up Screaming*, *Shadow of a Doubt* and *Mildred Pierce*, *The Letter* and *The Killers*, *Gilda* and *Detour*. The world of these films (from a variety of genres and budgetary levels) was bleaker, yet more dynamic for it. Shadows were deeper, angles sharper, camera movements and depth of focus more aggressively peculiar; stories had a way of beginning at a dead end and winding back to show how they had arrived there, with no last-minute reprieve for the hero and/or heroine; indeed, in these films hero and villain were harder to tell apart, sometimes even cohabiting in the same character—especially when it came to *heroine* and villain.

There was a new bloom in the Hollywood hothouse—lush, poisonous, fragrant with corruption, fascinatingly exotic even as it somehow took movies closer to imperfect real life than they were wont to go. No one had consciously planted it, but there it was. Having recognized the phenomenon, the French knew what to call it—*film noir:* black film, dark film.

Not that the term became current on this side of the Atlantic till much later, when English-language critics began to account for the fact that some of the most disreputable movies of Hollywood's Golden Age now looked like the era's richest and liveliest films (whereas many "prestige pictures" seemed like so much overstuffed furniture in a dusty attic). In his definitive Spring 1972 *Film Comment* article "Notes on Film Noir," critic and filmmaker-to-be Paul Schrader characterized noir as "American movies . . . in the throes of their deepest and most creative funk." That funk had its origins in a welter of historical, sociopolitical, and cinematic influences, many of which are outlined in Peter Rainer's piece "On Psychonoir" later in this chapter. Suffice it now to echo Schrader's point that film noir was not a genre (à la the Western, the screwball comedy, the gangster picture) so much as it was a style, a climate of mind and soul, a moment in history. Around 1953 the moment ran out; the dominant tone of American movies changed again; even cop films and crime films and movies about hard-luck heroes (Brando, Newman, et al.) no longer gave off the air of fatalism and the visual reek of the noirs. But noir is nothing if not perverse. Only after the bloom was off the belladonna did this nongenre cast up, in Schrader's opinion, "the masterpiece of film noir," Robert Aldrich's corrosive *Kiss Me Deadly,* in 1955 and, in 1958, "noir's epitaph," Orson Welles's nightmarishly phantasmagorical *Touch of Evil.*

But if film noir has been over with for three decades and counting, what is it that has been on view lately in the multiplexes of the land? For "film noir" is a household phrase now. Not only moviemakers and movie fans but also journalists, fashion mavens, rock aficionados, and other trendoids love to bandy it about. Music video directors have found noir an eminently appropriatable "look," even slipping into anachronistic black and white now and again; TV producers take notes from it to pump up the "cinematic" value of what was long a visually dull medium. Sometimes the results are exciting (say, the first season of Michael Mann's TV series "Miami Vice" and "Crime Story"). But too many aspiring noirs of our day deserve to be labeled not film noir but "designer noir." It's not a vision, it's attitude. You don't make it, you put it on and wear it.

Even honest filmmakers are self-aware about noir as classic *noiristes* never were. They live in a fallen, postnoir world, in which film noir *is* now a genre, with forms and conventions explicitly understood by the people who operate in it. But within this self-awareness, there's room for legitimate attempts to *reinvent* film noir, *reimagine* it in terms relevant to changed times and a changed film industry.

So on with the reinventing! Our survey begins with Carrie Rickey's short but comprehensive history of the gangster film, one of the classic genres that historically fed into noir and that has also enjoyed renewed prominence. Michael Sragow and Michael Wilmington discuss two epic gangster pictures of modern times, Sergio Leone's *Once Upon a Time in America* and Martin Scorsese's *Good-Fellas,* respectively. The Coen brothers' *Miller's Crossing* (reviewed by the editor) and Quentin Tarantino's *Reservoir Dogs* (Kenneth Turan) are movies *about* gangsters that take their imaginative thrust from the realm of noir—especially in their almost literary interest in the mysteries of character, and an impulse toward stylization as an article of both artistic and existential faith.

Moving into film noir proper, Peter Rainer enlarges our understanding of classic noir and posits the post-Vietnam, post-Reagan nineties as a logical time for noir to reassert itself. Lawrence Kasdan's *Body Heat* (Stephen Schiff) shows how to build on the legacy of films noirs past; Taylor Hackford's *Against All Odds* (RTJ), how not to. Peter Rainer finds Alan Rudolph's *Trouble in Mind* reimagining not only the myth of noir but also the sort of world, and time frame, in which it belongs. Time frame is also artfully elusive in *The Grifters,* which seems to transpire in a fifties version of the nineties —or vice versa; Julie Salamon praises this sleekest film adaptation of pulp writer Jim Thompson. And in his piece "On Copping a Plea," Dave Kehr considers the changing dynamics of movie cops and confirms that, somewhere in the night, we are all on dangerous ground.

ON MOB RULE

Carrie Rickey

Looking for a career instead of just another job? Consider a profession that offers unusual security and advancement. Benefits are impressive, hours flexible, starting salaries high, tax advantages unsurpassed (let's just say your income would be tax-free). Consider that this business is organized on the principles of brotherhood. Respect for your elders. Tradition. Loyalty. Honor. Consider that this diversified multinational larger than IBM wants you, even though you may lack a high school diploma. Energy and discipline are the only skills required, although knowledge of firearms could be useful. Consider, too, that the syndicate—excuse me, corporation—has an unmatched record in making nobodies into somebodies.

Sound like an offer you can't refuse? Consider yourself one of the Family.

Moralists say crime doesn't pay. Well, it does at the box office. Ever since the Snapper Kid strutted through D. W. Griffith's *The Musketeers of Pig Alley* ('12), hassling Lillian Gish while he slipped a wad of bills to a grateful cop, gangsters have made law-abiding citizens look square. Cigarette dangling from his leering lips, hat rakishly tilted, the Snapper Kid (played by Elmer Booth) epitomized the style of the new century: urban, kinetic, slanted. Next to him, languid Gish was a relic from the Victorian age.

Since the Snapper Kid's day, Hollywood has mythologized three types of heroes: the cowboy, the cop, and the gangster. Guys with guns in a world without women. Most durable is the gangster; without him, the cop has no adversary. And when he's also a modern cowboy whose frontier is the city—or, as with Michael Corleone in *The Godfather Part III,* the world—the gangster gives us hero and villain in the same character. That's why the taste for gangsters has abated only briefly—during World Wars I and II, when real armed conflicts sated any pangs for reel mob wars.

But at the end of this year, which offered more gangster movies (thirteen) than any since 1931 (when forty were released), you have to ask yourself, do I really like eating lead? Yeah, you do. You're in favor of gun control, just not on the screen. Movie gangsters evoke your simultaneous desire and fear. You'd love to live like them, but you're afraid to die like them.

You like it when Chester Morris, as the pirate—a euphemism for bootlegger—in *Corsair* (directed by Roland West, '31), rationalizes what he does for a living: "It doesn't matter how you make your money. It's how much you have when you quit." You like it when Paul Muni, as Tony Camonte in the 1932 *Scarface* (directed by Howard Hawks), blasts his tommy gun, grinning, "Get outta my way, I'm spittin'." You like it when Jack Nicholson as Charley Partanna in *Prizzi's Honor* (John Huston, '85) goes ballistic—in both senses of the expression—in the sack with his hit woman wife, Kathleen Turner.

But it's not only the fusillade that attracts you. Nor is it the dollars, the defiance, the strategies that would boggle a chessmaster. Nor is it, as essayist Robert Warshow suggested, the double satisfaction of participating vicariously in the gangster's sadism and then seeing that sadism turned against him. It's also this: in America, outlaws are tolerated—and celebrated—as long as they keep blazing new frontiers. The history of the gangster film is the history of where the frontier is, both morally and physically. For what is the mob movie but the saga of an enterprising pioneer seeing how far he (yes, it's almost invariably a he) goes before getting caught? From the Snapper Kid to Michael Corleone, the evolution of the movie gangster is the evolution of America, a nation riddled with bullets and contradictions.

In his earliest screen incarnation, the movie gangster was a social problem to be solved. Mob films such as *Are They Born or Made?* ('14) linked gangsters with corrupt pols. In D. W. Griffith's *Intolerance* ('16), a gangster exerts his political influence to frame the "Boy" (Robert Harron) who tries to go straight. Sometimes the mobsters posed double threats, as in *The Gangsters of New York* ('14), in which the saloon is the capital of machine politics. Get rid of the saloon, the film implied, and good morals and good government will bloom.

Such logic led in 1920 to Prohibition, which, ironically, gave real-life gangsters significant employment opportunities. By 1926 illegal liquor was a $3.6 billion business. That same year, Al Capone made $105 million, which, adjusted for inflation—$650 million in today's dollars—remains the highest gross income a private citizen (including Michael Milken) has ever enjoyed. Al Capone's career inspired more films than any other gangster: at least seven features, including *Little Caesar* (Mervyn LeRoy, '30) and *Scarface,* which makes him more popular than even Abraham Lincoln. Hollywood's preference for Dishonest Al over Honest Abe suggests that Capone's money and his IRS troubles were images every American could aspire to and identify with.

Capone was not heroized by name during his heyday because between 1920 and 1933 very few movies acknowledged bootleggers and rumrunners. The Hays Office, that self-censoring arm of the movie industry, forbade films undermining Prohibition. Nonetheless, *Twelve Miles Out* ('27)—the distance from the coast at which bootleggers loaded their schooners—starred John Gilbert as a dashing rumrunner who, before perishing, earns the devotion of a gaga Joan Crawford. In his jaunty trenchcoat and cap, Gilbert is the gangster as romantic hero, the first of a screen type that would be more popular after Prohibition. (After all, he was just guaranteeing citizens their inalienable right to a snort.)

But the first modern gangster film is generally regarded to be Josef von Sternberg's moody *Underworld* (also '27). Working from a screenplay by Chicago crime reporter Ben Hecht, von Sternberg depicted in *Underworld* a mirror image of the upper world. A successful gang boss (lout George Bancroft) hires a failed lawyer, now a skid row drunk (fop Clive Brook), as his henchman. Like Vito Corleone, whose violence and sensitivity are shown in *The Godfather* as he contemplates vengeance while fondling a cat, Bull Weed (Bancroft) in *Underworld* is equally capable of brutal murder and tenderness toward the kitten he adopts. Bull is a stray attracted to other strays, like Feathers (Evelyn Brent), whom he elects queen of what looks like the gangster prom. What's striking about the film that won an Oscar for first-time screenwriter Hecht is how poetically von Sternberg evoked Bull, his moll, and his henchman as trusting members of a family.

The gangster soon became a two-fisted symbol of American enterprise, proof that even during the Depression upward mobility was still possible. Pug-ugly and pugnacious, Edward G. Robinson interpreted Little Caesar as the nation's first antihero. Had he lived in the 1870s, Rico Bandello would have underpaid steelworkers while building a legitimate empire, but in 1930 the only way to achieve status was by gunning down the crime commissioner. Once hired-gun Rico becomes top gun, he is swiftly brought low; when shot dead by the cops, he looks like nothing but a bum. While the Hays Office believed *Little Caesar* was moralizing that crime doesn't pay, what movies like it did was to link success with death, a hopeless message for hopeless times.

The Public Enemy (William Wellman, '31) reinforced this message while making a star of the charismatic James Cagney. His insolent Tommy (as in gun?) Powers possesses a smile like a smirk and a saunter that repels bullets and attracts dames. As a kid, Tommy rejects school as "learning to be poor." While his brother Mike enlists in World War I, Tommy enlists in the gang wars. When Mike accuses him of being a murderer, Tommy answers: "You didn't get those medals holding hands with Germans." Murder is murder. Tommy enjoys the perks of his profession: booze and broads. He gets Mae Clarke and Jean Harlow. Tommy buzzes, full of sting and life. Despite the Hays Office, his inevitable death is preferable to his brother's half life. At least while Tommy lived, he lived.

Unlike Rico Bandello, who is killed by lawmen, or Tommy Powers, slain by a rival gang, *Scarface*'s Tony Camonte finds his greatest enemy is himself. His lust for his sister (Ann Dvorak) makes him behave recklessly, and his own hubris does him in. He is the first gangster tragic hero, which elevates him above contemporary events in Chicago and links him to the great figures of literature. In the film's chiaroscuro, he lurks in moral shadow.

The Hays Office was beside itself. The unholy trinity of *Caesar/ Enemy/Scarface* was glorifying violence. So the Office's guidelines for Hollywood productions became rules: from now on, the gangbuster, not the gangster, would be heroized. Thus, Public Enemy Jimmy Cagney became a Fed in *G-Men* (William Keighley, '35). And that same year, in John Ford's charming comedy *The Whole Town's Talking*, Edward G. Robinson played a dual role as a mild accountant and the ruthless mobster he helps trap. Still, the accountant enjoys being confused for the killer, proving that, as critic Carlos Clarens put it, "in every milquetoast beats the heart of a mobster."

But censorship had a perverse effect. By banishing the gangster as central character, it pushed him into the world of mythology. "The last great apostle of rugged individualism"—that's how poet Leslie Howard exalts killer Duke Mantee (Humphrey Bogart) in *The Petrified Forest* (Archie Mayo, '36). To another character, "He ain't a gangster, he's an old-time desperado. Gangsters is foreign. He's an American"—not a Greek, Irish, Italian, or Jewish immigrant, whom bigots saw as un-American.

The gangster achieved even saintliness in a pair of excellent Raoul Walsh films. *The Roaring Twenties* ('39) depicted bootlegger Jimmy Cagney as a good guy who turned bad because he couldn't find work after the war. *High Sierra* ('41) starred Humphrey Bogart as Roy Earle, a relic of the Dillinger gang. In both films, gangsterism is as basic to American history as the world wars and the Depression. In both, the gangster seeks redemption. Cagney dies for a noble act on the steps of the church. Bogart finds his last refuge in the Sierra Nevada, where he cleanses his soul of urban squalor. And in both films, each loves the good girl who rejects him (Priscilla Lane, Joan Leslie) and rejects the "bad" girl who loves him (Gladys George, Ida Lupino).

With few exceptions—Lurene Tuttle starring in *Ma Barker's Killer Brood* ('60), Shelley Winters as Barker in Roger Corman's *Bloody Mama* ('70)—women are a footnote to the mob movie. One reason the gangster genre is so popular is that it reinforces the impossibility of guys working it out with gals. It also validates the expression of male rage toward females. Violence toward women offers the moments everyone remembers best: Cagney squeezing grapefruit on Mae Clarke's mug in *The Public Enemy*, Eduardo Ciannelli disfiguring Bette Davis's face in *Marked Woman* (Lloyd Bacon, '37), Lee Marvin tossing scalding coffee at Gloria Grahame in *The Big Heat* (Fritz Lang, '53).

During World War II, the gangster movie again took a powder. Afterward, mobsters got psychoanalyzed, as in *Kiss of Death* (Henry Hathaway, '47), when mob informer Victor Mature complains to D.A. Brian Donlevy, "Your side of the fence is almost as dirty as mine." "With one difference," returns Donlevy: "We only hurt bad people." And Richard Widmark bears him out. In *Kiss of Death* Widmark creates the screen's first psychotic gangster, Tommy Udo, who cheerfully shoves a wheelchair-bound granny down the stairs. Perhaps the most memorable psycho-gangster was the now-jowly Cagney in Raoul Walsh's *White Heat* ('49) as Cody Jarrett, whose best friend was his Ma (Margaret Wycherly). This model son likes to sit in Ma's lap when not pumping his rivals full of bullets. The film's still-startling coda is a perversion of the American success story: wounded Cody stands on a flaming oil tank, crowing "Made it, Ma. Top of the world!" Shot by police, the tank explodes into a mushroom cloud. (The link between gangster and Bomb would be made even more explicit in Robert Aldrich's 1955 *Kiss Me Deadly*, where mobster Albert Dekker traffics in nuclear explosives.)

While Tommy and Cody were characterized as social undesirables, returning gangster Edward G. Robinson as Johnny Rocco in *Key Largo* (John Huston, '48) was politically undesirable, humiliated at having been deported during the war, "like I was a dirty Red or something." Rocco presaged the dark symbolism of screen gangsterism in the fifties, when virtually every movie mobster was evil. When communists replace mobsters as public enemies, *The Mob* (Robert Parrish, '51), *On the Waterfront* (Elia Kazan, '54), and *The Garment Jungle* (Robert Aldrich and Vincent Sherman, '57) suggest that gangsters are communists and that they are infiltrating unions. If that weren't scary enough, *The Big Heat* terrifyingly implies that their next frontier is the American suburb. Fritz Lang's potent vigilante fantasy stars Glenn Ford as a cop whose loving wife is murdered because he's too close to cracking a crime ring. When the police force won't let him use the unorthodox (i.e., illegal) methods he needs to fight gangsters, Ford quits in frustration and enlists disillusioned mob moll Gloria Grahame to exact his revenge.

During the 1950s, the most novel development of the screen gangster was flannel-suited Mr. Brown (Richard Conte) in Joseph H. Lewis's *The Big Combo* ('55). The mob boss resembles a powerful businessman. He counsels his henchmen to use creative persuasion. "I'm trying to run an impersonal business," explains the charismatic Mr. Brown. "Killing is very personal." Mr. Brown's businesslike facade erases the boundaries between legitimacy and illegitimacy.

During the next decade, Hollywood gangster dramas tended toward nostalgic biographies of past mobsters, as if to say organized crime existed then, not now: *Baby Face Nelson* (Don Siegel, '57), *Al Capone* (Richard Wilson, '59), *Pretty Boy Floyd* (Herbert J. Leder, '60), *The Rise and Fall of Legs Diamond* (Budd Boetticher, '60), and *Mad Dog Coll* (Burt Balaban, '61). Only occasionally was there symbolic evidence that the contemporary gangster, like *The Big Combo*'s Mr. Brown, had completely integrated himself into American business. One such case is Sam Fuller's pulpy *Underworld U.S.A.* ('61). No longer is the American gangster a habitué of urban streets and back alleys. Now he is comfortably housed in a gleaming skyscraper, just like any other American conglomerate CEO. When a freelance hood (Cliff Robertson) hellbent on avenging his criminal father's murder takes on the syndicate, he is as successful as the grandmother who challenges the electric company.

Francis Ford Coppola's *The Godfather* ('72) depicted the transition from the Old Country, honor-bound world of Don Vito Corleone (Marlon Brando) to the modern impersonal corporation headed by his son Michael (Al Pacino). Coppola conceived it as an epic and photographed it with Old Master lighting. Family rituals such as weddings and baptisms are intercut with ritual murders and baptisms by gunfire, lending a sacramental authority to the carnage. In *The Godfather* and its equally powerful 1974 sequel, Vito Corleone is a variation on the American success story. He is the immigrant who makes good in the New World, an ethicist and sage who metes out justice and answers to a higher authority than the criminal justice system. Interestingly, in the war-torn America of 1972, Don Corleone is a pacifist who arises from his hospital bed to end a bloody mob conflict by declaring, "The war stops now!" Like any good patriarch, Vito Corleone puts family—and Family—first. The only time we see him kill (in *The Godfather Part II*, played by Robert De Niro), he shoots a Little Italy padrino who threatens his wife and kids, and later dispatches the Sicilian capo who killed his parents. The movie doesn't specify from where the Corleone income and power derives, but you figure it's not just olive oil.

His son's detailed involvement with gambling casinos, prostitution, and other vices makes Michael a less sympathetic character. Michael is a cold-blooded businessman. Where Vito Corleone is a figure who wrests authority away from the Establishment and dispenses justice, Michael strives to legitimize injustice—about as effective a metaphor of American business practices as any gangster movie has ever attempted.

The extraordinary success of the *Godfather* sagas naturally prompted many inferior imitators: *Black Godfather* ('74), another *Capone* ('75), and *Lepke* ('75). But, unlike the films of the 1930s, almost no contemporary movie wanted to evoke the modern mob.

An exception was Brian DePalma's 1983 *Scarface,* a remake updated to Miami's Little Havana starring Al Pacino as a Cuban cocaine czar. This *Scarface* was a success tragedy about an immigrant smart enough to corner a commodity but dumb enough to get high on his own supply. As written by Oliver Stone, who likewise characterized Chinese-American ganglords in the 1985 *Year of the Dragon* (directed by Michael Cimino), *Scarface* projected movie gangsters from the past into the present rather than imagining an original vision.

Through most of the eighties, Hollywood dealt with the mob by making fun of it. There was John Huston's dark comedy *Prizzi's*

Honor, in which goddaughter Maerose Prizzi (Anjelica Huston) outwits her paternalistic family, and DePalma's *Wise Guys* ('86), wherein Joe Piscopo and Danny DeVito play two gangsters so dim-witted that a mob boss (Dan Hedaya) sets them up to kill each other. In 1988, David Mamet's *Things Change* and Jonathan Demme's *Married to the Mob* noted similarities between Feds and ganglords. When *Mob* heroine Michelle Pfeiffer complains to FBI chief Trey Wilson, "you guys are just like the mob," he replies, "The mob is run by murdering, thieving, lying psychopaths. We work for the President of the United States of America!"

The comparison between mobster and president was made more seriously in *GoodFellas,* Martin Scorsese's vivid case history of Henry Hill, when the mobster-turned-federal-witness (played by Ray Liotta) explains, "As far back as I remember, I always wanted to be a gangster. To me, it was better than being President of the United States. It meant being somebody in a neighborhood of nobodies." More effectively than any movie since *The Godfather, GoodFellas* rethinks the gangster in symbolic terms. Liotta escorts Lorraine Bracco through the underbelly of the Copacabana, up through the kitchen, and into the dining room, where they are seated at a front-row table. It's nothing less than the odyssey of the American mobster from underworld to ringside seat.

It's no coincidence that six decades after the gangsters exploded on the screens in 1931, another explosion occurred in 1990. Both the thirties and nineties followed decades of excess and boom economy. They share a loss of faith in legitimate institutions, a bust economy, diminishing jobs and expectations. Thus, the gangster movie may have reemerged to suggest that the only way to achieve success is by illegitimate means. Andrew Bergman's comedy *The Freshman* is one of several to say that the mob (as represented by a Vito Corleone look-alike played by Marlon Brando) is more honorable than the FBI. You could argue that that year's mob movies glamorize the gangster at the expense of the lawman. That the gangster has better clothes, all the fun, and most of the good lines. In Sidney Lumet's *Q&A,* police officer Nick Nolte is immoral compared to the honorable ganglord Armand Assante. In the Prohibition-era comedy *Dick Tracy* (directed by Warren Beatty), the bent Big Boy Caprice (Al Pacino) is much more in tune with the times than straight-arrow Tracy (Beatty). Big Boy's philosophy, which he attributes to Abraham Lincoln: "If you ain't for the people, you can't buy the people."

You could argue that 1990's mob movies were a condemnation of eighties materialism and corruption, that the mobsters in *Miller's Crossing* (Joel and Ethan Coen) who buy and sell the mayor and chief of police are not unlike the Charles Keatings who allegedly buy and sell senators. You could argue that that year's gangster films addressed the meltdown in the American melting pot. The ethnic divisions and divisiveness in *Q&A,* where the police department is run by the Irish, who lord it over their black and Latino lieutenants, where the district attorney's office is polarized between Italian and Jewish factions, and where the gangs are run by Puerto Ricans, show you how narrow ethnic loyalties obstruct a wider sense of community.

But isn't it true that whenever we worry about our security, our welfare, even our future, we always conjure images of violence, power, and retribution? When America is afraid of enemies from without, like demon rum or communism, we make the film gangster their symbol, the devil incarnate. When America is afraid of enemies from within, like the failure of its economy or its institutions, we choose the movie mobster for our avenging angel, our desperate grab at hope. This is why once again, in 1990, the commandment was: Honor thy Godfather.

Philadelphia Inquirer, December 23, 1990

ONCE UPON A TIME IN AMERICA

Michael Sragow

Now that it's arrived in its uncut, 227-minute, director-approved form, Sergio Leone's *Once Upon a Time in America* emerges as a pulp masterwork—at once the simplest and most indescribable of movies. In a sense, it's just what the title indicates: a bloody American fairy tale, the gangster movie to end all gangster movies, just as Leone's *Once Upon a Time in the West* ('69) was the ne plus ultra of Westerns. It's about the children of immigrants scraping the bottom of the American melting pot, on New York's Lower East Side. It's about a Jewish criminal kingpin, David "Noodles" Aaronson, who dreams of greatness "once upon a time" and spends the rest of his life wondering why his salad days wilted. Most of all, it's about time itself, and how Noodles learns that it's more important to start making sense of your own life, your own *history,* than it is to cream the competition. And as Noodles, Robert De Niro gives his fullest, most richly textured performance since *Taxi Driver* ('76); he is once again the Great American Actor.

When it was first released, the film was slammed by most critics (myself included); only after this version began wending its way from city to city did it begin turning up on Ten Best lists. You may wonder how a movie could seem so different with eighty-three minutes added. After all, it was easy to see the greatness of *The Seven Samurai* or *Children of Paradise* even when they were initially shown in severely truncated forms. The answer is twofold. First, this is not the kind of classically controlled work those films were, but a bold, lunging effort by an idiosyncratic artist who needs the freedom to sprawl—sometimes self-indulgently, often gloriously. And second, the editors of the studio-approved short version eliminated Leone's (i.e., Noodles's) point of view. They showed a killer instinct for every second of screen time that imbued Leone's narrative with its coherence—and its guttural, poetic intensity.

What played the theaters originally was a failed attempt to put a yarmulke on *The Godfather:* a blow-by-blow account of the rise and fall of Jewish criminals roughly modeled on Bugsy Siegel and Meyer Lansky, who start out rolling drunks and achieve their peak as Prohibition bootleggers. What you see in Leone's version is an audacious combination of shoot-'em-up and memory play: all the gang's tie-ins with rackets and unions, all the double-crosses and contract hits are filtered through Noodles's mind. The movie is framed by his getting stoned in an opium den, and the story skips and jumps across decades, from 1933 to 1968 to 1923 and back again, as Noodles plays Chinese checkers with his past.

In a fairy tale, of course, time is conquered: once the ogre, the wolf, or the wicked stepmother is defeated, the hero is free to live happily ever after—at least until the next challenge. *Once Upon a Time in America,* though, is a film noir fairy tale, and it puts Noodles in that existential prison shared by hard-boiled heroes and villains alike. For most of the movie he's "doing time," whether he's in jail or out of it, and the main antagonist is memory. Even after serving out his sentence for stabbing a cop and killing a competing gangster who had murdered one of his best buddies, Aaronson is haunted by wrong turns and misfires. Not only does he fail to win his upwardly mobile childhood sweetheart, Deborah (Elizabeth McGovern), but in his baffled mixture of anguish and rage he destroys their love by raping her. Not only does he fail to save his hyperactive partner, Max (James Woods), from self-destruction, he is also responsible (he thinks) for Max's murder. This prisoner of time rehabilitates himself three and a half decades after these disasters, when he finally looks the people he's let down in the face. To his surprise, he discovers that he's been truer than they to their shared childhood loyalties. In retrospect he realizes that his life has been an honorable saga: the tragedies he took on his own shoulders were not solely of his making. He learns that everyone's life is in part a work of fiction, a reordering of the past to make the present livable; and he writes himself a mellow epilogue, a wise old man's version of happily-ever-after.

Another director might have turned the same material into a rags-to-riches-to-rags story. Leone transcends clichés through reverie and metaphor, and through a layering of the action that treats the story's several eras like double and triple exposures. He starts *in medias res,* on the eve of Prohibition's end. Noodles, hoping to prevent Max from trying to rob the Federal Reserve Bank, tips off the cops to the gang's last bit of bootlegging. The plan backfires as Max and the other two musketeers, Patsy (James Hayden) and Cockeye (William Forsythe), end up as corpses in the street. Brutal gunsels murder Noodles's mistress (Darlanne Fleugel), torture speakeasy owner and gang mascot Fat Moe (Larry Rapp), and almost trap Noodles in the opium den. He escapes and hurries to a locker that's supposed to hold the gang's money. The briefcase locked inside is stuffed with newspapers instead. He has only enough cash for a one-way ticket to Buffalo. All this is suggested in bursts of action that alternate with glancing audiovisual brushstrokes—glimpses of a coffin-cake labeled PROHIBITION, the blaring of a phone that seems to ring for hours.

We don't even see Noodles's thirty-five years of exile: Leone cuts straight to his return, in 1968. Confused by a mysterious summons from a rabbi, Noodles finds his way back to Fat Moe's, now no longer a kosher deli or a speakeasy, just a timeworn pub—but still with the same Fat Moe. As the two friends put their heads together, the mystifying flow of action starts to cohere. Fat Moe leads Noodles to a back-room apartment adorned with pictures of their old friends, including the famous actress Deborah, the only one to become a big shot. Noodles loosens a brick in a bathroom/storeroom wall and is transformed into the "little cockroach" who used to spy on Deborah as she danced in the warehouse and wiggled out of her tights. Now it's 1923, the year when his life was formed, and Leone's extraordinary cinematographer, Tonino Delli Colli, irradiates the heavy earth-and-soot tones of the ghetto re-creations with an elegiac light. We see the young Noodles (Scott Tiler) as a leader among street kids, getting pocket money out of petty crime while, unseen, his father prays and his mother cries. We see him long in vain for the pristine Deborah (Jennifer Connelly) but settle for Peggy (Julie Cohen), who sells her favors for a charlotte russe a shot. We see him team up with new-boy-in-town Max (Rusty Jacobs) to embarrass Whitey the crooked cop (Richard Foronjy) and Bugsy (James Russo), the neighborhood's top thug. And we see him commit homicide to avenge his tiny friend Dominic (Noah Moazezi), who falls down and dies in Noodles's arms with the pathetic words "Noodles—I slipped."

It's in this flashback section that you first notice the film's biggest problem: aside from scraps of Yiddish and cracks about delicatessen food, there's nothing Jewish about these hoodlums. In fact, they occasionally imitate stage Italians: when Max is at the peak of his glory he buys the throne of a seventeenth-century pope. What turns Leone on are the pictorial possibilities of the ghetto—Chasidic robes and side curls here, Yiddish and Hebrew storefronts there. But it's to his credit that such primal scenes of tenement life as the young boy reading *Martin Eden* in the common lavatory—and ending up playing "looksies, not feelsies" with Peggy—reach the American screen for the first time, despite their presence throughout immigrant literature.

The crux of the movie, though, is not in its social cataclysms but in the metamorphosis of Noodles from a "little cockroach" into a man, the evolution of the reflexes that govern his existence. In an oft-repeated phrase, he and his buddies refuse to "take it up the ass," to be unmanned by the Law or their competitors or their women. Max establishes himself as the hothead, Noodles as his steady "Uncle"; and "Uncle" slowly takes on the stature of a Homeric epithet. Motifs that at first look fragile assume their proper weight with repetition, as when Max steals a watch and warns Noodles that he's going to mess with his "time." And in Leone's hands, the everlasting aches of Noodles's life tug at our hearts too—not just Dominic's death, but Deborah's special reading of the Song of Solomon, with lines like "He is altogether lovable . . . but he'll always be a two-bit punk, so he'll never be my sweetheart." Whenever the movie focuses on Noodles it's lucid and compelling. In the middle and culminating sections of the film, De Niro gives a moving interpretation of melancholia and aging, aided by one of the all-time great makeup jobs (credited to Nilo Jacoponi, Manlio Rocchetti, and Gino Zamprioli). From the moment he's released from prison, Noodles is a haunted man, and De Niro manages to make his ghosts real to us. It's a subtle performance (but not, as with most of his other recent performances, so subtle that it disappears). What De Niro gets across in split seconds of hesitation and indecision is that for the eternally arrested Noodles every pleasure and pain is filtered through childhood recollections.

Leone can't always sustain the film's odd aura of violent meditation. You may find yourself looking forward to his jolting spurts of action or, even better, to those seconds of tense anticipation when the clink of a spoon on a coffee cup threatens to turn into a death knell. A couple of plot strands still don't lead anywhere in this version, especially the entrance of the Max-Noodles gang into union organizing. (Reportedly, Leone has prepared a 265-minute version for Italian television; maybe it'll make sense there.) And Leone's emotional breadth isn't as rich as his vision. He has a genre director's view of character: his audacity, here as in his Westerns, is to present his violent heroes without apology and to show their violence extending into their emotional and sexual bonds. Tuesday Weld, for example, does an unsettling turn as Max's steady girl—a sort of loyalist slut. Leone doesn't enthrall you, as Peckinpah and Penn do, with how much humanity he finds in murderers; rather, he stuns you (and occasionally outrages you) with his willingness to pursue their single-minded logic to extremes. Yet there are moments in this movie so breathtakingly daring, so grand, that they're romantically transcendent. When the grown Noodles impresses Deborah by hiring a Long Island oceanfront restaurant out of season, complete with retinue and band, it's a Jazz Age vignette worthy of Fitzgerald. And the director's feeling for the size of his criminals, and the size of their guilty consciences, makes this movie something more. It's an amazing combination of pulp and Proust: Leone's *Remembrance of Crimes Past.*

Boston Phoenix, March 5, 1985

GOODFELLAS

███

Michael Wilmington

In Martin Scorsese's wacko, blood-chilling masterpiece *GoodFellas*, the main characters are sub-Mafiosi gangsters who haven't made the upper echelons. They take their style, their cues, and their clout from the guys at the top, but they're really cowboys. They don't have the self-discipline of the "made men," the Cosa Nostra kingpins; they get a sexual charge out of killing. Utterly amoral, they're childishly proud of being crooks; they maim or steal out of overheated *cojones* and adolescent pride.

Scorsese, who grew up with characters like this in Little Italy, takes one, the real-life Henry Hill (Ray Liotta), subject of coscenarist Nicholas Pileggi's book *Wise Guy*, and makes him the narrator–focal point of possibly the best movie ever made on American crime and criminals. (Even if it isn't, it's certainly on a level with the highest: the *Godfather* series, *Once Upon a Time in America*, Hawks's *Scarface, The Public Enemy, Bonnie and Clyde, Underworld*.) More than *Mean Streets* or *Raging Bull*, this is the ultimate Scorsese movie, a fantastic bravura display.

Technically, it's staggering: a feast of virtuoso Steadicam tracking shots, ironically pell-mell editing (by Thelma Schoonmaker), and a mix of baroque visual satire, off-key realism, and brilliant, scabrous dialogue that elevates gutter badinage to the high verbal style of a Jacobean drama or a thirties screwball comedy. Tying it all together is a barrage of period rock songs and an ingeniously shifting camera style (lit by cinematographer Michael Ballhaus) that evokes each decade from the fifties to the eighties for us.

The "GoodFellas" (the recent TV series "Wiseguy," and perhaps Brian DePalma's crime comedy *The Wise Guys* of a few years back, necessitated a new title for the movie) are pro criminals who live off heists, protection, and drugs, but they're not actual mob members—and only one of them, hothead Tommy DeVito (Joe Pesci), is even eligible to become a made man. His two buddies, Jimmy Conway (Robert De Niro) and Hill, can never be Cosa Nostra; they're part Irish. Still, they're drunk on the idea of the criminal as aristocrat. They drive Ferraris, wear Armani suits, go to Jerry Vale concerts, and stow their wives and mistresses in absurdly garish homes and apartments. They're lower-class guys who idolize big criminals like local boss Paulie Cicero (Paul Sorvino). Like modern versions of Peckinpah's Wild Bunch, they're brutes and killers—but they're comical brutes who, like all pros, have developed a half-crazy style of inside humor and sarcasm to cauterize their work wounds.

One thing that makes *GoodFellas* stand apart is its absolute lack of sentimentality. The movie is terrifying and visceral, but also wildly funny—by far the funniest Scorsese has ever made. The humor is lurid and pitched so fast and reckless that it continually catches you off guard. It slants life as the wise guys themselves see it—as a huge joke. Sadistic, but bursting with vitality, this humor may startle or offend some audiences. But the laughter is stinging, cathartic, and never divorced from moral awareness, the perception that these men are killers and scum.

Scorsese shows the comic side of the killers' sadism, so we can understand how they think and act; then he turns the screws and makes them pay the price. *GoodFellas* is shocking precisely because it shows the attractions of a criminal lifestyle—the buoyancy of doing anything you want, regardless of anyone else's pain. The wise guys' very slang for murder, "whacking," suggests something comical, screwy, or vaguely masturbatory. They're like the Three Stooges with guns: instead of eye jams or head butts, they blow each other's brains out.

In the movie's two key scenes, Pesci's Crazy Tommy shoots a bar-boy in the foot for bringing a drink late and talking back and then, at a second encounter, blows him away completely for answering vile abuse with a quiet, brave "Fuck you." Tommy's poker partners are shocked but not at a loss—they're ready to go get the shovels—while his pal Jimmy is amazed that Tommy can't take a joke. By giving us these appalling reactions to a pointless murder and sweeping us right into the callous, flip responses of the killers, Scorsese shows us how evil happens, how it isn't too far away, emotionally, from the way some "normal" people act. In showing the attractions of psychopathology, he goes past movies like *Bonnie and Clyde*. His gangsters aren't beautiful or ironically innocent; they're human scum—and if we like them at all, it's because they're energetic, colorful, funny scum.

Robert De Niro isn't the star of the movie; he isn't even the star character actor. Liotta, present for virtually every scene, has the lead role, while Pesci has the juiciest part. But it's De Niro who acts as the movie's anchor. When his character begins to tumble into paranoia and pathology in the movie's last third, it's as if the movie were cracking up with him. Mob boss Cicero has an impassive, apelike dignity, but De Niro is the grinning paterfamilias who becomes a monster. There's something monstrous about the Mafia women as well: Lorraine Bracco and the others with their teased hair, powdered, lacquered expressions, foul mouths, and knit pantsuits. They're suburban gargoyles in a sunny green world where immaculate lawns barely conceal the moral chaos.

Some masterpieces aren't fully recognized in their own time. Some, like *Psycho, Bonnie and Clyde,* or *The Wild Bunch,* are damned as immoral, overviolent, excessive, and deeply irresponsible. Rather than make facile condemnations of evil, Scorsese does something more important, trickier—and, in the end, far more moral. He takes us right into the criminal mind, into the wise guy life—a life of amorality, corruption, easy violence, and sudden death. He and his brilliant cast show us why killers kill, thieves steal, pushers push, rats squeal. He shows us why the Mafia has long been one of the most profitable American business entities, and—the core of his vision—exactly why young guys from poor city neighborhoods might make membership in organized crime their highest aspiration. He shows us the exhilaration of crime and also its consequences.

GoodFellas is a "pay the piper" movie, much like *Bonnie and Clyde,* and a ferocious one. It zooms us through a comical false paradise of the appetites, then sends us crashing into an inferno of paranoia and death. It shows us—and this may be what makes some critics nervous—how crime pays.

Isthmus, September 28, 1990

MILLER'S CROSSING

■■■

Richard T. Jameson

Ice dropping into a heavy-bottomed glass: cold, hard, sensuous. The first image in *Miller's Crossing* hits our ears before it hits the screen, but it's nonetheless an image for that. Tom Reagan (Gabriel Byrne) has traveled the length of a room to build a drink. Not that we saw him in transit, not that we yet know he is Tom Reagan, and not that we see him clearly now as he turns and stalks back up the room, a silent, out-of-focus enigma at the edge of someone else's closeup. Yet he is a story walking, as his deliberate, tangential progress, from background to middle distance and then out the side of the frame, is also a story—draining authority from the close-up Johnny Caspar (Jon Polito) who's come to insist, ironically enough, on the recognition of his territorial rights.

The place is a story, too, which we read as the scene unfolds. A private office; not Caspar's, but not Reagan's either—it's city boss Liam "Leo" O'Bannion (Albert Finney) who sits behind the camera and his big desk, listening. An upstairs office, we know from the muted street traffic (without stopping to think about why we know). Night outside, but sunlight would never be welcome, or relevant, here. A masculine space, green lampshades amid the dark luster of wood, leather, whiskey. A remote train whistle sounds, functional and intrinsically forlorn; the distance from which it reaches us locates the office in space and in history. This room exists in a city big enough to support a multiplicity of criminal fiefdoms and a political machine that rules by maintaining the balance among them, yet it is still a town whose municipal core lies within faint earshot of its outskirts. Urban dreams of empire have not entirely crowded out the memory of wilderness, of implacable places roads and railroads can't reach, even if one of them has been wishfully designated Miller's Crossing. Hence we are not entirely surprised (though the aesthetic shock is deeply satisfying) when the opening master-scene, with its magisterial interior setting and dialogue fragrant with cross-purpose, gives way to a silent (save for mournful Irish melody) credit sequence in an empty forest. And then to a title card announcing, almost superfluously, "An Eastern city in the United States, toward the end of the 1920s."

It has always been one of the special pleasures of movies that they dream worlds and map them at the same time. *Miller's Crossing* dreams a beaut, no less so for the fact that Joel and Ethan Coen's film is a reverent, rigorous reimagining of the world of Dashiell Hammett, especially as limned in *The Glass Key* and *Red Harvest*. (A phrase from *Red Harvest* supplied the title of the Coens' filmmaking debut, *Blood Simple*.) The look is right, from first frame to last—even the aural "look" of that ice: this is a movie that knows what drinking is about in Hammett, what it has to do with rumination and gravity, coolheadedness and rash error, and every coloration of brown study. The mood is instinct with the private pain that separates reticence from caring and conceals itself, with desperation and anger, in seeming not to care. Even the narrative spaces are true to Hammett. There is a man named "Rug" Daniels who enters the film dead, whose murder is the least insistent and finally least significant of the film's mysteries, offhandedly explained amid the backwash from gaudier mayhem ("I don't know, just a mixup"); the cast has to wonder—though the audience need not—why Daniels's corpse should be missing his eponymous toupée. Floyd Thursby might envy a death surrounded by such perplexity and pixilation.

The terrain is worthy of mapping. But more importantly, the mapping itself becomes cinematic terrain in *Miller's Crossing,* each adjustment of distance and perspective invested with exquisite sensibility. Sometimes the effect is startling, like the delayed revelation that the precariously politic dialogue between Leo and Caspar, with Tom kibitzing, also involves a fourth man: The Dane (J. E. Freeman), Caspar's partner in crime, who, though standing directly behind Caspar the entire time, is never seen by the audience till his fierce visage towers in sudden closeup several minutes into the scene. That silent detonation is the most effective shock cut since Dennis Hopper in *Blue Velvet* offered to "fuck anything that moves." But one takes no less satisfaction when, a moment later, after Caspar and The Dane's angry departure, Tom Reagan leaves off lounging at the window ledge behind his friend and boss, moves to a couch along the wall, settles in, takes a deep drink, and says, "Bad play, Leo." Ninety-nine directors out of a hundred would have played that line in closeup. Joel Coen frames Tom within enough space that we feel both director and character have a judicious respect for patterns, for the ways in which moves and designs can go wrong, and for the crisis whose resolution is going to drive Tom and Leo forever apart.

When John Wayne noticed that Dean Martin, as the drunk in need of redemption, seemed to have the ripest part in *Rio Bravo,* he asked Howard Hawks what he ought to do to hold up his own end of the screen. Hawks replied, "You look at him like he's your friend." Tom Reagan is Leo O'Bannion's friend in *Miller's Crossing,* but he has the devil's own time looking out for the interests of both of them. Johnny Caspar starts out wanting only to send a red letter to "The Schmatte," Bernie Bernbaum (John Turturro), a bookmaker who's been screwing the play every time Caspar fixes a prizefight. Leo refuses to lift protection on Bernie, partly to insist on his own authority, but also because Bernie is the cherished brother of Verna (Marcia Gay Harden), whose dark beauty has stirred banked fires in his heart. Tom wishes his friend could keep his mind on business. He also wishes he knew what to do about the fact that he himself is secretly Verna's lover.

Albert Finney came late to the role of Leo, after Trey Wilson, the 43-year-old actor who played the father of the quintuplets in the Coens' *Raising Arizona,* died of a stroke. Finney's extra decade introduces an imbalance into the friendship between Tom and Leo and adjusts the nature of their rivalry for Verna; besides being a hefty powerbroker ill-made for romantic conquest, his Leo takes on the pathos of age and last options. But if Finney's Leo is less than equal on the field of love, he's more than equal as a figure of estimable regard. The screenplay obliges Leo to disappear for most of the last two-thirds of the movie; excellent player that he was, it's doubtful whether Wilson could have loomed so large in absentia as Finney's Leo does. The sense of rueful aspiration that drives Tom Reagan during his often-mystifying maneuvers to set the cockeyed world of *Miller's Crossing* right finds expression mainly through the Irish music that marks his passage, and our memories of Leo—apart from his beefy authority and boyish candor—reverberate as a kind of music. Not only the playing of "Danny Boy" over the most audacious of the film's tour-de-force sequences (an exhilarating first-act high that would render the remainder of any other movie anticlimactic), but also the mortally wounded sighs Leo emits after learning of Tom and Verna's affair. And the way Finney gets the history of a long day and Leo's life and his friendship with Tom into responding to the offer of a late-night drink: "I wouldn't *mind."*

That line reading is one of a thousand things to love about *Miller's Crossing,* along with a zephyr of smoke through waxed floorboards, the rubbing together of stark trees above a killing ground, the arrival of a small man to conduct the beating a giant couldn't manage, the way men and guns fill up a night street like autumn leaves drifting. And one loves a screenplay with the fortitude to lay all its cards on the table in the first sequence and then demonstrate, with each succeeding scene, that there is still story to happen, there is still life and mystery in character, there is reason to sit patient and fascinated before a movie that loves and honors the rules of a game scarcely anyone else in Hollywood remembers anymore, let alone tries to play. Johnny Caspar is a brute posing as a philosopher, but he knows the word that fits the Coen brothers' moviemaking: "et'ics."

One of the Coens told a *New York Times* writer that *Miller's Crossing* had its genesis in the image of a black hat coming to rest in a forest clearing, then lifting to soar away down an avenue of trees. That image accompanies the main title, a talisman of the movie's respect for enigma and its dedication to the irreducible integrity of style. It also crops up verbally as a dream Tom describes to Verna—the closest he gets to sharing a confidence. Yeah, says Verna, and then you chased the hat and it changed into something else. "No," Tom says immediately, "it stayed a hat. And I didn't chase it." But one way or another, this man in grim flight from his heart, who cannot, must not "look at him like he's your friend" till the last world-closing shot of the film, chases his hat all through *Miller's Crossing*. So do the Coens. And that it doesn't change into something else is the best news for the American cinema at the dawn of the nineties.

Film Comment, September–October 1990

POSTSCRIPT: The brothers Coen are coauthors of their films. Both are credited as screenwriters; Ethan, as producer; and Joel, as director—because, as he has joked to interviewers, "I'm the older brother." But Ethan participates fully in the shooting, and the Cannes Film Festival tendered its 1991 award for Best Direction of *Barton Fink* to both of them.

RESERVOIR DOGS

Kenneth Turan

Like it or not (and many people will have their doubts), writer-director Quentin Tarantino has arrived, in your face and on the screen. His brash debut film, *Reservoir Dogs,* a showy but insubstantial comic opera of violence, is as much a calling card as a movie, an audacious high-wire act announcing that he is here and to be reckoned with. Strong violence is Tarantino's passion and he embraces it with gleeful, almost religious fervor. An energetic macho stunt, *Reservoir Dogs* glories in its excesses of blood and profanity, delighting—in classic Grand Guignol fashion—in going as far over the top as the man's imagination will take it.

Tarantino does have the filmmaking flair to go along with his zeal. Though *Reservoir Dogs'* storyline of what happens when a well-planned robbery goes wrong is a staple of both B pictures and pulp fiction, Tarantino's palpable enthusiasm, his unapologetic passion for what he's created, reinvigorate this venerable plot and, mayhem aside, make it involving for longer than you might anticipate.

His background is as an actor and he has a gift for writing great bursts of caustic, quirky dialogue, verbal arias that show off not only his facility with scabrous, tough-guy language but also the abilities of his performers. And it was his script that attracted excellent actors like Harvey Keitel (who also signed on as coproducer), Tim Roth, Michael Madsen, and Steve Buscemi to the film.

Tarantino's writing style is clear from *Dogs'* opening set-piece, focused around a table in a Los Angeles coffee shop where a group of seven nondescript men are just finishing up what looks to be a hearty breakfast. Tarantino himself, cast as "Mr. Brown," starts things off with an exaggeratedly profane exegesis on what Madonna's "Like a Virgin" is really all about, followed by a cranky riff by "Mr. Pink" (Buscemi) on why he doesn't believe in tipping.

Almost immediately after this meal, there is a sudden cut to the bloody interior of a late-model car, where "Mr. Orange" (Roth), shot so badly he seems almost to be drowning in his own blood, holds tight to the hand of a frantic "Mr. White" (Keitel) as he heads the car toward a prearranged rendezvous spot.

For five of those original seven breakfasters—each named (for security reasons) after a color and all identically dressed in black suits, white shirts, thin black ties, and sunglasses—turn out to be participants in a robbery of a diamond wholesaler planned by the other two, Joe (Lawrence Tierney) and his son, Nice Guy Eddie (Chris Penn). None of this is immediately obvious; it comes into focus in bits and pieces, for Tarantino has broken his story up and told it nonchronologically. Energetic scenes of the shootout alternate with quiet flashbacks to the planning as well as the emotionally unstable situation at the rendezvous point, as the surviving gang members scream bloody murder at each other, trying to figure out how an easy job turned into a fiasco, while Mr. Orange swoons in his own blood on the floor.

This is definitely not the Gang That Couldn't Shoot Straight, but rather a group of genuine hard guys, criminal professionals and proud of it, who know everything from how long the police take in responding to alarms to which parts of the body are the most painful to be shot in. The type of crowd that follows the question of "Did you kill anybody?" with a perfectly natural "Any real people or just cops?"

Part of the appeal of *Reservoir Dogs* is the way it makes all this feel terribly authentic, a veracity that is a tribute to the skill of its actors. Though it seems a shame to pick favorites in one of the year's most cohesive ensembles, three performers do stand out. Steve Buscemi is deadpan funny as the cranky Mr. Pink; veteran Lawrence Tierney (star of the 1947 cult classic *The Devil Thumbs a Ride*), with a voice like a tow-truck winch, is gruff as they get as the gang's rapacious boss; and Michael Madsen (Susan Sarandon's ambivalent lover in *Thelma & Louise*) plays the unforgettable "Mr. Blonde," the mellow sadist who loves seventies music and provides *Reservoir Dogs* with its most talked-about moments of gory violence.

Though it's impossible not to appreciate the undeniable skill and élan Tarantino brings to all this, it is also difficult not to wish *Reservoir Dogs* weren't so determinedly one-dimensional, so in love with operatic violence at the expense of everything else. The old gangster movies its creator idolizes were better at balancing things, at adding creditable emotional connection and regret to their dead-end proceedings. As Tarantino makes more films (and his dance card is already quite crowded), perhaps he will see his way clear to going that one step beyond what he's accomplished here. You could even, in the spirit of things, call it something to shoot for.

Los Angeles Times, October 23, 1992

ON PSYCHONOIR

Peter Rainer

In Alfred Hitchcock's 1951 *Strangers on a Train,* a handsome tennis pro, played by Farley Granger, is befriended by an engaging, screw-loose stranger, Robert Walker's Bruno, and, without his conscious awareness, inexorably enmeshed in a murder. In Curtis Hanson's *Bad Influence,* James Spader's securities analyst is befriended by an engaging, malevolent drifter, played by Rob Lowe, and drawn into a nightmare world of killing and retribution. Both films are ticklishly perverse examples of the psychological crime thriller—one subspecies of a phenomenon usually referred to as film noir. Both films carry a mood of dread and apprehension that is far more eloquent than their relatively straightforward crime-thriller plots can account for. This eloquent moodiness, this sense of larger and darker forces overwhelming the simple stories we're witnessing, is typical of the form. It's a demonstration of how in our popular culture the thriller drains a septic tank of contemporary anxieties, the kind that go unvoiced in most mainstream Hollywood entertainments.

If film noir is emerging as the most galvanizing and upsetting of modern genres, there's ample reason for this. The resurgence of noir thrills is a dramatic response to the dutiful feel-goodism of the times. In Mike Figgis's *Internal Affairs,* an excruciatingly crooked policeman (Richard Gere) squares off with an internal-affairs investigator (Andy Garcia) who believes that his wife may be cuckolding him with the cop. In Sondra Locke's *Impulse,* Theresa Russell plays a vice cop who moonlights as a decoy—i.e., prostitute—in drug busts. In Kathryn Bigelow's *Blue Steel,* Jamie Lee Curtis plays a rookie cop terrorized by the deranged commodities broker (Ron Silver) with whom she was romantically involved.

The quality of these films is highly variable: *Internal Affairs* and *Bad Influence* are smart, terrific, voluptuously nasty; *Blue Steel* is a reprehensibly effective porno-violent blowout; *Impulse* is dreary. But whatever their merits, these films draw on the conventions of their forties and early fifties antecedents in ways that point up both how far we've come from those times and how close we still are.

The first films noirs were products of the fallout from the Great

Depression. The peachy-keen classics of the Depression era—the great musicals and romantic comedies—represented Hollywood's signal response to the Depression, and they're among its most blissful and enduring entertainments. But they also represented an evasion of underlying pessimism. The World War II years allowed this pessimism expression; it took the immediate postwar years, after the requirements of patriotic tub-thumping had passed, before this pessimism became rampant in the movies.

The film noir, with its moody, rootless heroes and stark, demented bad guys and black widows, its rain-slicked streets and pervasive claustrophobic fatalism, was a genre made to order. Hollywood at the time boasted a concentration of refugee German, Austrian, and Hungarian directors and cinematographers whose Expressionistic skills were the ideal instruments with which to emblematize this homegrown angst. Their movies derived their psychological resonances from their style.

The film noir was, finally, about being trapped, and the patterns of entrapment were depicted in near-abstract visuals. Characters were rendered as half-shadowed, almost sculptural forms; the light from a street lamp through Venetian blinds functioned as ghostly prison bars on the sodden, aghast face peeping out the window. The gallery of mugs from the classic films noirs are a murderers' row any self-respecting police blotter would kill for: Richard Widmark's giggly, death's-head baby face in *Kiss of Death* ('47); Barbara Stanwyck's cruel, thin-lipped sensuality in *Double Indemnity* ('44), with her flesh glinting like gunmetal in the haze of Fred MacMurray's ardor; Robert Ryan, as the Howard Hughes–like tycoon in *Caught* ('49), jutting his hawk's profile out of the shadows and into the light.

The resurgence of the modern film noir parallels in many ways the psychosocial developments of the forties and fifties. As in that era, we are still coming to terms with both a great war and a species of economic depression. The confluence of Vietnam and Wall Street's 1987 crash provides fertile ground for the black orchid of film noir. A specific postwar malaise common to noir—a malaise built on the realization that our lives are not living up to the era's cozy shibboleths of prosperity and optimism—is just now beginning to seep like a bloodstain through our films. Even the yuppies, once the bright and shining icons of the consumerist culture, have now, in movies like *Bad Influence*, been dragooned into nightmarishness.

The city, that wellspring of film noir, has been deromanticized in the popular imagination by crime, violence, overcrowding, despair. The sexual paranoia that snakes through the old crime thrillers snakes through the new ones, too. In the forties postwar films, returning servicemen could never be sure what their women had been up to while they were gone. And when they did find out, a corpse usually ensued. (Perhaps the best serviceman-encounters-faithless-woman-who-then-becomes-corpse movie was *The Blue Dahlia*, '46, starring Alan Ladd and scripted by that corpsemaster par excellence, Raymond Chandler.) In the modern AIDS era, the sexual paranoia is comparable and free floating. And the sexual rage is even more pronounced: Richard Gere's character in *Internal Affairs* humiliates his women; Rob Lowe's character in *Bad Influence* murders them. In *Impulse,* Theresa Russell's cop returns the compliment. Her sharpest line is: "Inside every man is a pervert waiting to get out."

The new thrillers are an implicit rejection of the bland uplift and evasions that characterized the eighties, just as the films noirs of the forties and, even more so, the early fifties were a rejection of the homilies of the postwar world. By framing this rejection in terms of the thriller genre, these films are able to disguise their subversiveness and still satisfy the audience's desire for action. The ghettoization of genre is a convenient and, for now, necessary camouflage.

There are, of course, stylistic differences between the thrillers of then and now. Obviously, color has replaced black and white. Voiceover narration and time-sequence juggling are mostly gone; the sex and violence are more plentiful, more languorously shot and edited. The scripts derive less from hard-boiled pulp fiction than from its modern equivalent—the pulp TV thriller, which at its most rococo, in its Michael Mannerist phase in shows like "Crime Story," defines the hard-boiled raciness and shadowings of video noir.

Bad guys were often portrayed in the old days as gross, stubby, gelatinous specimens—most memorably Sydney Greenstreet in *The Maltese Falcon* ('41) or Edward G. Robinson in *Key Largo* ('48). Now they're much more likely to be Ward Cleaverish (like Terry O'Quinn in Joseph Ruben's *The Stepfather,* '87), sleekly handsome (like Lowe), or well conditioned (Ron Silver in *Blue Steel,* appropriately enough, has a psychotic break while working out on his Soloflex). But in most of the important ways, the modern thriller has simply shifted in key the basic chordal progression. In the new noirs mentioned above, the hero is someone with an uneasy, or nonexistent, psychosexual relationship at home, who is drawn by an avenging, seductive adversary into a reckoning with his or her own capacity for horror.

The primal film noir theme of the innocent drawn into a pact with one's dark double is the subtext of all these films. This doubling of innocence and malevolence is particularly conducive to noir stylistics: in the shadows, everybody is rendered equally featureless, anonymous. These films may be shot in color but they all find fulfillment in the muted end of the palette. *Internal Affairs* pays homage to its forebears by fading its final violent tableau to black and white.

The modern thrillers may dabble in character psychology but, like the earlier thrillers, they are not primarily psychological or sociological investigations. In the forties and fifties, a popularized Freudianism sometimes buttressed the thrills; social explanations—poverty, a bad upbringing, and so on—were occasionally hauled in to reason away the villainy. But most of the time the bad guys were just . . . bad. Faced with Richard Widmark's Tommy Udo in *Kiss of Death* pushing an old lady in a wheelchair down the stairs, any Psych 101 explanation is bound to be comically inadequate. In the new thrillers, the bad guys' motivations go equally undeciphered, which gives the films both a modernist and an archaic veneer. The characters played by Gere, Silver, Lowe are, we are made to feel, born bad. The films in which they figure express a particularly modern disillusionment: our helplessness, despite our vast stockpile of learning, to truly understand someone else's depravity.

Perhaps the greater disillusionment in these movies is with the supposed comforts of the middle class. Dissatisfied with the bourgeois blandishments that were supposed to make us all happier, or deprived even of the promise or continuance of those comforts, we become enraged at the wealthy. The film noir has always been one of the few genres that explicitly recognized, if only for the purposes of plot, the class system in America. So many of the plots—think of *They Live by Night* ('48)—have been about the poor trying to get rich. And in the new thrillers, as in the old, the rich are almost without exception rotters. Wealth becomes the hallmark of wickedness. In *Internal Affairs,* a mobster kingpin hires Richard Gere's Dennis Peck to kill his parents because they're standing in the way of a business deal; in *Blue Steel,* the rantings of Ron Silver's

Eugene on the floor of the stock exchange are masked as part of the money-grubbing din.

Since great wealth is portrayed as the entrance to all manner of corruption, it follows that the yuppies in these movies who aspire to such wealth are foredoomed. *Bad Influence* is the most fascinating because, as did Jonathan Demme's *Something Wild* ('86), it stands the yuppie stereotype on its head. Despite initial impressions, the James Spader character's fast-track job as securities analyst gives him no real satisfaction. His Deco condo is devoid of warmth; it has the appearance of wealth stripped of all human meaning. The gleaming home entertainment equipment and New Wave furnishings and objets d'art become talismans of corruption. Rob Lowe's character, inhumanly smooth, seems to be an emanation of these yuppie accoutrements; he pops out of the surroundings like a malevolent genie. The film noir, with its absolute reliance on style, is uniquely capable of setting and expressing its basic themes amid the gleaming surfaces of yuppieland.

What all of these movies are saying is that ultimately the laws of society cannot protect you. Its good-time reassurances are a con. The female leads in *Blue Steel* and *Impulse* may be cops but they're still victims—the traditional role for women in urban jungle scenarios. To the extent that these films all conclude with last-minute rescue operations by the forces of good, they seem phony.

The function of the law, of the police, in these movies is far more ambiguous than it was in the old B-thriller days. Back then, a renegade cop was the exception in a well-protected universe. Now the perception of corruption among our upholders of the law is widespread. The new thrillers are blatantly cynical, and in that cynicism is at least a measure of truth. It may be a bum's truth, but it connects up with the fearsomeness of contemporary urban life in a way that the comfy, feel-good movies don't. The modern crime thriller is the nightmare in the field of dreams.

Los Angeles Times, April 8, 1990

BODY HEAT

■■■

Stephen Schiff

We go to the movies for all sorts of reasons, but surely one of them is to watch people like ourselves live out our daydreams—the naughty ones we know *we'll* never act upon. Murder, illicit affairs, grand theft—it doesn't matter whether the dreams are nightmares, just so long as they're voluptuous nightmares. Daydreams are scenarios; burning inside them is the question "what if?" And there are movie genres that seem expressly designed to churn up those what-if fantasies. For a long time, people wanted to see disaster movies and political conspiracy movies, movies that asked "what if" on a grand social scale. Horror movies, I suppose, ask the same question in the voice of a morbid child. And there are also genres that try to be "realistic," that don't deal much in what ifs at all. War movies don't. Most Westerns don't. And on the whole, gangster films don't. But it is film noir, that dark demi-genre suspended somewhere between the "realistic" film and the voluptuous nightmare, that brings this enticing "what if" to a personal plane. Films noirs are about individual fates and individual holocausts: they're disaster movies of the spirit.

The great films noirs of the forties and fifties mirrored a realization that seemed to hit postwar America all at once: that even in utopia, in a land flushed with victory and prosperity, personal destinies could remain terrifying. These films navigated the cracks in the gleaming smile of *Saturday Evening Post* America. Most of the best noirs—*The Lady from Shanghai, Double Indemnity, Out of the Past, Gilda, Gun Crazy,* and so on—are about fairly ordinary men living dangerously ordinary lives, until something crosses their path and sets their darkest dreams aflame. If that something were a book or a movie or a job—the things that usually cross *our* paths—then the dreams would be fairly harmless. But in films noirs the black cats are usually women and extraordinary women at that—women who know that they're igniting dreams and know how to make those dreams seem to come true. Femmes fatales.

We don't often see films noirs these days, and maybe that's because we don't often see femmes fatales in the movies. This is a consequence of the age. As the eighties dawn, the willful, ravenous sexuality of a Rita Hayworth, a Barbara Stanwyck, or a Jane Greer is out of fashion, and that's not because women don't want to see it (the femme fatale is, after all, alive and well and living in the soap operas). It's because the men don't. Groping for the meaning of masculinity, eighties men may find the broad-shouldered she-wolves of the forties and fifties a bit threatening; how much easier it is to contemplate the innocent, vulnerable sexuality of child-women like Farrah Fawcett, Brooke Shields, and Bo Derek. But what would happen if an eighties schlub met a classic femme fatale? Perhaps he would turn away and dismiss her, thinking, "It's only a movie." Then again, he might be too big a dreamer for that. Perhaps he would be like the feckless lawyer William Hurt plays in Lawrence Kasdan's bewitching *Body Heat*—a movie in which the femme fatale returns to the screen and brings all the humid glamour of the film noir with her.

Kasdan, who wrote *Raiders of the Lost Ark* and cowrote *The Empire Strikes Back,* had never directed before, but right from the start one feels his calm and assurance. In a few deft strokes he introduces us to Ned Racine (Hurt), and very quickly we learn that Ned's a third-rate womanizer and a fourth-rate barrister, that he lives in a crummy little town near Miami, and that he probably always will. He goes for women in uniform—nurses, policewomen, waitresses—but only because they seem easy to him. His clients—crooks and boors—are easy, too. But one night, at an outdoor concert, while Ned is watching the band play "That Old Feeling," a woman rises out of the audience, a woman in a white dress, with cascading hair and a cool, sensual walk. Hurt plays the scene beautifully: when he sees her he looks as though he'd been slapped. The very existence of this elegant, long-legged beauty casts his whole life into shadow. The nurses, the clients, the town, the heat—all feel unutterably shabby and degrading. This woman is like a sex goddess from an old movie, but she seems more real than anything he knows. And so he has no choice. He follows her.

Her name is Matty Walker (Kathleen Turner) and she lives in a big, big house with her rich, weaselly husband, Edmund (Richard Crenna), who isn't around much. She hates him. Once these elements are in place, we know what's going to happen, because we've seen it so many times before, in movies like *Double Indemnity* and *The Postman Always Rings Twice.* Ned and Matty will fall in love, will kill Edmund, and then will sink into a morass of turnabouts, hidden clues, and betrayals. *Body Heat* has been roundly pooh-

poohed in some quarters for being such a calculatedly noirish picture, full of stylized dime-novel dialogue and byzantine plot twists, and graced by an atmosphere that, despite the modern cars and modern references, is strongly redolent of the past. I'm not sure what all the bother is about. *Body Heat*, certainly the best imitation of a film noir since *Chinatown* seven years before, isn't muffled and somber and period-bound like the remake of *The Postman Always Rings Twice* in early 1981; it's thoroughly entertaining, and its self-consciousness only enhances its hypnotic aura. *Body Heat* isn't—and can't be—a pure, contemporary film noir because it's about the *old* films noirs, about how they've crept into our dreams until they're part of our unconscious vocabulary.

That's why Kasdan's dialogue is so synthetic and slangy. Confronted with a forties sex goddess, Ned coughs up forties lines: terse, awful things like "We're not gonna get greedy; if we do, we'll get burned." Some of this stuff is pretty ponderous, and at times you can see the bare bones of the script poking through the movie's glistening skin. But the dialogue in *Body Heat* can't be removed from its context. Take away the smoke and mist, the thick, slicing shadows, the air of fatalism, and you've got the mundane present, a place where people speak plainly and no one is drawn into the night by a sultry woman in white. In *Body Heat* even the phoniest-sounding dialogue fits (the way Clifford Odets's purple speeches fit into a hyper movie like *Sweet Smell of Success*) because Ned and Matty make it fit. When Ned first comes on to her, Matty seems dubious ("Does chat like this work with most women?" she snarls). But a few moments later she's matching him quip for quip. She knows that all she has to do to trap this man is play the part of the goddess he sees her as, and because she's a preternaturally talented vamp she can do it: she can outplay Ned, and out–dirty-talk him, and outflirt him. When they make love, the spectres of pulp novels and old movies hover around them, making everything hotter, sexier. "You're not so tough after all, are you?" Ned tells Matty, trying to play Bogart to her Bacall. And Matty whispers, "No. I'm weak," and then plucks a kiss from him as if she were biting a grape off a vine. Ned loves this stuff, and Matty knows it. She locks him out of her house so he can break in and take her, and when he does, they twist themselves into movie poses and kiss movie kisses.

It's a pretty sexy picture, but the sexiness isn't all in the lovemaking scenes. It's in the very idea of Matty, and in the atmosphere her presence in a modern movie conjures up. The way shots dissolve together or lap up against one another like waves; the way smoke mingles with the hot fog; the way the camera glides in and down on love or murder, or else just waits, patiently, for an explosion that comes a heartbeat later than you expect it; the way the noir imagery (the shadows of Venetian blinds, the ceiling fans, the full skirts, the wind chimes and boathouses and gazebos) folds into the film's texture—all this lends a lazy, erotic tone. Even the omnipresent heat imagery comes to seem less obtrusive as the film ensnares us in its mood. The heat isn't just a stylized metaphor for deadly sex—it stylizes the movie's reality. When the night is hot, when rules and morals shimmer like a mirage, a little Florida town begins to feel unreal—movie-ish—and 1981 comes to seem a moment stranded in time. *Body Heat* is all about illusions, about the way our perceptions of things mix with our dreams and with our cultural pasts, until everything is fog. In the beginning of the movie, Kasdan uses golds and pastels to convey a hard, pedestrian world, but as we approach the murder scene a haze sets in and the colors evaporate. The night of the crime is etched in blacks, whites, and grays, and the killing takes place in a parlous fog, where things come at you out of nowhere: trees, guns, police cars, fire. Then, after the deed is done, the colors return. Only they're different this time: everything acquires a tawny, corroded look, like cheese that's been left out too long.

Even the supporting characters live movie-fed lives. Ned's wise-cracking buddy, an assistant D.A. named Lowenstein (Ted Danson), thinks he's a latter-day Fred Astaire, and his other pal, a police investigator named Oscar (J. A. Preston), is trying to be Sidney Poitier, a black cop with a halo. Teddy Lewis, pro arsonist (played by a punky young Mickey Rourke), first appears singing Bob Seger's "Feel Like a Number," and it's only after the camera pulls back to show us he's lip-synching that we realize he's not the hard rocker he imagines he is. In fact, Matty's husband, Edmund, is the one major character who hasn't built his identity out of spare parts, and this (along with Richard Crenna's exaggeratedly slimy performance) is precisely what makes him hateful. In a world of dreamers, Edmund has succeeded because he understands the bottom line, because he's "willing to do what's necessary." He despises the nerds who aren't, and when he says as much, Ned is forced to examine his own vague soul. "I know that kinda guy," Ned mutters. "I hate that; makes me sick." And then, blinking hard, "*I'm* a lot like that." From that moment on, poor Edmund's fate is sealed.

The movie stands or falls with Hurt's performance, and there are people I know who are so put off by the sight of his mustache that they never give his acting a chance. True, it's a ruinous mustache, a formless, slithery thing that looks as if it belonged in a sardine can. Before ten minutes had passed, though, I had forgotten about it; I was watching one of the most exciting movie performances of the year. Hurt (who starred in *Altered States* and *Eyewitness*) approaches his character in a way that ties up all the movie's themes. Since Ned has become the hero of his own little film noir, Hurt becomes an actor playing an actor, and as he tries to cover up his crime we can see how his friends investigating the case mistake his guilty discomfort for a weird nonchalance. Hurt is big and blond and handsome, and he gives off a movie star aura, but he's no bland dreamboat. His face has a grownup, lived-in look, and yet there's something pained and childlike behind those little eyes. His Ned can't believe he's sharp enough for Matty, and he's sure that those borrowings from Bogie will fall flat. And then, when Matty plays along, Ned grows bolder and more confident; the reinforcement she gives him compounds his own self-love. Hurt tries nutty things in this movie, but he doesn't push them at us. He maintains a sort of existential distance—the distance of a man watching himself methodically ruin his life.

But Kathleen Turner has some awkward scenes, and so does the movie. There's a terrible moment in which, at the height of his scheming, Ned watches a symbolic clown drive past (en route to a Fellini movie, no doubt), and Turner destroys a pivotal sequence in which she has to breathe one of Kasdan's worst lines: "I'd kill myself if I thought this thing would destroy us." She isn't a terrific actress, but she doesn't have to be: she only has to be a terrific image. If you leave *Body Heat* struggling to remember what she looks like, that's not because she's not memorable—with her flaring, hungry nostrils and her husky voice, she is. It's because Kasdan makes her flicker: she's the fire in *Body Heat*. And, like the femme fatale in every film noir, she's also the ice.

Boston Phoenix, September 22, 1981

AGAINST ALL ODDS

■■■

Richard T. Jameson

A car pulls into a gas station in a small town south of Tahoe, bringing bad news for the station's owner. An indeterminate amount of time earlier, under a different name and in another life, he had undertaken a job of work for a certain shady operator: to hunt down the beautiful woman who had put a bullet in the shady operator and run off with $40,000 of his money. He found the woman in Mexico but he didn't bring her back. Instead, he fell in love with her, joined her in her flight, and, in the wake of another, fatal shooting, was deserted by her. Now his former employer—and rival in romance—has found him. The guy has a new, dirtier job that needs doing, and he figures he's owed.

That accounts for about half the story tautly told by Daniel Mainwaring (under the pseudonym Geoffrey Homes), first as a novel, *Build My Gallows High,* and then as a 1947 RKO movie, *Out of the Past*—a title so instinct with legend, to pronounce it is to sigh. Almost certainly, no one who worked on the picture had any idea they were making one of the great films of the forties. Somehow, everything went together just right. The bleak inevitability of the plot was reinforced by its structure—beginning *in medias res* and winding back up to the present, via the hero's almost self-hypnotized narration, before moving toward fatal climax and denouement. The casting and performances of the young Robert Mitchum (whose existentialist-without-portfolio air was never more poetically exploited), Jane Greer, and Kirk Douglas as the mutually damned trio of lovers passed effortlessly beyond acting and into screen iconography. Director Jacques Tourneur did his best work ever: muting the savagery of the genre material as he had when shooting horror movies for Val Lewton; playing the fine cut-and-thrust dialogue in the softest of conversational tones; and lending the whole enterprise the fluid movement and haunted, filigreed look of a film noir fairy tale. *Out of the Past* is perhaps the one film noir that demands to be described as exquisite.

Unlike, say, that other flukey forties masterpiece *Casablanca,* the film didn't attract much attention upon initial release. Even now it tends to get filed under the patronizing rubric "cult

The twisted storyline of *Out of the Past* features plenty of murder and double cross, yet thanks to director Jacques Tourneur the prevailing mood of the film is eerie, delicate reverie—and the result is one of the masterworks of film noir. The complex homoerotic tensions among Paul Valentine, Kirk Douglas, and Robert Mitchum in this scene are barely hinted in the script. (Courtesy of Turner Entertainment Co. © 1947 RKO Pictures, Inc. All Rights Reserved. Photo from Museum of Modern Art Film Stills Archive.)

movie." So most people who go to see *Against All Odds,* Taylor Hackford's new telling of the tale, may be unaware they're watching a remake. They're still less likely to suspect that the original story was a good one.

That story's still there, in vague outline, but in straining to adapt it to the ethos of the eighties, Hackford comes very near ruining it. The hero (Jeff Bridges) can't be, as the Mitchum character had been in that earlier life, a forties-style private detective who takes on the wrong case. He has to be something, well, kinda Now: a pro football player? Make that an ex–pro football player, recently and unfairly deprived of his position on the team. Make that a team owned by the rich-bitch mother of the runaway lady. Give the rich bitch (no such character figured in the original) a mini-*Chinatown,* destroy-the-ecology-of-California scheme to be involved in—it can taint every other character who wanders through the action. And since, meanwhile, our nondetective hero has to have some justification for starting to make like a private eye and carrying out the Mexican quest, let him be obligated in advance to the shady operator figure, played by James Woods. Maybe Bridges once thought about—but didn't actually go through with—shaving points in a crucial game so Woods could win big on some bets. He's not really guilty, but he could be made to *look* guilty and in his heart he *feels* guilty, because we're *all* guilty. Ah, Malaise; Motivation; Meaning. But further and further away from a compelling movie.

Those are symptoms of a fundamental lack of narrative conviction. Here's a bigger one. How can you remake a film noir classic boasting one of the supreme manifestations of the femme fatale if you don't, at base, believe in femmes fatales? Jane Greer's Kathy Moffat in *Out of the Past* was an inspired monster. One could spend half the film wondering, with Mitchum, whether she was false or true, predator or victim, and then spend the second half knowing the truth about her, and knowing that that made no difference— she was still fascinating, irresistible, in the passionate intricacy of her falsehood, the absoluteness of her commitment to perversity. In *Against All Odds,* Rachel Ward's Jessie Wyler isn't perverse, just perplexed. Mostly she is perplexed about the muddle Hackford and his screenwriter, Eric Hughes, have made of her character.

First, they violate the machinery of the basic plot-and-character scheme that lay at the heart of *Gallows/Past.* They make Jessie a child of wealth, with a sizable bank account to draw on (even while in hiding—that's how Bridges tracks her, by tracing her withdrawals!). But why should such a creature have bothered to steal a few thousand bucks—pocket change—when she ran out on her mobster lover? It's necessary to the hero's evolving obsession with her that he (and we) wonder whether she struck out at Woods as a blow for personal freedom or may have also, among other things, wanted that money. A femme fatale will always try to have it both ways; beyond a certain point, a producer-director and his screenwriter can't.

When is a director reaching for a fresh interpretation of a scene and when is he simply blowing it? There's a scene in *Out of the Past* wherein Mitchum dukes it out with his former partner in the private-eye game (Steve Brodie), who has tracked him and Kathy down and wants to trade his silence for their money. Tourneur directed the scene so deftly, it's genuinely shocking when Kathy, forgotten on the sidelines, suddenly shoots the intruder in cold blood. In the counterpart scene here, the exact opposite effect is achieved: we see the shooting coming a mile away—soooo many shots of a certain pistol lying in the dirt, soooo many shots of Jessie in consternation at all this brute-male violence—and it seems, moreover, like what any decent movie heroine would do in such a situation.

Hackford doesn't really believe in the story Tourneur & Co. once told so powerfully. He must have found it too mythic, too "Hollywood," too relentless. He opts for Explaining Jessie. Explaining her so thoroughly, as one caught in the cross fire of too many L.A. power struggles, that she hasn't a prayer of coming across as anything but an overage battered child.

The great selling point of *Against All Odds* is the promise of hot stuff between Jeff Bridges and Rachel Ward, from the man who brought you *An Officer and a Gentleman.* Hackford has supplied sundry sandy caresses, underwater embraces, and even a literally steamy nude scene in an improbably reactivated Mayan sauna (though for my admittedly funny money Ward was sexier sucking bullets in *Dead Men Don't Wear Plaid*). Again, the original far surpasses the remake. Without arousing the wrath of any censor board, Tourneur not only succeeded in tapping the Mitchum-Greer love match for a headier erotic charge than the sum total of The Cinema of Taylor Hackford to date, but also managed (entirely through mise-en-scène and direction of actors) a homoerotic tension in the Mitchum-Douglas rivalry more complex and provocative than the clinical innuendos of Eric Hughes's dialogue for James Woods's stridently macho mobster.

There is, however, one factor that makes *Against All Odds* a must-see precisely for admirers of *Out of the Past.* The one decent use served by Hackford's burdensome additions to the plot is that they provided a role for Jane Greer herself to play. She's the mother of her original character, as it were, the aforementioned silver-haired rich bitch, Mrs. Wyler. She's still a beauty, and though she never gets near a gun this time out, I haven't the least doubt she's still very, very dangerous.

The Weekly (Seattle), March 7, 1984

TROUBLE IN MIND

Peter Rainer

Alan Rudolph has always had a prodigious ease as a filmmaker and a prodigious pretentiousness as an idea man. In movies like *Welcome to L.A.* ('76) and *Remember My Name* ('78) you could take pleasure in the way he moved the camera and framed his compositions, but his characters talked as if they had spent too much time in deprivation tanks. If you melted down their dialogue it would make a great paste wax—you could shine your furniture with it. Last year's *Choose Me* was dubbed the Rudolph movie for people who don't like Rudolph. I still didn't care much for it. A lot of what people took to be satirical and funny just seemed like the usual Rudolphisms to me, with a twirl or two.

Trouble in Mind is unmistakably an Alan Rudolph film: It retains some of his arch swooniness. But it's also a captivating, bizarre film noir fantasia. The best part of *Choose Me* was the lyrical opening sequence in the street, scored to Teddy Pendergrass; Rudolph extends the pleasure of that scene—its sensual tingle—throughout most of *Trouble in Mind*. He does in this film what I think he was mistakenly credited with doing in *Choose Me*. Along with his extraordinary cinematographer Toyomichi Kurita, he turns his pretensions into cracked, lyric flights of fancy. It's funny in the dank, brittle way some of the best films noirs were, when they were at their most tough-guy poetic; and it's as dreamy and trancelike as those films sometimes were, too. Rudolph can do anything he wants to in this movie: his style is so perfected that the film has the effect of a single, uninterrupted camera move through noir corridors and drizzly cityscapes.

Kris Kristofferson is the blasted, bitter hero who, in the best film noir tradition, sees his salvation in a young, unsullied woman. A former cop who spent a long stretch in the clink for the vengeance shooting of a mobster, Kristofferson's Hawk has returned to his haunt—the grayish RainCity, in an unspecified future where language and currency have subtly changed and the militia is a presence in the streets. He takes a room above the breakfast diner run by an old flame, Wanda (Geneviève Bujold), and spends a lot of time gazing out of his window (he constructs a cardboard miniature model of the street scene) and picking at his ham and eggs in the diner downstairs. The diner is Edward Hopperish, with a neon glow. Even in daylight, its denizens seem slugged and depleted. They're like vampires sapped of their strength when the cold light hits their faces. It's a familiar grungy tableau, and yet Rudolph makes it like nothing you've ever seen: a busboy swats roaches with addled aplomb; a black poet (Joe Morton) sits in a booth wreathed in plumes of cigarette smoke and spews screwy, philosophy-major blank verse.

This poet is also a low-level gangster looking for a partner. He finds him in Keith Carradine's Coop, a country boy who brings his girlfriend, Georgia (Lori Singer), and their baby girl to the big city to make a score. That's a great noir theme, the corrupting influence of the big bad city. It was also a central theme in silent films; Rudolph makes us understand the visual and thematic links between noir and movies like Murnau's *Sunrise* and *City Girl,* passages in Griffith, even Keaton. He plays around with this theme. Once Coop falls in with crooks, he whoops it up in sordid little fleabag hotel room orgies and leaves his girlfriend increasingly open to the tough-tender ministrations of Hawk, who's in love with her innocence. Every time we see Coop his clothes become flashier, his features more jagged; his hair, swooped into a warlock's pompadour, becomes more outré. By the end of the film Carradine resembles Willem Dafoe's comic-book villain in Walter Hill's *Streets of Fire,* with his lurid nostrils and vampire's widow's peak. And yet he's not scary, just pathetic. This rube is like a futurist noir version of the small-timers who come to Hollywood and immediately go for the open-shirt-and-medallion look. Rudolph turns Coop's corruptibleness into an absurdist joke.

He also turns Coop into something of an artwork. Noir characters, at their best, were always poetic conceits. Rudolph takes the conceit a step further. The people in *Trouble in Mind* are like centerpieces in their own private museum; they take the light like showcase sculptures, and they're coordinated with the decor—the huge Deco palace of RainCity's kingpin gangster Hilly Blue, played by Divine without the female impersonator accoutrements; Hawk's cinderblock apartment; a Chinese restaurant in loud reds and golds; Georgia's opium den–yellow room. Joe Morton (who played the mute title character in John Sayles's *Brother from Another Planet*) is an artwork, too; he's burnt ocher to Coop's gilded white lily. Rudolph has a jangly modern artist's love of visual collision. In *Choose Me,*

Susan Scott's image-text paintings were on the walls of Geneviève Bujold's apartment, and movie posters were used pop-art style in Rae Dawn Chong's digs. In *Trouble in Mind*, Rudolph uses sculptor Dale Chihuly's elegant glassworks; Joe Morton's apartment is like a Zen computer nut's pad; a towering cylindrical Lucite fish tank figures prominently in Divine's mansion. Rudolph filmed in Seattle and he uses the Space Needle in one scene as though it had been specially designed for the film. Like most of the movie, it has a piquant abstract quality.

Noir movies have always distinguished themselves with their look. The inky expressionist visual designs, framed in highly contrasting shades of black and white, were like the leopard skins of the characters, the stories. There have been a few color noirs (*Chinatown, Farewell My Lovely*), but no one has ever reworked the genre the way Rudolph has in *Trouble in Mind*. He's taken the genre's inherent visual elegance and brought it into the realm of abstract art. He's given film noir a modernist, out-of-the-mainstream flavoring. He can stage a shoot-out in a Deco mansion and make it look like *Hellzapoppin* at the Guggenheim. (That's partly because— here's another RainCity in-joke collision—it's really the Seattle Art Museum.)

You would expect the actors to fade into the ozone with a movie this designed-to-the-teeth, but they bring their own stylishness to the piece. Kristofferson is strong and brooding; Bujold is tart, like a nouveau Ida Lupino. Keith Carradine is loonily intense—he doesn't point up for the audience his overweening pompadour. Lori Singer could have been more resonant, and Divine—in the Sydney Greenstreet role—isn't wonderful (this is his first time playing a man). But even the bad acting in this film is all of a piece with Rudolph's off-kilter design. And he uses Mark Isham's pop-rock-jazz fusion score to lull the audience into the design, into the mood. It's true that you can grate your teeth on some of the lines in this movie; at one point Kristofferson says, "You gotta be nice to your friends because without them you're a total stranger." But highfalutin dialogue is no stranger to noir. Charles Brackett and Raymond Chandler and Ben Hecht came up with some lulus in their day. It's part of the texture of the movies. There was always something slightly absurd about film noir, with its doom-tinged aura and moody blues people. *Trouble in Mind* finally locates a filmic universe for Rudolph's artificial-world gifts. He's never seemed so at home, and his confidence is like a balm.

Los Angeles Herald Examiner, December 11, 1985

THE GRIFTERS

Julie Salamon

In the forties and fifties, Hollywood turned out plenty of taut, dark pictures about tough men and even tougher women who treated life as a con game and ended up hurt or dead. They usually lived in Los Angeles. Treating their melodramatic subjects with matter-of-fact irony, these films seemed wise rather than cynical.

In recent years filmmakers have tended to use ironic commentary to distance audiences from characters and their stories. David Lynch epitomizes this deliberate subversion: his stylized characters are so self-mocking, it's impossible to believe in them as anything more than parody. It's spin control applied to moviemaking. He knows how things should play, even if he doesn't know—or show—what they really mean.

The British director Stephen Frears proves that it is possible to reproduce the old films noirs through a contemporary sensibility. He lays out *The Grifters,* Jim Thompson's story of three hustlers in L.A., without mocking the subterranean universe they live in, or its rules. He never undercuts the story by imposing the outside world on his characters. He allows them to accept who they are: rebels who find that beating the system has put them in the position of having to conform to a code of conduct much harsher than the one from which they've escaped.

Thompson, the pulp writer who became a cult figure after he died in 1976, wrote characters so crisp and hard they could carry symbolic weight even if they weren't deep. An unsentimental moralist, he wrote about people trying to lift themselves up in the world by cheating, and he generally made them pay a price that seemed too big for their crimes. Screenwriter Donald Westlake, who wrote the terrific little thriller *The Stepfather* and—as Richard Stark—the novel that gave rise to *Point Blank,* has stayed true to Thompson's clean lines. Characters get at the heart of things in the most deceptively simple ways. "I guess I owe you my life," a son tells his mother after she's rushed him to the hospital. Without missing a beat she assesses her offspring coolly. "You always did," she reminds him.

In such diverse pictures as *My Beautiful Laundrette, Sammy and*

Rosie Get Laid, Prick Up Your Ears, and Dangerous Liaisons, director Frears has proved repeatedly that he knows good talk when he hears it and has the visual wit to match. His films connect to one another only in their view of the world as the playing field for all kinds of gamesmanship—between classes, between lovers. Here the subject is "the grift," the hustle—the hustle people play for money and the hustle for love. Incest lies at the heart of the triangular relationship of Lily, her son Roy, and Roy's lover Myra. Frears gets away with it by presenting the package without sentimentality or apology— and with plenty of spiky humor.

He pays his obligatory homage to the old movies right away, with a seductive black-and-white vision of Los Angeles. Elmer Bernstein, who's scored everything from *The Magnificent Seven* to *Bird Man of Alcatraz* to *Ghostbusters,* finds the right mood, nostalgia without the lump in the throat.

Then, in color, Frears introduces his three main characters so precisely that you feel as if you've known them forever the minute they hit the screen. There's Lily (Anjelica Huston), the sexy forty-year-old in a short tight skirt, high heels, and short platinum hair with a face that hasn't relaxed in about ten years. She's at the track, up to no good. There's Roy (John Cusack), the baby-faced man of twenty-five, cleancut and soft. He's at a bar, holding up twenty-dollar bills when he orders but slipping the bartender a ten when he pays, hoping to get change for a twenty. There's Myra (Annette Bening), who's the same as Lily but ten years younger, so she still thinks the grift is fun.

Lily hates Myra and vice versa because neither of them particularly likes seeing what they've been, what they will be. And because they love the same man—Roy. Huston's ability to shift from an appearance of vulnerability to brute strength no longer surprises, after her accomplishments of the past five years: *Prizzi's Honor, The Dead, Crimes and Misdemeanors,* and the miniseries "Lonesome Dove." The news is Bening, whose main success so far has been on stage, and who clearly emerges from this picture as a force to be reckoned with. Myra isn't a nice person at all, but she certainly is seductive. She isn't an ordinary femme fatale. Her power comes more from the naughty pleasure she takes from the way she knows men react to her sexuality. She isn't flirtatious; she presents herself as a favor and fully expects to be taken up on her offer. When she isn't, she'll try something else.

With his appealing little features, Cusack gives the right impression of earnestness and mischief for Roy. He delivers the most deadpan lines without flinching, which is all they need for believability.

Frears is as good with the small touches as he is with the big ones—and that means they're great. Everyone is a character, down to the sprightly desk clerk at the hotel where Roy lives (the whimsical Henry Jones) and Pat Hingle's viciously genial Bobo, Lily's boss.

Wall Street Journal, January 24, 1991

ON COPPING A PLEA

■■■

Dave Kehr

Two weeks after the Los Angeles riots, audiences were packing into theaters to enjoy the comic escapades of two L.A. cops, detectives Martin Riggs (Mel Gibson) and Roger Murtaugh (Danny Glover), as they roughed up suspects, conducted illegal searches, and launched high-speed car chases through the streets of the city.

There seems to be some ambivalence here. The difference between the Rodney King video and *Lethal Weapon 3* is that one makes people want to break windows and the other, box-office records.

The police have always existed in a volatile love-hate relationship with the civilian population, which is what makes cops such effective and enduring figures in mass entertainment. Like no other figures in our society, they are worshiped and feared, envied and despised. As much as moviegoers may fantasize over the evident freedom enjoyed by movie cops—the freedom to cross social and legal boundaries, to act out violent impulses, and to exercise an immediate, personal power over anyone who stands in their way—it's only natural that we also fear that freedom being turned against us.

Here, the distinction between hero and monster is strictly a matter of point of view, and point of view is something that the movies are uniquely well equipped to manipulate. Attitudes can be determined almost entirely by where a director chooses to place the camera—close in for empathy, farther back for irony and distance.

These are exactly the notions behind *Unlawful Entry*, an unusually intelligent and provocative thriller directed by Jonathan Kaplan. Kaplan develops a skillful, complex, and morally discomfiting manipulation of point of view through the film's very effective first half, before the movie degenerates into implausibility and a simplemindedness that reeks of studio interference.

Kaplan begins by establishing the impotence and frustration felt by his civilian protagonist, Michael Carr (Kurt Russell), when a burglar breaks into his Los Angeles home and holds his wife Karen (Madeleine Stowe) at knife point. Ludicrously brandishing a putting iron, Michael has no choice but to let the man escape, and his sense of failure adds another strain to his already decaying marriage.

Enter Patrolman Pete Davis (Ray Liotta of *GoodFellas,* in another extremely creative, charismatic performance), the coolly competent policeman who responds to Michael's call and subsequently helps put the Carrs' life back in order. He supervises the installation of a new security system, offers Michael his help with the downtown rock club he is promoting, and invites his new friend out on a nocturnal tour of duty, during which Pete happens to catch the thief who invaded Michael's home.

In a highly disturbing sequence, Pete offers Michael the opportunity to enjoy that secret cop freedom—to give vent to all of his anger and anxiety by beating the now helpless suspect to his heart's content. When Michael, appalled, steps back, Pete does the job himself, clubbing the man to the ground in images that powerfully suggest the King tape.

Pete has invited Michael to cross the line, to join him in that no-man's-land outside of normal social bounds that movie cops inhabit. For Pete, Michael's refusal is not a sign of moral integrity—of "civilization," as Pete contemptuously calls it—but of cowardice, and the proof that Michael's beautiful wife deserves someone far stronger and more masculine. Someone, Pete thinks, like himself.

Unlawful Entry, which was written for the screen by Lewis Colick, is occasionally guilty of pushing some psychological hot buttons, including the rape metaphor embedded in the title. Is Karen purely a victim, or is she—as hinted by her clear dissatisfaction with her husband and initial responsiveness to Pete—asking for it? And is Michael's hesitancy due to moral scruples, or a general impotence? These issues are sometimes examined and sometimes exploited—used to whip the audience into a vengeful frenzy for the final confrontation.

There are signs, however, that Kaplan means his climax to be less cathartic and less positive than the Saturday night audience takes it to be. Michael does turn to violence by the end of the film, but he has lost a significant portion of his humanity in the process. Tempted by the extralegal power of the policeman—by the opportunity to take the law into his own hands—Michael is shattered by the experience.

The ambiguous cop figure—partly admired, partly feared—dates back at least to Don Siegel's *Dirty Harry* ('71), which featured Clint Eastwood as a San Francisco detective given to voyeurism, excessive force, and the torture of suspects. Suggestively, the explanation for Harry's unbalanced behavior—the loss of his wife—is the same given sixteen years later for the suicidal depression of the Mel Gibson character in the first *Lethal Weapon* ('88). But where *Dirty Harry* saw a marginal psychopath, the *Lethal Weapon* series envisions an entertainingly impulsive free spirit, unburdened by trivial concerns for life and limb (his own or others'). As director Richard Donner's frequent references to Warner Bros. cartoons and the Three Stooges make clear, Gibson's Martin Riggs is meant to be taken as a comic figure whose use of violence, as in a cartoon, has no real physical consequences.

If Riggs stands outside of society, it is as a gloriously free man, not a threat. And when he wants to reenter civilization, he can always drop in on the staunchly bourgeois household of his partner, Murtaugh—himself a gruff but understanding father figure. Riggs has the best of both worlds, enjoying both the anarchic individualism of the movie cop and the warmth and support of a family.

Riggs is essentially a child, and the films in which he appears are children's films, dealing in untrammeled fantasies of irresponsibility and freedom from adult authority. It may be for that reason that sexuality, despite the alluring presences of Rene Russo and Patsy Kensit, has never taken hold in the series. Riggs, the eternal adolescent, isn't quite ready for that stuff yet.

But there have been plenty of other movie cops who are. Director William Friedkin, in such films as *Cruising* ('80) and *To Live and Die in L.A.* ('85), was one of the first filmmakers to eroticize police work, developing a whole range of fetishistic associations around the paraphernalia of the profession (lots of leather and glistening steel) and emphasizing the kinky power relationships that develop between cop and criminal, investigator and suspect. These themes were developed further in Harold Becker's *Sea of Love* ('89), Richard Tuggle's *Tightrope* ('86), Michael Mann's *Manhunter* ('87), Kathryn Bigelow's *Blue Steel* ('89), and, of course, Jonathan Demme's Oscar-winning *The Silence of the Lambs* ('91). The most blatant of them all was Mike Figgis's *Internal Affairs* ('90), in which rogue cop Richard Gere was treated as an icon of rampant male sexuality, seducing all comers, fathering hordes of children, and eliminating any lesser male who dared oppose him.

Lost in all of this is any notion of duty or calling—the traditional motivations of movie cops and, before them, the Western sheriffs who were their cinematic ancestors. The motto on the side of the squad cars may read "To Serve and Protect," but just who is being protected, much less served, is left an open question in most of these films. The civilian population vanishes, or is reduced to a few pesky, bewildered onlookers. The cops, working out their own internal psychodramas, are the sole identification figures.

It is possible that, in the end, the L.A. riots and *Lethal Weapon 3* do not exist in contradiction but serve related ends—those of throwing off constraints, of giving vent to built-up anger and frustration, of reveling in social irresponsibility and personal freedom. Agents of repression from one point of view, cops become vehicles of release from another. In real life, however, the windows stay broken, bullet wounds take a long time to heal, and the dead do not get up again when the director says "cut." The release is only temporary; the anger and its causes remain.

Chicago Tribune, July 12, 1992

WESTERNS

When the majority of contributors to this book were growing up, Saturday matinees at the Bijou and on most TV stations were dominated by what we then called "cowboy movies." These weren't the great Westerns, the *My Darling Clementine*s and *Red River*s and *Shane*s. They were program pictures, produced in the thirties, forties, and fifties by Poverty Row studios or the B units of the majors, featuring recurring cowboy stars playing recurring cowboy heroes who outgunned the villain—or outpunched him, preferably at the edge of a handy cliff—in time to bring the action to a close just under an hour after it had started. The villains were recurring as well; a friend recalls that whenever his father happened to pass through the living room and see the portly, mustachioed, invariably black-hatted Charles King on the TV screen, he would mutter, "There's that sonofabitch again!"

Probably writer-director Hugh Wilson (of TV's "WKRP in Cincinnati") would recognize that sonofabitch, too. Yet after Wilson had filmed *Rustler's Rhapsody,* a deadpan, dead-on parody of white-hat–black-hat cowboy movies for the amusement of mid-eighties ticket-buyers, he discovered that preview audiences were bewildered, not amused. They didn't get the jokes because they didn't have the generic references. Most of them hadn't seen a Western in years. A once-universal familiarity with a whole lexicon of codes, conventions, and clichés was no more. Wilson had to reshoot or drop scenes. His movie flopped at the box office anyway.

That was 1985, the same year Lawrence Kasdan's *Silverado* and Clint Eastwood's *Pale Rider* racked up grosses "disappointing in relation to [production] cost," and several years after a would-be Western renaissance had foundered, most spectacularly with Michael Cimino's megacatastrophe *Heaven's Gate*. Not for the first time, the Western was declared dead, its erstwhile popular eminence usurped by more high-octane action genres, its relevance and appeal supposedly discredited by more than a decade of political revisionism.

Yet in 1990, against all odds and industry wisdom, director-producer-star Kevin Costner made *Dances With Wolves* and saw it become the highest-grossing Western in history and only the second (since 1931's *Cimarron*) to win the Academy Award as Best Picture of its year. Two years later, *Unforgiven*—Clint Eastwood's top-grossing film ever—became the third. As this book goes to press, Mario Van Peebles's Afrocentric *Posse* is going into release, and more than a dozen other oaters are in production. The reports of the Western's demise may have been greatly exaggerated. Yet again, in their very different ways, both *Dances With Wolves* and *Unforgiven* are highly accomplished and admirable films, and it may be that audiences simply know what to do with a good movie when they're given one. The success of the good ones doesn't necessarily betoken a continuing renaissance for the genre at large. But, as even the most terminally effete uptowner can no longer deny, when Westerns are good they are very good indeed.

Meanwhile, this chapter maps the latest bends in the Big Trail. "On How the Western Was Lost" is J. Hoberman's analysis of the genre's tortuous evolution in the era of Vietnam. For further historical perspective—and to focus attention to an underrated but magnificent body of work now happily available in the video stores—Dave Kehr writes about the remarkable series of Western collaborations between actor James Stewart and master director Anthony Mann in the 1950s. Stephen Schiff celebrates the ferocious beauty of Walter Hill's *Long Riders;* the editor cherishes *Silverado* as a throwback to a time when Westerns were a dime a dozen and worth every penny; Michael Wilmington places *Dances With Wolves* among both revisionist and unabashedly classical Westerns; and Dave Kehr traces Clint Eastwood's career to show how he came to his greatest achievement, *Unforgiven*.

ON HOW THE WESTERN WAS LOST

J. Hoberman

They tell me everything isn't black and white. Well I say why the hell not?

—John Wayne, 1969

The buffalo are gone. The railroad is finished. The red men are in disarray. The sun sets on Monument Valley. Once the quintessential Hollywood genre, the Western, as we knew it, is virtually extinct.

The cowboy movie was typically the vehicle America used to explain itself to itself. Who makes the law? What is the order? Where is the frontier? Which ones are the good guys? Why is it that a man's gotta do what a man's gotta do—and how does he do it? Each Hollywood Western, no matter how trite, was a national ritual, a passion play dramatizing and redramatizing the triumph of civilization over "savage" Indians or outlaws. It is the Western that was our true Fourth of July celebration. As historian Richard Slotkin has pointed out, in the national imagination America's real founding fathers are less those celebrated gentlemen who composed a nation in the genteel city of Philadelphia than "the rogues, adventurers, and land-boomers, the Indian fighters, traders, missionaries, explorers, and hunters who killed and were killed until they had mastered the wilderness." Add to these the cavalrymen and demobilized soldiers, freed slaves and impoverished homesteaders, picturesque immigrants and miscellaneous riffraff who went west after the Civil War—as well as "the Indians themselves, both as they were and as they appeared to the settlers, for whom they were the special demonic personification of the American wilderness"—and you have the characters for what seemed the pageant that could not die.

Like baseball, the Western is a sacred part of America's post–Civil War national mythology—a shared language, a unifying set of symbols and metaphors, and a source of (mainly male) identity. But baseball is all form; the Western is heavy, heavy, heavy on content. That the national pastime was successfully integrated after World War II while the demographics of the Western remained overwhelmingly white up until the eve of the genre's demise—despite the fact that at least a quarter of the working cowboys in the late nineteenth century were of African descent—should alert us to the possibility that the Western was as concerned with concealing as enacting historical truth.

As a genre, the Western was most often confined to a relatively brief era of American history—the twenty-five-year-long mop-up operation between Lee's surrender at Appomattox and the defeat of the Sioux at Wounded Knee. The Hollywood Western enjoyed its Golden Age during a quarter-century Pax Americana that followed World War II, a mainstay of early television no less than of "grind" movie theaters. Between 1865 and 1890, individuals were armed and the violence was constant; between 1948 and 1973, the nation was mobilized and the fear of war endemic. By focusing on the distinction between legal and illegal killing, the Western supported American hypervigilance during an age when, it was feared, widespread affluence might lull the nation into decadent complacence. Not for nothing did John F. Kennedy name his program the New Frontier, or Stanley Kubrick choose cowboy icon Slim Pickens to ride a hydrogen bomb, in *Dr. Strangelove,* bareback to Armageddon.

The celebration of national expansion intrinsic to the Western implicitly supported the Cold War ethos of limitless growth and personal freedom. The Cinerama spectacular *How the West Was Won* ('62), which climaxed its epic saga with a vision of freeways, conveniently designates the high-water mark of this optimistic worldview. Thereafter, confidence in the Western began to ebb in response to the struggle for civil rights at home and the questioning of imperial ambition abroad. If the Eisenhower era represented the Western's high noon, an era in which the U.S. appointed itself global sheriff and the gunslinger supplanted the cowboy as the archetypal Western hero, shadows had lengthened by the time Kennedy reached the White House. The old stars and veteran directors were aging. Sam Peckinpah's *Ride the High Country* and John Ford's *The Man Who Shot Liberty Valance* (both '62) introduced the crepuscular mood that deepened in Ford's *Cheyenne Autumn* ('64) and Howard Hawks's *El Dorado* ('67).

The sixties brought unprecedented domestic and foreign upheaval and, given its privileged place in American popular culture, the Western could hardly remain immune. In Italy, Sergio Leone made the genre more immediately relevant by raising the body count. At once more abstract and more violently naturalistic than Hollywood Westerns, Leone's *Dollars* trilogy not only unveiled the last Western hero, Clint Eastwood—the "dirty" icon who would preside over the end of the Western and the birth of the urban anti-Miranda *policier*—but invented a new mode. Excessive, operatic, thoroughly cynical in its representation of frontier heroism, the so-called spaghetti Western liberated the furies within Sam Peckinpah, inspiring Hollywood to new heights of carnage and a greater degree of naturalism.

By the mid sixties the Western had outgrown the screen. As many have observed, the men who fought in Vietnam were raised on Westerns—presented with cap-firing six-guns and Davy Crockett coonskin caps and deposited at Saturday matinees to watch the adventures of Hopalong Cassidy and Gene Autry. The average recruit had entered his teens at a time when eight of the top prime time TV shows were Westerns. Small wonder that John Wayne, the greatest of movie cowboys, became a talisman for a substantial number of American soldiers in Vietnam, or that he took the war as his personal crusade. Wayne's base in *The Green Berets* ('68) is called Dodge City. Meanwhile, in the actual Vietnam, where dangerous areas were known as "Indian country," Vietnamese scouts were termed "Kit Carsons" and Americans painted the slogan "The Only Good Gook Is a Dead Gook" on their flak jackets. There is a celebrated passage in Michael Herr's book *Dispatches* in which a combat reporter is invited out on a search-and-destroy mission against the Viet Cong: "'Come on,' the captain said, 'we'll take you out to play Cowboys and Indians.'"

In the national dream life, Indochina was an extension of the Western frontier and Americans were once again settlers, cavalrymen, schoolmarms, gunslingers, and marshals on a mission of protection and progress. The metaphor was irresistible, but this time there was no consensus on who were the good guys and who were the bad guys. Lyndon Johnson called upon the U.S. Army to "nail the coonskin to the cabin door"; the counterculture opposing his war identified itself with outlaws or worse. . . .

The Western mythology played itself out in Vietnam and vice versa. Peckinpah's *The Wild Bunch* and the William Goldman–George Roy Hill *Butch Cassidy and the Sundance Kid*—both key 1969 releases—embodied a striking inversion of values. At once cynical and romantic, both movies presented the unregenerate criminal as a sympathetic figure and were regretful at his elimination by the agents of law and order. In the wake of *The Wild Bunch* and the My Lai massacre, the genre grew increasingly apocalyptic. *The Green Berets* aside, Hollywood produced no movies on the war while the war was being waged. Instead, there were such revisionist and counter-revisionist essays as *Little Big Man* (Arthur Penn, '70), *The Cowboys* (Mark Rydell, '71), *Bad Company* (Robert Benton, '72), *Ulzana's Raid* (Robert Aldrich, '72), and *High Plains Drifter* (Eastwood's first Western as a director, '73), crypto-Vietnam films all. The Western split into radical right- and left-wing camps. Those starring John Wayne and, to a lesser extent, Clint Eastwood took up the cudgels against those directed by Arthur Penn and Robert Altman (*McCabe and Mrs. Miller*, '71; *Buffalo Bill and the Indians*, '76), while Peckinpah's Westerns were divided against themselves (*The Ballad of Cable Hogue*, '70; *Junior Bonner*, '72; *Pat Garrett & Billy the Kid*, '73). Common to all, however, was a sense of social breakdown, disillusionment, and the distrust of "liberal" mainstream values.

The most overtly ideological of revisionist Westerns concerned the Indian wars. The revelation of American atrocities in Vietnam only reinforced the argument that the slaughter of Native Americans was less the distortion than the essence of the white man's wars. *Little Big Man*, *Soldier Blue* (Ralph Nelson), and *A Man Called Horse* (Elliot Silverstein) identified with the Indians so strongly as to be the equivalent of marching against the war beneath a Viet Cong flag. Released in 1970 and coinciding with the publication of two influential histories, *Custer Died for Your Sins* and *Bury My Heart at Wounded Knee,* these films proposed that any and all Indian barbarities paled before the enormity of white genocide. Indeed, Sidney Poitier's *Buck and the Preacher* ('72) proposed an alliance of red and black men.

By the middle of Richard Nixon's first term, the quintessential Hollywood genre had clearly come unglued. But, in addition to widespread confusion, the extraordinary succession of revisionist and parody Westerns that appeared around the turn of the decade did embody a desire to acknowledge a multiplicity of perspectives on the winning (or losing) of the West. The ultimate desecration of the genre, Mel Brooks's *Blazing Saddles* ('74), the highest-grossing Western before *Dances With Wolves,* capped the assorted anti-, post-, spaghetti, revisionist, psychedelic, black, and burlesque Westerns of the early seventies. (It is appropriate that the concept for Michael Cimino's 1981 *Heaven's Gate,* blamed by some for the demise of the genre, also dates from this period.) By that time, *The Godfather* had emerged as a new sort of national epic and, as presaged by East-wood's Western-lawman-in-New-York *Coogan's Bluff* (Donald Siegel, '68), Fort Apache was relocated to the urban wilderness of the Bronx.

From 1910 through the end of the fifties, a quarter of all Holly-wood films had been Westerns. As late as 1972, the high point of genre revisionism, the year of *Jeremiah Johnson* (Sydney Pollack) and *The Life and Times of Judge Roy Bean* (John Huston), *The Great Northfield Minnesota Raid* (Philip Kaufman) and *The Culpepper Cattle Company* (Dick Richards), *Buck and the Preacher* (Sidney Poitier) and *Greaser's Palace* (Robert Downey), Westerns still represented twelve percent of Hollywood's output. But the year that brought Nixon's triumphant reelection was the last in which Western releases would reach double figures. The subsequent falloff was dramatic: four Westerns were released in 1973, two in 1974, five in 1975, seven for the Bicentennial, two in 1977, three in 1978, and a total of three between 1979 and 1984, the year of TV Western host Ronald Reagan's even more spectacular reelection. As J. Fred MacDonald put it in his history of the television Western, "no form of mass entertainment has been so dominant and then so insignificant."

Though the Western has bequeathed such enduring American totems as Marlboros and blue jeans, its decline effectively redefined the masculine screen image. There were no new heroic cowboys after Eastwood. When Dustin Hoffman made a Western he imper-sonated an Indian. Robert Redford played a notorious outlaw; Warren Beatty, a failed pimp. The seventies gave us an entire gen-eration of movie stars who have never donned Stetsons (De Niro, Stallone, Pacino, Dreyfuss). At the same time, the issues that preoc-cupied the Western have either been repressed or dispersed to other genres—including the Vietnam war film.

That the Western landscape still holds the promise of liberation and/or redemption, rebirth or reinvention, can be seen in such dis-parate nineties hits as *Thelma & Louise* and *City Slickers,* not to men-tion the phenomenal success of *Dances With Wolves* and the TV miniseries "Lonesome Dove." That the Western itself, save for a handful of releases, has remained defunct since the fall of Saigon suggests that the spectacle by which America came to be America has proved resistant to the reillusionment of the past dozen years. The rhetoric that supported Desert Storm and the celebrations that followed were notable for a paucity of Western imagery, despite the leadership of our first Texan president since Lyndon Johnson. (It's striking that the yellow ribbon, symbol of Americans held hostage overseas, is habitually located in a 1973 Tony Orlando song rather than a 1949 John Ford cavalry Western.)

Yet the popularity of Kevin Costner's *Dances With Wolves* ('90), a softer version of the Indian Westerns of 1970, demonstrates our enduring fascination with the classic Western situation—the confrontation in the wilderness between the European and the native American. It will be more difficult, I suspect, to make so "universal" a movie on the subject of the Alamo or the Mexican War. Although acknowledging the presence of blacks and Asians and thus grudgingly "urbanizing" the West, the two most ambitious Reagan-era Westerns, Clint Eastwood's *Pale Rider* ('85) and Lawrence Kasdan's *Silverado* ('85), were noticeably uncomplicated by the presence of Indians or Hispanics. Indeed, *Dances With Wolves* is itself so antiseptic and well regulated as to reduce our national dark-and-bloody ground to campsite proportions.

If nothing else, the hysterical response to the Smithsonian's recent exhibition "The West as America"—centering, for the most part, on the unremarkable curatorial suggestion that the Western art of the nineteenth and early twentieth centuries may have had its own ideological agenda—shows how contested and problematic this territory is. In that sense, the Western is still at the impasse it reached twenty years ago. Bloody and confused, the iconoclastic last Westerns took moviegoers to the end of a long and winding trail and found a thicket of ambiguities. It remains to be seen whether the first post-Western generation has any pathfinders with the nerve to push deeper still into that wilderness and reignite a genre that once epitomized America to itself and to the world.

Village Voice, August 27, 1991

ON ANTHONY MANN

Dave Kehr

Between 1950 and 1955, director Anthony Mann made five Westerns starring James Stewart. Though they remain oddly unappreciated in the United States (their exposure mostly limited to patchy prints on the late show), these movies have long been counted abroad as major classics of American film.

For French critic Jacques Lourcelles, the series constitutes "the most beautiful 'defense and illustration of the modern Western' that one can find." For Bertrand Tavernier and Jean-Pierre Coursodon, writing in their definitive *50 Years of American Cinema,* the Mann-Stewart Westerns are "that which the genre has given of the most perfect and the most pure." *The Far Country,* the penultimate film in the series, is for Lourcelles "*tout simplement, le plus beau Western du cinéma américain.*"

It may be that the Mann-Stewart films are too dark and complex for today's audiences, who tend to value the simple mythmaking of Fred Zinnemann's *High Noon* and George Stevens's *Shane* over the moral paradoxes and difficult psychologies that Mann, John Ford, Budd Boetticher, and Raoul Walsh were exploring in their more modest Westerns of the same period. Today's audiences certainly prefer the naïve, boyish James Stewart of Frank Capra's films over the driven, often violent persona Stewart created in his postwar movies, under the direction of Mann and Alfred Hitchcock.

Yet it was Stewart himself who initiated the Mann cycle, when he brought *Winchester '73* to Universal as part of a pioneering independent production deal. The legendary Fritz Lang was signed to direct but dropped out at the last minute. Mann, who had passed his early career creating resourceful, modestly budgeted films noirs (*T-Men, Raw Deal*) largely for independent release, was brought in as Lang's replacement. The result was one of the most financially successful films of the decade, and the movie that, with Raoul Walsh's *Pursued* ('47), introduced the so-called adult Western.

The stark, black-and-white *Winchester '73* ('50) still reflects the Teutonic Lang's influence in its casting (Dan Duryea as a giggling killer), cyclical structure (the film follows the title weapon, a rifle that is passed from hand to hand until it returns to Stewart's possession), and revenge theme (Stewart's character is searching for the man who killed his father—it turns out to be his brother). But Mann's signature is immediately visible in his use of the Western landscape—a rugged, treacherous, variable terrain that Mann used, uniquely and unobtrusively, as a projection of the interior landscapes of his characters. Mann's West is not the great social expanse of Ford, with its serene horizon line of history, but a crabbed, subjective environment, full of jagged rocks, dense forests, and deep precipices that reflect the dark obsessions and conflicted impulses of his heroes.

With the 1952 *Bend of the River* Mann moved into color and beyond the simple moral divisions of *Winchester '73*. Good brother and bad brother now inhabit the same skin: Glyn McLyntock (Stewart), a former border raider (with a rope burn around his neck) who is struggling to go straight as the leader of a wagon train on its way to Oregon. But because of his past, McLyntock can't help but befriend Emerson Cole (Arthur Kennedy), a horsethief with whom he shares a Missouri history.

Winchester's itinerary of an object here becomes the journey of an individual; the same strongly marked symbolic stages are present but without the earlier film's structural rigidity. Like the rifle, McLyntock is morally neutral, able to lend himself to good or evil, depending on the context in which he finds himself. But with Cole as a kind of double, representing a McLyntock that might have been (or still could be), the hero has something to react against. The final confrontation is not an act of revenge as much as the violent resolution of an interior conflict.

More violent still is *The Naked Spur* ('53), the harshest and most rigorous film in the cycle. A five-character drama, the film strongly suggests the psychological poker games of Budd Boetticher's Randolph Scott Westerns (*Seven Men from Now, The Tall T,* etc.), with an itchy anger in place of Boetticher's elegance and irony.

Stewart is a bounty hunter fighting to transport a wanted killer (Robert Ryan) across a mountain terrain, alternately helped and hindered by three hangers-on who may or may not be on his side: an old prospector (Millard Mitchell), a renegade cavalryman (Ralph Meeker), and a young woman (Janet Leigh). Changing screenwriters (Sam Rolfe and Harold Jack Bloom instead of the usual, and excellent, Borden Chase), Mann accedes to a new level of hysteria, emphasizing the nightmarish contortions of the landscape and presenting Stewart as a marginal sociopath, driven half mad by the collapse of his marriage and the loss of his ranch. In contrast to the raging hero is the cool, collected villain, who dominates those around him not through violence but by insinuation and seduction. Pointedly, Ryan is shown as a master of the landscape, defending himself at various points by arranging little avalanches.

The Far Country ('55) reunited Mann and Stewart with Chase, for what remains the masterpiece of the series. After the miniaturism of *The Naked Spur,* Mann introduces a sweeping social and historical context that seems straight out of Ford. Stewart is Jeff Webster, a trail driver with a cloudy past that includes at least two recent killings. Trying, with the help of grizzled pal Walter Brennan, to transport a herd of beef to the gold rush country in Alaska, he comes up against an eccentric local lawman (John McIntire) who impounds the herd for his own.

With entire populations at stake, rather than individual destinies, Mann's revenge theme takes on a new urgency. The loner hero seems to be surrounded by forces beckoning him into couples, unions, communities (not the least of which is Ruth Roman as a smart, profit-minded saloon owner), with only his own deep suspiciousness holding him apart. In the end, however, it is revenge that returns him to the fold, when Brennan is killed by McIntire's forces and Stewart must take sides. The irony is so elegantly understated as to be all but invisible.

If *The Far Country* is the culmination of Mann's classicism, *The Man from Laramie* ('55) suggests the opening of a new gothic phase, which would be continued with Gary Cooper in 1958's *Man of the West*. Working for the first time in CinemaScope, Mann seems to have smoothed out his jagged landscapes to suit the strong horizontals of the new format. The action in *Laramie* takes place largely in a single flat and arid setting—the ranch belonging to an aging, distinctly Lear-like cattle baron (Donald Crisp). Stewart's Will Lockhart (the name is worthy of Hawthorne) takes his place as one of the old man's three "sons"—one literal, a crazed sadist (Alex Nicol), one adoptive (Arthur Kennedy as a crafty, mercenary foreman), and one idealized and unavailable (Stewart).

Revenge remains a motive (Lockhart is ostensibly searching for the gun merchants responsible for his cavalryman brother's death), but the violence of this world has grown increasingly irrational and out of scale. In the film's most famous sequence, Nicol has two of his henchmen hold Stewart down while he fires a bullet through his hand. There is something in the extremity of this scene, in its sheer cruelty and arbitrariness, that points its way completely out of the classical Western tradition. After *The Man from Laramie*, the next stop is the chaos and absurdity perceived in the Western in the sixties by the genre's last two great practitioners, Sam Peckinpah and Sergio Leone.

Chicago Tribune, July 5, 1992

EDITOR'S NOTE: During this same period Mann also directed Stewart in the non-Western *Thunder Bay* ('53), *The Glenn Miller Story* ('54), and *Strategic Air Command* ('55). Mann also cast, prepared, and directed the classically integral first scene of *Night Passage* ('57).

THE LONG RIDERS

■■■

Stephen Schiff

Director Walter Hill says that the most important shot in his films is the first one. And his latest film, *The Long Riders,* begins with a shot that looks as though it came from Bergman's *The Seventh Seal:* a procession of silent riders, silhouetted against the empty dusk, cantering in single file along the arc of a hilltop. The movie recounts the saga of the Jesse James–Cole Younger gang, and as the credits flash, the camera pulls closer and closer to the gang; the riders bound toward us in slow motion, their cowboy hats rising and falling, their beige dust-coats flapping, the hooves of their horses splashing luxuriously in the tall grass. Watching those horses fly across the screen, you're astonished by the pleasure they give, a pleasure so keen it's almost painful; it's like the sudden, piercing memory of a dream. Hill, you see, wants us to know what we've been missing. If his film's opening shot bespeaks myth and metaphysics, the next few shots announce a special occasion: the return of the Western.

Yet this is a horse opera of a different color, a movie that breaks away from the New Western, the revisionist Western, the Western that killed the Western. True, Hill is a very self-conscious director and he sprinkles his film with references and cinematic wisecracks. The influence of *The Wild Bunch* and *Bonnie and Clyde* and Kurosawa and even Eisenstein is obvious in his work, but he turns their lessons to his own ends. His film isn't a spoof or a debunking, a misty dream of the West or a metaphor for the present. In its classic structure, its sensuousness, and its love of violent action, *The Long Riders* seems to reinvent the Western from the ground up,

The brothers Carradine—Robert (left), David (on horseback), and Keith—play the Younger boys of Missouri in Walter Hill's epic Western *The Long Riders*. (© 1980 United Artists Corporation. All Rights Reserved. Photo courtesy of MGM/UA Home Video, Inc., a subsidiary of Metro-Goldwyn-Mayer, Inc.)

reveling in the wonder of thunderous gallops and erupting six-guns as if no one had ever seen them before.

The French critic André Bazin once defined the classic Western as a combination of elements—"social myth, historical reconstruction, psychological truth, and the traditional theme of the Western mise-en-scène"—that reached its peak in John Ford's *Stagecoach* ('39). When directors tried to justify or revitalize the genre by adding relevance, social comment, "adult concerns," they were creating what Bazin called the *sur*-Western: "a Western that would be ashamed to be just itself." The *sur*-Western had its value, of course, but somehow it lost the immediacy and force that the good old Western had—and that *The Long Riders* brings back. Bazin's argument isn't always convincing, but his reverence for the genre is: ever since the West was won, our horse operas have entertained us, educated our morality, and reflected the ebb and flow of the American dream. It's no accident that the Western disappeared in the late seventies, in the wake of Vietnam, Watergate, the CIA scandals, and a host of other revelations that called the dream into question.

I don't think the return of the Western necessarily heralds a dawning era of American certainty and vision, but *The Long Riders,* despite its old-fashioned structures and formulas, does reflect contemporary concerns. As we huddle in the gloom of yet another recession, banding together against foreign enemies and corporate heedlessness, *The Long Riders* gives us an outlaw myth that fits.

Set in Missouri after the Civil War (it was shot in Georgia), the film takes place in a land of deep-green forests and muddy fields, of wheat farms and waterfalls and humid weather. It's the West as American heartland, a frontier without the exoticism of sagebrush and howling coyotes. And if most outlaw yarns are about misfits and outsiders, *The Long Riders* beckons us into a rich and vital community, a world that supports the James-Younger gang, lives off its earnings, and dies to protect it. Ex-Confederates all, the James-Younger boys are family men who refuse to give up the battle against the Union. In robbing banks and trains and eluding Pinkerton agents, they believe they're defending the independence and dignity of the South against the depredations of the Yankee corporations. As Hill told *Film Comment,* "I think that their popularity really lies in the fact that they robbed and stole from the railroads and banks, which the Missouri farmers hated more than we hate the oil companies." Does this sort of "relevance" turn *The Long Riders* into a *sur*-Western? Not at all. The film's center of gravity isn't in its social vision, but in the splendor of its images, in the eloquent iconography of its characters and the rough beauty of its shootouts, barn dances, and poker games.

Hill began as a screenwriter (he wrote *The Getaway* for Sam Peckinpah and *The Thief Who Came to Dinner* for Bud Yorkin and wrote and directed *Hard Times, The Driver,* and *The Warriors*). But his films aren't talky; they're ecstatically visual. In *The Long Riders,* the way things look becomes the way they feel. Textures, compositions, patterns of light and shadow possess a mysterious emotional force. When I heard that producer-stars James and Stacy Keach had decided to cast several sets of Hollywood brothers in the lead roles, I thought it sounded like a pretty silly gimmick. I was wrong. James and Stacy Keach play Jesse and Frank James; David, Keith, and Robert Carradine play Cole, Jim, and Bob Younger; Randy and Dennis Quaid are Clell and Ed Miller; the Ford boys, Bob and Charlie, who try to join the gang and later turn on them, are played by *National Lampoon* writer Christopher Guest and his brother Nicholas. Shortly after the credits, when the scene switches to a deserted beach, Hill poses the brothers against a luminous sky, singly and in pairs. As he cuts from one face to another, we realize we're being shown something new in movies. We're actually *seeing* kinship—not in any overt camaraderie, but in the way the brothers' features rhyme, in the minute ways they respond to fraternal similarities, in a thousand ineffable expressions and gestures that the actors may not even be aware of. You can feel the magnetism of blood.

Very quickly, then, the action is rooted in a sense of family. And almost as quickly, Hill brings us into the community that nourishes the gang. He shows us breathtaking robbery sequences, each done in a different style, and, in between, he depicts courtships and night life and funerals and other civilized rituals. Jesse James marries Zee (Savannah Smith) and there's a big wedding that the whole county attends. There you get a sense of what the gang means to its neighbors: everyone wants to join, but only the best and the brightest are chosen. And yet, standing up for the gang is part of the community's unwritten code. When Ed Miller, whom the gang has kicked out, refuses to carry a gun because he has no personal quarrel with the Pinkertons, his girlfriend leaves him in an instant.

The Long Riders is that rare thing: a Western with complex relationships and sharp, fascinating female characters. Hill has never been particularly interested in exploring character, but he's a brilliant portraitist in the tradition of John Ford, and the beauty and nuance he reveals in his closeups of faces knocks the wind out of you. Mostly, though, we learn about the outlaws by observing how they get along with the women in their lives. James Keach gives Jesse James an Old Testament brand of purity and fervor, and when he's courting Savannah Smith their scenes together are all thrust jaws and burning gazes; one night, when he comes to her after a long absence, the expectant light in his eyes is almost otherworldly. They're a tough, humorless pair, these two, and at first it's strange to think of Jesse James as a family man. But they share a strength not unlike that of Puritans and founding fathers and zealots: we can see what it is in Jesse that makes him the gang's leader. As David Carradine plays him, Cole Younger is Jesse's opposite. Hard-drinking, freewheeling, a lover of long card games and good fights, he's the old-style Western hero, mean and slit-eyed and fast on the draw. Carradine's performance is the best in the film. He's sly, sardonic, yet disarmingly direct, and he's almost matched, take for take, by a smoldering newcomer named Pamela Reed, who plays his girlfriend, the gunslinging prostitute Belle Starr. Reed isn't pretty, exactly—she has coarse features and the beginnings of a mustache—but innuendo slithers through her husky voice, and her knowing, fearless stare could set the drapes on fire. When Cole and Belle make love they grab each other in fistfuls, and they take an infectious, dirty delight in exchanging raw remarks. If this isn't chemistry, I don't know what is. Even young Beth (Amy Stryker), the girl who drops Ed Miller to pursue Jim Younger, is more than the ordinary ingenue. Looking into her wide blue eyes, you'd think her the picture of innocence, but when she opens her mouth the voice that comes out is unexpectedly smoky and cynical. She and Belle, you imagine, are just the sort of tough, sexy, likable women who *must* have won the West.

The unexpectedness of the characterizations heightens the authenticity one feels in the casting. Indeed, authenticity might well be the film's watchword. *The Long Riders* is probably the most historically accurate of the Jesse James movies (and there have been dozens); Hill has taken remarkable care to get the period details right. The cards in the poker games are hand painted; the scratchy-looking nighties the bordello girls wear appear homemade; Ry Cooder's soundtrack, full of banjos and fiddles, Jew's harps and slide guitars, is never false, never distracting. And in one robbery scene, I was startled to notice that the beset train wasn't the usual perfectly preserved antique: when Keith Carradine climbs atop it, you can see that the roof is worn and corroded. The authenticity in this movie is more than mere decoration. In order to retell the Jesse James story yet again, Hill has to make us feel as though we're seeing it for the first time. He succeeds because he's made the details so exciting: the faces, the props, the colors. In this movie, it's the decor that's most deeply felt, the surface that's profound.

And yet many who see it will come away disappointed because of what they *have* seen before: the slow-motion violence that's out of Peckinpah, especially *The Wild Bunch*. Peckinpah's ballet-of-death technique, in which wounds spew blood in slow fountains and bodies flop through the air like laundry, dominates the climactic shootout during the gang's disastrous raid on Northfield, Minnesota. When Peckinpah tried this in *The Wild Bunch* he wanted to make the death scenes shockingly real, to hit us with them and knock out of us whatever amusement or detachment we felt. But the ballet of death turned out to be so entrancing that it became an aesthetic experience; its beauty distanced us from the pain it depicted. This distancing is what interests Hill. In his Northfield sequence, he is trying to show what happens when the community of outlaws, debilitated by separation and bickering, leaves the magically protected homeland of Missouri and encounters a newer, stronger mythic community: the industrious Swedes of Northfield, the people the outlaws dismiss as "squareheads." "We should never have left home," Jesse tells Frank, and he's right; the destruction and pain in the Northfield sequence are overwhelming. Yet by turning that sequence into a Peckinpah-style ballet, Hill changes its nature. Some scenes become wild flurries of color, like abstract Expressionist paintings; others have an oddly pastoral quality, and the soundtrack, which is filled with strange electronic whirrings that actually tell us when a bullet is about to hit, undercuts the realism. Hill has gone beyond Peckinpah, purposely manipulating the master's methods (which, after all, had been pioneered by Arthur Penn and Akira Kurosawa before him) to draw us away from the pain. What we are seeing becomes less the destruction of individual characters than a dismantling of pure form, a collective disintegration— the death of a myth.

As action, as special effects, it all works beautifully. But I'm afraid Hill hasn't prepared for it properly. The film's second half feels elliptical, truncated, vague. Something's missing, and the trouble begins when, very suddenly, the gang takes a sort of sabbatical. The outlaws go their separate ways, and Hill follows just one of them, Cole Younger (and then only in order to watch him have a rip-roaring knife fight with Belle Starr's Texan husband, played by James Remar). When the gang regroups, though, something has changed. There are arguments, unexplained shifts of attitude, cloudy decisions—decisions that lead to Northfield. Jesse becomes utterly enigmatic, and his bitter confrontations with Cole Younger seem to emerge from nowhere. What has gone wrong? We never find out. If the death-of-a-myth ballet is to work, we have to know why the myth is dying, what has wounded it, why family has turned against family, how the seemingly invulnerable circle has been broken. The answers, evidently, wound up on the cutting-room floor, and it's a pity. *The Long Riders* is good at an hour and a half, but as a three-hour epic it might well have been a masterpiece.

And yet, the meanings that are missing in the narrative glint at us in the images. Hill never pretends to explain his heroes—too much explanation can smother a legend. He believes that the truth about them is there for everyone to see, in the canyons of their faces, in the way they throw a punch or aim a shotgun. And his film proves his point. Imperfect, incomplete, mystifying though it is, *The Long Riders* is still the richest movie to come out of Hollywood in months, because Hill understands the poetry of horses and guns and big skies. He understands how to make movie magic.

Boston Phoenix, May 20, 1980

SILVERADO

∎∎∎

Richard T. Jameson

I said I liked *Silverado* and the editor said mostly he didn't. I said it had given me a grand time; he grumbled something about structural problems. I allowed as how it bordered on the miraculous that some wised-up, thoroughly contemporary filmmakers had managed to rediscover the pleasures of the pure Western without parodying, tarting up, or otherwise condescending to the genre. He said he only liked Westerns that transcended the genre, and as far as he was concerned the genre needed all the transcending it could get. I said, "I *like* Westerns. I grew up with Westerns!" He chuckled, pleasantly: "Ken Maynard?" "Among others." That put the discussion on hold for about two weeks.

Well, I *did* grow up with Westerns—Jack Randall and Hopalong Cassidy on Saturday afternoon TV, occasional Technicolor excursions with Audie Murphy, Alan Ladd, Jimmy Stewart at the moviehouse. Something other than nostalgia accounts for my continuing fondness for those youthful experiences. Some of those Westerns would turn out years later to be films de Anthony Mann or "the George Stevens classic, *Shane.*" Others would recede in the memory as simply movies with Audie Murphy or Jack Randall in them. Cumulatively, all left their mark. In some fundamental ways, my pleasure in the ultrastylized look, movements, and behaviors of Westerns shaped my sense of what movies at large ought to be, what sorts of texture, ritual, and discovery we should require of them.

Is any other kind of movie more purely aesthetic? Although Westerns speak to a dream of America and uniquely American

Scott Glenn and Kevin Kline (center) supplied the primary heroics in Lawrence Kasdan's lovingly old-fashioned Western *Silverado,* and Danny Glover (right) was their equal in nobility and marksmanship. But it was Kevin Costner (left) as Glenn's irrepressible kid brother who ran away with the audience's affections and started a swift climb to superstardom. (© 1985 Columbia Pictures Industries, Inc. All Rights Reserved. Photo courtesy of Columbia Pictures, Inc.)

codes of honor and integrity, I never seriously confused the genre (specific exceptions aside) with an even halfway literal record of historical events and personages. The first time I heard Westerns likened to tales of King Arthur's Round Table, I figured, "Yeah, well, *sure!*" The pure Western is as abstract and fanciful—and just as true to human aspirations and the hunger for legend.

The great thing is, Westerns turn narrative itself into legend. We follow the storylines about range feuds, families decimated, old friends falling out, new alliances being forged in the crucible of action and history, and if someone asks of a given movie "What's it about?" we probably answer with a few phrases of plot summary. But what we really watch, what makes the hair on the backs of our necks shiver and our faces spread in glee is something else entirely. It's the recognition we share of a privileged code, the evolution of signs: the way a certain Henry rifle or a pair of pearl-handled .45s or the brand on the flank of a pinto keeps turning up; whether there's cut whiskey in the bottle on the table; how long it takes before we know why some people persist in greeting one fellow in *Silverado* by inquiring, "Where's the dog?"

Lawrence Kasdan, who produced and directed *Silverado* and wrote it with his brother Mark, obviously loves and understands this elemental aspect of the Western and wanted to reclaim it from decades of parody and revisionism. He's taken pains that his movie should be "about" nothing beyond its own patterns of incident, character, and the characters' apprehension of one another. The endeavor constitutes neither an excursion into camp preciosity nor an aridly academic exercise in restoring an archaic genre. Rather (if my own experiences and the rapt delight of three separate general audiences are any indication), *Silverado* marks the rediscovery of a truly popular art form as supple as it is formalized, as accessible as it is exotic, and prodigiously entertaining.

The trick is that the prodigious entertainment necessarily springs from extreme concentration. This plays into one of the fundamental tensions in the genre: between the vast, apparently endless potentiality of the landscape and the life-or-death consequentiality of the smallest, most mundane detail. At the beginning of the film, Emmett (Scott Glenn) is bushwhacked by several gunmen, whom he succeeds in dispatching handily. Two of their horses run off; Emmett finds the third tethered nearby and leads it behind him as he continues his journey. When he comes upon Paden (Kevin Kline), horseless, stripped to his long johns, and left by four no-goods to parch in the desert, he revives the fellow and trades terse introductions with him. "Where're you goin'?" Emmett asks. "Where's the pinto goin'?" Paden responds agreeably, and the next cut discloses the two horsemen approaching an outpost together. Rapport is all well and good, but at base Paden rides that pinto or he dies.

Kasdan pursues this logic of survival and advancement, and builds a wry narrative structure on it. The pinto carries Paden to that outpost where, with money Emmett loans him to buy new clothes, he obtains instead a secondhand revolver and kills one of the men who had left him to die. That man had Paden's bay horse ("the only thing I really miss"), aboard which Paden now accompanies Emmett to the town of Turley. (It's no longer a matter of life and death, but Emmett's a decent guy and Turley sounds as good a place as any.) There Paden spots another of his victimizers under a black hat with a silver band ("After the bay, the only thing I really miss . . ."). Guns are drawn, Paden blasts the lowlife out from under the hat, which plops on the floor in a closeup all its own—and in the next cut, the hat goes to jail.

I've shorthanded a good deal here, overleaping such crucial business as the introduction of the two other principals in *Silverado's* heroic foursome: Mal (Danny Glover), a less-than-stoic black who's just about "had enough o' what ain't right" in the wild white West, and Emmett's kid brother Jake (Kevin Costner), who's already occupying that jail cell before Paden is shoved into it under his reclaimed headgear. No "structural problems" here. The Kasdans' script contains nary a wasted line or move, inventing crackling-good crisis situations (how does a man in long johns with ten borrowed dollars to his name obtain a gun, load it, and accurately fire it before an unscrupulous man across the street either rides his stolen horse away or shoots him down?) and layering one spare, generic transaction over another until a persuasive fictive life emerges.

Silverado is the kind of Western in which characters have absolutely no existence beyond the moves they eloquently make onscreen. They're as thin and transparent as a strip of celluloid, but if they and their actions are interlayered right, patterns assert themselves and the interplay of coded gestures can suggest the shape and possibility of real human connection. Values that are defined even as they are acted on form the essence of Western conduct and, not coincidentally, of every film defining its own unique principles of meaning, style, and substance in the act of unreeling.

The suppleness of the Western as art form lets Kasdan hearken back to the basic forms of the program Western (that is, to Ken Maynard rather than John Ford), while at the same time adapting the models to the present day. For instance, when the sheriff of Turley has to intercede in an altercation involving the principal characters, there is no hard and exclusive reason why the sheriff should not be an Englishman who's carved out his own frontier fiefdom by force of cosmopolitan peculiarity as well as quick wit and strong will. Hence, though John Cleese arrives upon the scene with a characteristically Pythonesque "What's all this then?" the shock of dislocating recognition on the audience's part is only momentary, and our delight increases geometrically as Cleese goes on to meet all the generic obligations this lawman figure owes to the furtherance of the plot, while also agreeably seasoning the flavor of the picaresque adventure. By the same token, the arrival of Jeff

Goldblum as a fur-collared gentleman gambler in the immediate aftermath of a killing on the main street of Silverado plucks at the fine line of period credibility just enough to set it vibrating amusingly. There's room for even a long absurdist drink of water like Goldblum in the mythopoetic spaces of the Western, if not necessarily the Old West.

Clearly, whatever he may have scripted and shot, Kasdan ultimately elected to cut *Silverado* along a steady, masculine action line. Not surprisingly, the leathery, laconic Scott Glenn fits the classic Gary Cooper mold as though it had been struck for him. Kevin Kline is inescapably a more contemporary presence, and urban-contemporary at that—or, as the estimable Peter Hogue put it, "He's got a quiche-eater's streak in him." Kline and Kasdan cannily accommodate this quality, even turn it into a virtue by translating it into Paden's penchant for irony and guile. And to Western habitués nervously guarding the genre's frontiers against incursion by supercilious yuppies, there were few scenes in 1985 more gratifying than the string of exchanges between Kline and Linda Hunt as a saloonkeeper of exemplary civility. This pair, two of the hippest, most esteemed theaterfolk of their generation, slip right into the rigorously ethical, self-aware behavior and communication that constitutes the genre's most privileged mode of being. Saying what needs saying and understanding reams left unsaid, they make a marriage of true minds across the bar of Silverado's Midnight Star.

Stylistically as well, Kasdan has his modes of being straight, and straight to the generic point. The director takes his pleasure in the dynamics of a classic genre rather than contriving *hommages* to classics of the genre: *Silverado* reminds me of a hundred Westerns I've seen, but none in particular. A couple dozen people get killed, but a single gunshot is usually bloodlessly fatal, and accuracy tends to be a function of deterministic frame composition. It's worth noting that the most communicably painful wounds in the movie aren't fatal: a vicious, dying thrust of a gunman's arm that sends a bullet into Mal's sister's stomach during a jailbreak; and the meaty *punch!* of a rifle slug entering Emmett's thigh at the final showdown.

As for that showdown, with the four heroes converging on the hilltop town of Silverado, realistic strategy plays no part in it. Within a distinctly limited assortment of streets and buildings, each knight-errant seeks out his opposite number and sends him (and the occasional crony) to his reward. The fights do not overlap; every arena is a private space bearing no relation to the rest. The same Western connoisseur who prizes the scrupulous attention to trajectory and topography in an Anthony Mann shootout can also value the rarefied ritual of this final clearing of the books. It compels an order of exultation all its own, of a kind with that moment around the middle of the second reel when Kasdan gives us an auspicious horizon shot, and the four male leads, who had not previously made common cause, now appear together, riding abreast.

The communal satisfaction of the audience at that moment is palpable—satisfaction in the moment itself and what it signifies about the nature of the action that will follow, and also satisfaction in the unstated but felt-in-the-blood awareness that it's been far too long since a Western reached for this kind of recognition. It's scarcely the highest order of recognition the Western at its greatest can yield; but then, the charm and gratification of *Silverado* inhere in the good faith with which it reaches for something other than greatness.

These peak gestures in *Silverado* recall nothing so much as those penultimate passages when the Bar-20 riders saddled up and thundered off to the showdown, Gluck's "Dance of the Furies" surging on the soundtrack; or when Buck Jones, Tim McCoy, and Raymond Hatton at last forswore their separate-agent status and gathered their reins with a signatory "Let's go, Rough Riders!" You don't learn about this level of the Western in film courses, but the filmgoer or film critic who has entered upon maturity bereft of such cultural conditioning is poorer for it.

At least, that's how this legatee of a misspent youth chooses to see it. With what awe and wonder I used to attend the esoteric transactions of that alien race up there on the screen. What they said and didn't have to say, comprehended without my comprehending how, yet somehow succeeded in resolving through clear and direct action, constituted a simulacrum of adult capability to my pre-adolescent heart and mind. When I grew up, I hoped, I'd understand stuff like that. Meanwhile, it was wondrous.

In this connection, the varmint who steals *Silverado* for his own is Brian Dennehy. He plays my favorite Western type, the guy who turns up early in the proceedings, trades some cryptic dialogue with the hero (in this case, Paden), gives plenty of indication that he and the hero have shared some history, been friends, but somehow no longer are. Looking at this fellow, one can't help liking him. When he shows up again, we're glad to see him. We don't even mind if he kills one or two minor characters nobody will miss, just to confirm him as a worthy and talented adversary. One senses in his ever-appraising grin not just danger but also a relish for life's little ironies, like the fact that he's unashamedly corrupt and will eventually have to kill or be killed by precisely the one fellow he holds in esteem, his old chum with a weakness for values. Dennehy, a great silvery bear, crawls inside this Western archetype as if it were an irresistible oversized coat, and wears it with rare style. Basically, that's what *Silverado* does with the long-neglected mantle of the Western.

Film Comment, September 1985

POSTSCRIPT: One of the first Hollywood Westerns in a long while to be shot on location in the States (in New Mexico), *Silverado* was seen—and mostly loved—by legions of fans, became a hot ticket on the video-buying and -renting circuit, and marked the beginning of Kevin Costner's stardom. Yet it went into the annals as a flop. Go figure.

DANCES WITH WOLVES

Michael Wilmington

Let's face it, we've treated [the Indians] very badly; it's a blot on our shield. We've cheated and robbed, killed, murdered, massacred and everything else. . . . But they kill one white man and, God, out come the troops!

There are two sides to every story, but I wanted to show their point of view for a change [in *Cheyenne Autumn,* '64]. I had wanted to make it for a long time [because, in my movies] I've killed more Indians than Custer, Beecher and Chivington put together.

—John Ford

Early on in *Dances With Wolves*—a movie in which director-star Kevin Costner gives new life and vigor to the Western genre—we see a huge, ramshackle wagon silhouetted against an endless sky and a vast, rolling plain. In it, Costner's John Dunbar and a foul-mouthed guide (Robert Pastorelli) are making their way to an abandoned fort. Dunbar is on a fool's mission. He became a hero after an unsuccessful suicide attempt turned into a glorious Civil War charge. He received his orders from a lunatic (Maury Chaykin), who killed himself immediately afterward. In this wild realm, absurdity, chance, and sudden death seem to rule.

There shouldn't be glory in the ride. But there is. The widescreen compositions, the hard but lyrical palette of colors, the effortless rolling motion of the wagon and horses, all create something thrilling: a sense of plunging into a mystery vast and dark, an adventure of endless exhilaration and ambivalent promise. It's the frontier itself, which Costner, in an earlier closeup pregnant with portent, tells us he wants to see . . . before it's gone.

It's a quintessential Western moment.

If you love Westerns, you're often made to feel apologetic about it—as if a taste for *The Searchers* or *The Wild Bunch* were an automatic sign of questionable intelligence or dubious morals. And that was particularly true in the eighties, when the genre seemed to have expired. Since 1976, when John Wayne made his last movie, *The Shootist,* Westerns seemed a moribund form, surviving mainly in TV revivals and insurance commercials.

It's often suggested that the 1981 debacle *Heaven's Gate* killed them off completely. And I think many detractors of Westerns believe that they should die, that the entire genre is a dangerous perversion of historical fact and a huge, over-rowdy repository of unhealthy macho fantasies. Not-so-subtle hints of class or urban prejudice often surface in diatribes against Westerns. And when new Westerns turn up—including such interesting entries as Fred Schepisi's *Barbarosa* ('82), Clint Eastwood's *Pale Rider* ('85), and Anthony Harvey's *Eagle's Wing* ('79)—they tend to be judged, not as themselves, but as test cases for the entire genre.

That's what's so exciting about the widespread admiration for *Dances With Wolves.* A big commercial and critical hit, almost assuredly a multiple Oscar nominee, this three-hour epic about an idealistic cavalry man and his relations with a Sioux tribe is both fresh and iconoclastic, and it's a Western in the old, classic sense: a work of range and sweep, humor, lyricism, and action. No genre is moribund if it still produces works that connect with audiences in this way.

It has also been suggested that *Wolves'* impact lies in myth debunking or in some new cinematic take on Western history. But that's only partly true. The movie's major departures are in its use of the Lakota language—subtitles appear during conversations between American Indian actors—and in its strenuous efforts to be true to Indian culture.

There's nothing new about its pro-Indian viewpoint; major Westerns have taken the American Indian side since the 1926 silent film *The Vanishing American,* and I think it can be argued that, since 1950 and Delmer Daves's *Broken Arrow,* sympathy with Indian protagonists has been the rule rather than the exception. The tendency peaked in Arthur Penn's *Little Big Man* ('71)—a movie almost identical in viewpoint, sympathy, and historical overview to *Dances With Wolves.*

But, true to its devotion to the Sioux culture, *Dances With Wolves* uses Indian actors in Indian roles. It doesn't cast a Jeff Chandler (Oscar-nominated for his Cochise in *Broken Arrow*) or a Rock Hudson (in the title role of Douglas Sirk's *Taza, Son of Cochise*) or even a Don Ameche (Alessandro, the tragic swain of the early Technicolor *Ramona,* '36) in the tribe. (Ironically, the Indian actor playing tribal elder Kicking Bird has an Anglo name; he's an Oneida named Graham Greene.)

The writer, Michael Blake, is the great-grandson of an Indian fighter in the old Sixth Cavalry, and he bends over backward here. Perhaps he feels he's paying for a few family sins: the Sioux are wise and pure, the whites mostly hateful or ridiculous.

Beyond all this, *Dances With Wolves* has the same appeal as most classic Westerns, even the same sort of flaws. The buffalo stampede, the shootouts, the ribald portrayals of the secondary characters, the devotion to landscapes, the tender scenes with animals—when Costner's horse and pet wolf are hurt, it's an annihilating experience—all are almost paradigmatic Western scenes. So is the rather ritualized treatment of the love interest: a white female captive (Mary McDonnell), rescued by the Sioux from a Pawnee massacre, conveniently turns up.

And so is the rescue of the hero by a last-minute charge—this time by the Sioux rather than the cavalry; a similar turnabout climaxes the 1953 Budd Boetticher movie *Seminole.* It may also be argued that because *Dances With Wolves* boasts a feisty heroine named Stands With a Fist, it contains a feminist subtext. But feisty heroines are common in Westerns, all the way back to Claire Trevor's defiant prostitute Dallas in the 1939 *Stagecoach.* Those who say that *Wolves* is a radical departure, that it corrects or reverses all the bad archetypes of Westerns, probably haven't seen very many Westerns.

Even so, the altered angle of vision in *Dances With Wolves* accomplishes something important. It allows an audience that may be very wary of depictions of Indians to respond anew to the genre's greatest strengths: the mixture of grand vision and low humor, lyrical views of untamed land, and explosive, unpredictable violence. These qualities, seen in most of the great Westerns of the past, have been absent, in large part, from American movie screens since 1976.

In 1976, Ford was dead and Wayne was dying. Howard Hawks, Sam Peckinpah, and Sergio Leone had all, unknown to us at the time, directed their last Westerns. Clint Eastwood, then the world's most consistently popular movie star, had just finished *The Outlaw Josey Wales* and was about to move more decisively into urban crime movies. For the rest of the decade and the one to come, Westerns went into a commercial eclipse.

Of course, there were historical and cultural reasons. Between 1950 and 1980, the period encompassing the Western's postwar boom and slow decline, a communications explosion changed the way we viewed ourselves and the world. Television dissolved borders, creating a huge, homogenous cultural and visual web. The idea of an isolated frontier, surrounded by wide, unreachable spaces and populated by settlers from a faraway place, began to seem even more foreign. New discoveries in American history brought into question the popular myths and heroes on which the Western was erected. New attitudes toward minorities and the meaning of the American Dream made the cultural background of the genre seem obsolete. The Western itself, which had hardened into a repetitive set of ritual plots and characters, seemed to lose its meaning.

Yet in some ways the Western didn't die. It transmuted into other genres: science fiction space operas (*Star Wars*), urban buddy-cop thrillers (*48HRS., Lethal Weapon*), war movies (*Rambo*), and, most obvious, the contemporary revenge movie (*Walking Tall*). In most cases, the movies borrowed the structure of a typical fifties or sixties Western and grafted it onto a supposedly modern setting—with an outsider or principled loner face to face with outlaws or sadists, prodded into a final showdown. The old Western had historical background and archetypal meaning that "placed" the patterns of violence and revenge. These new versions were more gross, more absurd. They ignored modern society, pretending that someone in

Los Angeles, New York, or a small Southern town would act precisely as the hero of a Western set in old Abilene or on the Texas-Mexico border, and suffer absolutely no consequences. These movies drained idealism from the form, replacing it with law-and-order slogans or clichéd depictions of social evils. They became, in general, more vicious, more cynical, more divorced from reality. We accepted the old Western as either history or a dream; its modern hybrid was much more of a nightmare.

It's a pity that the Western generated such knee-jerk critical scorn and suspicion during its two richest recent periods—1948–62 and 1967–76—because, in many ways, it's an ideal movie genre. The beauty of the landscapes, the development of drama through constant tension and eruptions of action, and the contradictions in American history during the Western's time frame (1850 through the early twentieth century) offer filmmakers tremendous scope, a great canvas, and numerous opportunities for bravura visual touches.

I've loved Westerns since the age of seven, and I've never understood the hostility they arouse in some audiences and critics. Is it literary prejudice? An antipathy toward horses? Why would *Lawrence of Arabia* or *The Seven Samurai*—which play almost like transplanted Westerns—gain immediate critical acceptance, but not *The Searchers* or *Once Upon a Time in the West?* And why don't contemporary filmmakers seize upon the tools that might make a Western even more physically beautiful: new photographic equipment, new formats such as IMAX?

The view among some writers that Westerns are bad because they celebrate the spread of an empire and soft-pedal the persecution of Indians is a superficial one. Westerns are capable of many different social and political inflections, from the extreme right (Cecil B. DeMille's *The Plainsman,* '36) to the extreme left (Abraham Polonsky's *Tell Them Willie Boy Is Here,* '69) and many points in between. And they commonly express many sentiments—the need for community spirit, fair play, courage, self-sacrifice, a sense of one's historical position—that are among the most potent and stirring American ideals.

The highest achievement of *Dances With Wolves* is that it returns the context—dreamlike and vivid as ever, but as we see it now, rather than as we saw it in the Western's heyday. Probably we can never return to the purity and simplicity of John Ford's vision of the West. But we diminish Ford by not recognizing his complexity, by forgetting that the rich sympathy toward other cultures we see in *Dances With Wolves* was always present—buried or overt—in such movies as *Fort Apache* or *Wagon Master*. Ford, after all, became a Navajo himself—an honorary tribal member whose Indian name was Natani Nez, or Tall Soldier. Like all great artists, he knew very well the tragedies his own people had caused—because the victims were his people as well.

Los Angeles Times, December 16, 1990

UNFORGIVEN

Dave Kehr

The Western will always seem the central genre in the career of Clint Eastwood, in spite of the fact that, in a filmography that now covers nearly forty years, *Unforgiven* is only Eastwood's fourth Western as a director and, astonishingly, only his tenth as a star.

Beginnings count for a lot, of course, and Eastwood's fame began with his eight seasons as a regular on TV's "Rawhide" and the three revolutionary Italian Westerns directed by Sergio Leone: *A Fistful of Dollars* ('64), *For a Few Dollars More* ('65), and *The Good, the Bad and the Ugly* ('66). Still, if Eastwood's image remains inseparable from the wide-brimmed hat and the long-barreled gun, it's because his star persona incorporates so many of the themes and interests of the Western and carries them forward into other genres.

Eastwood's second American film upon his triumphant return from Italy was Don Siegel's *Coogan's Bluff* ('68), in which he played a present-day Arizona sheriff tracking a killer in New York City. The transition from Western lawman to urban cop was completed with Siegel's 1971 *Dirty Harry*.

But Eastwood has never played the traditional, idealized Western hero, as epitomized by the Gary Cooper character in *High Noon*. He has even poked affectionate fun at that gallant, pure archetype in his 1980 *Bronco Billy,* in which the mythic hero of the West turns out to be a shoe salesman from New Jersey performing for a bunch of schoolkids. But, mostly, Eastwood's Westerners tend to be edgy loners—cynical and self-interested in the Leone films, neurotic in the Siegel titles, eerie and otherworldly in the Westerns Eastwood has directed himself.

Each phase in the evolution of Eastwood's persona can be defined by the relationship of the individual to society—the central subject of most Westerns, and one of the key themes of the American cinema. Where the earliest movie Westerns—those of Tom Mix or Buck Jones—offered a hero who was a simple, knightly protector of society, part of it and honored by it, the darker variations brought to the genre by John Ford, Howard Hawks, and Fritz Lang cast the hero as an outsider, forever forbidden to join society because of the very talents—for violence and aggression—he used to defend it.

For Ford, in such films as *Stagecoach* ('39) and *My Darling Clementine* ('46), the hero occupied an unstable middle ground between civilization and savagery, often defending the rule of law through his own lawlessness. By the time of Ford's searing *The Searchers* ('56), the hero's quest for justice had become indistinguishable from a neurotic obsession with revenge—a theme that would come to occupy a central place in Eastwood's work.

Throughout the fifties, Western heroes became more and more alienated from the social body—driven by private demons in the films of Anthony Mann; shrewdly independent in the Westerns of Budd Boetticher; too large for the cramped confines of modern society in the convulsive, elegiac work of Sam Peckinpah.

Leone's films, which introduced the Western's final phase of mass popularity, pushed these antisocial tendencies to the extreme. So alienated was Leone's protagonist that he lacked even a social appellation—he was the Man With No Name. As smart and cunningly manipulative as a Boetticher hero, though without Boetticher's romantic ideals, the Man With No Name placed himself on the far periphery of the social struggle. Refusing to take sides—in a conflict that amounted to the venal versus the grotesque in any case—Leone's hero would intervene only to provoke more chaos and then swoop down to take his spoils. Law and order was a game to be played only for profit, as the idealistic sheriff ceded his place to the self-interested bounty hunter.

Working with Leone, Eastwood developed a fiercely retentive acting style. He hid his emotions behind an even, laconic speaking voice, the direction of his gaze behind a perpetual squint, and his movements beneath a loose-fitting serape. Rational and removed, the Man With No Name seemed a barely corporeal presence, a projection of pure intellect.

All of that changed with Eastwood's return to Hollywood in 1968, for Ted Post's underrated Western *Hang 'Em High*. Though still operating outside of society, Eastwood's character was motivated not by profit but rather by revenge as he hunted down the nine men—civic leaders and corrupt officials—who had attempted to lynch him.

Two themes that would become very important in Eastwood's own films make their first appearances here: the idea of the quasi-supernatural hero, who has somehow survived his own death, and that of the implacability of feminine anger, embodied here by Inger Stevens as the first in the long line of sharp-featured blondes to haunt Eastwood's work.

Eastwood's association with Don Siegel, begun that same year with *Coogan's Bluff,* produced a series of tightly collaborative films as significant as those of Anthony Mann and James Stewart or Boetticher and Randolph Scott. Siegel returned Eastwood's character to a social and psychological context, filling out his heretofore obscure interior life with a full range of fears and insecurities.

On the one hand there is Dirty Harry, the San Francisco police detective who carries the classical dilemma of the Western hero— the need to break the law in order to maintain the law—to new heights of neurosis and hysteria. Harry's fierce belief in justice at any price springs not so much from abstract idealism as a desperate need to deny his own violent and sadistic tendencies, which, Siegel suggests through careful cross-cutting, run almost exactly parallel to those of the psychotic killer Harry is pursuing.

On the other hand there is Corporal McBirney, the wounded Union soldier of Siegel's still-astonishing *The Beguiled* ('70), who is taken in by the staff and students of a Southern female boarding school. McBirney's presence unleashes a wave of sexual tension, culminating in the calculated decision of headmistress Geraldine Page to amputate his gangrenous leg, in a sequence attended by its full Freudian implications. McBirney's attempts to manipulate the situation, through smooth talk and seductiveness, are consistently undermined by his inability to control his clumsiest male impulses— for drink, sex, or explosions of anger. Meanwhile, the women remain coolly in charge, focusing their icy, unwavering hate.

Unforgiven is dedicated to "Sergio and Don" and it stands as a masterfully synthetic work, paying tribute to both of Eastwood's most important mentors while bringing in a full complement of his own themes and inflections. The protagonist, William Munny, could be the Man With No Name living in uneasy retirement—a former outlaw and bounty hunter whose attempt to settle down with a wife, family, and Kansas farm has turned sour with his wife's recent death.

The plot is set in motion by a group of angry women, not far removed from those of *The Beguiled*. A prostitute in the town of Big Whiskey, Wyoming, has been cut up by a sadistic ranch hand; her coworkers have established a pool to buy themselves a bounty hunter and the justice that the corrupt local sheriff (Gene Hackman) won't provide. Provoked by an aspiring teenage gunslinger, the Schofield Kid (Jaimz Woolvett), Munny decides to pursue the bounty and enlists the help of an old colleague from his outlaw days, the peaceably retired Ned Logan (Morgan Freeman). But Munny has lived too long in the world to maintain the bounty hunter's detachment—the Man With No Name has become the Man with Wife and Kids. Though the violent impulses are still there—Munny is too restless, too driven, to ever really settle down—they can no longer be so easily acknowledged or indulged.

Like the Siegel films, *Unforgiven* proceeds through a complex process of contrast and comparison, drawing its characters into a dense web of moral relativism. At one extreme there is the cold-blooded bounty hunter English Bob (Richard Harris, costumed to suggest Lee Van Cleef in the Leone films), whose interest in the case is purely mercenary; at the other is Strawberry Alice (Frances Fisher), the leader of the prostitutes, whose pursuit of justice masks what may be a deeply justified vengeance on the entire male sex, although her own quest is obsessive and extreme (she is strongly suggestive of the Sondra Locke character in 1983's *Sudden Impact,* the finest of the later Dirty Harry films).

Eastwood's own Westerns have pushed the genre to a level of stylization beyond Leone and Siegel. Drawing on Biblical references, Eastwood creates an aura of supernatural invulnerability around the hero, a ghostly figure who has returned from a previous life to exact revenge (*High Plains Drifter,* '73), provide redemption (*The Outlaw Josey Wales,* '76), or offer an ambiguous, difficult combination of the two (*Pale Rider,* '85).

Munny is not a ghost in *Unforgiven*—he may, in fact, be the most warmly human and socially integrated of all of Eastwood's characters—but he becomes one as the action unfolds. The escalating violence eats away at him; wounded, his face comes to resemble a death's-head, and when he strides through a saloon door for the film's extremely disturbing final confrontation, he has again turned into an angel of death, his eyes steely and his jaw set.

In the 1990s, the Western itself seems a ghostly survivor of another time, a reminder of an era in American filmmaking when popular entertainments routinely tackled the most serious moral and social questions. Clint Eastwood's *Unforgiven* is a film fully worthy of its genre—gripping and profound, the product of a great tradition and the summit of a great career.

Chicago Tribune, August 2, 1992

COMEDY

One autumn not long ago, a publicist invited me to an early screening of a comedy, hoping to encourage an article around the time of the film's spring release. When the follow-up phone call came the next morning, I sighed regretfully (this was a very nice publicist) and said, "If I were to run an article on your movie, the theme would be how completely Hollywood has forgotten how to make movies like this. The star's a good actor, as we know; your new actress is funny and charming, and I'm sure she'll have a terrific career; a couple of the supporting players are people I always enjoy; I'll remember some of the big laughs and line-readings. But that's not enough.

"In the thirties and forties, Hollywood made dozens of movies built around similar plots and situations, and almost all of them were better than your movie. Forget about Howard Hawks, Preston Sturges, Billy Wilder—I'm talking about *average,* no-big-deal comedies. Even journeyman writers and directors knew how to give a picture texture and cohesion. If it took place in a small town, you knew the town, knew how its spaces added up. You knew a dozen characters who lived in it, even if most of the time they just hovered on the sidelines. If the plot was set in motion by a violent incident, and then the action shifted into comedy, directors and camera crew knew how to shoot both kinds of scenes so that they flowed together, instead of having one part of the movie feel unhinged from the other.

"Your movie doesn't even *begin* until after the dramatic setup—a whole reel. And then, when characters from the opening reappear to prepare for the climax, you wonder where they've *been* all this time. I mean, it *is* a small town. Yet your director concentrated so exclusively on the main characters, he couldn't show the continuity of life going on around them. And without that kind of interaction, that kind of texture, you're just connecting the dots, leaping between high points that aren't very high because there's nothing for them to stand in relief against. Which, come to think of it, is a pretty interesting point to make about what's wrong with a lot of contemporary filmmaking . . ."

But the publicist preferred that we forget the whole thing.

The films discussed in this chapter mostly stand in relief against the prevailing flatness, witlessness, and want of elegance and grace that have characterized recent screen comedy. Stumbling upon the unexpected pleasures of the Bill Murray–Harold Ramis *Groundhog Day,* Andrew Sarris finds new hope for the "Saturday Night Live"–"SCTV" alums who have generally followed up their small-screen triumphs with alarmingly coarse (and alarmingly lucrative) feature comedies. Michael Wilmington salutes the shamelessly, sublimely silly *Airplane!* gang and their *Naked Gun* franchise. Mel Brooks's riposte to George Lucas, *Spaceballs,* gladdens the heart of J. Hoberman. Peter Keough has mixed responses to the cartoonish mode adopted by the brothers Coen in *Raising Arizona.* The editor applauds Joe Dante's wild fusion of comedy and horror movie in *Gremlins,* but feels Ivan Reitman botched both in *Ghostbusters.* Owen Gleiberman introduces an American original, Richard Linklater's *Slacker.* The truly black comedy of Michael Lehmann's *Heathers* and Danny DeVito's *War of the Roses* is plumbed by J. Hoberman and David Ansen, respectively. And Henry Sheehan offers Albert Brooks, writer-director-star of *Defending Your Life,* as our most seriously underrated comic auteur. (Woody Allen gets his innings in a later chapter, "The Director as Genre.")

GROUNDHOG DAY

Andrew Sarris

Harold Ramis's *Groundhog Day,* from a screenplay by Ramis and Danny Rubin, based on a story by Rubin, generates enough warmth, wit, humor, sexual chemistry, and spiritual resonance to light up a whole season of Valentine's Days. Unfortunately, the combination of Bill Murray and a misleadingly facetious title may keep away moviegoers who bemoan the decline of Romantic Comedy on the screen since the supposedly Golden Age of the thirties and forties. By the same token, the targeted adolescent mass audience may be disappointed by an unexpected serving of caviar when mountains of meatballs were eagerly awaited.

Whatever the box office verdict may be, *Groundhog Day* is bound to have a long shelf life at the videocassette outlets, along with such previously underrated movie romances as John Carpenter's *Memoirs of an Invisible Man* and Frank Oz's *Housesitter.* Curiously, all three of these incongruously tender and delicate love stories feature as their male leads uproariously funny veterans of the first generation of "Saturday Night Live." Hence, while Hollywood's male hunks have been admiring their pects and bonding with their male partners, Chevy Chase (*Invisible*), Steve Martin (*Housesitter*), and Bill Murray (*Groundhog*) have been falling in love on the screen, each with one and only one beautiful woman every bit his equal in the almost-forgotten game of heterosexual love, with its civilized rules of conversational courtship and mutual respect.

Despite its title, *Groundhog Day* does not play at all like the current grossness-for-grosses productions. Even the caricatures are mercifully modulated into subtle variations on the general theme of hopelessly square provincialism. For example, Stephen Tobolowsky's marvelously unwelcome Ned, the comic crystallization of every class bore you never wanted to meet again in this lifetime, materializes in the middle of the Main Street of Punxsutawney, Pennsylvania, and proceeds to try to sell you life insurance. This is the horrifying situation that Bill Murray's city-smart weather reporter, Phil, encounters not only on Groundhog Day in Punxsutawney (actually, Woodstock, Illinois), but every day or, rather, on the same day repeated again and again for him alone and no one else. This is the comic premise of Danny Rubin's ingenious story, which exploits Murray's penchant for redemptive themes to play off his cynically deadpan persona. He has followed this path disastrously on two occasions in the past, John Byrum's *The Razor's Edge* ('84) and Richard Donner's *Scrooged* ('88). Harold Ramis, of all people, has finally enabled Murray to hit the comic and emotional jackpot with as graceful a job of mainstream movie direction as I have seen in a long time.

For her part, the beautifully engaging Andie MacDowell seems to have overcome the peculiar career jinx that has afflicted her since her electrifying breakthrough in Steven Soderbergh's *sex, lies & videotape* ('89). As a television producer named Rita, she projects from her first entrance a mix of intelligent curiosity and unsuspicious sweetness that is the stuff of which male dreams are made. The heart of the film involves, at first, a series of manipulative maneuvers by Phil to exploit a time machine for himself. Ultimately, however, he surrenders unconditionally to his own emotional imperatives. Here I felt that the predominantly young audience began to stir restlessly in their seats: Hey, Bill, don't go noble on us. Screw the bitch like the selfish bastard you've always been. Don't be gentle and respectful. That's sissy stuff.

Actually, most of the big laughs come in the first part of the movie, when Murray's Phil is only slightly less cantankerous than Phil, the scene-stealing groundhog himself. The late surge of Capraesque altruism is occasionally a bit much, but the Murray-MacDowell explosion of wit and charm sweeps everything before it. I only hope that *Groundhog Day* doesn't prove to be too enlightened for today's depraved audiences, thus compelling Murray to return to a steady diet of meatballs in order to retain his commercial viability. In other words, down with Mike Myers and Dana Carvey, and up with Bill Murray, Steve Martin, and Chevy Chase. Or is my generation gap showing?

New York Observer, February 22, 1993

THE NAKED GUN

■■■

Michael Wilmington

Some movies make you laugh. Some movies don't. *The Naked Gun: From the Files of "Police Squad!"* definitely falls into the first category.

Here is a vulgar collection of cheesy jokes, bald-faced stick-it-in-your-eye slapstick, appalling parodies of old TV cop shows, and puns for which someone should be half-shot at sunrise. There are inane Abbott and Costello word games that resemble the demented prattle of crazed infants. There are lewd innuendos of every type. And there's enough bad taste and cornball humor to choke Wilbur and Mr. Ed and capsize Gilligan's Island. Somehow, the movie kills you anyway.

Maybe it's sheer density. *The Naked Gun* was written by the Zucker-Abrahams-Zucker *Airplane!–Kentucky Fried Movie* team. Their method, as before, is to throw up a blizzard of gags and goofs, one every twenty seconds or so, while bringing on a parade of TV and sports stars—from Priscilla Presley to O. J. Simpson to song parodist "Weird Al" Yankovic.

The Naked Gun is a continuation of ZAZ's short-lived 1982 TV series, "Police Squad! (in color)." That show was a send-up of the standard fifties–sixties TV cop thriller of the "Adam-12" level, reconceived as if it were invaded by the Three Stooges and done by half-asleep actors, emptily bombastic announcers, and jaded old pros too bored with everything to scrub out the obvious boo-boos. Here, Leslie Nielsen, the dourly impassive Detective Lt. Frank Drebin of "Police Squad!" who can't park a squad car without knocking over every trash can in the neighborhood, is flung straight-faced into the maw of world communism and terrorism. Before the story begins, Drebin takes on Castro, Qaddafi, the Ayatollah Khomeini, even poor Gorbachev, in a Stallone/ Schwarzenegger one-against-a-bunch bust-up. Soon, more serious threats intervene: an impending goodwill tour by Queen Elizabeth (played here by Jeanette Charles, who also resembles Dr. Ruth), during which HRH is scheduled to be assassinated by the dapper, perfidious Victor Ludwig (Ricardo Montalban), the kind of smoothie who should be hawking Paul Masson.

In the years since he first played Drebin, Nielsen has deepened the role, made it more subtle, more universal, more paramount. He's brought out an almost preternatural mellowness in a character who began as a relatively uncomplicated dimwit. Now, when Drebin bangs into a trash can, or crosses his eyes and falls over his foot, or sets fire to an apartment while trying to light a match, one can sense profound world-weariness, an overpowering angst. Or maybe one only thinks one can. In any case, Nielsen looks as natty as Merv Griffin, mugs like Red Skelton, and has a richer, deeper monotone than Jack Webb. Andrew McCarthy, eat your heart out.

Jim Abrahams and the Zucker brothers, David and Jerry, are the ultimate couch-potato gangsters. They're unashamed boob-tube exploiters, who seem to see the world through a TV screen, darkly. The way they use actors like Nielsen, Montalban, and George Kennedy (promoted over Alan North as Drebin's sidekick) shows their frenziedly ironic devotion to media trash. Actors who have made a career of keeping straight faces through preposterous lines are ideal for a movie like *The Naked Gun*. And David Zucker, directing alone this time, handles them like an equally straight-faced, jaded young hack who can't understand why the set keeps blowing up. The result is, no kidding, funnier than all six "Police Squad! (in color)" shows put together.

The Naked Gun has one major flaw: the scene where an obese woman falls on Reggie Jackson, as a hypnotized zombie rightfielder royal assassin. Isn't it painfully obvious that Jackson should be squashed not by this rotund interloper but by George Steinbrenner, in the throes of an apoplectic fit, followed by Billy Martin and Margaret Thatcher? Never mind. No one achieves perfection in this vale of tears, this chaos, this naked gun of a world we live in. Not even "Weird Al" Yankovic.

Los Angeles Times, December 2, 1988

SPACEBALLS

J. Hoberman

The spirit of desecration rules Mel Brooks's *Spaceballs*. Buoyant, unsentimental low comedy, this manic *Star Wars* parody is continually vulgar without ever seeming smarmy. "Shall I have Snotty beam you down?" someone wants to know, randomly smearing yet another cosmos. When the order comes to "jam" enemy radar, you know exactly what sort of mess to expect. Unlike *Star Wars, Spaceballs* is regression that knows its name.

A long decade ago, George Lucas's lethal combination of bombastic special effects and simpleminded morality arrived (alongside *Rocky* and *Close Encounters*) to herald a new era in American mythmaking. At once more and less than "only a movie," *Star Wars* is that nexus of banal platitude, childish fantasy, and obsession with technology that not only defines our entertainment but bids to become the most pathetic, delusionary boondoggle in human history. *Star Wars* is stupidity on a cosmic scale, but Brooks is shameless. He'll plaster an I ♥ URANUS bumper sticker on the back of a rocket ship or give a character a name just to set up one ridiculous gag ("What's the matter, Colonel Sandurz—chicken?"). Almost every joke in *Spaceballs* gets repeated in one form or another, but the picture seldom drags. Brooks's redundancy seems less a failure of imagination than exuberant generosity. He's like a Coney Island barker who lets the ride go around twice.

Spaceballs is Brooks's first film in five years, and it's so pure an expression of his particular worldview you almost expect to see him play each role the way he insinuated himself into every epoch in *History of the World, Part I*. He limits himself to two—one of which has no *Star Wars* equivalent—while farming out the plums of the Darth Vader clone, here Dark Helmet (Rick Moranis in his most petulant nerd mode) and the Chewbacca simulacrum, one Barf (John Candy), a sort of inflated Pekinese *cum* Cowardly Lion, introduced dancing to heavy metal and pigging out on Milk Bones. There's also a special effects creation named Pizza the Hut and a C3PO-type 'droid, Dot Matrix (mime Lorene Yarnell) with a voice supplied by Joan Rivers. However one might miss the actual Joan, her manicure-protective clapping and metallic coiffure, it's still priceless to hear that breathy rasp exuding from a skinny chrome robot with the saucer-eyed stare and idiotically gaping mouth of a plastic sex doll.

Dot notwithstanding, Brooks's effects are no great advance over *Flash Gordon*'s. Indeed, mocking the solemnly mystified *Star Wars* hardware is one of *Spaceballs*' running gags. ("Dim the lights. *Dimming the lights. Go to red. Going to red.* Pray to God. *Praying to God.*") *Spaceballs* is stocked with monstrous, fallible consumer appliances: flying Winnebagos, industrial-strength hair dryers, colossal vacuum cleaners, doomsday machines that wish you a nice day. There's no religious certainty here—as someone irascibly points out, "even in the future nothing works."

The spaceships in Brooks's universe accelerate from light speed to ludicrous speed, and, at times, so does the film. (Silly as it is, *Spaceballs* contains passages of inspired moviemaking: a disco-scored rocket evacuation, an ingenious blend of *Alien* and Chuck Jones's *One Froggy Evening*.) The giddiest shpritz comes some forty-five minutes into the action, when Brooks appears, beigely dipped in QT Tan, as Yogurt, "the everlasting know-it-all" and keeper of "the Schwartz." This latest incarnation of the 2,000-Year-Old Man doubles as the proprietor of *Spaceballs*' awesome shlock shop: "We put the picture's name on everything. This is where the real money is made," he explains, showing Spaceballs—The Doll, Spaceballs—The Sheets, and (inevitably) Spaceballs—The Toilet Paper. "God willing, we'll all meet again in *Spaceballs II—The Search for More Money.*"

Spaceballs' fiesta of ancillary products caps a number of self-reflexive gags, ranging from some of the principals gaining access to *Spaceballs—The Videotape* ("Prepare to fast-forward") to a riff on stunt doubles I've been waiting fifteen years to see. If not exactly Brechtian, *Spaceballs* isn't affirmative either. In some respects, *Spaceballs* is that "Jews in Space" movie Brooks promised at the end of *History of the World*. Brooks usually ignores the tortuous Good Father–Bad Father dichotomy of Lucas's saga: the key to his revision of *Star Wars* is his perception of Carrie Fisher as a JAP manqué. Bringing Lucas violently down to earth, he reads the whole extravaganza back into Beverly Hills.

Like some madcap farce of the Yiddish theater, *Spaceballs* is a universe ruled by crass Jewish aristocrats. ("My cousin Prince Murray has a dealership in the Valley.") As the resident "Druish" princess, Daphne Zuniga is compelled to wear a gradually decomposing crinoline wedding dress all movie long. (When she's captured by the villains they threaten to give her back her old nose.) Brooks has a connoisseur's appreciation for Jewish paranoia, but the film is also an expression of Jewish confidence.

More than any other filmmaker, Brooks gives full vent to the sense Jews have of being at once inside and outside America's mass culture. For a long time and perhaps even today, Jews have made show biz from behind a mask. That's one more false face that's abandoned in *Spaceballs'* carnival. Brooks uses the wisdom of an immigrant Jewish huckster to deflate and devalue Lucas's ostentatious spectacle—the antithesis of *The Producers* in its appropriation of fascist kitsch. *Young Frankenstein* was tempered by affection, *High Anxiety* bridled by respect, but *Spaceballs* is filled with healthy contempt.

At once tawdry and sanctimonious, a seamless blend of Leni Riefenstahl, Walt Disney, John Ford, and Buck Rogers, *Star Wars* brought the movies back to some imagined, born-again, guns-and-cuddles dreamland where the past disguised itself as the future and the shopworn shone like new. Brooks disassembles Lucas's universe with the utmost disrespect. The grotesque Biblical pretensions of the *Star Wars* trilogy are treated as one more ridiculous sublimation of Gentile power: "It looks like the Temple of Doom," someone quivers. "Sure ain't Temple Beth Israel," Joan Rivers snaps back.

Village Voice, June 24, 1987

RAISING ARIZONA

■■■

Peter Keough

Formal mastery without feeling makes people uneasy. Perhaps Joel and Ethan Coen sensed this in the wake of (and despite) the resounding critical and popular success of their first feature, *Blood Simple,* and decided to include a little compassion and optimism next time out. Regrettably, in their new film *Raising Arizona,* humanism is just so much baggage. It's handled the way the film's two escaped cons handle the infant they have kidnapped: Off to pull a bank heist, they leave the kid on the roof of the car when they take off down the highway. Discovering the mistake, they U-turn and tear howling back, screeching to a halt inches from the baby, who sits vaguely annoyed on the center line. Moments later, the robbers burst into the bank, toting mean-looking 12-gauges and a bemused eight-month-old in a car seat. Splendidly self-parodic, this is one of the Coens' funniest moments in the movie.

But the baby, in the end, not only foils the outlaws' plans, he undoes the Coens' chief virtue: their ebullient, blackly nihilistic sense of the absurd. *Blood Simple* unnerved viewers even as it delighted them, because it demonstrated that a vastly entertaining film could spring not from any reverence for the human soul but from a callow joy in cinematic artifice, from exuberance in technical expertise, and from the same morbid fascination and good-natured sadism that compels little boys to buy ant farms and reptiles. Raised on movies and TV, the Coens are masters of the *form* of film genres, if not their spirit; in *Blood Simple* they indulged their gift by creating a wild and elegant Rube Goldberg movie that was a virtual lexicon of film styles, techniques, and allusions. Basically, *Blood Simple* melded the two disparate genres of film noir and silent comedy, borrowing plot, characters, and textures from the former and a worldview from the latter. Buster Keaton, whose films are set in a world based on a sublime conspiracy of the inanimate against the human, is the closest parallel. But there's a difference: pathetic, impassive, and comically noble, the human nonetheless prevails in Keaton's films; for the Coens, the world is a machine of devious plot twists and sudden unpleasant disclosures, and the human characters, ignorant, selfish, and corrupt, haven't got a chance. When it comes down to the conflict between man and the indifferent universe, the Coens will side with the universe every time. That's the source of the dark, Olympian hilarity of *Blood Simple,* and it's one of the Coens' greatest strengths.

Raising Arizona is again a chimerical fusion of alien film forms. The dominant genre is changed from the fatalistic film noir to the sunny screwball comedy, a form rooted in the happy reconciliation of individualism and conformity. The Coens' formulation of this process is clever, if blatant; their main problem is taking the theme seriously long enough to make it funny.

Their hero, H. I. "Hi" McDonough (Nicolas Cage), for example, has neither the humanity of a Jimmy Stewart nor the urbanity of a Cary Grant. He's a crude and smug caricature, a gangly puppet with jerky arms and legs and a triangular, toplike head emphasized by unlikely tufts of hair, a greasy swipe of a mustache, and Cage's overbitten chinlessness. Since the Coens are incapable of pure cliché, Hi is redeemed somewhat by a weird polyglot diction composed of prison slang, *People* magazine, folk ballads, and Shakespeare. His crackbrained dialogues, philosophical observations, and running commentary are reminiscent of M. Emmet Walsh's oddities in *Blood Simple.*

In the film's blackout-style opening, Hi is shown to be a descendant of pioneers who fulfills his yen for anarchy, independence, and wide open spaces by repeatedly botching convenience-store holdups and going to jail. In the course of his many incarcerations, he develops a passion for Ed (Holly Hunter), the officer who takes his mug shots. She's a stiff, petal-mouthed woman in blue who resembles a more robust version of the fretful daughter in Grant Wood's *American Gothic.* Hi's passion is requited, and the two wed in a union of wild individualism and nurturing order that promises a paradise in the midst of John Ford's Arizona wilderness.

But the unlikely match does not prove fruitful and the desert remains sterile. "Her insides," intones Hi in one of his many poetic flights, "were a rocky place where my seed could find no purchase." Notoriously fecund, on the other hand, are Nathan Arizona—the unpainted-furniture tycoon—and his wife Polly. Their "Arizona Quintuplets" are front-page news, and Ed and Hi decide to fill their need by stealing one from the Arizonas' abundance. The deed is done, and the flash of Hi's camera as he photographs the illicitly contrived family is followed by a bolt of lightning. The flash reveals an orifice opening in the mud outside the state penitentiary, which gives birth to the Faulknerian-monikered brothers Gale and Evelle Snopes (John Goodman and William Forsythe), Hi's old prison pals.

Hi and Ed's well-intended crime thus releases their dark side— not sufficiently, though, for the filmmakers. Inspired perhaps by the Arizonas, the Coens spawn yet another dark double for Hi—the "Lone Biker of the Apocalypse," aka Leonard Smalls (Randall "Tex" Cobb), a green-toothed and hairy road warrior equipped with furry leather duds, hand grenades, and a Harley Davidson, who may or may not be Hi's lost brother. Rounding out the crew of alter egos is Glen (Sam McMurray), Hi's smarmy boss, a paterfamilias of a host of hideous adopted children whose food-throwing, wall-defacing, and overall destructive depravity finally convinces Hi to give up family life and join the Snopeses in their bank job.

The heist doesn't quite come off as planned, and the movie degenerates into slapstick as the baby, Nathan Jr., becomes a soccer ball kicked from Hi to Glen to the Snopeses and then to Smalls. The comedy is cartoonish in its broadness and frenzy, and the cartoon is, in fact, the film form with which the Coens couple their screwball comedy. They supplement Sturges with Bugs Bunny, Wile E. Coyote, and Woody Woodpecker, and for a while it seems as if this audacious ploy might work. They strive hard to mimic the surreal skewing of physical laws that is the virtue of their animated models. A cactus leaps into the frame to smack a running man in the face; a doberman leaps for a throat, his teeth caught inches short of a jugular by a suddenly revealed restraining chain. A ubiquitous wide-angle lens (the cinematography is by Barry Sonnenfeld) makes feet loom disproportionately large over lounge chairs, lavender hair curlers spring from heads like pinwheels, and baby bottoms swell like the sails of galleons. The tracking shot, a mild fetish in *Blood Simple,* is here an obsession as the Coens seek to re-create the surreal freedom of the animator's sketch pad. The Steadicam tracks a motorcycle over a car, up a ladder, through a window, and into a screaming woman's mouth; it pursues a pack of dogs, a crawling toddler, and a fleeing felon with pantyhose on his head. In one memorable scene, Hi's kidnapping of Nathan Jr. is interrupted by the release of all the quints from their crib. They spread over the nursery floor like an overturned bucket of live bait, and the camera follows them accompanied by abrupt closeups, point-of-view shots, and the music of *Jaws* on the soundtrack. It is a bizarre moment, unsettling and hilarious, but somehow gratuitous. The Coens are merely showing off, but their virtuosity is not enough.

The initial inspiration sags into the worst aspects of Saturday morning TV—its repetitiousness, banality, and bald sadism. Instead of invention, *Raising Arizona* settles for gags that were stale when the Three Stooges used them. Long before the end, the Coens abandon comedy altogether for a Mad Max romp of car chases and explosions and an endless, Capraesque homily that leaves the stunned viewer waiting, in vain, for a punchline.

The Coens have not achieved the maturity needed to appreciate the vision of a Capra or Sturges, and their gifts are too rich and deep for the likes of Heckle and Jeckle. The unlikely formal marriage of *Raising Arizona* is barren, and the theme the Coens adopt to fill the gap is nominal at best. One of the motifs recurrent in this picture is suggestive of their failure: a copy of Dr. Spock's *Baby and*

Child Care that passes from hand to hand along with the charmingly photographed child. Dog-eared, singed, broken-spined, it survives every catastrophe. But it is never read. Whether raising babies for real or exploiting them in movies, it usually helps to take a look at the instructions. When the Coens grow up enough to regard people as mysteries to be probed and not props with which to provide cheap laughs and thrills, the brilliant promise of their talents might be fulfilled.

Chicago Reader, April 10, 1987

GREMLINS; GHOSTBUSTERS

■■■

Richard T. Jameson

There is a moment early in Joe Dante's *The Howling* ('81) when the heroine, a TV reporter on the trail of a mad killer, steps into a phone booth in a very dark corner of L.A. nighttown. As she checks in with the cops on the periphery of the hunt, she fails to notice that a man has appeared behind her, just outside the booth. He bulks there, sinister, back to her and to the camera, till she finishes her call and prepares to exit. Then she sees him, gasps, draws back. He turns, favors her with a what-the-hell-lady? look. She edges out of the booth; he steps in. He was just a guy waiting to use the phone.

For the casual viewer, a standard horror-movie tease; for film buffs, something more. The anonymous lurker happens to be none other than shlockmeister-supreme Roger Corman, the producer and studio boss under whom Dante apprenticed in the movie business. OK, an inside joke. But Dante's jokes have layers and layers. This one's an in-joke for superbuffs like Joe Dante himself, because it also refers to a specific movie moment. Back in 1968, when Roman Polanski worked a similar phone booth tease in *Rosemary's Baby,* the menacing/innocuous presence behind Mia Farrow turned out to be *that* film's producer, former shlockmeister-supreme William Castle.

I bring up this (in itself trivial) gag because it affords an insight into how Dante's movie mind operates, and it points toward what's so exciting and gratifying about his new film, *Gremlins*—a horror comedy whose ferocious originality inheres largely in the way it plays off the audience's familiarity with and cozy reliance on movie prototypes, then deliciously confounds them.

The storyline is basic fifties monster mash. While flogging his wares in Chinatown, genially daft inventor Rand Peltzer (Hoyt Axton) comes across an exotic breed of cuddly pet and takes it back to his all-American small town. The creature, called a *mogwai,* coos, croons, and charms the bejeezus out of everybody within range. However, having a mogwai around entails three dire responsibilities: you don't expose it to bright light, don't get it wet, and don't, absolutely *do* NOT feed it after midnight. Let no one doubt that all three prohibitions get summarily violated, with the result that the Christmas-card town of Kingston Falls is soon at the mercy of the original mogwai's hundred thoroughly uncuddly offspring. They bite, they kill, they interfere with TV reception. Only the sweet young hero and heroine (Zach Galligan and Phoebe Cates) have a prayer of stopping them and saving the human race.

As with any good film, the storyline doesn't begin to tell the whole story. Dante gleefully develops his own peculiar film world and savors it for some time before the titular gremlins are ready to wreak their mayhem. His small town, unlike the essentially realistic suburbia of *E. T.* and *Poltergeist,* has conspicuously been built for the occasion and set within a matte-painted landscape from a bygone film era innocent of location shooting. Frank Capra is its cinematic patron saint, up to a point: *It's a Wonderful Life,* besides turning up on afternoon TV, supplies the model for the main street and a key rich-old-meanie character (Polly Holliday in the Lionel Barrymore part). In addition, a recurring bit of business in the Peltzer household is adapted from a homey shtick in *You Can't Take It With You,* the junior high science teacher shows one of Capra's Bell Telephone documentaries (*Hemo the Magnificent*), and there's a wild sight gag featuring a photograph of favorite Capra villain Edward Arnold.

The nice-folks characters would fit right into Capra country, too, though unlike Capra's wonderful heroes full of gawky planes and other humanizing imperfections, Zach Galligan and Phoebe Cates look as if they'd been cast in molds and polished till they shine. They're *cartoon* versions of young nice-folk—which brings us to another patron saint, the great Warner Bros. animator Chuck Jones (who makes a cameo appearance in this live-action Warner Bros.

movie). Like Jones, especially in his Roadrunner mode, Dante is going to disassemble his already stylized film world and put it back together according to a demonic pattern wherein the funnier things get, the more horrific they get. And vice versa.

For the full measure of Dante's insidiousness, consider that *Gremlins* was produced under the aegis of Steven Spielberg (who also shows up as an extra), and its best joke consists in the way Dante is biting the hand that feeds him—though presumably not after midnight. As designed by Chris Walas, the original, unmutated mogwai incorporates the adorability of E.T. and raises it to the *n*th power. His eyes are big and soft as Bambi's, and he bats them shamelessly; the voice murmurs like a fussy kitten and the furry little stubby-legged body seems made to nestle in the palm of one's hand. Peltzer's family sighs "Aaaahh!" when they first see him. So does the audience, even as we feel that—damn it!—it would be ever so much more cool to resist the manipulation. We know that this *thing* is no real animal, after all, but a mechanical (and eminently merchandisable) toy. Peltzer is even permitted to name him "Gizmo"—a natural-enough term of affection for a Rube Goldberg type to come up with, but also a bit of rubbing-our-noses-in-it audacity on the part of Dante & Co.

The joke darkens when Gizmo's unholy descendants get loose. If Giz was a too-much version of E.T., the gremlins are the flip side of Giz's cuteness. The strokable ears become batlike, the murmuring a mad gibber, the fur something saurian. More unsettling than the physical transformation is the gremlins' behavior. And here Dante seems to say: you didn't know quite what to do with too much cute—what are you gonna make of the mischief these babies do?

For, like the evolving identity of the poltergeist(s) in the Spielberg production of that name, the gremlins keep shifting valences on us. They're merry pranksters but they also kill: practical jokes or murder, all's one to them. Are they a giddy manifestation of archetypal Evil loosed upon the world, or humankind in a distorting mirror? They like to put on costumes and act out grotesque variations of human pastimes (and incidentally deliver what I'd like to think was the coup de grâce to the breakdancing craze). Of course, much of this behavior seems less an imitation of life than wild-hair embellishments of *movie* versions of life. Dante's japery reaches its most perverse when he admits the gibbering horde to the local Bijou and suddenly we're looking at, er, a movie audience going merrily apeshit (with *Snow White and the Seven Dwarfs* as target of opportunity) in much the way we've been doing for the past hour or so.

Not to worry, Joe Dante is One Of Us. He's also that rarity among the new generation of moviemakers—someone who doesn't slavishly feed off the movie formulae of the past but instead truly celebrates the popular art form he's loved and been shaped by. Like Spielberg, his current sponsor, he's reinventing the movies by investing them with his own wit and love, his sharp technical skills and stylistic sense, his (dare we say) diabolical energy and imagination. In *Gremlins* he's given us what may be the best horror movie *and* the best comedy of the year.

☆

Gremlins cost about eleven million dollars to make, most of it occasioned by technical complications in animating the gremlin puppets. *Ghostbusters*, 1984's other oddball comedy–*cum*–horror movie, came in at thirty-eight mil. Watching it, one is struck by the waste—not so much of all that money but, rather, of the potential for a really extraordinary comic film. Every now and then, through the murk of Ivan (*Meatballs/Stripes*) Reitman's inchoate direction and the literally sketchy movement of the scenario, it's possible to catch glimpses of an epically zany movie in which the off-the-wall humor of the "Saturday Night Live"–"SCTV"–*National Lampoon* crowd would merge crazily with the spectral wonders of the wide screen and the Brobdingnagian heft of the occult genre. I'd still like to see that movie someday.

Bill Murray, Dan Aykroyd, and Harold Ramis play three variously uptight and hang-loose parapsychologists who get kicked out of their university lab and into the private sector, where, as somebody ruefully remarks, "they actually expect results." Either they're on the right track or New York City is experiencing an undue infestation of disembodied spirits this season (the film is vague on this point and many others from one scene to the next). After a stagnant period they swiftly become a success, and overnight media celebrities, as Ghostbusters. And eventually they too get the opportunity to save the world for democracy, or corporeality, or something.

Ghostbusters is a mess (a rather well-photographed mess, thanks to Laszlo Kovacs), but it's also a lot more fun than it deserves to be. Aykroyd and Ramis, both very funny guys and the authors of the screenplay, have unaccountably written themselves pretty much into the background and left the principal ghostbusting, and the movie, to Bill Murray. In part this may be due to the fact that his role was originally intended for the late John Belushi, and a lot of overcompensating may be going on. Whatever put Murray at the center of the film, we should be thankful, because he's in excelsis and he's hilarious. Whether putting the moves on client Sigourney Weaver (also funny, sexy, and mostly wasted) or the shaft to an obnoxious bureaucrat (William Atherton), he fairly exudes comedic self-confidence.

The Weekly (Seattle), June 6, 1984

SLACKER

Owen Gleiberman

The characters in Richard Linklater's wonderfully original independent feature are a series of young, talkative, semi-employed hangers-on living in the quaintly dilapidated, sunbaked college town of Austin, Texas: people on the fringes of the fringe. At the beginning of the movie a handsome, long-haired young man (played by Linklater) climbs into a cab and launches into an earnest monologue about his theory of alternate realities. The cabbie makes no acknowledgment of anything he's saying, and the young man never registers that he isn't being listened to.

Moments later, he wanders off, and the camera drifts over to another person, then another, then another still. There are ninety-seven characters in *Slacker,* and each arrives onscreen for a brief scene; spins out some pet idea, obsession, or philosophy; and then leaves. Linklater's restless, gliding camera eases down sidewalks and into bedrooms, coffee shops, and bars, achieving a hypnotic community of time; it feels as if each character were passing a baton to the next. No one in the film ever makes a reappearance, and—as in that cab—no one really listens to anybody else. After a while, we begin to realize that we're never going to "know" these people. Yet in a sense, just by hearing each character's unique style of prattling on, we know them completely—and the more we listen to them, the more they sound a lot like you and me. *Slacker,* which owes much to the punk-deadpan mood of Jim Jarmusch's *Stranger Than Paradise* (and to the Robert Altman of *Nashville*), doesn't simply satirize the new, indolent generation of middle-class bohemian dropouts. The movie is a kind of metaphysical comedy about an era in which people, more and more, are living inside their own heads. *This,* the film seems to be saying, is the true legacy of the sixties—the dazed, media-blitzed narcissism of young Americans who can afford to soak up their lives with private, cultish belief systems. At times the film is like a low-end-of-the-economic-spectrum version of last year's indie hit *Metropolitan.* Linklater, though, doesn't underline his wit in red Magic Marker. *Slacker* has a marvelously low-key observational cool. Whether we're listening to a Kennedy assassination conspiracy buff, a woman who claims to be the proud owner of a Madonna Pap smear, or two homegrown intellectuals exchanging perfectly serious sociological theories about the Smurfs, the movie never loses its affectionate, shaggy-dog sense of America as a place in which people, by now, have almost too much freedom on their hands.

Entertainment Weekly, August 2, 1991

HEATHERS

J. Hoberman

When it comes to the survival arts, the high school in *Heathers,* a surefire cult film, is as epic an arena as the Roman Colosseum. This black comedy of young (blood) lust, semiconscious desire, and rampant antisocial urges is the most audacious of teenpix, as well as one of the most stylish. Articulating an adolescent hyperreality that's more pop and lurid than the teen Kafka of *Sixteen Candles,* the secular-humanist verisimilitude of *Fast Times at Ridgemont High,* and the morbid muckraking of *River's Edge, Heathers* is a brazen provocation.

There probably hasn't been as clever a teen cartoon since *Lord Love a Duck* apotheosized Tuesday Weld some twenty-odd years ago, but, hilarious and irresponsible, *Heathers* invites adult outrage by satirizing the sensitive subject of teenage suicide. At the same time, it feeds youthful solidarity with a brutally entertaining representation of the high school caste system and sensational use of adolescent patois. The movie resounds with audience echo lines. "Fuck me gently with a chainsaw. Do I look like Mother Theresa?" the rhetorical question delivered with crushing disdain by the school's reigning sixteen-year-old megabitch, is only the most irresistibly quotable of half a dozen instant classics.

Immediately establishing its métier as the lunchroom theater of cruelty, *Heathers* plunges into the glamour and callousness of adolescence, with Westerburg High's "most powerful clique" patrolling the school cafeteria—three suavely diffident ultrababes named Heather, plus their ambivalent pal Veronica, picking their way past the earnest dweebs who collect food for famine victims, pausing to prank the most unfortunate of fat girls, Martha "Dumptruck," while dazzling star jocks and hapless geeks alike with the trick question of their lunchtime poll. (You win five million dollars two days before aliens announce they'll blow up the earth—so how do you spend the money?)

The caf in this densely textured, highly choreographed scene is as redolent as a locker room—you can almost smell the mixture of hormones and anxiety, the avid yearning of the Heather-smitten masses (and the Heathers' loathing for the physically unlovely), the visceral embarrassment of a member of the elite encountering a childhood friend outgrown, the ferocious pressure that traps Veronica in her need for Heather acceptance. Fetching sixteen-year-old Winona Ryder, who plays the conflicted Veronica with deeper-than-Method conviction, has the unself-consciously contorted facial expressions of youth down pat. "These are people I work with, and our job is being popular and shit," she lamely tells J. D. (Christian Slater), the rebellious hipster who catches her eye and seduces her into a clandestine anti-Heather war of attrition.

Irritating at first, Slater's ongoing Jack Nicholson imitation becomes a Kabuki representation of high school cool. (It also links *Heathers* to *The Witches of Eastwick* as Americanized *Faust*.) Ostensibly set in Sherwood (sic), Ohio, *Heathers* seems spiritually more attuned to Beverly Hills or the San Fernando Valley. The twenty-six-year-old screenwriter, Daniel Waters, wrote the script while working behind the counter of an L.A. video store. *Heathers'* protagonists are filthy rich, fearfully sophisticated, and heavily into arcane slang ("Get crucial"). The ridiculously smooth and snottily self-assured Heather Chandler (Kim Walker) even has a Barbara Kruger "I Shop Therefore I Am" postcard pasted up in her locker. These cool, sarcastic creatures are the children of the blessed. Still, *Heathers* is something like *The Breakfast Club in Hell*. Once J. D. and Veronica send Heather C. to that great prom night in the sky, covering their tracks with a masterfully forged suicide note ("I die knowing nobody knew the real me"), the movie successfully navigates a difficult transition from the realm of John Hughes to that of Alfred Hitchcock. Heather's "suicide" is not without unexpected side effects. Bulimics can suddenly keep down their lunch, while her poignant missive becomes feeling fodder for an aging hippie's English class. ("Are we gonna be tested on this?" one student demands to know.) More popular than ever, Heather becomes the subject of a two-page spread in the yearbook as well as an ongoing role model. The hapless Dumptruck tapes a note to her chest and walks into traffic, "another case of a geek trying to imitate the cool people and failing miserably."

Michael Lehmann, the thirty-one-year-old neophyte director, handles this material with a modulated DePalma style (caressing crane shots, dramatic overheads, tricky color coordination), drifting in and out of a casual pop surrealism that owes more to MTV than to Dali and Buñuel. (Cinematographer Francis Kenney shot "Girls Just Want to Have Fun," among other videos.) The movie is smartly paced and skillfully acted, but what continually astonishes is Waters's stunning dialogue. ("Dan handed me this 200-page tome," Lehmann told *Premier*, "unreadable, unfilmable, and one of the funniest, strangest scripts I'd ever seen." In the press kit Waters describes reading *Seventeen* as "science fiction.") In certain venues *Heathers* should provoke as much live feedback as *The Rocky Horror Picture Show:* "What's your damage, Heather? Did you have a brain tumor for breakfast?"

No teenpic is without its exploitation aspects and, having prudently softened Veronica's persona, *Heathers* can't quite achieve closure. After flirting with slasherdom, Lehmann and Waters ultimately make a less-than-successful attempt to go genre-realistic. Still, much of *Heathers* is stylized in unpredictable ways. (The screening room in which I saw the film was full of nervous giggling, with individual hysterics for specific bits of business.) Just as the austere use of pop music renders Waters's dialogue all the more crucial, the total absence of mall culture serves to exaggerate the two basic rhythms of adolescent life—namely, the endless, droning repetition of parental injunctions and the exciting, unpredictable torture of school.

Peer pressure rules—and so does impulse behavior. With the exception of J. D.'s appropriately demonic dad, the film's adults are universally brain damaged. ("Grow up" is the most cutting of the movie's many insults.) What gives *Heathers* its particular edge, however, is its identification with adolescent acting out. *Heathers* is a comedy in which urges can't be squelched, the thought is identical to the deed. "You believed [me] because you wanted to believe —your true feelings were too gross and icky to face," J. D. tells Veronica after she has confided in her diary that her "teen angst bullshit has a body count." Conceptually gross and icky almost to the max, *Heathers* invites comparisons with *Carrie.* But it is really more like *Carrie* in reverse: the destructive power resides not in the wretched and the repressed but in the privileged and libidinal.

Heathers' real precursor is Dutch director Renee Dalder's 1976 drive-in flick *Massacre at Central High,* a complex political allegory about revolution and authority that, far more alienated than *Zéro de conduit,* substitutes a high school for George Orwell's barnyard. The American public high school is, after all, the closest institution this society has to a democratic meritocracy—it's virtually the last place where all economic classes have the opportunity to meet and interact on a more or less equal footing. In this sense, *Heathers* is antiutopian for more than just attacking teenage innocence. As the satanic J. D. points out, "The only place different social types can genuinely get along is Heaven." Given the demographic preponderance of youthful filmgoers, *Heathers* may be the most socially realistic American movie released in early 1989.

Village Voice, April 4, 1989

THE WAR OF THE ROSES

■■■

David Ansen

It's been many a moon since Hollywood has produced a comedy as black as *The War of the Roses.* Is black comedy about to make a comeback? The feel-good Reagan years weren't conducive to a jaundiced point of view: black comedy had its heyday under the dark apocalyptic skies of the sixties, when all sacred cows were led directly to the slaughterhouse. There was no room for a *Dr. Strangelove* in the new morning declared by our national cheerleader. Instead we got Bill Murray, Eddie Murphy, *Police Academy,* and the harmless high concept of *Twins.*

The War of the Roses, a comedy of escalating marital warfare, doesn't hark back to the sixties satirical mode. It's about domestic, sexual demons. Director Danny DeVito goes back to the romantic comedy formulas of the thirties and forties and attempts to twist them into grotesque new shapes, with brutally startling élan.

Adapted by Michael Leeson from Warren Adler's novel, *The War of the Roses* is a worst-case cautionary fable about divorce, a kind of slapstick *Who's Afraid of Virginia Woolf?* Oliver and Barbara Rose (Michael Douglas and Kathleen Turner) have all the appurtenances of a perfect marriage. They fell in love on Nantucket when he was a brilliant Harvard law student and she was a star collegiate gymnast. They married, had two kids, and, as Oliver rose to make junior partner, moved into a beautiful suburban home which Barbara has furnished with only the most exquisite antiques and objets d'art. Thinking, in his workaholic myopia, that their lives are picture-perfect, Oliver is stunned one night when Barbara announces she wants a divorce. He demands to know why. "Because when I watch you eat . . . I just want to smash your face in," she says, shortly before slugging him.

The real nastiness begins when Barbara announces that in lieu of alimony she wants the house and all its contents. Suddenly these sane, successful paragons of the upper middle class are fighting over property, and no holds are barred. She locks him in the sauna, he saws off the heels of her shoes. And that's just for starters. Before this battle royal reaches its hair-raising conclusion, every pretense of civility lies in ruins, along with the house.

This is funny, you ask? Indeed it is, though the laughter mixes with gasps. Certainly not everyone is going to cotton to a comedy this down and dirty. But there's no denying that Danny DeVito (*Throw Momma from the Train,* '87) is emerging as a director with a distinctively dark comic style. *The War of the Roses* unfolds in flashback, as a tall tale told by Oliver's divorce lawyer (played by DeVito), and DeVito's bold, simplified images and surprising camera angles give the story the patina of a fairy tale, albeit a nightmarish one in which no one lives happily ever after.

Douglas and Turner and DeVito worked together twice before (as actors in *Romancing the Stone* and *Jewel of the Nile*), but never so well. This may be the most finely shaded performance Douglas has given: with delicious comic shading he shows you both Oliver's charm and his wimpishness, his mania and his confusion, and when he slurps his food you understand just why Barbara wants to slug him. Turner, with her breathless vocal tics and unlocatable accent, is a strangely unsettling actress: she's both a powerful and unstable presence, and in some roles you just can't get beyond her mannerisms. Here the ambiguity works to her advantage, suggesting all the inchoate rage sloshing around Barbara's restless soul. She's a formidable foe. And DeVito, with his bulldog tenacity, makes the perfect master of nasty ceremonies. *The War of the Roses* is a brave comedy to unleash on the holiday season: lovable it's not. But it snarls in your memory long after it's over.

Newsweek, December 11, 1989

DEFENDING YOUR LIFE

■■■

Henry Sheehan

Albert Brooks's hilarious *Defending Your Life* opens and closes with Brooks's character, adman Daniel Miller, enjoying applause from small, admiring crowds. The first time, the ovation is for telling jokes; the second time it is for . . . well, let's just say Miller has gone through a lot of changes, not the least of which are death and imminent rebirth. Always credited with being among the funniest filmmakers around, Brooks has received the proper due for his stylistic and thematic sophistication. But Brooks is not only funny, he is also one of the most talented and ingenious actor-directors working in cinema—period. With this, his fourth feature as a director, he stakes a claim for the artistic freedom his talent is due, and that claim is extremely persuasive.

Brooks's movies have a bold candor; rather than being undercut by a rash of jokes, they are enhanced by the contrast between the ostensible seriousness of their titles and the actual subversion of their protagonists' (always played by Brooks) self-esteem. *Real Life* ('79), *Modern Romance* ('81), and *Lost in America* ('85) may depend for their laughs on the foundering of serious intentions, but their deliberate and precise reversals always reinforce or elaborate on their proposed meanings. By contrasting pretentious ends with deflating means, Brooks actually does end up talking about real life and modern romance while being lost in America.

Like every actor-director, Brooks has a big enough ego to make himself the core subject of his films. The first time out, he went as far as playing a director named Albert Brooks, while in *Modern Romance* he invoked minimal shadow play by impersonating a professionally established but low-budget film editor. He moved a little further afield with *Lost in America* when he dropped the film-making guise for that of a successful midechelon "creative" advertising executive, a plainly analogous vocation. In *Defending Your Life,* Brooks, or Miller, is back in advertising. But since most of the film takes place in a screening room where Brooks and a largely hostile audience watch films starring Brooks, the camouflage, though amusing, is transparent enough to betray the filmmaker's intentions. Brooks *is* defending his life—his artistic life.

The defense opens with Daniel Miller's office birthday party, the occasion of his little standup routine when, thanking his work friends for their gifts, he tells a few gags. From there, Daniel goes off to the BMW lot where he picks up his present to himself, a new black Beemer, and, while tooling through Los Angeles streets, runs smack into an RTD bus and dies.

When he comes to, Daniel discovers he is in Judgment City, an Other Side cross between Century City and a resort community. Along with the afterlife's good news—you can eat as much as you want and not put on any weight, for example—he is shocked to discover that he must defend his life in an adversarial hearing. Judgment City is just a way station between lives; those who have used their time on earth to conquer their fears and anxieties, and thus cleared the way for a loving life, are allowed to go on to ensuing, undefined planes of existence. In contrast, those who have let their worries dominate them are doomed to be sent back to earth over and over until they finally get it right.

The whole procedure is one of the wackiest, funniest exercises in logical lunacy Brooks has ever concocted. The hearing chamber is a glorified screening room where participants watch scenes from the subject's life in what one of the hearing officers defines as a kind of 3-D, although it looks like any movie clips to us. Daniel's life is mercilessly skewered by prosecutorial dragon lady Lena Foster (well played by an unusually prickly and evil-eyed Lee Grant), while his defense is handled by an alternately unctuous and brusque three-piece–suit type, Bob Diamond.

As played by Rip Torn, Diamond is one of Brooks's funniest creations, certainly the funniest character Brooks didn't play himself. Diamond explains the whole comic setup to Daniel with a patronizing regard for Daniel's lack of comprehension. As it turns out, we earthlings only use about three percent of our brains, while members of Judgment City's permanent legal bureaucracy, such as Diamond, use about half. They think of new arrivals as "Little Brains." Whenever Daniel feels depressed, Diamond chimes in with ostensibly cheering but doubly depressing digs such as "Still don't get the Big Brain thing, do you, Daniel?"

As funny as the exchanges between Daniel and Diamond are—and they are very, very funny—they're essentially a sideshow to the main action, which follows a parallel track. For, as Daniel's days are taken up with screenings of scenes from his life—scenes whose interpretations are argued by Diamond (positively) and Foster (negatively)—his nights are spent courting another earthling. Julia (Meryl Streep) is a youngish mother whose life was apparently just one loving and noble moment after another. However, despite the fact that Daniel seems to have spent his life equivocating and weaseling out of trouble, Julia falls for him and, during their four nights together—at the end of which they may be separated by judgment—they fall passionately in love.

Daniel and Julia joke around, but their scenes steadily grow less funny and more serious and loving. In fact, they meet at a comedy club where the outrageously bad performance by a local comedian provokes Daniel to remark that brains are no insurance of a sense of humor, an observation key to the film's thematic progression.

Brooks's humor has always bordered on the anxiety ridden; it would take little to tilt his films from comedy to horror shows of psychic disintegration. And the films of his life that Daniel watches are perfect examples. From childhood to adulthood, and even beyond, these scenes are not just weighed by the performers for their value as evidence but, implicitly at least, are also analyzed for their essential natures. Are they comedy or tragedy; do they portray a fool or a guy just trying to negotiate life in all its mundane pain and difficulty? In assessing how we differentiate between the two, Brooks pulls off a stylistic coup that proves he is an outstanding master of cinematic form as well as a funny guy.

In *Real Life* and *Modern Romance,* Brooks concerned himself explicitly with the process of filmmaking. That concern receded in *Lost in America,* but not the accompanying preoccupation with the idea of performance in everyday life, of how people go to great lengths to present a certain image. Both concerns come to the front of *Defending Your Life* with a vengeance.

The scenes Daniel and company watch in that legalistic screening room are shot with contemporary Hollywood cinema's regular panoply of establishing shots, insert shots, and closeups, all edited together in the traditional style that relies on one central bit of audience identification. The point of view is dictated by the shots, but the maneuvering of the shots, as well as the decision on when to end a sequence and when to enlarge it, is absolutely manipulative. Thus, Diamond and Foster are correct when they offer up contrasting interpretations of the action; a constructed point of view is always there to back them up.

Brooks originates this process in a childhood scene where baby Daniel uses his tears to control his father, who is raging about his wife's spending habits and on the verge of striking her. This episode, in which Daniel uses what his father sees to calm him, introduces the idea of performance as a control and is inextricably tied to Daniel's lifelong behavior.

The use of editing crops up in a scene from Daniel's childhood, when facing down—actually, *not* facing down—a schoolyard bully becomes a chorus of shots in which Daniel is humiliated in front of his friends and, in particular, a little girl. This is all done through editing, and Daniel appears utterly humiliated. Yet Diamond's insistence that Daniel was restrained, not scared, holds water if you play the scene back in your head from different angles. The editing emphasizes how awful the occurrence was and how it stayed in Daniel's mind for the rest of his life. But just because the scene is pumped up by that editing does not mean, as Daniel and Diamond insist, that he really cares much about it.

Defending Your Life moves from general observation into specific artistic biography in a later scene, a particularly devastating one, when Daniel is overcome by paralyzing stage fright when addressing a business convention, a paralysis that surely must be like what a standup comedian—which Brooks was for years—feels before going on stage. Foster helps emphasize the autobiographical aspect when she introduces a sequence meant to show Daniel's general stupidity and incompetence, which turns out to be a reel of slapstick movie gags, one after another.

While all these highly edited sequences are going on, Brooks films the rest of the movie in a completely different style. He shoots a scene in a long, unbroken take whenever possible. In fact, he seems so worried that the audience might not know what he is doing that he precedes Daniel's accident with a long sequence of leisurely shots just showing Daniel driving in traffic and listening to his CD player. The scene goes on far longer than any utilitarian need for a mere setup.

More important, the courtship scenes between Daniel and Julia are essentially a series of long tracking shots during which they just talk about themselves. Brooks lets go a number of one-liners and Streep demonstrates her newly acquired—or admired, anyway—gift for light comic repartee. The essence of the scenes lies not in what they say but in the fact that they are saying it not in alternating closeups but in long, steady shots that depend on the re-created reality the two actors, the two human beings, can create for themselves. (It is no coincidence that the one collaborator Brooks has kept through all his films, including his shorts for "Saturday Night Live," is editor David Finfer.)

In a brilliant stroke, Brooks has thus reached deep into the nature of cinema's ability to reconstruct reality and made a profound plea for the efficacy of free will. His is a cinema that resents being dominated by the exigencies of narrative form and insists on a meaning that emanates from within the presence of a human being. The actions of the performer, the person who exposes himself on film, will determine the shot and thus the meaning of a scene; the mechanics of the camera will not coerce meaning from the actor. That argument is once in a while (not often, mind you, but once in a while) undercut by Julia's lack of depth as a character, a deficiency disguised by Streep's overwhelming acting ability, and a feeling that Brooks is arguing for a chance to make romances instead of comedies. (The film is loaded with digs at the very idea of telling jokes and the underlying cruelty of it.)

But any minor shortcomings lurking at the film's periphery are dwarfed by its overwhelming accomplishment. From life to art and back out to life again, Brooks profoundly engages our notions of ourselves and how we mitigate that notion with the perceptions of others.

Funny and profound. This is a great film.

Los Angeles Reader, March 22, 1991

ROMANCE

t's entirely conceivable that, in any year but the year of *The Crying Game,* the editor wouldn't have proposed a chapter on Romance. Love (and sex) preoccupies us all, but the love story itself—as in *Love Story*—is simply not a terribly interesting form to contemplate. The Astaire-Rogers movies of the thirties were love stories, but no one would remember them if Fred and Ginger hadn't danced their romance. The other most enduring love stories of the Golden Age tended to be comedies, and screwball comedies at that; "The love impulse in man frequently expresses itself in terms of conflict," Katharine Hepburn burbled to Cary Grant in *Bringing Up Baby* (she'd just heard it from a psychiatrist in a night-club), and it's the crazy, careening energy of their epic conflict we cherish, not the final clinch. Hepburn and Tracy didn't even kiss in *Pat and Mike,* but we still knew that what they had was cherce.

Solemn, soggy, straight-ahead love stories? Catch the miniseries. This chapter looks for love in all the wrong places, or at any rate unexpected places. Jay Carr zeroes in on the mutual yearning, unrequited passion, and ethical queasiness of the very adult love story between Gene Hackman and Frances McDormand in Alan Parker's *Mississippi Burning,* itself a pretty ethically queasy essay in the genre of historical docudrama. Roger Ebert recommends Harold Pinter's chilling contemplation of an affair in reverse, *Betrayal.* Peter Rainer finds *Roxanne* not so much a Steve Martin comedy (though it's very funny) as a lyric tribute to the spirit of romance. Peter Keough assesses, in *Love at Large,* how many genres can dance on the head of Alan Rudolph, a filmmaker who is perhaps more romantic than anyone else on the contemporary scene when it comes to the magic of telling stories. Michael Sragow takes a look at what is nominally a spy movie, Fred Schepisi's film of John le Carré's *The Russia House,* and locates its beating heart in the relationship between Sean Connery and Michelle Pfeiffer. Finally, Andy Klein leads us through the rich, resonant, masterly complications of the best screen love story in many a season, but—never fear—without giving away the secret of *The Crying Game.*

(For further variations on Romance, see the later chapter "The Women.")

ON ADULT LOVE STORIES

Jay Carr

Love may not exactly be sweeping the country, but it started showing up at the end of the eighties a lot more often than it used to in Hollywood movies. Adult love, I mean. Three Hollywood movies released within one month were built around complicated adult relationships: *The Accidental Tourist, Dangerous Liaisons,* and, less obviously, *Mississippi Burning.* And in the months before them came *Moonstruck, Crossing Delancey, Torch Song Trilogy, The Good Mother,* the sterling *Unbearable Lightness of Being,* and *Working Girl*—the last a stylish throwback to thirties comedy. Clearly, Hollywood is rediscovering the mature moviegoer, heeding demographic studies that point to an aging America and at least tentatively abandoning an exclusive devotion to the teen market and its adoration of macho biff-bam-pow.

What sets *Accidental Tourist, Dangerous Liaisons,* and *Mississippi Burning* apart from the other films (with the always notable exception of *Unbearable Lightness of Being*) is that it's the women who keep taking the big chances first, never the men, who either flee love or are in no way inclined to match what the women are feeling. In this sense, these aren't so much postfeminist films, as some critics have called them, as films that challenge men, emotionally speaking, to come out of hiding. As one of the characters (a woman) in Anne Tyler's novel *The Accidental Tourist* says whenever a new man appears on the scene, the question is: whom is he going to love?

That line of Tyler's doesn't make it into the film, but almost all of her beautifully worked out symmetry does, along with her resonant metaphors and her balance between the comic and the poignant. In genuflecting to the regenerative power of love, Tyler draws us into a world in which loving is too important to be left to men. William Hurt's Macon Leary, the story's protagonist, is a travel writer who hates travel. He makes his living writing guidebooks that enable leery businessmen to travel without ever experiencing the places they're traveling to. Ever since his young son was accidentally killed by a gunman's bullet in a hamburger joint, he's been cocooning himself in Baltimore drabness.

This, added to his normal remoteness, is too much for his more conventionally grieving wife (Kathleen Turner), who moves out, leaving him with his son's dog. The latter's disintegrating sociability opens the door to Tyler's key figure, the screwball heroine dog trainer who yanks Macon out of his reclusiveness and bombards him with outlandish, burgeoning, messy life. Muriel, the dog trainer, is a triumph for Tyler and also for actress Geena Davis. Her voice is too insistent, her fingernails too magenta, her fake tigerskin skirt too mini. But Tyler has faith in her and in Macon's demure, compulsively methodical sister (Amy Wright), who stands up to her selfish brothers when they try to sabotage her chances with Macon's publisher (Bill Pullman). Even Macon's wife hangs in there, once she gets through her grief.

The book's point—and the movie's—is to go with the flow, to realize that we're all accidental tourists, taking our chances on unscheduled flights, unchecked spouses, lost children, unforeseen destinations. In this, *Accidental Tourist* is to *Dangerous Liaisons* as matter is to antimatter. Beneath its sexual gamesmanship among decadent aristocrats on the eve of the French Revolution, *Dangerous Liaisons* is a moral and even cautionary tale, showing what can happen when the courage to love is absent. Like *Accidental Tourist,* it was a hot property—not a novel (although it began as one in 1782) but a Royal Shakespeare Company stage hit in London and on Broadway.

It's been Hollywoodized, with Glenn Close playing the pitilessly manipulative marquise who suggests to her first lover and longtime ally, the Vicomte de Valmont (John Malkovich), that he seduce the virginal fiancée (Uma Thurman) of a man who threw the marquise over. The dandy complies, but lets it be known he's more interested in seducing the virtuous young bourgeois wife (Michelle Pfeiffer) of another member of their circle. As the flow of letters, keys, whispered treacheries, and assignations accelerates in ways as elaborate and formal as the châteaux in which they unfold, everything comes unglued when the vicomte finds himself, to his surprise and dismay, falling in love with the woman he seduces.

Close's marquise reveals that she never stopped loving the vicomte even though she subsequently steeled herself against any and all passionate flights. When she realizes he's in love, she loses control, unsheathes her claws, takes advantage of the fact that the vicomte's ego is shakier than his heart is strong, and moves to kill his new love. Frankly, the American cast never musters the requisite aristocratic mien, and it costs the picture. But it does have moments, and the best ones come when the two women in love with the vicomte—Close and Pfeiffer—unfurl their feelings.

Compared to the original, this *Dangerous Liaisons* is a coarsened and otherwise flawed look at the connections between love and power, but it does put those connections on screen as few American movies even try to do. So does *Mississippi Burning*. Although it's mostly about the FBI bringing to light the murderers of three civil rights workers in Mississippi in 1964, it pivots on an extraordinarily subtle and powerful man-woman relationship involving Gene Hackman's sly FBI man, once a backwoods sheriff, and Frances McDormand's decent woman trapped in a corrosive marriage to a sheriff's deputy (Brad Dourif) who was in on the murders. In real life, the FBI cracked the case mundanely, relying on a paid informant. In this fictionalized version, Hackman does exactly as the vicomte does to the married woman he wants to seduce—he appeals to her goodness.

Although the film falls away from a promising beginning into meretricious vigilante formula, it never makes a wrong move in delineating the slow, insidious development of the complicity into which Hackman draws the only woman who can give him the evidence he needs to crack the case. More than director Stephen Frears ever does in *Dangerous Liaisons,* his compatriot Alan Parker nails down the tension between being genuinely attracted to a person and using that person. One of the reasons Hackman succeeds in getting to McDormand's conscience and exploiting it is that he never goes too far. At his insistence and McDormand's, there's nothing like a sex scene, nothing heavyhanded between them. But neither are we in any doubt that Hackman's agent is courting the deputy's wife, with honeyed words, with flowers, with sincere admiration.

And all the time, he's using her, and she knows it. "My father used to call these Ladies from Hell," McDormand says when Hackman hands her a bouquet of flowers. "They're car . . . carnivorous. Is that the word? The pretty color is the bait and the insects just home in there and . . . wham! They're dead before they've even got their shoes off!" McDormand's face as moral battleground is the film's most compelling sight. She knows she's being soft-soaped, but she also knows Hackman genuinely admires her, and she's not indifferent to his good opinion. Watching her sort out her feelings and decide in favor of conscience over caution saves the film from its retreat to the simplistic.

In interviews, McDormand has cleared up the mystery of how her scenes with Hackman are so subtle, so full of rightness, when the rest of the film is so skewed to the bold, two-dimensional stroke. Put simply, the scenes work because she and Hackman developed the characters largely on their own. They talked Parker out of three scripted versions of their scenes before he allowed them to go with what they knew would be right for the characters. In the first version, they sleep together, then she tells him the secret. In the second, she tells him the secret and they sleep together. In the third, they fall panting to the floor of the beauty shop where she works.

Not until a fourth version was shaped to their mutual satisfaction do they give us what we get from them in the film—subtle, highly charged face-offs, tense with unspoken feelings. The chemistry between them is heartstopping. The measure of the tension they generate becomes clear at the end, when Hackman shoots McDormand a fat, phony wink, and you're relieved to be let off the hook, down onto a more comfortable level of worldliness. The FBI man and the deputy's wife who knows what she's risking by talking to him are giving us the season's really dangerous liaison.

Boston Globe, January 22, 1989

BETRAYAL

Roger Ebert

Love stories have beginnings, but affairs . . . affairs have endings, too. Even sad love stories begin in gladness, when the world is young and the future reaches out cheerfully forever. Then, of course, eventually you get Romeo and Juliet dead in the tomb, but that's the price you have to pay. Life isn't a free ride. Think how much *more* tragic a sad love story would be, however, if you could see into the future, so that even *this* moment, *this* kiss, is in the shadow of eventual despair.

The absolutely brilliant thing about *Betrayal* ('83) is that it is a love story told backward. There is a lot in this movie that is wonderful—the performances, the screenplay by Harold Pinter—but what makes it all work is the structure. When Pinter's stage version first appeared, back in the late seventies, there was a tendency to dismiss his reverse chronology as a gimmick. Not so. It is the very heart and soul of this story. It means that we in the audience know more about the unhappy romantic fortunes of Jerry and Robert and Emma at *every moment* than they know about themselves. Even their joy is painful to see.

Jerry is a youngish London literary agent, clever, good-looking, confused about his feelings. Robert, his best friend, is a publisher. Robert is older, stronger, smarter, and more bitter. Emma is Robert's wife and becomes Jerry's lover. But that is telling the story chronologically. And the story begins at the end, with Robert and Emma fighting and with Robert slapping her, and with Emma and Jerry meeting in a pub for a painful reunion two years after their affair is over. Each additional scene takes place further back in time, and the sections have uncanny titles: TWO YEARS EARLIER. THREE YEARS EARLIER. We aren't used to this. At a public preview of the film, some people in the audience actually *resisted* the backward time frame, as if the purpose of the playwright were just to get on with the story, damn it all, and stop this confounded fooling around.

The *Betrayal* structure strips away all artifice. It shows, heartlessly, that the very capacity for love itself is sometimes based on betraying not only other loved ones but even ourselves. The movie is told mostly in encounters between two of the characters; all three are not often onscreen together, and we never meet Jerry's wife. These people are smart and they talk a lot—too much, maybe, because there is a peculiarly British reserve about them that sometimes prevents them from saying quite what they mean. They lie and they half-lie. There are universes left unspoken in their unfinished sentences. They are all a little embarrassed that the messy urges of sex are pumping away down there beneath their civilized deceptions.

The performances are perfectly matched. Ben Kingsley (of *Gandhi*) plays Robert, the publisher, with such painfully controlled fury that there are times when he actually is frightening. Jeremy Irons, as Jerry, creates a man whose desires are stronger than his convictions, even though he spends a lot of time talking about his convictions, and almost none acknowledging his desires. Patricia Hodge, as Emma, loves them both and hates them both and would have led a much happier life if they had not been her two choices. But how could she know that when, in life, you're required by the rules to start at the beginning?

Roger Ebert's Video Companion

ROXANNE

███

Peter Rainer

Roxanne is one of the most beautiful, elating romantic comedies ever made in this country. It makes you feel mysteriously, unreasonably happy, as if you were watching colors being added to a sunset. The glow from this film stays with you; it has a radiance like no other movie. Steve Martin, the writer-star, and his director, Fred Schepisi, create a cockeyed higgledy-piggledy universe that's as magically stylized as anything the great silent comedians came up with. The comedy comes out of the delicately illuminated setting, and the romance does, too. The movie is about the *rightness* of true love, and everything in nature—the quality of the light, the steep slope of the streets, the pure, wide mountain vistas—seems to conspire in the annunciation. We're watching a world where purity of feeling counts for as much as the purity of the glorious natural surroundings; a world where love—poetically, inevitably—will out.

By reworking Edmond Rostand's 1897 *Cyrano de Bergerac* to a Washington ski resort in off-season, Steve Martin, playing the long-nosed town fire chief C. D. Bales, courts disaster. Instead, the preposterousness of updating this glorious old warhorse works in the film's favor; it's part of the storybook charm. C. D. is the town's natural aristocrat; his off-kilter athleticism and courtly, self-absorbed quirkiness set him apart from his neighbors. He's more like a heightened version of eccentric. His long, tapered nose gives him a surreal handsomeness.

That nose is C. D.'s shame, but it's so much a part of who he is that he's unimaginable with anything smaller. A normal-sized nose would diminish him, make him seem less fantastic—in the same way that a smiling Buster Keaton would be a reduction of his character's poetic possibilities. The Keaton reference is central: no comic actor since the great Buster has been able to work up such an abundance of physical comedy. Martin works with such precision that there isn't a movement that doesn't contribute to what we know about C. D.; the sheer joy of physical release is in every step and skedaddle.

C. D. is so deeply ashamed of his nose that he compensates by becoming a connoisseur of his fine points; he moves about in a state of fine-tuned calisthenic rapture. He can shimmy up the side of a house to the roof in a few quick pull-ups. He walks up and down the slanty streets at gravity-defying angles; he's never on quite the same plane as anybody else but always just a bit askew from the horizon. C. D. *conspires* with gravity (as all the great silent comics did). He uses the loopiness of nature's forces to assert his specialness and turns stunts into dream walks.

It's a measure of Martin's performance that he manages to give C. D. a romantic core, without pathos. In this movie's supernal setting, pathos would seem as jarringly out of place as a shout in a canyon. When C. D. first meets Roxanne (Daryl Hannah) he's flabbergasted, as we are, by her beauty. But we see his awe in small, self-revelatory ways. He doesn't work against the planes of his surroundings quite so much when he's around her. Roxanne moves in a lyrical sweep, and C. D. acquiesces in that movement. It's a way of romancing her, of keying into her cycles.

To C. D., Roxanne is a heavenly vision—the apotheosis of the

Roxanne is a movie filled with beguiling asymmetries—in the architecture of its airy small-town locations, in Fred Schepisi and Ian Baker's winsome widescreen compositions, and most of all in the unlikely love-match of Daryl Hannah's Roxanne and Steve Martin's modern-day Cyrano. (Copyright © by Universal City Studios, Inc. Courtesy of MCA Publishing Rights, a Division of MCA Inc.)

beauty that surrounds him. (The whole town sparkles like an upturned planetarium; C. D. is its honorary moon man.) She's an astronomy student searching the skies for a new comet she believes is out there, waiting to be discovered. Closer to earth, she has eyes for one of C. D.'s new volunteer fire fighters, the hunky but painfully shy Chris (Rick Rossovich), who runs for cover whenever he gets close to Roxanne. Just as in *Cyrano,* she and Chris are brought together by the man who loves her most. C. D. is prevailed upon by Chris to ghostwrite love letters to her; then he prompts Chris's speeches to her under her balcony, finally taking over himself, shadowed from recognition. Roxanne is in love with C. D.— embodied by Chris. He's the go-between in the demolition of his own true love, and yet he keeps on going, writing reams of letters, devising speeches. When C. D. is in love, even gravity seems to have lost its tug on him. He's cometlike, carried away by his ardor, his folly.

C. D.'s wooing of Roxanne, through Chris, is done almost entirely with language. Martin's script for *Roxanne* is in love with words and their power to entrance. C. D. is agile and he can punch, too, but words are what carry him away. When a guy in a bar makes a dumb crack about his nose, C. D. one-ups the lout by improvising twenty proboscis put-downs in a row, in a heightened, exhilarated patter. (It's a variation on the most famous scene in *Cyrano.*) C. D.'s infatuation with language comes out of his most private precincts: when he's revved up, his speeches have the frantic, lickety-split velocity of a lonely man suddenly trumpeting his own inner dialogues for all to hear. His florid, triumphant love pronouncements are really a triumph of spirit, and that's where the real romance in *Roxanne* lies. What we immediately respond to in C. D. is what Roxanne finally responds to as well: not the beauty of his words so much as the beauty of the spirit behind those words.

This awareness of the primacy of the spirit makes *Roxanne* a deeply humane comedy. Schepisi and Martin embrace C. D. because they recognize his value; they recognize the beauty in his stumbly troupe of volunteer fire fighters, too. (The standout crew includes Michael J. Pollard, John Kapelos, Steve Mittleman, and Matt Lattanzi.) But it's not just the romantics and the outcasts the filmmakers side with. They also confer their blessings on Chris by eventually pairing him off with a more suitable soulmate (Shandra Beri), a waitress-cutie for whom his lunky muteness is as enticing as C. D.'s verbal ravishments. All of the movie's characters are haloed by the filmmakers' good graces, and that includes Fred Willard's tinhorn mayor and Shelley Duvall's café owner—C. D.'s best friend. Schepisi, with the help of his great cinematographer Ian Baker, creates a cuckoo, cloud-borne community, part Brigadoon, part Milkwood (the actual location is British Columbia); its inhabitants are magical versions of the everyday. Everything seems anointed in this town, newly minted: the fire fighters' bumblings are like the beginnings of slapstick; the starry heavens are like the first big night sky you can remember looking up at as a kid; C. D.'s love for Roxanne is like the first love. The freshness of this world matches the freshness of Schepisi and Martin's vision. Like C. D., they're romantics, too. Their movie sends you into a swoon.

Los Angeles Herald Examiner, June 19, 1987

LOVE AT LARGE

Peter Keough

Desire, illusion, and generic conventions are the mainstay of the movies, and they're Alan Rudolph's stock-in-trade, too. But Rudolph's passionate confections will never be mistaken for the standard commercial fare they so exuberantly parody.

Most movies refer to recognizable realities; Rudolph's refer to the movie artifice itself, creating a metaworld of movie time and movie place made strange by the director's puckish and perverse imagination. Aristotle would censure Rudolph's art as a reflection of a shadow four times removed from the real thing. But when Rudolph's films work—and in many ways *Love at Large* works better than anything he's done before—his jubilant dances of appearances have the numinous look of cinema archetypes.

As in *Choose Me* ('84) and *Trouble in Mind* ('85), the setting of *Love at Large* is an unreal city (actually Portland, Oregon) at once comfortably familiar and beguilingly alien. The props look commonplace enough, yet when you look closer you see the cigarettes bear brand names like Metro and the cars are ambiguous composites of twenty-year-old Dodges and Studebakers with model names like Superclassic. Rudolph's eclectic sets don't sprout the grotesquerie of a *Brazil* or a *Batman:* theirs is a subtle surreality, exactly but nonspecifically detailed, a Nabokovian alternative universe where everything has the glow, the cheesiness, and the immanence of a musical comedy.

Harry Dobbs (Tom Berenger), feckless private eye, fits right in with this world's jovial motleyness. In a rare and irrepressible comic performance, Berenger makes Harry a combination of several ineffectual and ingenuous imitations of more successful detectives. Aspiring to the crusty savoir faire of Sam Spade, he achieves the nimbleness of Inspector Clouseau, and in his chic dark-on-dark shirts and ties topped by a Totes rain hat, he resembles a Peter Falk fumbling in the wardrobe of Don Johnson. Like all detectives since Oedipus, Harry is on the trail of something beyond the accidental mysteries of his latest assignment. In his case, it's love—and like Oedipus, he's the last person to figure out what he's really looking for.

The love he's used to is the kind he'd like to escape, not track down. His girlfriend Doris (Ann Magnuson) is the jealous type, apt to smash crockery whenever a gossamer-voiced client calls up offering Harry a case, as she does when sultry Miss Dolan (Anne Archer) hires him to tail her errant thug lover Rick (Neil Young). Harry makes a rendezvous with Miss Dolan in the thickly tinted atmosphere of the Blue Danube club, where Archer demonstrates her pipes in a brief but convincing rendition of "You Don't Know What Love Is." Harry gets a cursory description of Rick. ("Dresses well. Smells nice," coos Miss Dolan. "That's a relief!" Harry guffaws.) He sets out at once, following the wrong man.

Of course, in a deeper sense the innocent tailee proves to be the right man. Taking a cue from *Blue Velvet,* Harry follows the false Rick into suburbia and finds beneath the split-level surface an uneasily realistic world of double lives, treachery, and bigamy. He stumbles into a *La Ronde* of inept two-timings and love triangles, and gets caught up in it himself. Unknown to Harry, Doris has hired another gumshoe to keep an eye on *him.* Like Harry, Stella Wynkowski (Elizabeth Perkins) is trying to elude her own love woes by spying on those of others. When the distance between these two hired voyeurs breaks down, so does Rudolph's from his subject: passion and violence erupt, first disrupting and then vindicating the film's blithe aesthetic surface.

Crucial to the success of such a soufflé of a movie is the manipulation of tone, and *Love at Large* does this better than any previous Rudolph film—probably because it is less ambitious. The mood in *Choose Me, Trouble in Mind,* and especially *The Moderns* ('88) could career to extremes, and not always with felicitous results. In *Love at Large,* Rudolph limits himself mostly to an impeccable irony, the kind in which the joke is on everyone and everyone is in on the joke. When he does shift gears it is for sound dramatic—or comic—reasons.

His is the kind of parody that transcends the object satirized and becomes a type of its own. And he is blessed with splendid actors who can galvanize such material. A case in point is Anne Archer's Miss Dolan, the airheaded, treacherous siren who has been a genre stereotype since Raymond Chandler. Archer doesn't eschew the cliché elements of the part, she radiates them. And she filigrees her archetypical vamp with the canny details Rudolph's script provides. Augmenting a voice as characteristic as Berenger's with a stunning, slightly dazed come-hither smile, she adds minute, hilarious nuance to lines like "Come Rick, I'm ever so ready!" and "Shall we be glad and dizzy the rest of our lives or will we destroy ourselves?"

Not all Rudolph's lines are winners. His penchant for the self-consciously gnomic phrase rears occasionally, in particular during an overlong philosophical discussion about love between a plane-bound Stella and Harry. Lines like "The lover is the one who waits" and "In falling for someone, is it the smile or the situation one goes for?" might look fine on the page, but even for these actors they drop like bowling trophies in performance.

In Rudolph's previous films, this preciosity in dialogue was matched by a contrivance in invention. Striving for exhilarating flights of fancy, he would sink into implausibility or even inanity. But in *Love at Large,* the frame shimmers with nascent revelation. As in a dream, anything seems likely to happen, and when it does, it seems the only thing that *could* happen. *Love at Large* is a master-piece in three genres: the hard-boiled detective film, the romantic comedy, and the chimerical and unique entity that is the Alan Rudolph movie.

Boston Phoenix, March 30, 1990

THE RUSSIA HOUSE

■■■

Michael Sragow

Watching the vistas in *The Russia House,* it's easy to feel the exhil-aration of the reluctant hero, Barley Blair (Sean Connery), a British publisher who becomes embroiled in the attempt of a visionary Soviet physicist nicknamed "Dante" (Klaus Maria Brandauer) to publish Soviet military secrets in the West. Cinematographer Ian Baker's images of Old Russia's churches and the Soviet Union's mammoth public architecture have a vibrancy and sweep that go beyond travelogue pictorialism. There's a hum of discovery to them. They express the chivalric, adventurous feelings that emerge with a rush as soon as Barley sees Dante's courier, Katya (Michelle Pfeiffer), whom he describes jocularly yet accurately as the Soviet answer to the Venus de Milo.

Katya, Dante's sometime lover (and exemplar), is an editor, so there's no suspicion when she stops by an audiocassette booth at a Moscow book fair and drops off Dante's journals. Divorced ("like everyone else in Moscow"), she lives with her two young children and favorite uncle. Like Dante, she's a Soviet idealist who doesn't trust the authorities now flacking for glasnost. Barley is something completely different: a bookish boozer and jazz fan who gets a chance to act on his instincts and become actively humane when he enlists with Dante and Katya.

In one of the most amusing subplots in *The Third Man,* the pulp Western writer played by Joseph Cotten is mistaken for an E. M. Forster–type novelist. The plot of *The Russia House*—adapted by Tom Stoppard from the John le Carré novel—is set off by a similar case of mistaken literary identity. Barley, lolling in his cups at the Soviet writers' village, Peredelkino, starts mouthing off about world peace. He's indulging in a liberal highbrow version of bar talk, but Dante takes him at his word. Barley argues that people everywhere have to wrest control of man's fate from big governments of any stripe. He adapts the May Sarton line that serves as le Carré's epigraph—"One must think like a hero in order to behave like a merely decent human being"—and it hits home to Dante. Dante makes Barley promise that if a poetic Soviet renegade like himself acts like a hero, Barley will behave like a merely decent human being. Dante sends his secrets-spilling journals via Katya so that Barley will publish them without any government intervention, Soviet or British. But when Katya shows up at the book fair Barley isn't there. She hands the journals to another bookseller, who, frightened of the consequences, turns them over to British authorities.

The Russia House is a trailblazing espionage film not only because it's the first Western movie made in the Soviet Union without coproduction status, but also because it's the first film to raze the wall between heroes and villains East and West. It takes the "plague on both your houses" approach of all le Carré's fiction (including 1962's *The Spy Who Came In from the Cold,* the basis of the previous best le Carré movie) and transforms it into something more stirring and positive: a fresh "us versus them" outlook in which the "us" are human beings and the "them" are bloodless bureaucrats. The movie isn't pretentious about this division; in fact, it uses the new setup as an opportunity to make light of the "grey men" who run security services.

Director Fred Schepisi (*Roxanne, A Cry in the Dark*) has never done craftier work than with the actors playing the British Intelligence and CIA men who surround and indoctrinate Barley—particularly, on the British side, James Fox, Michael Kitchen, and director-turned-actor Ken Russell. Fox has been a wonderful character actor in many different moods, but here is my favorite kind of Fox: the sly Fox. He embodies the best of the intelligence community—upright, empathic, and wily—while Kitchen is a shrewd weasel. Russell is a wild card. It will be ticklish for film buffs to see the madcap auteur behind *Women in Love* and *The Lair of the White Worm* behaving just as peculiarly and gleefully in front of the camera. With a shock of white hair, impossible-to-read eyes, and a touch of the Edwardian dandy to his vested clothing, Russell plays the opposite of an absentminded professor. He's a *prescient* professor who checks off every point of information Barley discovers about Dante as if he were grading a prize protégé.

The men in Her Majesty's service revel in their own Englishness; even their betrayal or craziness takes a literate, civilized form. The Americans, led by Roy Scheider, have a forced warmth, a crude energy, a scatological zing. The contrast is uproarious. Scheider and Fox share an unexpected chemistry—one of the drollest moments comes when Scheider pats the Brit's head and Fox calmly smooths his hair down afterward. J. T. Walsh, playing the main American military liaison, is as deadpan-funny as Don Davis's starchy military dad in "Twin Peaks"; John Mahoney does a cunning (if futile) bit of ingratiation, affecting a perfect hands-across-the-sea manner when first confronting Barley. These scenes perk the movie.

The grey men provide the pacemakers; Connery and Pfeiffer provide the heart. They're triumphant star casting, ardent in different yet complementary ways. Connery has the sort of power that illuminates every scene he's in, even when his character is dissembling. (His whole performance in the otherwise paralyzingly dull *The Hunt for Red October* was the pinnacle of scene-stealing dissemblement.) Pfeiffer's charisma, despite her obvious beauty, is more submerged and mysterious; the more she plays against her allure, the more she draws you in.

They're also, of course, terrific actors. Connery exults in Barley's impulses and appetites. His exuberance here recalls his Danny Dravot in Huston's *The Man Who Would Be King*, except Barley has no desire to be even a prince—he's an enlightened, sympathetic muddler. Connery brings out the romance of a man whose instinctive disillusionment masks real feeling. His bouts of boozy camaraderie and jazz (whether with a comb or a musical instrument) are irresistible. He may not look totally at home with a sax, but the filmmakers have given him the ideal theme song—Cole Porter's "What Is This Thing Called Love?" (played by Branford Marsalis with a lilting, bluesy quality). Pfeiffer's Katya defines that thing called love for him: one of the joys of the film is watching it dawn in Connery's eyes and gradually reach a blazing noon. Pfeiffer, astutely, doesn't meet his gaze too fervently, too quickly. She's mastered a Russian accent that's so unself-conscious it puts most of Meryl Streep's dialect work to shame. But what's most remarkable about her performance is its touch of Russian soulfulness. Pfeiffer's Katya has gravity. She's formidable enough to create an emotional world that Connery's Barley can live in. She won't give herself to a man until she's sure he can behave like a hero—or at least a decent human being.

Their romance would be even more satisfying if the filmmakers had dared to depart decisively from le Carré and twist the voltage up a notch. Le Carré, a master plotter, works in shades of gray even when he's pushing his characters to leave the twilight of espionage behind. By making the book's narrator a British Intelligence officer who envies Barley's free will and emotionality, le Carré deliberately holds down a reader's emotional expectations. By eliminating this character, the filmmakers both increase the drama's directness and allow Barley's ebullience to set the mood. Their approach is touched with exultation; the problem is, it leaves you wanting more.

On the whole, both Schepisi and screenwriter Stoppard (in his most ingenious adaptation) perform miracles with the material. Along with the nimble, lucid editor, Pete Honess, they speed up the narrative. Aurally and visually, they intercut the opening flashbacks—of Katya handing off Dante's manuscript, Barley living it up at Peredelkino, and British Intelligence tracking him down in Lisbon—with Barley's initial interrogation. They imbue all the action with present-tense intensity. When British Intelligence bugs Barley, and later when the wired Barley bugs Katya, Schepisi often lets the audience hear only the tape recording. When the West uses Barley to embroil Dante in spy games, Schepisi darts between the increasingly ambiguous action as it unfolds in Soviet streets and the clues that come into the Anglo-American situation room via tape and computer.

This swirling activity works both as virtuoso storytelling and as vivacious metaphor: Fox, Scheider, and the rest of the old-style Cold Warriors are operating in a tenuous universe of their own creation, one that's spinning apart as it loses all connection to life as it is lived. *The Russia House* is a genre movie but its themes break the bounds of the genre—and Schepisi expresses them visually. It's better for Barley and Katya (and then Dante) to meet in open spaces, where it would be difficult for Soviet authorities to tap their conversations. This gives Schepisi the excuse to photograph them in the most lyrical, capacious settings.

Leningrad's Field of Mars, a bell tower in Zagorsk (the City of Churches), or Kolomenskoye, the old country estate of the czars, all seem to fill up with Barley and Katya's expansive feelings. When the lovers move through claustrophobic and chaotic settings—a bright, overcrowded department store, a teeming (remarkably clean) subway—you can sense the fresh air pressing against the doors and the windowpanes. The tight corners in which the espionage agents operate reflect the confines of their minds.

In its use of atmosphere and irony, and in its bittersweet romantic feeling, *The Russia House* is one of the few East-West suspense films that bear comparison with *The Third Man*. An espionage film in the purest sense, it gets its kicks not from chases and bloodshed, but from thought and empathy. *The Russia House* makes intelligence thrilling.

San Francisco Examiner, December 21, 1990

THE CRYING GAME

Andy Klein

The career of writer-director Neil Jordan has been divided between small "personal" films like *Mona Lisa* ('86) and *The Company of Wolves* ('84) and bigger-budget Hollywood star vehicles like *High Spirits* ('88) and *We're No Angels* ('89). The history of film is full of directors who do their best work in the studio system, but it's painfully obvious that Jordan isn't one of them. With *The Crying Game* Jordan is back on his home turf—Ireland (at first, anyway)—

and back, more significantly, at the same sort of subject matter that motivated *Mona Lisa,* arguably his best previous film: the complicated and deceptive ways of romance, with all its political and personal ramifications.

The movie starts with a long, slow tracking shot of a carnival, seen from beneath a bridge, while Percy Sledge sings "When a Man Loves a Woman" on the soundtrack; the notions of a bridge and a carnival are no less metaphorically relevant to the film's themes than are the lyrics of the song. We see Jude (Miranda Richardson), a hard-edged blonde, pick up Jody (Forest Whitaker), a black British soldier. The two go off to a secluded spot for sex, but within moments a group of Jude's IRA pals show up and put the snatch on Jody. They drag him to a shack in the middle of the countryside, where they hold him hostage in exchange for one of their own in a British prison. Jody knows as well as they do that their scheme is futile and that he is, for all practical purposes, a dead man.

Jude's boyfriend, Fergus (Stephen Rea), is put in charge of guarding Jody. In military terms, he's certainly the wrong man for the job. Despite his best efforts at being coldhearted, he is basically a gentle soul. What's more, Jody is a charmer, and knows it. He sees that his one slim hope for survival is to convert himself in Fergus's eyes from an unfortunate political casualty to a real human being. More than a third of the film is taken up with Jody and Fergus's male bonding. They talk about sports and war and girlfriends. By the end of this sequence, Fergus feels closer to Jody than he does to his own mates; we know that he can't possibly kill him.

This opening act is tense and involving; it's also no warning for the disorienting tailspin the movie is about to go into. There are surprises in store: suffice it to say that Jody's execution does not go as planned.

The film skips ahead: after the kidnapping debacle, Fergus has fled to London, taking a new name and trying to obliterate his former life, most particularly any connection to the IRA. But, like all of us, he carries his past around within him; he can't escape his memories and guilt about his involvement. Inevitably, he seeks out Dil (Jaye Davidson), Jody's sexy ex-girlfriend, whose picture Jody had proudly shown him. In the film's unfolding, it's as inevitable as the rising of the moon that more will grow between the two than Fergus (consciously, at least) is counting on.

It's a nice piece of symmetry, a weird, politically tinged version of the partner-switching in a bedroom farce. At the beginning, Jude came on to Jody under false pretenses; now Fergus (hiding under the alias Jimmy) makes contact with Dil. But, just as both Jude and Jody ended up being something different underneath than they at first seemed, so will Dil. It's also appropriate that, as soon as Fergus and Dil get involved, the IRA almost supernaturally pops up again, like a manifestation of the hero's guilty conscience.

For all its virtues, which include yet another terrific performance from Whitaker, the first third is the least interesting part of the movie. In many ways, it's a setup, just like the kidnapping—seducing us into one sort of story, before knocking us down, hog-tying us, and dragging us into a different drama altogether. Nonetheless, it's full of tiny, unnoticeable hints of what's to come. While a first viewing is most pleasurable if you don't know what plot twists are in store, *The Crying Game* is even more rewarding the second time around, when foreknowledge enables you to pick up all the little thematic strands and patterns that Jordan has deftly woven through the entire tale.

All the identity-shifting and transferred guilt invokes memories of Hitchcock; but, in its droll tone and structure, the film is like a more serious version of *Zardoz,* the 1974 sci-fi "epic" by Jordan's old boss, John Boorman (who produced Jordan's 1982 directorial debut *Angel,* aka *Danny Boy*). It's also a much, much better movie than *Zardoz,* whose pleasures came entirely from its surprises, leaving very little for a second viewing.

This ability to maintain interest through further screenings is the critical test of whether a trick story is more than just the sum of its tricks. With most Agatha Christie books, for instance, there is nothing left after you find out the ending. With a work like *Psycho,* however, multiple viewings continue to be enlightening, even if they never exactly recapture the shock of the first time through.

Part of *The Crying Game*'s aesthetic validity derives from a set of rich performances at its center. Besides Whitaker, there is a sharp turn by Jim Broadbent (who starred in Mike Leigh's *Life Is Sweet*) as Col the bartender, as well as a surprising and unforgettable debut from Davidson. More than anything, however, the film rests on the shoulders of Rea, who gives great dignity and humanity to perhaps the most passive film protagonist in recent memory.

Early press screenings of *The Crying Game* drew radically diverse reactions. But even its detractors walked out arguing, which is a positive sign of some sort. It seems to strike some sort of deep emotional chord in audiences, albeit in many cases a disturbing one. But, as Col jokingly asks, near the midpoint of the story, "Who knows the secrets of the human heart?"

Los Angeles Reader, November 27, 1992

THE DIRECTOR AS GENRE

Some directors work in genres; others bring such an absolute sense of their own vision, style, and preoccupations to bear, regardless of what type of film they're making, that they virtually supplant—even become their own—genre. Is *The Seventh Seal* "a medieval movie," *Persona* "a vampire film," *Fanny and Alexander* "a family saga"? Well, yes, but the main thing is they're all Ingmar Bergman pictures, and the rest is just sorting and filing.

This proposition is developed at length in the editor's consideration of *The Shining*—muddled horror movie (as reviewers generally found it to be) or icily majestic and malignant Stanley Kubrick film? In an essay written for this volume, Michael Wilmington pays tribute to the most versatile of all American directors, Howard Hawks, who may have filmed the definitive example of just about any genre you might name but also rarely failed to make it uniquely his own. No one more decisively exemplifies The Director as Genre than Alfred Hitchcock, whose *Rear Window* is reassessed through Michael Sragow's lens. All of Woody Allen's movies go into production with WOODY ALLEN FILM chalked on the slates; we trace how the meaning of that phrase has evolved and richened over two decades, from *Bananas* (David Denby) through *A Midsummer Night's Sex Comedy* (Bruce Williamson), *The Purple Rose of Cairo* (Michael Wilmington), and *Another Woman* (David Ansen) to *Crimes and Misdemeanors* (Richard Schickel). John

Huston's directorial career began at a high gallop in 1941, variously raced and stumbled through some thirty movies into the 1970s, and hit a quietly amazing winning streak during the last decade and a half of his life; Michael Sragow honors the 1985 *Prizzi's Honor* as one of his finest. Michael Wilmington charts Francis Coppola's tortuous road to *The Godfather Part III* and finds the film—warts and all—movingly autobiographical. Robert Altman, the great American director of the seventies all but written off by Hollywood in the eighties, scored a triumphantly cheeky comeback with *The Player* in 1992; Stephen Schiff lets us in on the fun. Lastly, Richard Corliss's X ray of Spike Lee's *Malcolm X* discloses a latent image: The Director as Wannabe.

STANLEY KUBRICK: THE SHINING

Richard T. Jameson

Camera comes in low over an immense Western lake, its destination apparently a small island at center that seems to consist of nothing but treetops. Draw nearer, then sweep over and pass the island, skewing slightly now in search of a central focus at the juncture of lake surface and the surrounding escarpment, glowing in J. M. W. Turner sunlight. Cut to God's-eye view of a yellow Volkswagen far below, winding up a mountain road through an infinite stand of tall pines and long, early-morning shadows; climbing for the top of the frame and gaining no ground. Subsequent cuts, angling us down nearer the horizontal trajectory of the car as it moves along the face of the mountainside. Thrilling near-lineup of camera vector and roadway, then the shot sheers off on a course all its own and a valley drops away beneath us. More cuts, more views, miles of terrain—bleak magnificence. Aerial approach to a snow-covered mountain crest and, below it, a vast resort hotel, The Overlook. Screen goes black.

Did Stanley Kubrick really say that *The Shining,* his film of Stephen King's novel, would be the scariest horror movie of all time? He shouldn't have. On one very important level, the remark may be true. But that isn't the first level people are going to consider (even though it's right there in front of us on the movie screen). What people hear when somebody drops a catchphrase like "the scariest horror movie of all time" is: you joined the summer crowds flocking to *The Amityville Horror,* you writhed and jumped through *Alien,* you watched half of *Halloween* from behind your fingers, but you ain't seen nothing yet! And a response: OK, zap me, make me flinch, gross me out. And they find that, mostly, Kubrick's long, underpopulated, deliberately paced telling of an unremarkable story with a "Twilight Zone" twist at the end doesn't do it for them—although it may do a lot of *other* things to them while they're waiting.

So Kubrick, who is celebrated for controlling the publicity for his films as closely as the various aspects of their creation, is largely to blame for the initial, strongly negative feedback to his movie. Maybe he didn't know, when *The Shining* started its way to the screen several years back, that the horror genre would be in full cry, the most marketable field in filmmaking, by the time his movie was ready for delivery. But he could have seen that, say, a year ago. And still he pressed on with the horror sales hook, counting on it— along with his own eminence—to fill theaters and to pay off the $18 million cost of the most expensive Underground movie ever made.

The action of the film can be synopsized in terms that seem to fulfill the horror movie recipe. Jack Torrance (Jack Nicholson)— sometime schoolteacher, shakily ex-alcoholic, and would-be writer—signs on as caretaker of this resort hotel in the Colorado Rockies, deserted and cut off from human contact five months of the year. Sharing the vigil will be his quiet-spoken, rather simple wife Wendy (Shelley Duvall) and their just-school-age son Danny (Danny Lloyd).

Danny secretly possesses the gift of "shining"—the ability to pick up psychic vibrations from past, present, and future, long distance or closer up. Before he ever gets to The Overlook, he is receiving messages from "Tony," the make-believe playmate who is Danny's way of accounting to himself for his special powers. The Overlook has framed its share of bad scenes since its construction in 1907, and more of the same—indeed, some of the same—seem to be in store for the Torrance family.

Jack has no acknowledged powers of shining, but he appears to be in tune with the hotel in his own way. Supposedly, he plans to take advantage of his undemanding work schedule as caretaker to get into "a big writing project" he has outlined, and periodically we see or hear him typing away. But we also begin to get ample indication that he will follow in the footsteps of the previous caretaker, Grady, a steady-seeming fellow who chopped up his wife and daughters one winter's day and then blew his brains out.

This likelihood is apparent from the first. Among the prime sources of irritation to horror-zap buffs is that Kubrick (writing with novelist Diane Johnson) has thrown out most of Stephen King's ectoplasmic and otherwise preternatural inventions—most of the more outré ghosts, the demonic elevator, the deadly drainpipe, the sinister hedge animals (an insoluble special-effects problem?)—to concentrate on the three principal characters and The Overlook as a collection of abstract spaces. He has also—and not entirely for reasons of cinematic streamlining—dispensed with virtually all of Jack Torrance's troubled history, so that his "motivations" and the degree of his complicity with whatever forces inhabit the hotel become much more elusive. Neither is Torrance permitted a very traceable descent into madness—he simply arrives there. Moreover, Kubrick has decentralized Danny as psychic focus of the action and target of acquisition (because of his gift of shining) for the hotel's master demons, encouraged Jack Nicholson in the most outrageous displays of drooling mania, and directed Shelley Duvall so grotesquely that Wendy Torrance becomes nearly as much a case for treatment as her husband. He has, in short, deprived the audience of any real opportunity for identifying with his characters in their hour (rather, 146 minutes) of menace, thereby violating conventional theory on how to bring off a jolly good scareshow.

Now it can be told: *The Shining* is a horror movie only in the sense that all Kubrick's mature work has been horror movies—films that constitute a Swiftian vision of inscrutable cosmic order, and of "the most pernicious race of little vermin that nature ever suffered to crawl upon the surface of the earth." The Stephen King origins and haunted-house conventions notwithstanding, the director is so little interested in the genre for its own sake that he hasn't even systematically subverted it so much as displaced it with a genre all his own. And why should this come as a surprise? Who bothers to characterize *Dr. Strangelove* as "an antiwar film," or sees merit in rating *2001: A Space Odyssey* as "an outer-space pic," or finds particular utility in considering *Barry Lyndon* as "a costume picture"? *The Shining* is "A Stanley Kubrick Film," and as such it makes impeccable—if also horrific—sense.

It seems poetically apt that, at the time Stanley Kubrick was describing arabesques round space stations and star corridors and the history of human consciousness in *Space Odyssey*, Michael Snow was making *Wavelength*, "the *Birth of a Nation* in Underground films" (Manny Farber's phrase). A forty-five-minute film "about" a loft, it consists of a single continuous zoom across eighty feet of horizontal space, beginning with a full view of the room and ending on a closeup of a photograph on the opposite wall. Actually, a dissolve is necessary to get to a second, very brief shot of the photo, which, when the shot/film began, we didn't even recognize as a photo: a wave about to break on the shore. Formal pun: optically move down the length of a room to look at a picture of a wave (the dissolve enabling specific perception and "understanding" after the comprehensive inventory of the whole space)—and the name of this moving picture is *Wavelength*.

I've no doubt that Kubrick has seen *Wavelength*, and not just because his new film ends with a shot that moves down a corridor and into a photograph, after which we dissolve for still closer scrutiny of the photo's elements. After all, he appropriated the visionary techniques of Jordan Belson, another Underground filmmaker, for *2001*. And maybe the avoidance of orthodox motivational analysis in his treatment of characters has its analogue in Snow's cheeky rebuke to our susceptibility to melodrama in *Wavelength*, when a wounded man staggers into the empty loft, collapses on the floor, and is summarily lost sight of—and left unaccounted for—as the zoom penetrates deeper into the room-space, leaving him outside the frame of visibility.

To be sure, Kubrick is a track man rather than a zoom man. Indeed, his tracking—in this film, freed of all physical restraints thanks to the development of the Steadicam—has long since become notorious, if not infamous, among critic types: an obscurely embarrassing fetish. ("Of *course* there's a lot of tracking—he's Kubrick! So what else is new?") Nevertheless, the tracking in *The Shining* is consecrated to a good deal more than satisfying the director's lust for technology or providing a grand tour of a Napoleonically lavish set. It personifies space, analyzes potentiality in spatial terms, maps the conditions of expectations within a neo-Gothic environment that is finite, however imposing its scale. And if this sounds like an arid exercise to pass off as a popular entertainment, consider that Kubrick twice provides the formal nudge of Roadrunner cartoons heard playing on a TV offscreen somewhere.

Tell a casual filmgoer that he's caught between comic and emotional hysteria because Wile E. Coyote's multifariously misfired stratagems describe a systematic reinterpretation of spatial and temporal possibility, the trading-off of kinetic and potential energy, and he'll think you're pulling his chain; but that's still why he's laughing.

The Steadicam sits low, mere inches off the floor behind Danny Torrance as he rides his tricycle round and round the ground floor of the hotel early in the film. We follow him for a complete circuit, incidentally getting our bearings on what's where in relation to what else (kitchen, office, lobby entrance, the Colorado Lounge where Jack does his writing). Kubrick gets away with this establishing tracking shot because even the most antifetishistic observer must find the technical achievement exhilarating, and also because the action is punctuated with one of those vivid, lushly particular moment-of-cinematic-discovery effects that has virtually an atavistic appeal: the clump-*whoosh,* clump-*whoosh* sound as the child trikes, with blithe relentlessness, across the polished floor and deep-pile carpet.

Yet even as we get off on this wonderful movement, we look for it to disclose more. Will the kid round a corner and run smack into a ghost? Every turn, every new avenue of perception, is approached with anticipation; and nothing happens. Anticipation, anticlimax, anticipation. It has a lot to do with the quality of the Torrances' lives.

For Jack Torrance's life has nowhere to go. The wrinkle in Kubrick's haunted-house concept is not that The Overlook Hotel, with its layer on layer of sordid, largely silly (in Kubrick's selection from King) atrocity, taints Jack—it is the setting he was born to occupy, the snow-walled zone in which he can achieve an apotheosis he is clearly unequipped to achieve in any other way. To be a writer, for instance, is not within Jack's grasp. It is sufficient self-justification that his former wage-earning job of schoolteaching got in the way of his writing; or that his wife Wendy so little comprehends the reality of writing (she thinks he just needs to get into the habit of doing it every day) that he can stay points ahead simply by being more sophisticated on the subject than she. The Overlook's spaces mirror Jack's bankruptcy. The sterility of its vastness, the spaces that proliferate yet really connect with each other in a continuum that encloses rather than releases, frustrates rather than liberates—all this becomes an extension of his own barrenness of mind and spirit.

Those spaces draw Jack. Kubrick sees to it that they draw us as well. It's not merely a matter of corridors obsessively tracked. Virtually every shot in the film (whether the setting be The Overlook or not) is built around a central hole, a vacancy, a tear in the membrane of reality: a door that would lead us down another hallway, a panel of bright color that somehow seems more permeable than the surrounding dark tones, an infinite white glow behind a central closeup face, a mirror, a TV screen . . . a photograph. From the moment we lose the consoling sense of focus and destination supplied by that island picturesquely centered in the lake, we are careening through space.

There's a moment quite early in the Torrances' residency when Wendy and Danny go to explore the Overlook Maze, a carefully sculpted hedge as old, and very nearly as large, as the hotel itself. Kubrick cuts from them to Jack, drifting in an eerie lope through the hotel interior. He stops at a table bearing a scale model of the Maze outside. A low-angle shot of Jack registering bemused interest is followed by a downward gaze, absolutely perpendicular, at the Maze. This frame is pure geometry until we notice two figures (cartoonlike or real?) moving, and casting individual shadows, in the central aisle. The overhead view has been descending steadily (camera movement? zoom?) since the cut to it, and faintly, like mouse squeaks, we begin to pick up Wendy-and-Danny voices.

What is the scale here? Are we looking at the table model or the actual Maze? If the actual Maze, those figures are the real Wendy and Danny foreshortened from a great height, as in the film's opening aerial views; perhaps Kubrick has just reverted to his fond, God's-eye view that turns the world into a chessboard. If the scale model, then those figures are grotesque projections of Wendy and Danny—projected in Jack's imagination, or somehow duplicated in a demonic, child's-toy accessory of the hotel. Or is the actual Maze, the real Wendy and Danny diminished by distance, being seen by Jack in sympathetic phase with the hovering spirit of the "Overlook" itself? We can't be sure. Any or all of the above might be true (and the descending view never gets far enough to plug us back into life-sized visual relation to mother and son; that is achieved only by a cut back to them seen from normal eye level). We aren't sure where we stand in this game. And it won't be the last time.

In a moment of intense distraction sometime later, Jack lurches into the hotel bar, the Gold Room, and climbs onto a stool. The place is empty, not only of people (of course . . .) but also of booze, which the management always removes during the off-season to cut insurance costs. Still, it's the sort of space in which Jack used to find solace. And now, having awakened from a nightmare of Grady-like atrocity, and having been accused of hurting his son as he (inadvertently?) did once before, he sags with self-pity and sighs, "God, I'd give anything for a drink! Give my god-damned soul for just a glass of beer!"

Up to this point we have been observing Jack from a diagonal, behind the bar but some distance down its length. Now we cut to a position directly opposite him. He drags his hands down over his face and then peers straight at us. His face is brightly—too brightly —flooded by the warm glow of a lighting strip built right into the bar; and now the fluorescence is increased by a sudden, hail-fellow-well-met grin. "Why *hello*, Lloyd!" And Jack slides into a well-rehearsed litany of world-weary wisdom, a soliloquy pretending to be a monologue, delivered to a composite image of all the bartenders in his past. *We* have been cast as "Lloyd." The role is bizarre, but not intolerable. Then Kubrick reverse-cuts and there, where we figuratively stood, *is* Lloyd (Joe Turkel).

Jack goes on talking; he isn't the least surprised that Lloyd is visible, for real, and pouring him a bourbon, as a matter of lovely fact. We are now the ones distracted. Here at last is an authentic Overlook ghost, vouchsafed to us ever so naturalistically (if eerily gilded by the lambency of the Gold Room) without benefit of any "shining" from Danny. Not only that: we have no way of knowing (and never will know) whether this is the first time in a month or more of occupancy at the hotel that Jack has seen Lloyd. Nor is there any consolation in the fact that, when Wendy arrives on the scene a moment later, neither Lloyd nor his bourbon is in evidence.

Kubrick makes limited, straightforward use of the standard reality-illusion device of mirrors in *The Shining*. But as narrative details, the bits and pieces of many possible Overlook stories, accumulate, and as the editorial design of the film becomes increasingly oblique and suggestive, more and more one feels trapped in an infinity of facing mirrors. Identity and reference are deliberately confused: Wendy comes to tell Jack, "There's a crazy woman in the hotel," and he giddily responds, "Are you out of your fucking mind?!" It is only the first tremor in an extraordinary concatenation that escalates toward the final crisis.

The brutalization of Danny (of which Jack had been accused) took place in the mysterious Room 237, whose vibrations had tempted the boy several times previously. We watched through his eyes as he passed through the door, but were spirited away by Kubrick's cutting to Wendy, who in turn led us to Jack in the throes of "the worst nightmare I've ever had," the gory murder of his family. Hence, though technically innocent, Jack has been formally implicated in whatever transpired in 237.

As Jack answers Wendy's summons to investigate the room, we suddenly find ourselves locked in on the compartmentalized logo of a television news program. A slow zoom-out, and we are in the Miami home of Dick Hallorann (Scatman Crothers), The Overlook's black cook, who also "shines," and who had earlier established rapport with Danny in one of the few sequences free (up to a crucial point) of the central-vacancy principle. Reverse-cut and zoom-in on Hallorann as he suddenly registers horror.

Cut to a closeup of Danny Torrance, shivering in a trance, a froth of spittle on his lips (as Jack had visibly drooled when coming out of his nightmare). Then the camera begins describing a subjective penetration of Room 237—Danny shining to Dick about his experience? Dick remembering an experience of his own in 237 (his fear of the room having been planted earlier)? Not until we see an adult Caucasian hand reaching out to push open the bathroom door can we be sure exactly what is happening.

Beyond the bathtub curtain, a hazy figure moves, then draws the curtain aside. A nude woman, young, lovely, but mannequinlike, looks across the room at the camera for a moment—and then we reverse-cut to Jack Torrance in the doorway. The young woman rises, steps from the bath, pauses. Cut again to Jack, who slowly begins to leer in anticipation and starts toward her. They embrace, kiss—and over her shoulder Jack beholds the reflection of a thick, ancient, partially decomposed hag in his arms. He backs away; the hag advances, cackling, arms extended. Intercut with this are images of the same old woman seen from above, lying dead in the tub, then beginning to stir to life. It is a perspective Jack never had, but presumably either Danny or Dick Hallorann did; a reality from the past (Danny's, Dick's, or one still more distant) is juxtaposed against the immediate reality of Jack's experiences in 237 at that moment. Who and which is where and when? And does it matter?

Jack Torrance returns from the encounter denying that there was anything to see in 237. Moreover, he seeks to placate Wendy with the resonant cliché, "I'm sure [Danny]'ll be himself again in the morning." (But he won't: he'll be "Tony.") Wendy isn't buying; she insists they get Danny out of the hotel. Threatened for the first time with separation from The Overlook, Jack explodes: "You've been fucking up my whole life! But you won't fuck this up!"

Storming off, Jack finds the hotel corridors strewn with balloons and confetti, and the sound of a twenties dance band floating on the air. A fluid lateral track brings him from the hallway into the Gold Room once more. The nightclub is full of subdued revelers in period dress. Jack passes among them, affecting unconcern about his caretaker togs, and adjusting his stride to approximate an elegant dance stroll. Good old Lloyd is on duty, there's bourbon for Jack's glass, and "the management" has given instructions that "Your money is no good here, Mr. Torrance." Jack, though unremarked by the assembly as he has surely been unremarked through life, will momentarily be assured: "You're the only one that matters."

But *The Shining* is something much more complex than an exercise in solipsism. Lloyd's respectful salute upon both of Jack's visits —"What will it be, Mr. Torrance?"—is tinged with quiet irony. And Jack, far from being able to join the party, is instead shunted off from it: a collision with the waiter, a spilled drink, and his and the camera's course is deflected into . . . another powder room.

As he has so often played hyperkinetic sequences off against grindingly slow ones, here Kubrick condemns Jack to a long, maddeningly static and formalized talk scene—off the back hall of life, as it were, like the seedy servants' quarters he is given to occupy in this luxury hotel—while the music and the crowd murmur on the other side of the red, red wall. It is a conversation that self-destructs in its logic: the waiter, Jack's interlocutor, is none other than Mr. Grady (Philip Stone), the former caretaker, who in short order assures Jack: 1) that he has never seen him before, 2) that he himself has no memory of ever having been the caretaker, 3) that Jack has *always* been the caretaker—"I should know, sir, I have always been here," and 4) that he indeed had to "correct" his family when they interfered with his caretaking!

Roles shift in other ways: Grady is the unctuous servant deferring to his superior at the same time he becomes the steely master of the scene and issues The Overlook's definitive warning that Jack is now expected to "correct" his own family. He even introduces Jack to the quaint snobbery of his anachronistic, English-accented cultural frame: Danny has tried to bring "an outside party, a *nigger,* a nigger *cook*" into the action; and Jack repeats, "A *'nigger'?*" (a superb reading by Nicholson) in a tone that suggests he is not used to considering negritude an offense, is on the verge of disbelieving laughter, and yet is also fascinated by the new ripple of self-congratulating possibility here. Whose sensibility is in charge? What role does Jack play in The Overlook narrative that would have Grady as its center? Indeed, how many of those other guests out in the Gold Room are "the only ones that matter" in *their* scenarios—cut off from Jack and from us the way the promising panoply of possibilities in a dream are lost when we detour into a peripheral line of development that never carries us back to the main scene?

Surely this distraction of the self is Hell, not the seamy, vicious gestures by which the lost soul expresses its violence. Jack Torrance is presented with an oneiric environment in which only he matters —and then he doesn't matter at all. This is the final vacancy. This is the bankrupt script. This is the horror that we feel when Wendy Torrance, come to look for her husband in his writing den, at last manages to see The Overlook manuscript, the outpourings of his creativity: the endless reiteration, in myriad configurations, of the same formulaic line, the same lyric bad joke—"All work and no play makes Jack a dull boy." Jack the dull boy becomes Jack the bright boy when, having done murder at last, he rises into a previously neutral frame: this time the vacancy is fulfilled in his wide, white, shining face.

Has there ever been a more perverse feature film than *The Shining* in general release? No one but Kubrick could have, would have, made it. Certainly no one but Kubrick could come as close to getting away with it. And it is impossible to suggest another contemporary star besides Jack Nicholson who could have served to hold its ferocious strategies together. Both director and star have been criticized for showcasing a mugging, transparently implausible geek performance. Transparent is the operative word. The devastating subtlety of Nicholson's Torrance lies in its obviousness. We watch Jack Nicholson—and we *will* watch Jack Nicholson, note every raised eyebrow, every mongrel twitch of limb—from the fatuous, blatantly phony man-of-the-worldliness and patronizing deference in the opening interview scene (with Barry Nelson—a Kubrick casting coup—as The Overlook manager), through the smarmy tolerance of Wendy's naïveté, to the raging, aggressively self-defensive rationalizations of his contractual eminence in The

Overlook establishment. Scarcely a reviewer has failed to sneer that Nicholson has regressed to playing Roger Corman mad scenes—but that's *it,* that's what works: Nicholson the Corman flake become Nicholson the easy-riding superstar, Bad-Ass Buddusky, J. J. Gittes, R. P. McMurphy, super-hip, so sardonically self-aware that he cuts through the garden variety of cynical Hollywood corruption like a laser, and lays back bored.

Jack Nicholson plays Jack Nicholson playing Jack Torrance playing Jack Torrance as King of the Mountain. Everything Jack Torrance says in the extremity of his derangement is pixilated in the viciousness of its banality ("Heeeeeeere's *Johnny!*"); his loathsome bum jokes are gauntlets flung in the face of his significant others, his family, his audience—and they are loathsome most of all because they rebound on him, because he tells them badly, as he plays the furtive madman badly. But not Jack Nicholson. Nicholson plays the madman badly *brilliantly.*

And Kubrick, the king of his own cinematic mountain, the lone, hush-hush contriver of Skinner boxes for the contemplation of his fellow creatures, or his idea of them? Kubrick flings the stingingest gauntlet of them all. He makes a horror movie that isn't a horror movie, that the audience has to get into and finish for him.

The Maze: shivers of goose-pimply expectation from the audience. But the Maze is quite benign. Indeed, Danny Torrance knows it like his own hand. Danny the Kubrick Child gets free of bathrooms, slides magically down a personal snowhill, leads the Daddy Monster a merry chase through that Maze. And the Maze, hole after hole opening before us as the Steadicam rushes down tunnel after tunnel, is not a trap but an escape hatch. Child's play: Danny backs up in his own footsteps in the snow, nobody else's; but Stanley Kubrick will not permit the viewer to share in the reversing of relentless tracks.

Danny and Wendy will escape, but we stay behind with the monster of banality. We track into the frozen moment of time in a film where time, finally, is as abstract and terrible as space. Once a Kubrick monster threw a bone into the air and became man; now the man regresses to monster, grunting, incapable finally of even pronouncing its own bad jokes. Illumination is poisonous: we cannot learn: "we have always been here." The hole—the photograph that the last track penetrates—is the screen. The face grinning imbecilically out at us is our own. Shining.

Film Comment, July–August 1980

HOWARD HAWKS, GENRE-KILLER

■■■

Michael Wilmington

People who affect us the most, often embody wild contradictions; we can never quite catch them. Howard Hawks, the favorite film-maker of my young manhood (18–35 or so), the Hollywood genre moviemaker par excellence, described himself as a man who talked slowly but could make things go fast.

Hawks's talk indeed was laconic, cool, very dry, always right on the nose. And the "things" he could refine to their maximum speed—racing cars, boats, planes, actors and actresses, and, most particularly, movies—were all in some way vehicles for human travel: tools for fun, which could kill or wound if they got out of control.

"The Master of Hollywood genres": it's almost the first thing any biographer or memorialist says about Hawks. It's his signature card, like Hitchcock's suspense, Ford's Westerns, Minnelli's musi-cals, Antonioni's ennui, Bergman's angst, Bresson's Catholicism, or Welles's blasted greatness. After that, we invariably get an amazing laundry list of titles, recalling Hawks's formidable all-around expertise: Westerns (*Red River, The Big Sky, Rio Bravo, El Dorado*), romantic comedies (*Bringing Up Baby, Ball of Fire, I Was a Male War Bride, Monkey Business*), gangster movies (the original *Scarface*), flying pictures (*Ceiling Zero, Only Angels Have Wings*), musicals (*Gentlemen Prefer Blondes*), biographies (*Sergeant York*), war movies (*The Dawn Patrol*—again, the original—and *Air Force*), science fiction (the Christian Nyby–directed, Hawks-produced *The Thing*), and film noir (*The Big Sleep*).

Do we need further specialization? There are newspaper comedy (*His Girl Friday*), WW II intrigue-romance (*To Have and Have Not*), backstage theater farce (*Twentieth Century*), historical epics (*Land of the Pharaohs,* most of *Viva Villa!*), hunting adventures (*Hatari!*), fish-ing films (*Tiger Shark, Man's Favorite Sport?*), prison pictures (*The Criminal Code*), movies about children ("The Ransom of Red Chief" in *O. Henry's Full House*), "buddy" movies (*A Girl in Every Port*), antiwar films (the 1936 *Road to Glory*), sports or racing movies (*The Crowd Roars, Red Line 7000*), and even—most unHawksian—family domestic dramas (the underrated *Come and*

At a South American airfield closed in by sea, fog, and mountains, a band of strong-willed individuals united by a love of professionalism and danger plays improvisational games with life and death. *Only Angels Have Wings* is the definitive Howard Hawks picture. Graced with superlative flying sequences, but dominated by crackling dialogue scenes in which characters trade loving insults, the film boasts a glorious cast, of which only a fraction is visible here: Thomas Mitchell, Jean Arthur, Allyn Joslyn, Cary Grant, and Victor Kilian. (© 1993. Photo courtesy of Columbia Pictures, Inc. All Rights Reserved. Museum of Modern Art Film Stills Archive.)

Get It, which was completed by William Wyler; tellingly, though Wyler was a real master in this genre, Hawks's scenes are better, livelier).

One can even prowl through the lower reaches of Hawks's credits and nose out a murder mystery (*Trent's Last Case*), a Ruritanian romance (*Paid to Love*), an Arabian soap opera (*Fazil*), and a Roaring Twenties college comedy (*The Cradle Snatchers*). But for Paramount's insistence—against the desires of friends Gary Cooper and Ernest Hemingway—that Sam Wood and not Hawks direct *For Whom the Bell Tolls* (one of the major director-casting blunders of the forties), he would have, in one stroke, knocked off the classic literary adaptation and left-wing problem picture genres as well.

And, I'll bet, brilliantly. (Hawks was ready and willing to make *Bell*; Hemingway's *The Sun Also Rises,* whose movie rights he owned for more than a decade, apparently stumped him.)

Examine that list further and you find, over and over, movies that combine or cross-fertilize genres: Western and comedy (*Rio Bravo, El Dorado*); thriller, romance, and comedy (*The Big Sleep*); farce and romance (*Bringing Up Baby*); science fiction and horror (*The Thing*); musical, gangster, and romantic comedy (*Ball of Fire*); romantic comedy and aviation thriller (*Only Angels Have Wings*); romantic comedy and science fiction (*Monkey Business*) . . . and movies that have unlikely genre sources: *To Have and Have Not* is not just a semi-adaptation of the Hemingway novel, but an answer to *Casablanca* (a project Hawks rejected). The chamber Western *Rio Bravo* is an answer to two "message" suspense Westerns, *High Noon* and *The 3:10 to Yuma,* but it's also in the minimalist-backdrop, character-humor-and-dialogue style of the late-fifties Warner Bros. TV Westerns ("Maverick" and the rest).

No matter what the type, humor keeps popping in. Farce snuggles up to tragedy, suspense and romance embrace, and everywhere we are constantly aware of movie forms underneath. But also, in every case, we see people who act as if they weren't enclosed at all, as if they had perfectly free will and could move where they wanted—even comment on the movie they're in, as does Cary Grant ("He looks like that actor, you know, Ralph Bellamy") in *His Girl Friday.* The use of genre is a trap: the machine which the maker (Hawks) understands fully—and within which the players seem to have (illusory?) freedom.

That dichotomy of freedom and entrapment is the key to Hawks's style and his life-view, even more than the idea of the all-male group (which, after all, almost every action director shares). Mastery and ease of movement is what his heroes attain after repeating the same tasks over and over. And competence, as François Truffaut remarked, is the wellspring of Hawks's personality, the real subject of his films. They're about people who do things well—handled by a director who did nearly everything well, whose major flaw may have been his impatience with (fear of?) failure and people who fail.

That fear may be part of what stings all these films to life. No matter when they were shot or what period they re-create, Hawks's movies always unfailingly suggest the here and now. Of all the great Hollywood genre directors—and perhaps of all great directors, period—his is the most complete and intense sense of the present tense. (That's why his strongest admirers include the French "New Wave" directors, and revolutionary improvisers like Robert Altman.)

Spontaneity and "improvisatory" dialogue and acting mark his work. But so does an eerie feeling that the movie is happening to you as you watch it, that Hawks's angle of vision and your own are identical, that the characters—even minor ones, like the sarcastic delivery boy who speaks two lines to Cary Grant in *Bringing Up Baby* and disappears—are all alive and fully functioning humans. Everything contributes to this: the consistent eye-level (or, to be precise, slightly lower than eye level) camera shots, the understated, non-"theatrical" acting, the realistic rendering of the mechanics of action, work, and sport.

And yet Hawks's films are not "real" in the sense that Rossellini's or De Sica's—or Ken Loach's and Gianni Amelio's—are. The genre gives them a sense of déjà vu. They're all stories we've heard before, in other gangster movies, Westerns, comedies, etc.—but not quite this way.

Hawks bends genres, collides genre forms and naturalistic behavior in the same way he sets up all those other dichotomies nosed out by critics, semiologists, and assorted structure-hunters: male-female, comedy-tragedy, child-adult, human-animal, war-pacifism, work-play. Because we've heard the story before, we relax. Then something—a vivid gesture, a piece of offbeat dialogue, a curious interchange—jars us, stimulates us. "I just went *gay* all of a sudden," shrieks *Bringing Up Baby*'s frazzled Cary Grant, haplessly dressed in Katie Hepburn's aunt's frilly bathrobe and trying to explain himself; "Was you ever bit by a dead bee?" rummy Walter Brennan queries repeatedly in *To Have and Have Not;* and when Claude Akins in *Rio Bravo,* afraid for his life in Duke Wayne's jail, says of guard Brennan "He's crazy," Brennan screams joyously, "He's right!"

"Make five or six good scenes," was Hawks's oft-repeated strategy, "and then don't annoy the audience the rest of the time." That constant sense of the audience, that game with the audience, is part of what makes Hawks's movies so ideal for film buffs, the kind who obsessively see all of a director's (or writer's, or actor's) movies, and who often see movies more than once. Each one of his movies improves when you think of them all. And with very few exceptions, each one improves or holds its magic every time you see it. His pictures are a world unto themselves: alive.

We're often reminded that Hawks was a flyer and an engineer

who built racing cars, planes, and *Hatari!*'s bounceless camera trucks, just as we're reminded of his athletic skills (he was a U.S. junior tennis champion) and his life-style of Beverly Hills derring-do and suave machismo. But just as important a key to Hawks the creator is his "voracious reading" and love of writing and writers. William Faulkner and Ernest Hemingway, of course, were his friends—and Faulkner one of his most frequent screenwriters (five films credited, and parts of others)—but his taste was broad ranging and populist. He plucked young science-fantasy writer Leigh Brackett out of the pages of *Thrilling Wonder* and *Planet Stories* and put her to work on *The Big Sleep* with Faulkner and Jules Furthman. And the smartest, funniest scribes in Hollywood were usually the ones he wanted: Furthman, Ben Hecht and Charles MacArthur, Dudley Nichols, John Huston, Charles Lederer, Harry Kurnitz, Charles Brackett, and Billy Wilder (who lingered on *Ball of Fire* to observe Hawks closely and made his American directing debut shortly afterward). "I'm such a coward," Hawks told Joseph McBride, "that unless I get a great writer I don't want to make a picture."

Hawks, who claimed that Hemingway, Faulkner, Raymond Chandler, and Dashiell Hammett were his favorite authors (on another occasion he cited Willa Cather), clearly regarded good writing as de rigueur. But of all Hollywood Golden Age moviemakers he was one of the most cavalier once he had a script. He would change scenarios liberally (especially in his later years), scribbling new lines on his famous yellow legal pads throughout the filming. This freeness rhymes with his approach to genre: Get a solidly established genre and subvert it. Get a good script and switch the lines. Change sex roles (*Gentlemen Prefer Blondes, Bringing Up Baby*). Change sexes (*His Girl Friday*). Change ages (*Monkey Business*). Collide the structure with the humanity inside; let life explode or reshape the plan.

Many longtime Golden Age Hollywood filmmakers hopped around among different genres as much as Hawks—William Wellman, Henry Hathaway, and George Marshall, for example—before settling down with one or two. But none were as universally skillful. Hawks's incessant genre-hopping, like the lady-killer's bed-hopping, was never a matter of job assignment—since he initiated or controlled most of his films from the thirties on—but always from design, personal choice. He wanted to be a jack-of-all-movie-trades; what drove him on was probably a mixture of competitiveness and a scientific detachment about his métier. To McBride, he once described his youthful strategy for learning directing: For six months he went to a movie every night and stayed twice if he liked it. He soaked in all the strategies, and his choice of a model shows real taste and prescience: John Ford, years before *The Informer*. Hawks was movie critic as well as moviemaker—perhaps the best critic of all among his colleagues.

There is one solidly established genre absent from Hawks's canon: the female weepie (though *Come and Get It* is a weepie from the male angle, a soap opera without tears). Perhaps this is fitting for a notoriously and self-consciously masculine director, who—according to his bitter ex-wife Lady "Slim" Keith—never cried, rarely displayed emotion, and had eyes, described by Roz Russell as "like two blue cubes of ice." Hawks was aware of his seeming coldness. He once mentioned that his brother Kenneth, who died while filming a 1929 flying sequence, would have been a "warmer" director than he—"more like Frank Borzage"—and perhaps, by saying this, he admitted a lack, a secret frustration.

But you can't win 'em all—and Hawks, as his beautiful, snobbish, and witty ex-wife reminds us, was a lady-killer. (At the age of 81, when he was taken home from the hospital to die, he made a date with two nurses.) It was, according to Slim, his incessant philandering, compulsive gambling, and "coldness" that broke up their marriage. And though Slim tends to exaggerate Howard's flaws to make him look bad, those two traits—lady-killing and gambling—are suggestive. Along with his attraction to high-risk sports, they tend to turn much of life into a dangerous game, a match with love or death.

Hawks was described by his second cousin Carole Lombard as a "sneaky" fellow who could get into a woman's pants before she knew it—and, in a way, that encapsulates his narrative strategy as well. He sneaks up on you, slides into your life and affections, conquers his audience with a mixture of the "same old line" (subjected to endlessly fascinating new twists), and then, restless, strikes out for something new. A new challenge, a new conquest, a new genre.

His goal is almost always the same: to have "fun," and to make his audiences have it too. (And to have fun, like the compulsive Casanova, in many settings, with many partners.) When fun is absent, Hawks's view of life and the world becomes terribly bleak. He has fewer illusions than most. The cycle, as in *The Dawn Patrol, Scarface, Ceiling Zero,* can become one of endless tragedy, ferocious danger, inevitable death—a meaningless destiny against a featureless horizon, from which no religious solace or romantic sentimentality gives succor. "To live or to die? What drama is greater?" he once asked two French interviewers, and we see in his films both a preoccupation with rejuvenation and eternal youth and a near-obsession with death—or cheating it. Betting against the house.

Perhaps one reason for the nightmarish intensity of Hawks's gangster classic and personal favorite film, the 1932 *Scarface,* is the way death shapes it. The use of anachronistic-seeming visual distortions or oddball viewpoints and angles, which he usually eschews; the virtuosic tracking shots and machine-gun montages; the persistent, fatalistic repetition of the X motif in Tony Camonte's (Paul Muni) murders—this stylization is German Expressionism at a slow boogie beat, crime mixed with comedy. But it also suggests an extreme psychosis: the nightworld as a killer might see it, as a huge, shadow-thronged, deadly trap, X-ing out, closing in.

Scarface's opposite number is *Hatari!,* an African hunting picture made thirty years later and the most characteristically Hawksian movie of all: a show shot with an absolutely sunny, calm, crystalline lucidity and good humor, probably the best example ever of "transparent" moviemaking. Some critics dismiss *Hatari!* as a collection of spectacular hunting sequences yoked to clumsy, meandering formula romantic comedy. But those hunt scenes, of rhino, giraffe, and wildebeest (executed without doubles by John Wayne, Hardy Kruger, Red Buttons, and the other actors, playing members of a Tanganyika zoo-procurement team), are no less lively or seductive than the low-key, casually goofy scenes of camaraderie in the camp.

Hatari! probably has a model as well, John Ford's 1953 *Mogambo,* and if you compare the two you can instantly see the hallmark of Hawks. *Mogambo* is crafted, easygoing classicism, a movie-movie with obvious antecedents; *Hatari!* is something that, damn it, just seems to be happening—more modern and experimental, in 1962, than anyone recognized. That illusion of spontaneity—in which all the clumsiness, *longueur,* and tensions of life have their place—may be what alienated those *Hatari!*-haters who wanted more obvious artfulness in their art.

Hawks disliked the obvious. To him, a movie was a living organism that might change as it grew. One starts with a structure, a job; then the humans within the structure begin to alter it. The jazzplayer takes the melody, knowing it completely, embellishing at will. That change is central to Hawks's art. Sexuality, passion, emotion, love, sympathy (everything that Slim says she couldn't see) is the blast that opens up the routine, sweeps it away. Critics often set out to nominate which are Hawks's masterpieces—and the selections can be quite different. Some prefer the comedies to the action films, and vice versa. But it's a matter of temperament. Almost all the movies are good; Hawks has a disarming consistency. But since the movies are in different genres, different mixtures of genres, they sometimes go off at different angles, aimed at slightly different parts of the house.

It's claimed that Hawks's films present a childish, limited view of life basically geared toward men who don't want to grow up, who want to bond together and play games—sexual, among others—while ignoring life's ripening. (Who just went gay all of a sudden.) There's some truth in that, and it may well describe part of Hawks's own character. And yet, in the end, it's spectacularly irrelevant. Hawks's movies do not appeal exclusively to a select, elect clique, even though that's what they often portray. They appeal, literally, to almost everyone of a certain intelligence, taste, and looseness—even though they're among the most personally revealing, highly individual, even autobiographical movies ever made within the Old Hollywood studio system.

What I loved most about his work, I think, when I was nineteen, was the sense of self his movies gave me. Howard Hawks was a true cinematic paterfamilias, a role model—not for the machismo, but for the competence, the undemonstrative sympathy, the nonsadistic strength, the perfect balance, suave wit, and cool grace. In his movies one sees the world differently. Better. One sees it as an athlete, playing at the peak, might see the court or field. Fiercely, lucidly, bright, every detail in place, with a smack-in-your-face clarity and depth. A world where everything suddenly makes sense—except when, suddenly, it doesn't. The world from eye level, presented by a man who talks slowly and makes things fast.

Written for this book, March 1993

ALFRED HITCHCOCK: REAR WINDOW

Michael Sragow

Rear Window is more than one of Alfred Hitchcock's greatest comedies of terrors. Set in a Greenwich Village apartment and its adjoining courtyards, this urban variation on the backyard-murder story is a once-over-lightly satire of the quality of modern life and a once-over-thoroughly exploration of the allure of voyeurism. Always a Hitchcock personal favorite, *Rear Window* (like *Vertigo, The Trouble With Harry,* the remake of *The Man Who Knew Too Much,* and *Rope*) was owned outright by the director; and since he wanted these films' theatrical value to appreciate over the years, he made sure they would not get thrown into the dustbin of TV syndication. Only after his death, in 1980, did the Hitchcock estate negotiate for a rerelease. And the twenty-one-year hiatus after *Rear Window*'s last public screening prevented it from taking its proper place in film history—not merely as the predecessor to such search-and-destroy melodramas as John Carpenter's *Someone Is Watching Me!* but also as the inspiration for such inquiries into perceptual truth as Antonioni's *Blow-Up,* Coppola's *The Conversation,* and Brian DePalma's *Blow Out.* Still, the movie couldn't have returned at a better time. DePalma aside, the decade preceding *Rear Window*'s return has been a horrible one for suspense movies—too many potential thrillmasters have succumbed to cheap tricks. The notion of suspense not as shock but as a heightening of the essential narrative question "What's gonna happen next?" has gone right out the window. It comes back through *Rear Window:* the best thriller of 1954 becomes the best thriller in 1983.

Often condemned during its first release as a celebration of the peeping Tom, this movie is actually a rigorously structured morality play. It revolves around the apartment of L. B. Jeffries, nick-named Jeff (James Stewart), a photojournalist laid up in a wheelchair with injuries he received while shooting the Indianapolis 500. To get his mind off the pain, the summer heat, and his troubled romance with gorgeous fashion plate Lisa Fremont (Grace Kelly), he takes to looking out the window (eventually using his camera as a telescope) and immersing himself in the lives of his neighbors. The joke lies in how Jeff confronts the mélange of sights and sounds in his own Village backyard—from a hefty female sculptor chiseling a figure with a hole in place of its stomach (she calls it "Hunger") and an unemployed composer battling the piano keys to such sitcom types as the ravenous newlyweds or the childless couple pampering the family dog. Then there's the hubbub of the boulevard beyond, which he can glimpse through an alleyway. It's a typically congested, modern middle-class environment—and Hitchcock makes us understand how city dwellers grow to see their neighbors as just part of the world's clutter.

Jeff's approach to life is to siphon it all into his camera lens while carefully delimiting what he allows to touch his heart. He's even hesitating to marry the warm, sweet, and witty, altogether perfect Lisa because he's afraid that she wouldn't fit into his peripatetic journalistic life—and that, as a result, she'd try to shackle him. Lisa, for her part, filters life through her own standards of good taste; for all her seductiveness she may be a little too chic to shake any sense into her dream boy. The only major character who's got it together is Jeff's nurse Stella (Thelma Ritter), who thinks that any analytic approach to life, and especially to love, is a lot of hooey: in her day, she says, you saw each other, you got excited, you got married.

The amorous sparring goes on until Jeff is roused from sleep one night by a scream and a crash; after that, he begins to notice strange comings and goings in the apartment of a traveling costume-jewelry salesman, Lars Thorvald (Raymond Burr), and his invalid wife (Irene Winston). Jeff tries to interest the police through an old wartime buddy, Detective Tom Doyle (Wendell Corey), but he can't come up with enough evidence to warrant a search of the Thorvalds' apartment. And though Doyle is a voice of reason that urges respect for the neighbors' privacy, law alone will not make sense out of the urban chaos. So Jeff, Lisa, and Stella become an unlikely trio of sleuths, and their life-or-death adventures peel away Jeff's journalistic smugness and Lisa's haute couture (some of the movie's funniest moments are those in which Grace Kelly performs derring-do in glamorous Edith Head getups).

By the time of *Rear Window*, Hitchcock had already refined his use of subjective camera—putting the audience in the mind of the characters; in this film he pushes the technique to new heights. As our heroes gibe and quibble over the suspected murder (which we never see), we take refuge in the anonymity and safe distance of Jeff's flattening long lens—until the terrifying moment when Thorvald stares right back. It's an astonishing visual and psychological coup, like those instances in the "live" theater when the houselights are thrown up during the performance and the actors can stare at the theatergoers. In the movie's context, it shocks us into realizing that mass communications media—and photojournalists like Jeff—have created a surface realism that reduces people to manipulable images and blinds us to their capacity for an independent, even hostile, life.

In the course of the famous interviews François Truffaut conducted with Hitchcock (published by Simon and Schuster), the Master made a crucial distinction between the art of suspense and the trick of surprise:

> We are now having a very innocent little chat. Let us suppose that there is a bomb underneath the table between us. Nothing happens and then, all of a sudden, "Boom!" There is an explosion. The public is *surprised,* but prior to this surprise, it has been an absolutely ordinary scene. Now, let us take a *suspense* situation. The bomb is underneath the table and the public *knows* it, probably because they have seen the anarchist place it there. The public *is aware* that the bomb is going to explode at one o'clock and there is a clock in the decor. The public can see that it is a quarter to one. In these conditions the same innocuous conversation becomes fascinating because the public is participating in the scene. The audience is longing to warn the characters on the screen: "You shouldn't be talking about such trivial matters! There's a bomb beneath you and it's about to explode!"

Rear Window is probably Hitchcock's most involving audience-participation film: we're given Jeff's data as he gets them, and when in one instance he misses something, *we* pick up on it—one of Hitchcock's gifts to the attentive.

It's all like a gripping game of Clue. Rebuilding a Greenwich Village street on a Paramount soundstage was a technical feat, and Hitchcock used the parallel apartment windows for a split-screen effect, achieving multiple perspectives in the most offhand way. But we don't think of any of that when we watch the movie: instead, we perceive the apartment buildings as giant game boards, and the lit apartment windows as precious squares—we're made to think that by taking in as many split images as possible we can solve the mystery and win the game. The film is full of unemphatic but vital sequences, such as the long opening shot that establishes the geography of the courtyards, then moves into Jeff's window and, by what it picks out—a thermometer, his sweating face, his foot-to-hip cast, magazines, framed photographs, a smashed camera—establishes his character. Hitchcock challenges us to make our thoughts catch up with our simple perceptions: we study objective measures of information, like that thermometer; our eyes grow attuned to the different degrees of daylight. We find ourselves checking Jeff's watch—indeed, Hitchcock uses his own trademark cameo to reset a clock. The entire movie does nothing less than test the limits of empirical evidence.

Just as important is Hitchcock's canny use of movie stars. Few contemporary directors have the knack of playing off their stars' established personas. But Hitchcock knew how to exploit James Stewart's nice-guy image. Initially, when Jeff observes his neighbors, he seems to share in their common humanity; but when he gives in to insupportable curiosities, we're made to feel queasy and embarrassed for Stewart. Few other directors ever tapped Stewart's capacities for prurient interest and self-disgust, and for half the movie the actor turns in what amounts to a terrific silent performance. And given Hitchcock's obsessive food-for-sex metaphors (which clearly predate *Tom Jones*), it's appropriate to say that he served up a mouthwatering Grace Kelly. The most obvious visual effect in the movie is produced by her first kiss with Stewart; because of a slight camera jiggling they seem to pulsate together, in slow motion. Everything Kelly does is "proper" yet enchantingly sexual. Rolling out her character's full name while showing off a dress, she turns a modeling session into a sort of full-dress striptease. (Later, she does pose for Stewart in a nightgown, as a "preview of coming attractions.") If some of the bit players aren't all they might be (the jokes about "Miss Torso," a dancer who practices in her underwear, are a little broad), Thelma Ritter's Stella is wonderfully salty. As with Selma Diamond in *My Favorite Year*, you hear the New York subway system in her voice.

Although both Hitchcock and die-hard auteurists tend to pass over his literary sources, he and screenwriter John Michael Hayes remain faithful to the general outlines of Cornell Woolrich's story (published under the pseudonym William Irish in the collection *After-Dinner Story*), even borrowing a line or two of dialogue. Hitchcock shares Woolrich's reductive view of human possibilities, his almost Hobbesian vision of humanity holding its lives together with habits (to which Hitchcock adds his own sour overlay by portraying marriage as the ultimate bad habit). Woolrich spells out the concept of "delayed action"—the time it takes for modern man to synchronize impulse, thought, and deed; and Hitchcock makes that theme implicit in the fabric of the action. But the differences are, of course, as significant as the similarities. It was Hitchcock and Hayes who made the hero a photojournalist; and it was Hitchcock and Hayes who cooked up the love story.

Hitchcock, who used several Woolrich stories for his long-running TV show, probably shared a profound psychological affinity with the author—one that goes deeper than anyone would have expected before the emergence of posthumous biographical accounts. A Woolrich anthologist once compared *Rear Window*'s author to *Psycho*'s Norman Bates: "Both men were dominated by their mothers throughout their lives and long after their mother's death; both were trapped by accident of birth, through no fault of their own, in the most wretched psychological conditions; each was gifted (cursed?) with an unobtrusive yet penetrating intelligence that made him deeply aware of his own and all men's trappedness." We now know that this description could apply to Hitchcock himself. Yet in his fifties movies he had a cool handle on his hang-ups. Reading "Rear Window" leaves a mild, sweaty taint; watching the film, you feel titillated, horrified, and then purged—and sublimely entertained.

Boston Phoenix, October 11, 1983

WOODY ALLEN: BANANAS

■■■

David Denby

Woody Allen is probably the best comic talent working in American movies today, but also about the most erratic. *Bananas,* of which he is director, star, and writer (in collaboration with Mickey Rose), has some ideas that are so bad we may laugh simply because he's really going through with them; at other moments it seems he may yet become a popular satirist of genius.

Much of his humor is intentionally "stupid," intentionally sophomoric; like an irrepressible college humorist who somehow never graduated, he is always freshly enthralled by the world's absurdity, always eager to prove the power of far-out humor to take the measure of that absurdity. Occasionally, his stupid jokes have a rather sneaky force if you're aware of the reality behind them. The film opens with a television show: It's "ABC's Wide World of Sports" bringing us live coverage of the assassination of the president of a small Latin American republic. The sequence features real sports announcers—Don Dunphy and ineffable Howard Cosell, looking like an inquisitive eel. Cosell interviews the participants: "Well, of course you're upset and that's understandable under the circumstances," he says to the dying president.

At his best Allen mocks the dead language of television, movies, and advertising by placing the clichés in an absurd context or by gleefully exaggerating them. (He has written his own blurbs for the newspaper ads: "Moving, rich, tense, taut, filigreed, and gossamer.") Most of his ideas, however, are closer to free-flying nonsense humor, exhilirating and undisciplined, but without the aggressive force of the film's opening. One has to speak of separate ideas rather than an overall conception because Allen hasn't bothered to impose a unified style or theme on his material. Satire, burlesque, slapstick, and parody are all jumbled together. A courtroom sequence in which Allen is tried for subversive activities is simultaneously a half-hearted satire on the Chicago conspiracy trial and a parody of Perry Mason; a burlesque of revolutionary heroism and privation (Fidel Castro in the Sierra Maestre) is interrupted with parodies of contemporary movie clichés.

Allen is so impatient that he can't sustain or develop anything, and his movie keeps darting off in odd directions or pausing demurely for little interludes. Some of the gags are linked by a kind of comic free association, and the plot—Allen gets involved in a Latin American revolution to impress his ex-girlfriend—is so casual and intermittent that it seems to be there mainly to tease our assumption that a movie *needs* a plot. He unfortunately lacks the physical abilities of the great movie comics of the past—the athleticism and balletic grace that allowed them to recover from the most compromising mishaps with such brilliant panache that the recovery became the basis for the next gag. When Allen takes a pratfall he looks genuinely clumsy, and the sequence has to end. It is this failure to give his work any overall comic line—both physically and intellectually—that holds his pictures down to the middling-good level.

Like those great men of the past, he is trying to create a consistent character for himself from movie to movie. The bank robber who couldn't write a legible holdup note in *Take the Money and Run* is the same man who gets an invitation to dine with a military dictator in *Bananas* and arrives at the palace carrying a pastry assortment for his host. He is a man who would gladly ingratiate himself wherever possible if he could only overcome his truly radical incompetence. Terrifically inert by nature, he's so other-directed that he winds up performing heroic deeds just because people ask him. And when he acts, he's bound to run through the entire Yiddish lexicon for comic ineptitude: a *shlimazl* one minute, a *schmendrick* the next, a something-else the third. His contretemps with the talcum powder when he's preparing for his girl betrays the ingrained sloppiness of a man irrevocably removed from physical graciousness; the scene falls just short of being very ugly. Of course, he always manages to rob the bank, lead the revolution, and get the girl, so his clumsiness makes a rather feeble ironic point: if this fellow can succeed, then the world must be run by even greater idiots and worse incompetents.

As a satirist, Allen is not without the diffidence of his screen character. It's good that he's not protecting any of the conventional pieties (he's free, for instance to attack Castro *and* the CIA), and he has the originality to change an old emphasis or shift a familiar target (in a spoof of psychoanalysis he makes fun of the patient's revelations rather than the analyst's jargon). With the whole of American culture as his province he'll probably never run out of absurdities to work up into sharp little bits, but the lack of any moral or political position whatsoever prevents his work from having much bite. He has the sophistication for a truly cleansing American satire but at present not the guts.

The Atlantic, August 1971

WOODY ALLEN: A MIDSUMMER NIGHT'S SEX COMEDY

Bruce Williamson

Doggedly loyal Woody Allen fans are welcome to *A Midsummer Night's Sex Comedy,* which sets Woody back a giant step into his oh-to-be-Ingmar-Bergman phase. This costumed period piece is generally sophomoric, soporific, and left me wishing that Woody would just go back to being himself. I'll defend to the death a filmmaker's right to try something new and different. But what is new about an indifferent rehash of Bergman's masterly *Smiles of a Summer Night,* made in 1955 and already rehashed by Stephen Sondheim in the stage musical *A Little Night Music?* Anachronisms of morals and manners abound in *Sex Comedy,* a turn-of-the-century romance reeking of 1982 that has Mia Farrow doing a so-so Diane Keaton imitation. Mary Steenburgen, José Ferrer, and Tony Roberts also wade through Allen's sluggish country weekend, but the only memorable houseguest, for my money, was Julie Hagerty—chief flight attendant of *Airplane!*—as a horny nurse. Too bad Woody neglected to invite a show doctor. Neither Julie's charms nor limpid cinematography by Gordon Willis nor Allen's undeniable talent can do much to rescue a terminal case of trivial, derivative blah.

Playboy, November 1982

WOODY ALLEN: THE PURPLE ROSE OF CAIRO

Michael Wilmington

The Purple Rose of Cairo is the title of the new Woody Allen movie: a sweet film, funny, smart, lovely, sad . . . human. Other American filmmakers accomplish this kind of miracle occasionally, but few with the regularity of Allen.

It is also, Allen would have us believe, the title of a third-rate romance released in 1935 in the depths of the Depression. That *Purple Rose* was a throwaway programmer, shot at high speed by a studio hack. Its subject: the romantic antics of the idle rich—flitting with glamorous élan before painted skylines and paper moons, nothing weightier on their minds than the successful climax of Boy Meets Girl.

Flat, styleless, it has one devoted fan. Watching it at the Jewel Theater, night after night, is a waitress named Cecilia, one of many leading lives of unquiet desperation. Abused by her layabout husband, tormented at work by a carping boss, Cecilia dreams at *The Purple Rose*. One of the minor characters—a pith-helmeted young idealist named Tom Baxter—thrills her. He signifies a world of kindness, beauty, high adventure, monochrome bliss. He incarnates Romance, as movies have done for millions, dreamy-eyed, chewing their popcorn in the damp and fragrant darkness. If only, we can almost hear Cecilia breathe, if only he were real . . .

Then, a miracle: Baxter, weary of two-dimensional life, climbs down from the screen, approaches Cecilia, declares his love. He is everything she dreams of, everything life will never give her, unwavering, forever true. Just like in the movies . . .

That's the premise, and Allen has not simply milked it for a few cute jokes and star turns. As Buster Keaton did in 1924's *Sherlock Jr.*, he has taken this gimmick to its limits and—within the lines of its limpid craziness—has made it live. He does this with his writing, with the matchlessly brisk, supple flow of his dialogue . . . a cataract of wit where most movies have sporadic burps. He does it with ingenious, subtle effects; the ravishingly stylized cinematography of Gordon Willis (as virtuosic here as he was in *Pennies from Heaven*). He does it with his actors: Mia Farrow, radiant as Cecilia; Danny Aiello, believably mundane and monstrous as her husband; Jeff Daniels, both as a gleaming Tom Baxter and as the callow actor who created him; and with everyone else as well. (But not himself, though the entire film breathes with his presence, sings with his rhythms, skips to his beat.)

The Purple Rose of Cairo is a small, gentle film; it won't imperil *Variety*'s box-office champs. It may even appear too fragile or wistful. But, in its way, it's a jewel, a wonder. In its way, it's perfect.

The theme is easy to extract: reality and illusion, the fragility of romance, the danger of heart's desire. It plays with our special relationship to movies with depth and passion. It shows why these dreams exist and flourish—why they die. One shot of Farrow, shivery with yearning, watching the screen, is withering, perhaps the most moving that Allen has ever made—a directorial epiphany just as the close of *City Lights* was Chaplin's.

Chaplin and Keaton are a good measure; Allen long since deserves a ranking with them both. It doesn't matter whether he achieves the laugh quota of *Bananas* or *Love and Death*. Stretching himself each time out, operating away from the frustrations that bedevil his colleagues, he has become the one among them all who always speaks with his own voice, who increasingly deepens his art.

Purple Rose of Cairo is his tribute, not to the best the cinema can offer, but to what it offers even at its slightest: the tenderness it can raise, the dreams it can satisfy, the light of laughter, the shadow of tears; a tribute to all those foolish and impermanent sequins that glow and vanish but can be more precious, in that flickering instant, than a diamond worth a *Ghostbusters* gross.

Los Angeles Times, March 1, 1985

WOODY ALLEN: ANOTHER WOMAN

David Ansen

Why is it that Woody Allen's Ultraserious movies—*Interiors* ('78), *September* ('87), and now *Another Woman*—are always about WASPs? What does it mean (and what does it say about Allen) that his comedies are fundamentally Jewish and his tragedies Gentile? Can it be that in some strange corner of his paradoxical mind he believes that only the *goyim* can achieve tragic stature, that their problems require a special solemnity? Or is this rather a subtly disguised act of social criticism: a dissection of the arid lives that non-Jews are condemned to live? Or perhaps the issue is more one of style: since the model for his "art film" mode is clearly his idol Ingmar Bergman, does he find it too imaginatively incongruous to fit the Jewish experience into his New York Nordic movies? *Wild Strawberries* is one thing; *Wild Matzos* another.

The question needs to be asked, particularly after the disaster of *September,* a movie written with such a maladroit ear that you had to wonder why one of our most talented filmmakers was so stubbornly going against his own grain. It's not that Allen shouldn't be serious, but it did seem that when he abandoned comedy altogether his movies felt like imitations of other people's work—Bergman in *Interiors,* watered-down Eugene O'Neill in *September.*

Another Woman is a step forward. It's still self-consciously "literary" and its themes are laid out so schematically that the audience can anticipate exactly where it's headed, yet it has an emotional urgency that keeps you plugged in. You have the feeling that Allen is exposing some raw nerve endings this time, that he's not just hiding behind Art.

His heroine, Marion (Gena Rowlands), is a woman who does just that. A philosophy professor, she's been using the life of the mind to block out feelings all her life. Having devoted her life to studying great thoughts, she's led a complacently unexamined life, and now, having turned fifty, her life bites back. While working on a new book in a rented office, she overhears with mesmerizing clarity the psychoanalytic sessions in the next-door office. The sobbing voice of a patient (Mia Farrow) begins to obsess her and unleashes her own painful memories. The mysterious woman next door is the catalyst for her own belated journey of self-discovery.

There are echoes of both *Wild Strawberries* and *Persona* in Marion's voyage, but Allen's detail work is *echt* New York—a savage sketch of the Upper West Side intelligentsia at grim play. (Santo Loquasto's shabby-genteel sets are letter perfect.) Marion's second husband (Ian Holm) is a priggish, philandering physician, whom she cautiously chose to marry instead of the man who truly loved her (Gene Hackman). Marion is forced to confront the people she's hurt in her past—the brother (Harris Yulin) who's had to live in the shadow of her academic achievements, a bitter actress (Sandy Dennis) whose boyfriend she unconsciously stole, her mentor and first husband (Philip Bosco).

Another Woman flares to life when Hackman and Yulin and Dennis are onscreen, and it also has wonderful bits from Blythe Danner and Martha Plimpton. (There's a long and much too literal dream sequence that's a mistake, as are all the hand-me-down symbols of panthers and masks.) Gena Rowlands is, as always, fascinating to watch, but it seems odd to cast her, of all people, as a woman radically out of touch with her own feelings. Few actresses are as unrepressed as Rowlands—or as unacademic. Yet none of these flaws proves fatal, because in the end you feel that Allen is grappling with a theme close to his heart. There's little subtlety to his on-the-nose approach, but there's genuine urgency in Marion's struggle to overcome a life of self-deception. Perhaps what we are watching is Woody Allen's own ongoing struggle to free himself from a kind of artistic bondage. Attention must be paid.

Newsweek, October 24, 1988

WOODY ALLEN: CRIMES AND MISDEMEANORS

■■■

Richard Schickel

Judah Rosenthal (Martin Landau) is possessed by a primal memory. It is of a rabbi instructing him, as a boy, that the eye of God is all-seeing. No crime ever escapes it. Now successful and middle-aged, Judah self-deprecatingly suggests to an audience at a testimonial dinner on his behalf that perhaps he became an ophthalmologist because he is haunted by that recollection.

Seeing is also a subject that aptly named Cliff Stern (Woody Allen) takes seriously. A documentary filmmaker, he is driven not by God, but by the demands of an unyielding conscience to make his camera—his eye—bear witness to the inequities of his careless time. Needless to say, by its material standards he is a terrible flop.

His only connection to Judah—until the concluding sequence of Allen's thematically unified but narratively bifurcated movie—is through a saintly rabbi (Sam Waterston), who is the doctor's patient and Cliff's friend. His eye trouble is quite literal—by the end of the movie he has gone blind. But this blindness is also symbolic. By visiting this affliction on the only character in his movie who has remained close to God, Allen is suggesting that if the deity himself is not dead, then he must be suffering from severly impaired vision.

For all the *Crimes and Misdemeanors* Allen records in this film go not merely unpunished, they are generously rewarded. Upstairs, on the seriously melodramatic storyline, hypocritical Judah actually gets away with murder, arranging for the assassination of his mistress (Anjelica Huston), who threatens to make their affair—and his equally shabby financial affairs—public, thereby destroying his family, wealth, and social postion.

Downstairs, on the funny line, Cliff's brother-in-law Lester (Alan

The influence of Ingmar Bergman on Woody Allen was detectable even in Allen's "early, funny movies" such as *Love and Death* ('75). In such later efforts as *Another Woman* and *Crimes and Misdemeanors,* it's become explicit both thematically and stylistically—up to and including the participation of Bergman's premier cinematographer, Sven Nykvist (at right, working with Allen on *Crimes).* (Photo by Brian Hamill. Courtesy of Rollins & Joffe.)

Alda, bursting through his cool persona with a gloriously fashioned comic performance) offers him a sinecure. Do a documentary about Lester that will make him look like a philosopher-king among the pompous multimillionaire nitwits who produce prime time TV. Needing money to complete his film about a genuine philosopher, a gentle humanist who is also a Holocaust survivor, Cliff agrees but tries to turn Lester's story into an exposé. He is, of course, kicked off the project. Just by the way, Halley (Mia Farrow), Cliff's true love and his one hope of escape from a dreadful marriage, ends up engaged to Lester. And—oh yes—Cliff's revered philosopher enigmatically commits suicide, rendering the filmmaker's footage valueless, his reverence questionable.

This is the funny stuff? Yes, because of the deliberately farcical spin Allen puts on Cliff's frenzies. It is good showmanship, of course, a way of relieving the itchy ironies of Judah's discomfiting story. It may also be good theology. If neither Judah's guilty musings on his own crimes—and he does exhibit a strong desire to be caught and punished—nor decent Cliff's frantic quest for some kind of fulfillment can awaken Heaven's sleeping eye, then what in this world can? If *Manhattan,* coming at the end of the seventies, was Woody Allen's summarizing comment on that decade's besetting sin of self-absorption, then this is his concluding unscientific postscript on the besetting sin of the eighties, which is greed. Sometimes the joins in the movie's carpentry are awkward, sometimes its mood swings are jarring. But they also stir us from our comfortable stupor and vivify a true, moral, always acute and often hilarious meditation on the psychological economy of the Reagan years.

Time, October 16, 1989

JOHN HUSTON: PRIZZI'S HONOR

Michael Sragow

If satire is what closes on Saturday night, irony is what never gets a chance to open. These days, it's the missing ingredient in our culture—imagine how relieved you'd have felt about Reagan if you had known that he was somebody's joke on us. Irony has almost disappeared from American movies, and even when it's revived it has a hard time attracting audiences weaned on the Mars bars of Lucas films, the corrosive soda pop of slasher flicks, or the jerky comedy of *Porky's* movies. I've watched *Dr. Strangelove* with college crowds who didn't realize it was a comedy—they'd just seen the same material treated relatively straight in *WarGames* or on TV. So it's a rare pleasure to report that irony returns with a bang in a Mafia love story called *Prizzi's Honor,* the *Dr. Strangelove* of the *Godfather* movies and John Huston's best film in the decade since *The Man Who Would Be King* ('75). Because it's played with such vibrancy and panache by the three leads, Jack Nicholson, Kathleen Turner, and Anjelica Huston (as well as by a cast of supporting grotesques, including William Hickey, Robert Loggia, John Randolph, and

Lee Richardson), it should win over a lot of those viewers starving for 100-proof entertainment while Hollywood continues to serve up frappes.

First, though, they've got to know what to expect. Seeing *Prizzi's Honor* cold, you may wonder about everything from the leisurely pace to the anywhere-from-1959-to-1970 time period and the wavering tone. I saw it right after one of summer 1985's imitation-*E. T.* heartwarmers (*Cocoon*) and it had the emotional effect of insulin shock. It seemed curdled and distant, an "old man's movie"; it didn't evince the instinct for dynamic moviemaking that's distinguished Huston's prime work. But on second viewing I realized this isn't just Huston redux—it's Huston reborn. He has the same disillusioned view of life's graspers and overreachers (categories to which he consigns most of us), but now there's a mellow, absurdist touch that resembles late Buñuel as much as it does the Huston of *The Maltese Falcon* ('41) and *Beat the Devil* ('53). In Huston's 1948 *Key Largo*, the Mafia represented all the commercialism and corruption threatening postwar America; in *Prizzi's Honor*, its victory is complete. Yet Huston doesn't wring his hands, as he did back then, over its vicious, patriarchal tyranny. He's saying that despite their Old World machismo and blood vendettas, these rich aren't that different from you and me. As film critic David Ehrenstein put it to me, "It's not an old man's movie—it's a foxy grandpa's movie." Or a foxy godfather's.

It's no trick to take a film like *Rambo* ironically; millions of moviegoers have already managed that. What's unique about *Prizzi's Honor* in the eighties movie climate is that it takes an ironic outlook toward its own subject matter. It's a complete, structured vision of gangland morality—and, by extension, of the contemporary ethics we're all stuck with—that keeps a cleansing distance from its own characters. We see through their pretenses; what's true about the movie is Huston's ironic art.

The hero is Charley Partanna (Nicholson), the enforcer for the Prizzi family, "straight-arrow Charley, the all-American hood" who's sworn his allegiance to the clan since birth but finds himself testing family ties when he marries a "Polack" beauty named Irene Walker (Turner). She's naturally distrustful of marrying into the Sicilian clan: her late husband always told her, "The Jews in this business are bad enough, but the Sicilians would rather eat their children than part with their money" (and they *love* their children). Partanna has his own reason to be distrustful: Irene is a freelance hit woman who may have been part of a scam to fleece one of the Prizzis' casinos of exactly $722,085. Then again, every character is in a position to pull off a double-cross (or even a triple). That goes not only for Charley and Irene but also for Maerose Prizzi (Anjelica Huston), the don's granddaughter. She once intended to marry Charley herself; instead, after a jealous quarrel, she brought shame on Charley, her family, and herself by shacking up with another man. For four years she's wanted Charley back; her father, Dom (Richardson), would love to have Charley killed to avenge her shame. Meanwhile, her grandfather, Don Corrado (Hickey), tries to balance the demands of the younger Prizzis with those of enforcer Charley—whom he needs (as director Huston does) "to hold everything together."

Huston adroitly depicts the Prizzis' honor in all its carnivorous vainglory while making it seem no more or less shocking than the insular pride of any American family, immigrant or otherwise. The opening credit sequence sets up his vision of the Italian-American underworld as a compendium of cracked binational clichés: God, godfather, and pizza pie. Huston gives us a gangland bio of Charley in three tableaux that establish the air of macabre kidding: the proud consiglière papa and his don share the first peek at newborn Charley in the hospital; the Cub Scout gets brass knuckles as a Christmas gift; adolescent Charley enters mob manhood by making like blood brothers with the don. Although Huston doesn't sustain that tone all the way through, he rarely lapses into silliness, so the aura is never destroyed. He allows the gravity of the Prizzis to sink in without letting us forget that the pride and moralism of this rat pack isn't that different from Scout's honor.

With long, unbroken takes, lingering portraiture, and the glittering Rossini-Verdi-Puccini pastiche by soundtrack composer Alex North, Huston gives us not just irony but a luxurious, baroque irony. He doesn't go at the Prizzis' perversity halfheartedly— he exults in it. That's what's daring (and possibly off-putting) about the movie, and also what's refulgent about it. The wedding scene that starts the movie proper is almost the exact opposite of *The Godfather's*, which swept audiences up in the Corleones' dash and warmth. (Some of the echoes seem deliberate: at the reception you hear one of the same Italian wedding tunes.) Here Andrzej Bartkowiak's camera crawls down from the stained-glass window to the bride and groom before the altar and then down through the congregation; editor Rudi Fehr slyly inserts candid shots of the onlookers, starting with William Hickey's vampiric don, who looks to be in a dead sleep until he checks in on the goings-on—and then resumes his slumber. At moments like that you imagine Huston behind the camera, cackling softly.

Richard Condon (who adapted his own novel, with Janet Roach) has written his plot on a Mobius strip—all the double crosses fit onto one twisted strand of subterfuge. Despite some slow moments, his story allows Huston to demythify the Mob in the most direct way: by showing how each Mafioso, from the base of every family pyramid to its apex, has a carefully triangulated existence. We never even see Don Corrado Prizzi outside Brooklyn; and until Charley marries Irene and removes Maerose's stigma, this Prizzi granddaughter isn't allowed *inside* Brooklyn, except on "special occasions." Charley Partanna is considered "a thinker" (never mind that he's a slow one) because he checks carefully all the unwritten codes of his clan and trade before embarking on any course of action. But it's the liberated Irene (a sometime tax consultant) who introduces the gang to some facts of modern life, such as companies' treating their ransom payments as tax write-offs, and Charley who processes the info with sluggish wonder. What's funny is, he acts the same way in his romance: he demands to know whether Irene "loves" him or is simply "in love," which he's learned is "temporary," a result of "hormonal secretions."

With this man at the center, less seasoned directors might have wanted to rush matters along. Huston resists the temptation to hustle his actors out of character, and they almost all come through for him. When the smart, self-mocking Nicholson has played dumb or semi-dumb characters in the past, his eyeball-rolling antics have had filmgoers rolling in the aisles—even when, in *The Shining,* they were meant to be riveted to their seats. Nicholson gives those eyebrows a workout here, too, but he incorporates his mannerisms in a consistent, overscaled performance; as in the entire movie, there are subtleties contained in his absurdities. Here the roll of the eyes and the strange events around his forehead signal more than crazed desire or disbelief; we're watching a little boy's inverted emotions. Nicholson's Charley is still pretty much a Cub Scout. Even when he rolls his lip Bogart-high on the right side, the effect is disconcertingly jejune. When Maerose asks him to "do it," his eyebrows become darting vectors and his cheeks puff up and his mouth tightens as he asks, "With all the lights on?" When he's with Irene that same tentativeness takes on different colorings as he makes flustered attempts to appear debonair and sophisticated. Kathleen Turner's Irene is just the woman to bring out the failed cosmopolite in him. She orders a "jugo de piña Bacardi" with the right savoir faire to make Charley ask whether it's "Puerto Rican or something." Turner always seems to be at her most actressy when she plays femmes fatales, as if she were self-conscious about being glamorous. She's more original—and risible—lampooning those roles in *The Man with Two Brains* or *Romancing the Stone*. In this movie, her slight self-consciousness is in character—in fact, for the first time Turner is allowed to strike a middle ground between passion and self-parody.

And the film introduces a great high-style comedian in Anjelica Huston, John's daughter, who creates the brand-new archetype of the IAP—the Italian-American Princess. Maerose Prizzi grew up with Charley and stayed close to him until their plans fell through: when she explains to him that Art Deco is a style, not a person, it's with sisterly affection. But she also gives off husky overtones of hunger and rejection. And when Charley's marriage to Irene allows Maerose to reenter her family—because the man she "wronged" has achieved happiness without her—Anjelica Huston becomes a princess of irony, too. As Maerose exposes Irene's double-dealings to the don, or taunts her father by recounting how Charley "forced himself" on her, she pours on the love and the hate, the hurt and the revenge. She's a nifty split-level actress, and a striking one, with a black-rose luster to match Turner's blond beauty.

The dialogue is like a cross between Mario Puzo and David Mamet: there's an uproariously terse matter-of-factness to statements such as "Cops don't like it when we hit one of their wives" and questions like "If Maxie Heller's so fucking smart, how come he's so fucking dead?" But the man-woman scenes have a jagged verbal distinction all their own. Irene and Charley are caught in a perilous mating dance—he's always trying to pin her down, she's always trying to smooth over crises or straighten out their affairs. In a typical bit of domestic diplomacy, she impresses him with her independent means by bragging of doing three or four hits a year, most for "full price"; when Charley says that's a lot, she plummily replies, "It's not that many if you consider the size of the population."

In order to float this sort of fantastical gangland effrontery, Huston concocts a potpourri of effects: like Twyla Tharp's Sinatra dances, *Prizzi's Honor* both sends up and salutes America's showbiz-colored vision of the high life. Charley goes to sleep on chessboard pillowcases, reading one of those grand old oversized *Esquire* magazines, and his favorite sportcoat is colored a canary yellow so loud you can almost hear it chirp. Bartkowiak's cinematography is both austere and glitzy—soft-toned, but with spooky blues and garish burgundies shining through. If most of the supporting performances stay within the boundaries of realism—indeed, Richardson, Robert Loggia (Maerose's uncle), and John Randolph (Charley's father) would make a first-rate company for *Glengarry Glen Ross*—Hickey bursts those bounds with his godfather parody, all parchment skin and death's-head grin.

But Huston's finest effects are much quieter, and to do them justice I have to borrow from his friend, the late James Agee, who saluted Charles Chaplin's black comedy of murder, *Monsieur Verdoux,* in words that apply just as well to *Prizzi's Honor.* Huston, like Chaplin, subdues most of his outrageous fun to his appetite for cold nihilistic irony. He directs like a sardonic ringmaster, an inspired emcee. He obviously believes that if you can invent something worth watching, the camera should hold still and clear so that you can watch it. That remains one of the best possible ways to use a camera; Huston is the one great man who still stands up for it. We are just smart enough to recognize a cliché, never smart enough to see how brilliantly a master can use it. So we may sneer at Huston's frequent use of airplanes jetting across the screen this way and that, to mark another business trip or return, just as forties audiences sneered at Chaplin's trains. But these airplanes do a lot at once. They are in the best sense economical; they are cumulatively funny and express Charley and Irene's ever-more-frantic busyness; and they wind up the film like a tight spring. Most important of all, Huston dares to portray Charley, Irene, and friends as Chaplin did Verdoux: as business realists. And according to that realism, the only difference between free enterprise in murder and free enterprise in the sale of elastic stockings is in legal liability and net income. Huston dares to use their personalities as a constant metaphor for modern civilization, in which creative power is paralyzed except in the interest of gain and destruction; in those interests it is vigorous as never before.

It was Agee who first canonized Huston, after such triumphs as *The Maltese Falcon, The Treasure of the Sierra Madre* ('48), and *The Asphalt Jungle* ('50)—movies that established him as the American director most likely to combine popular and artistic success in the classic D. W. Griffith tradition. Agee died in 1955 while Huston was struggling with the Great White Whale, *Moby Dick* ('56); ever since, the legendary director has wandered between commercial larks—from *Heaven Knows, Mr. Allison* ('57) to *Annie* ('80) or *Victory* ('81)—and self-conscious attempts at art—from *The Misfits* ('61) to *Under the Volcano* ('84)—only occasionally combining the best elements of each. With *Prizzi's Honor* he's made a film that seems guaranteed critical success. It would be the ultimate justification of his art if it meets with popular success as well—and the ultimate irony if it doesn't.

Boston Phoenix, June 18, 1985

FRANCIS COPPOLA: THE GODFATHER PART III

■■■

Michael Wilmington

It's not personal, Sonny. It's strictly business.

—Michael Corleone, *The Godfather*

After sixteen years, it was an offer Francis Ford Coppola couldn't refuse. In *The Godfather Part III*, he and Mario Puzo return to their franchise: the Corleone Family Saga. Once again they take up the violent, virtuosic, densely detailed epic of gangsters and American society—of *omertà* and *famiglia,* bullets and cannoli, blood ties and bloodstained vendettas—that they spun with such staggering aplomb and worldwide impact in *The Godfather* ('72) and *The Godfather Part II* ('74).

This new sequel, in which Don Michael Corleone (Al Pacino) tries to go straight and crash the Vatican itself, is another rich, broadly scaled work, shot through with brutality and brio. It has arias and grand moments to match either of its predecessors: the coldly festive opening at a celebration of a Mafia don's charities; a nervous, panoramic Little Italy assassination; a jolting comic-violent scene in which Andy Garcia, playing the newest Corleone, faces down two would-be assassins who interrupt him in the middle of an assignation.

Al Pacino re-creates his role as Michael Corleone in Francis Coppola's *The Godfather Part III*. Moving up in the background is the next don-to-be, Andy Garcia as Vincent Mancini. (Photo by Fabian. © 1993 Paramount Pictures. All Rights Reserved. Photo appears courtesy of Paramount Pictures.)

The movie carries the trilogy's recurring major figure, Pacino's Michael, from 1979 to his death, knitting together dozens of old plot strands, themes, and symbolic motifs. It brings back the original cinematographer, Gordon Willis, that master of deep shadows, metallic sunlight, and deceptively flat perspectives. It reintroduces a gallery of familiar faces—including sister Connie (Talia Shire), divorced wife Kay (Diane Keaton), and ultradisturbing background figure torpedo Al Neri (Richard Bright)—and drives them toward an operatic climax, where, to the strains of Mascagni's "Cavalleria Rusticana," Michael meets a family destiny out of Verdi, Shakespeare, or James M. Cain.

Yet, though *Godfather III* is definitely one of the best American movies of 1990—a work of high ensemble talent and intelligence, gorgeously mounted and crafted, artistically audacious in ways that most American movies don't even attempt—it's still a disappointment. It fails on the highest level.

It's a matter, perhaps, of both script and tone. The first two *Godfathers*, dominated by Pacino's menacingly passive Michael and by the magisterial gravelly croak of Marlon Brando or Robert De Niro as the old and young Don Vito Corleone, were violent tales done with incongruous subtlety and discretion. Back then, in his early thirties, Coppola's narrative style was marvelously circumspect. He bathed those earlier films in a tender melancholy, a sense of reverie that stood in eerie counterpoint to the lurid events and horrific gangland killings. Part I is more boisterous and bloody; Part II, more complex, poetic, and charged with grief. But neither ever seemed to raise a voice unnecessarily, or strain for an effect.

Part III, by contrast, has scenes or plot twists—a flabbergasting helicopter attack on a Cosa Nostra commission meeting; the incongruously rapid rise of Sonny Corleone's illegitimate son, Vincent Mancini (Garcia); a Byzantine hive of intrigue revealed at the Vatican—where the tone seems forced, underfelt, almost strident. Is that copter rubout an allusion to "The Ride of the Valkyries" in *Apocalypse Now?* What prompts the operatic vocation of Michael's son Anthony (Franc D'Ambrosio), beyond Coppola's own musical family? Why are dialogues between the partially reconciled Michael and Kay so bland and perfunctory? And how can Michael muster the muscle to stave off attacks from other Mafiosi after going completely "legitimate"?

Since *Apocalypse Now* ('79), Coppola has changed into a very different filmmaker. Now he regularly goes for visual opulence, extravagant effect; his masterpiece of the eighties was the film noir, German Expressionist, neorealist teen melodrama *Rumble Fish* ('83). But *Godfather III,* for all its obvious quality and visual bravura, lacks the fullness or inevitability of the first two films: the ways Coppola and Puzo seemed to skim easily over the social and criminal terrain of the first half of the twentieth century. In a way, this movie seems to come from a whole different world—and not simply because it's set in 1979, five years after the release of *Godfather II,* and twenty years after the conclusion of the events it portrays.

In *Godfather III* there's something sad, slightly vacant, and dourly dreamy in Pacino's eyes as the fifty-nine-year-old Michael. Set deep in a bulldog mug, with a receding crewcut, they're the eyes of a man who'd rather be almost anywhere but in his immediate surroundings, a man who—like the Misfit in Flannery O'Connor's "A Good Man Is Hard to Find"—believes "there ain't no real pleasure in life."

It's Pacino's face—its wasted, bitter, ravaged resignation—that many people will recall longest from *Godfather III.* And they'll also remember the leaner, slicker, more wolfish features of Andy Garcia as the up-and-coming, new-style don. Garcia seizes the screen here, and gives an explosive, tigerishly self-confident performance. Playing a character conceived during the wedding scene of the first *Godfather,* he creates a tense, narcissistic killer. Unlike Michael, Vincent is supremely equipped by instinct to be a gangster: a man of fast reflexes, intense ambition, and no moral qualms. In his first confrontation with Joey Zaza (Joe Mantegna), Michael's successor and rival, Vincent nearly bites off his ear.

Pacino, on the other hand, plays Michael as a tough, self-contained pro, trapped in gloomy self-examination after a life of brutal, near-reflexive decisions and actions. He's rotting inside. His disease—diabetes—suggests here spiritual as well as physical decay. And, after rising to the top, he's now trying to go beyond, to move hundreds of millions of dollars, buy God's emissaries, and enter Heaven through the back door.

"Michael Corleone, do you renounce Satan?" a priest asked during the baptism of Michael's godson in the first film—a scene that was shockingly intercut with the systematic execution of the Corleones' enemies. The irony of that legendary climax lay in the juxtaposition of outward piety or conformity and covert slaughter. It's extended more heavily here, with one church scene after another, and Michael actually confessing three decades of crimes to the future Pope John Paul I (Raf Vallone). Michael, an outsider in a family of gangsters, had become the most dangerous criminal of all: the soured idealist, the man who knows and hates evil, but does it anyway. He was the murderer who fully accepted La Rochefoucauld's maxim, "Hypocrisy is the debt vice pays to virtue."

There's always been an obvious connection between Coppola and Michael; Coppola deliberately played it up in *The Godfather,* giving the character the middle name Francis. In *Godfather III* the identification becomes almost eerie. Michael is a man from a tight-knit family, risen to the top, living a life of tension and near financial ruin, desperately trying to pull away from a business that won't let him go. When Coppola decides to end the film with the possible sacrifice of a child, it obviously has personal reverberations. So do Michael's financial takeovers. And so does his tight-knit family: the newly icy, resolute fury of Talia Shire (Coppola's own sister) as Connie; the artistic aspirations of Anthony; Kay's moral superiority.

Coppola and Puzo notably ignore politics this time around, but as they focus on the last ravages of the Corleone family, driven to its dissolution, they also create an awesome incestuous tangle among the worlds of crime, business, religion, and art. In this corrupt alliance, only the world of art is presented as uncompromised and pure. It's the world that the idealists like Anthony try to escape into; it's also a world that, as in the performance of "Cavalleria Rusticana," bizarrely mirrors everything that happens outside it.

But religion is just as tainted as the other worlds, polluted by its vast acquisition of wealth and power. Coppola and Puzo deliberately play here with references to the Vatican Bank scandal, as well as rumors about the possible murder of the Pope. "All my life I kept trying to go up in society," Michael remarks to Vincent. "Where everything higher up was legal. But the higher I go, the crookeder it gets. Where the hell does it end?"

In hell, obviously, which is exactly where *Godfather III* leaves Michael: the emotional Hades of a man who has sacrificed the only thing that gave all his crimes meaning—*famiglia*. In the last shot of the movie, an orange—a fruit that has had numerous sinister connotations through all the episodes of the saga—slips from his fingers.

In 1972, when he made the first of the *Godfather* movies, Coppola scored an unprecedented coup. He seemed to have made a movie that was *Citizen Kane* and *Gone With the Wind* simultaneously: a huge blockbuster, biggest of its time, that also had depth, social vision, and multiple layers of meaning, a film that satisfied both the pop-culture audience and the intelligentsia. For this, he became a hero to many film critics, some of whom were all too eager to cast him as villain or betrayer—or fool—later on.

The Corleone saga was something unusual in gangster movies: a crime epic that presented the Mafia family and, especially, their leonine, mumbling patriarch Vito Corleone (Brando) in the kind of sweepingly romantic terms that characterized more conventional, affirmative family epics. And part of its widespread audience clearly ignored Coppola's dark subversion of their image; they found the Corleones endearing, Michael almost heroic. Coppola brilliantly used actors—Brando, Pacino, Keaton, Shire, James Caan, Robert Duvall, John Cazale—whose sensibility opened up their parts in unique ways. They seemed—still seem—more like a family of artists than a family of criminals. As a group, they had incongruous sensitivity, delicacy, and grace—and vulnerability as well.

Coppola didn't cast gangster "types" except in the non-Corleone roles, and that's what gives the first movie its tense undercurrents.

The most moving moment in all three films came from the late John Cazale as brother Fredo in *Godfather II:* delicate, enervated, reclining painfully beside Michael, who will soon kill him, crying out his rage and pain at being passed over. Sweet, ineffectual, doomed Fredo didn't belong in the average gangster movie. But then, none of them did: not even James Caan's Sonny, the hotheaded ladies' man.

But time's passage has destroyed or altered the context in which those first two *Godfathers* were produced—a momentarily fertile climate for offbeat movies in the early seventies—and replaced it with another, shallower era in which financial stakes are huge and artistic gambles minimal. The daringly structured *Godfather II* probably couldn't have been made in 1990, and sixteen horrifyingly intense and sometimes brutal years intervened for Coppola: years filled with sudden success, financial catastrophes, spectacular public and artistic reversals, and family tragedies.

In a way, we can sense all of this in Part III. Perhaps because the first script was written too hastily, in six weeks instead of the six months Coppola requested, the writing is both overly formulaic and strangely unguarded and open. Despite frequent rewriting afterward, Coppola hasn't let his attitudes and feelings get swallowed up in the material. They keep jutting out: most obviously in the way he uses his lightly experienced and miscast daughter Sofia (a last-minute replacement for Winona Ryder) as Michael's daughter Mary, lavishing an almost defiant paternal affection on every shot. Oddly enough, *Godfather III* is in some ways a typical, perhaps too typical, movie sequel and, in others, a startlingly confessional film. Real anguish and pain keep seeping up through the predictable kinks of the story.

One of the most attractive things about Coppola is the very intensity and range of his ambition, the way he wants to be a superfilmmaker, master of everything: a fine writer, a visual virtuoso, a technical whizbang, a maestro of complex effects and camera movements, and an actor's director generating the raw, improvisatory magic of a Cassavetes or Scorsese. But sometimes you can't be everything, and this movie's major weakness lies in the area that's always been one of Coppola's prime assets: his screenwriting. The frequent rewriting after the original six-week wonder can't overcome flimsiness or broadness in the framework. In the end, *Godfather III* is more conventional than its antecedents.

It's inevitable. On short notice, Coppola and Puzo get what you would expect: the broad symbolic outlines and motifs and the big "aria" scenes. But they haven't been able to tie everything together, fill in all the connections, remove scenes that just don't work, re-create the seamless embellishment and profusion of the earlier films. Six weeks was an offer they should have refused.

Almost equally damaging: the defection of Robert Duvall, due to a salary dispute. In 1974, *Godfather II* also lost Richard Castellano's Clemenza to salary demands; Coppola had to kill off the character and give his lines to Michael Gazzo's Frankie Pentangeli. But Duvall's Tom Hagen is more crucial than Clemenza. As the Corleones' adopted son and consiglière, he's so inextricably tied into the whole texture and emotional weave of the story that he's always seemed indispensable, perhaps even part of some inevitable, slowly ripening climax, a last bloody act where Hagen would play combatant in a final betrayal and clash with Michael. Writing Duvall out of the movie seems painfully unnecessary. Leaving a priestly son (John Savage's Andrew Hagen) in his place, while handing over some of his lines to George Hamilton, as a silken new consiglière, is a poor substitute.

In light of all this, it may seem perverse to call *Godfather III* one of 1990's best American movies. But it is. The brilliance and fertility of Coppola's talents and the excellence of his cast and crew pull him through once again. He's always been a great assembler of talent; if he's a dream-castle builder, he's a supremely generous one. Visually, this is the most gorgeous of the three *Godfathers;* Willis and production designer Dean Tavoularis have outdone themselves. And it's loaded with fascinating moments: Garcia's magnetic psychopathology, Pacino's weary pursuit of grace, Eli Wallach's angelic duplicities as Don Altobello, and, especially, that climactic opera house set-piece, with its bravura echoes of Visconti's *Senso* and Hitchcock's second *The Man Who Knew Too Much.* And if the movie loses some—maybe even most—of the battles you wish it had won, it still scores a magnificent final victory by rounding out a series that ranks with the most ambitious and extraordinary creations in American movies.

When you try so hard for beauty, complexity, and richness, you can leave the audience with a banquet even when you fail. That's what Coppola does here. The problems that afflict him in this compromised *Godfather III* are ones perhaps endemic to today's big-budget moviemaking. Its triumphs are the victories—partial, but certainly precious—of moviemakers working together, of artistic devotion and ambition, of the ensemble, the *famiglia*. The *Godfather* series—like *Kane* for Orson Welles—has perhaps been Coppola's crown jewel and also his curse. He hasn't completed it perfectly, but he's completed it with a passion. And passion is something that should never have a price.

Los Angeles Times, December 23, 1990

ROBERT ALTMAN: THE PLAYER

■■■

Stephen Schiff

After years of rebellion and exile and failure, the veteran director Robert Altman has finally made a great big funny movie that's going to ring bells, knock socks off, throw people for loops, and in general create the commotion of the year. Which is all very well. But does that mean he's about to become a Player?

In Hollywood, a Player is someone the big boys have to reckon with, someone who's decidedly on the game board, whose calls you take, whose dinner invitations you accept, someone who can make a difference to your movie or your studio or your prospects of ever owning beachfront property.

By those standards, it's been a very long time since Altman qualified—if indeed he ever did. Critics and movie buffs rightly regarded him as the colossus of Hollywood's last Golden Age: between 1970 and 1975 he turned out eight films, six of them out-and-out masterpieces (*M*A*S*H, McCabe and Mrs. Miller, The Long Goodbye, Thieves Like Us, California Split,* and *Nashville*). But audiences have generally snubbed him. His most recent box-office hit was *Popeye* in 1980, and the only one before that was *M*A*S*H,* way back in 1970. *Nashville*—with its 24 characters, its magically interlinked narratives, and its swirling layers of emotion and sound—changed the world's idea of what an American film could be, but it too gasped and died at the box office in 1975. After that, Altman's genius seemed to unravel all at once. He drank hard and partied hard and made bad movies, and by the end of the seventies his personal chaos threatened to swallow him alive.

Altman retreated to Paris, burning bridges as he went, and there he spent America's yuppie years working on odd projects: theater adaptations (some good, some terrible), TV shows (his "Tanner '88" series for HBO won him an Emmy), and finally his splendid van Gogh biography, *Vincent & Theo* ('90). A howl of dismay about how artists inevitably bleed to death on the cross of commerce, *Vincent & Theo* excited art-house audiences and even wound up on some critics' ten-best lists, but in Hollywood's mind Robert Altman's song had been sung. He was a tottering has-been, a wanderer in the wilderness who, through some combination of booze, burnout, and infernal cussedness, had marginalized himself into the ozone.

But all that's about to change. Altman's new movie, *The Player,* is—why mince words?—another masterpiece, the first Altman has managed since *Nashville* almost twenty years ago. Adapted from the well-regarded novel by Michael Tolkin (who is credited with writing the screenplay), the movie towers over its source in every way. It's a real Altman film: exuberantly atmospheric, masterly without being show-offy, complicated yet understated, opulent and light-headed at the same time. It is also one of the smartest, funniest, most penetrating movies about moviemaking ever made.

Movies-about-moviemaking tend to come in two flavors: the celebratory (*Day for Night, Singin' in the Rain*) and the sardonic (*Sunset Boulevard, The Bad and the Beautiful, Barton Fink*). But *The Player* skips blithely beyond both categories to something far richer and stranger, something at once antic and metaphysical. In this film, the usual "scathing satire" of Hollywood is just the beginning. Yes, Altman's studio hotshots are laughable monsters; yes, their language is hilariously tortured and their cars are hilariously shiny and they seem to know more about the varieties of mineral water than about the classic films whose posters glower reprovingly from their walls. Altman is good at this stuff, but he knows that's the easy part. What he really wants to reveal is the psychology beneath the familiar Hollywood hypocrisies. If we expect the usual Us vs. Them scenario, with brilliant "creatives" getting the spunk stomped out of them by Armani-clad philistines, Altman's view proves much subtler—and much truer. *The Player* is about how the industry crushes the originality out of anyone who participates in it—any Player: writer, director, or production chief.

And that's because the Hollywood system makes it impossible to view the world afresh, to derive inspiration or even information from it. Enter the game and you can't help yourself; everything, from the morning headlines to the person you love, gets ground to movie fodder. Daily life is transformed into a storyline, with arcs and plot points and climaxes you can manipulate; the people around you turn into characters—heroes, villains, the Sidekick, the Girl. And perception itself becomes a glittering widescreen process, with Dolbyized stereophonic sound.

That Altman demonstrates all this without getting windy about it is a feat in itself. That he does so in a movie that is at once a hugely entertaining suspense thriller, a sultry romance, and an irresistibly hip comedy makes for the sweetest revenge.

☆

It almost didn't happen that way. When producer David Brown optioned Tolkin's novel four years ago (for $2,500), Robert Altman wasn't even on his mind. He shopped it around to James Dearden (who had written *Fatal Attraction* and written and directed *Pascali's Island*) and to director Joseph Ruben, whose *True Believer* was being touted as a hit in the making (it wasn't); neither package could lure the necessary financing. Chevy Chase wanted to star in the movie for a while, but the honchos at Warner Bros., where Chase has an exclusive contract, convinced him it would ruin his image. Then director Sidney Lumet signed on; *The Player* was on its way to becoming a slick studio thriller. But Lumet is an expensive piece of talent. His going rate of around $2 million a picture proved hard to raise, and in the end Lumet accepted another picture instead.

Which is when Robert Altman showed up. Over breakfast at New York's Westbury Hotel, he told Brown he was born to direct *The Player,* but he was worried, according to Brown, that the moneymen were going to "fuck it up and give him trouble." As a studio executive, Brown had worked with Altman on *M*A*S*H* and *McCabe and Mrs. Miller;* he had seen the director at his best. "I'm a cockeyed optimist," says Brown, "and I thought Altman was a brilliant idea. He wasn't drinking and he wasn't smoking—this film meant something to him." Altman was hired and he may get yet another taste of revenge. *The Player* could prove a small-scale hit.

Why not? In one of the movie's most sublime scenes, our "hero," a studio production executive named Griffin Mill (played by Tim Robbins), defines "certain elements that we need to market a film successfully: Suspense. Laughter. Violence. Hope. Heart. Nudity. Sex. And happy endings. Mainly happy endings." Altman's joke is

that his big anti-Hollywood picture actually has all these things—
plus one other crucial marketing requirement.

It has stars. Not just two or three or even five. This movie has
fifty stars. Maybe more. It's Altman's Revenge, Part III: You want
stars? I'll give you more stars than any studio could sign, more stars
than Spielberg or Levinson or Joel Silver could attract, more stars
than there are in a year of *People* magazine, more stars than Mike
Ovitz can cram into his breakfast Rolodex.

Even during his bridge-burning days, when he industriously
alienated scores of writers, producers, and studio executives, Altman never stopped cultivating stars. He gave actors chances they
couldn't have had without him, listened to their ideas, incorporated
their ad-libs into his famous overlapping dialogues. Altman has
always been an actor's idea of a great director: patriarchal, collaborative, admiring, a little bit indulgent. And now the actors are
returning the favor. First there are the ones who actually play characters in the film: Tim Robbins, Greta Scacchi, Whoopi Goldberg,
Fred Ward, Peter Gallagher, Brion James, Vincent D'Onofrio,
Dean Stockwell, Cynthia Stevenson, Richard E. Grant, Sydney
Pollack, Lyle Lovett, and Dina Merrill. Unimpressed? All right. But
then there are all the other stars, the ones who play themselves in
the movie's party and restaurant and movie-within-a-movie scenes:
Cher, Julia Roberts, Bruce Willis, Nick Nolte, Anjelica Huston,
Susan Sarandon, Jack Lemmon, Andie MacDowell, Lily Tomlin,
John Cusack, Jeff Goldblum, Rod Steiger, Harry Belafonte, Shari
Belafonte, James Coburn, Malcolm McDowell, Joel Grey, Peter
Falk, Steve Allen, Jayne Meadows, Gary Busey, Buck Henry, Elliott
Gould, Robert Wagner, Jill St. John, the late Brad Davis, Karen
Black, Louise Fletcher, Marlee Matlin, Burt Reynolds, Scott
Glenn, Teri Garr, Mimi Rogers, and on and on and on.

That all-you-can-eat movie star buffet is, among other things, a
daunting demonstration of the sheer clout Altman still reserves.
Sheer clout, and perhaps something else—perhaps a sense that if
Altman calls you, you go, because at the very least it will be fun,
and at the most it might be magic.

"Bob would call the stars and ask them for a day's work," says
David Brown, "and they would just come. And those who weren't
invited were offended."

"The reason I did it was because of Bob," says Jack Lemmon,
who is seen playing the piano in one of the movie's party scenes. "I
hadn't had a chance to work with him before, and I love his work,

and I love him personally. He called up and said, 'Listen, I'm throwing a party.' I said, 'That's terrific. We're there.' He said, 'Well, you're going to be photographed.' I said, 'That's terrific. I'll get a suit.' He said, 'You'll be my orchestra.' I said, 'It's getting better by the minute.' And, God, everybody and their mother's uncle was there. So Felicia and I got all dolled up and away we went, and he said, '"Here's the piano,' and I said, 'How about a little Gershwin?' And he said, 'There goes $500,000—for the rights, you know.' He said, 'Make something up.' And I did. It really was like a party—we just sat around and schmoozed. We were all there for the same damn reason: isn't it great to be here for Bob?"

Altman calls the movie stars "extras," which gives you an idea of what he's up to. He's using cameo performances in a way they've never been used before: for verisimilitude. Altman places movie stars in his restaurant and party scenes because if you go to certain restaurants and parties in Hollywood those stars are really there. He wants to convey the flavor of a world in which magazine-cover faces show up all around you: they're in line with you at the drugstore; they nod and grin from the next table. If you swim among the stars, life outside the fish tank can start to look remote and unreal. Just like a movie.

☆

But Altman's vengeance doesn't end there. *The Player* begins with a display of directorial virtuosity so dazzling it amounts to an act of defiance. We're on the lot of an unnamed studio, where Griffin Mill has long been heir apparent to the studio boss, Joel Levison (perfectly played by Brion James, an actor who has heretofore distinguished himself portraying a variety of killers and thugs). Rumor has it that Levison is about to hire a hot young executive named Larry Levy (Peter Gallagher) and that Griffin's star is consequently falling. He may even lose his job. "Quiet on the set," and a clapper appears in front of us, announcing the tenth take of a scene in Robert Altman's film *The Player*. In short, we're watching a movie within a movie—the very movie, in fact, that we'll hear described by an unhinged screenwriter some two hours later. *The Player* hasn't even begun and already Altman is beckoning us to question what's real.

Now begins the most astonishing trick Altman has performed since the great traffic jam opening of Nashville. A master of the fluid, gliding camera, Altman has always used zoom lenses (which still lend his work a pleasantly anachronistic sixties look) and his custom-made "jib arm" to slither in and out of characters' lives. In an Altman movie, the world looks like a solar system: we enter one planet's orbit only to spin off into another's, and then we rocket out to the wide shot, there to view the harmony of all his dancing spheres. As *The Player*'s opening credits roll, the audience gets its first look at the studio's interlocking jigs. During the next several minutes, we will meet most of the movie's characters, we'll hear a variety of crack-brained "pitches"—"*Ghost* meets *The Manchurian Candidate*," for instance, and "*The Gods Must Be Crazy*, except the Coke bottle is now a television actress"—and we'll glimpse the first clue in the movie's thriller plot.

But that's not all. Among the characters trotting in and out of view is the security chief, Walter Stuckel, played by Fred Ward, and although Altman customarily keeps so many conversations buzzing at once that it's impossible to follow them all, we do catch a bit of Walter's. He's nattering on about the greatness of old movies, and particularly about the wonders of the long take—the endless opening crane shot of Orson Welles's *Touch of Evil*, for instance, or the 1948 movie *Rope*, which Alfred Hitchcock directed without any cuts. Walter despises contemporary movies. "I hate all this cut, cut, cut," he says. And then he's gone, and along comes a trio of finance people, and then a tour group of Japanese investors, and then a dozen other plotters and schemers. Finally the credits end, and we recognize what Altman himself has just accomplished: he's shot this entire, dizzying, eight-minute sequence exactly the way Walter would have wanted him to, in a single, swooping crane shot. Without a cut.

Altman spends a lot of that shot peeping into studio windows, the ones where deals are made and pitches delivered. It isn't long before you realize that the windows are like movie screens, and that every time we watch a pitch delivered through one, we're seeing a little movie—a story is being told on a screen.

In fact, screens become a leitmotif in *The Player*; they crop up in nearly every scene, and they're there for a reason. Altman is working out a kind of Hollywood metaphysics. In the eighteenth century, Immanuel Kant caused a "Copernican revolution" in philosophy when he announced that man could never truly know the real world because he was doomed to perceive it through his five limited senses and through the distorting lenses of space and time. Altman adds one more layer of distortion. *Homo hollywoodus* knows even less of the real world because he perceives everything as if it were happening on a screen. It's a sickness, this distortion, and in Tinseltown the sickness is systemic: nobody's immune and nobody's happy about it. And the self-loathing it generates among suspendered honchos and ink-stained wretches alike inevitably arouses alienation and even paranoia.

Which is probably why Griffin becomes so unhinged when he starts receiving menacing unsigned poscards from a struggling screenwriter—apparently one Griffin never got back to. The postcards are fairly explicit. That writer, whoever it is, wants to kill him.

The Player isn't much on plot, but what there is thickens quickly. Griffin tracks down the screenwriter he thinks is threatening him, one David Kahane (Vincent D'Onofrio), whom he finds in a movie theater watching *The Bicycle Thief*. Here is another one of Altman's screens, and there's yet another in the karaoke bar where Kahane takes Griffin for a drink. But the most important screen in *The Player* is the metaphorical one on which Griffin has already discovered Kahane's girlfriend, June (Greta Scacchi). Looking for Kahane, Griffin drives to the writer's house, dials Kahane's number on his mobile phone, and then, under cover of night, peers through the window as June answers. Watching her talk to him on the phone gives Griffin a voyeuristic jolt, a frisson that he can't shake. "It was so exciting and new and strange," he will later tell June, but what he means is that looking at her in this way, as if her window were a movie screen, has made her seem like a star to him—like the costar he requires for the film he's living. (Later, Griffin takes June to Desert Hot Springs, an immaculate spa whose only denizens are so beautiful they look as though they were sent straight from the agency. "Do places like this really exist?" June asks. "Only in the movies," Griffin replies.)

Tim Robbins, who is probably best remembered as the half-crazy minor-league pitcher Nuke Laloosh in *Bull Durham,* is wonderfully cast as Griffin—not just because he's a terrific actor, but also because he has the squinched-up, rubbery face of a newborn baby. That face is like unmolded clay; you can do anything with it. And since Griffin is busily striving to turn himself into the suave leading man of his own living movie, the poses he strikes—of mastery, of sophistication, of know-how—stand out on that baby face in high relief.

Altman has always pretended that he doesn't know much about directing actors, but his work here betrays him. The character of June, for instance, is little more than a postliterate cipher, but Altman draws from Greta Scacchi the warmest, most genuinely sensual performance she's ever given. He lets Dean Stockwell go bananas as a hustling movie producer, lets Richard E. Grant get all neurasthenic and quavery as a hard-pitching screenwriter, and gives the director and sometime actor Sydney Pollack room to chew gum and spout tough-guy aphorisms as Griffin's lawyer; Pollack responds by carving out the perfect portrait of a Player. Best of all, Altman gets an exhilarating, loosey-goosey performance from Whoopi Goldberg, as a police detective who suspects Griffin of murder. There's a scene in the Pasadena police station, with Goldberg twirling a Tampax as she questions Griffin about his sex life, that's destined to be a classic; its capper comes when Griffin tries to defend himself with the kind of high-minded harangue that works only in the movies—and the whole station cracks up in disbelief.

☆

There's a chill at the center of *The Player*. Altman gets us rooting for Griffin by subtle degrees—first, because his job is threatened; later because he's in love and in trouble. But the movie needles us by degrees, too, by gradually exposing Griffin's corruption. If we're cheering Griffin on even though he's a cad (and worse), that makes us somehow accomplices in his perfidy. And, in the end, when he prevails while the nice but decidedly less glamorous folk around him tumble, Altman slathers on the triumphant music and sunshine in a way that may make us squirm. He's not letting anyone off the hook—not even the audience. After all, we're part of the system, too. We're the ones clamoring for "*Ghost* meets *The Manchurian Candidate*"; we're the ones drooling over Bruce and Arnold and Julia and Mel. No one leaves *The Player* with a clear conscience.

Yet what finally keeps this movie from being downright distasteful is its unquenchable glee. "It's a bright guilty world," observed Orson Welles in *The Lady from Shanghai;* he might have been describing the sunbaked, irremediably trivial planet on which Altman's insects scrabble and claw. Coming only two years after the gloom of *Vincent & Theo, The Player* is surprisingly high-spirited and ebullient. For long stretches, Altman's restless camera roams

Lotusland like a merry truffle pig, snurfing out all manner of nuttiness and pretension and squealing with joy as the schemes and reversals and in-jokes fly overhead.

In other words, *The Player* feels like a party. It's layered and trenchant and even profound, but it's also an awful lot of fun. Better still, it looks as though poor, bedeviled Robert Altman had a lot of fun making it. That, in the end, may be the sweetest revenge of all.

Vanity Fair, April 1992

SPIKE LEE: MALCOLM X

Richard Corliss

The movie's first minutes promise fire this time. A *Patton*-size U.S. flag fills the screen and is set ablaze. Video clips of Los Angeles cops pummeling a helpless Rodney King are underlaid with the words of Malcolm X fulminating against the white devil. Flames of black rage gnaw at the fabric of the flag until it is burned into a huge *X*. America, the image says, created Malcolm X in a centuries-old crucible of race hatred. And the legacy of Malcolm, murdered in 1965, helped define the battered field of today's Stars and Stripes.

Spike Lee is a logo maker of genius. It seems as if half of the baseball caps worn by American kids carry the defiant initial *X*—a clever device that raised consciousness of Malcolm and, not incidentally, advertised Lee's movie biography a year before its release.

Now the film arrives, in more than the usual storm of tumult and hype that attends the premiere of a Spike Lee Joint. Even before the shooting began, Lee conferred with Black Muslim minister Louis Farrakhan, an early associate of Malcolm's who has vexed many with his antiwhite, anti-Jewish harangues. Lee also hired a Black Muslim security force as bodyguards on the set. He fought publicly with his distributor (Warner Bros.) and insurer (the Completion Bond Co.) when work on the overbudget film was suspended. Then he solicited and received gifts from black entertainers (Bill Cosby, Oprah Winfrey) to help him complete postproduction. He urged kids to skip school and see *Malcolm X* on its opening day. He discouraged white reporters from interviewing him about the film.

Whatever rancorous agenda this served, it got the film's name in the papers. Lee is also a self-promoter of genius.

He is no filmmaker of genius. And yet you have to cherish, like a guilty conscience, any writer-director who can outrage so many people with a melodrama set in the ghetto tinderbox (*Do the Right Thing*), a musical about skin-tone prejudice among blacks (*School Daze*), and an interracial love and lust story (*Jungle Fever*).

So the big surprise about *Malcolm X* is how ordinary it is. The film is a lavish, linear, way-too-long (three hours plus) storybook of Malcolm's career, the movie equivalent of an authorized biography, a cautious primer for black pride. It is Lee's biggest film, and the least Spikey. At one point in producer Marvin Worth's twenty-six-year hajj to get this movie made, and before he was persuaded that an African American should direct the movie, Norman Jewison (*A Soldier's Story*) wanted to do it. If Jewison had, the product would be about the same. Only the label would be different.

The lure of movie biography is to show the contours in a life of significance. Working from a screenplay written in the late sixties by James Baldwin and Arnold Perl, Lee splays Malcolm's story across a forty-year panorama of Americana (the film cost thirty-four million dollars, but it looks twice as expensive and expansive). In the mid twenties, Malcolm Little's parents are threatened by the Ku Klux Klan. In the thirties he finds both acceptance and isolation in white foster homes and white schools. In the forties Malcolm (embodied with potent charm by Denzel Washington) is a rakish dude, running numbers and lording it over his white mistress Sophia. In the fifties he finds Allah in jail and becomes a minister of the Black Muslim faith under the sect's founder, Elijah Muhammad. In the sixties, with the encouragement of his wife Betty, he breaks from the racist Nation of Islam and pays for this social enlightenment with his life.

Lee sketches Malcolm's life colorfully, if by the numbers. But he falls victim to the danger of movie biography: he elevates Malcolm's importance until the vital historical context is obscured. Malcolm came to prominence in an era of great black oratory. Baldwin, Martin Luther King Jr., Adam Clayton Powell, Eldridge Cleaver, Maya Angelou had no power but in their minds and throats and pens. And what force, what rage, what music they found there.

Malcolm's style was cooler than King's, more lawyerly than evangelical; its bitter logic cut like a knife at the throat of complacent white America. Even in the time of Malcolm's most toxic demagoguery—defaming liberals as white devils, civil rights heroes as Uncle Toms, and Jews as sapping "the very lifeblood of the so-called Negroes to maintain the state of Israel"—his steely charisma beguiled the white media. In Harlem he was something more than a diversion: he was the prophet of the black male underclass. "It was manhood time," says Al Freeman Jr., who played Malcolm in the TV miniseries "Roots II" and is Elijah Muhammad here.

Lee could have scared folks by foregrounding Malcolm's seductive racism. But he takes the safe route, viewing his subject less as a flamethrower of incendiary rhetoric than as a victim. Until his late break with the Black Muslims, Malcolm is mostly a tool: of white racists, black gangsters, jail-cell preachers, and the Hon. Elijah Muhammad. Malcolm's uniqueness is lost, his personality blurred. He begins as Little and ends as X: still the unknown.

Lee is more a producer—a hustler after the big picture, an entrepreneur of scalding emotions—than a director. He is not one to attend to the shading of character. As Washington says, "He basically left me alone and let me run with it." Lee's moods had opposite effects on the excellent actresses who play Malcolm's wife and his white hussy. "He laughs, laughs large," says Angela Bassett (Betty). "He's energy plus." But Kate Vernon (Sophia) says, "He was belligerent and disrespectful in tone toward me. There's a boys' club, and women are not allowed—especially white women. I hated the idea of feeling excluded because I was white. The set was tense. I've heard all his sets are tense."

If so, that's because the director sees so much riding on each of his films: the future of cinema, precious testimony from an African American perspective, and, not least, the reputation—carefully nourished, always vulnerable—of Spike Lee. "Spike was on the set," recalls an observer who was close to the shooting, "and a guy comes up and tells him, 'I know you! I saw your film *Boyz N the Hood*.'" Lee was miffed, but the crew members laughed seditiously. They surely knew that John Singleton's *Boyz N the Hood* earned about as much money as *Jungle Fever* and *Do the Right Thing* did together. Lee doesn't care to be overtaken by the young black directors whose careers his success helped make possible.

Nor would he settle for a Malcolm-like niche in movie history: the radical prophet who achieved his stature posthumously. Lee would rather be a top-grossing auteur now than a biopic subject later. Perhaps that is why his movie is so stately, reverent, and academic, so suitable for the Oscars with which Hollywood rewards high-minded mediocrity. Some other director will have to find a way to merge the danger of a brilliant, racist orator with the seismic jolt of energized filmmaking. That picture will be worth skipping school for.

Moviegoers may accept Lee's burning logo and tepid melodrama as cinema's vision of Malcolm X now. They can hope for the fire next time.

Time, November 23, 1992

THE STAR AS GENRE

The earliest moguls didn't announce the names of their films' leading players because they were afraid of the talent becoming power brokers. Then, in 1910, a rival producer revealed that "the Biograph Girl" was actually one Florence Lawrence, and the rest has been alternately beguiling and maddening history.

"The little fellow" became Charlie Chaplin—and Charles Chaplin ended up owning, and bankrolling, his own studio. He was a rare exception. For others, the power of stardom could prove as illusory as the glamour worlds they inhabited on screen. To take just one ferinstance: MGM, the studio that boasted "more stars than there are in heaven," produced and released "Crawford pictures," not tearjerkers with Joan Crawford in them; but when, after a decade and a half of popularity, Crawford pictures stopped being box office, L. B. Mayer gave Joan her walking papers.

In today's dubiously evolved Hollywood, studios still have power, but they don't have stars. For better and for worse, stars are independent agents and they have power, too—enough, in some cases, to get a picture made independently and then find a studio to buy it. Others still need to be asked. And ask the studios will; no ticket buyer is enticed to the multiplex to watch a corporate logo. And if a previously unremarked (and perhaps still unremarkable) toiler in the cinevineyard ends up a key component of a runaway hit film, the world awakens the next morning to learn that Sharon Stone's new deal is in the multimillions.

But we're above that sort of thing here. This chapter concerns itself with who's hot and who's not only insofar as it affects the quality of film experience that results: the movies that are conceived and made in a particular way because a star exists to be showcased, and the movies that somehow change, in or after the act of making, because a star has emerged. Jay Carr takes a look at some of today's putative stars—and undeniably terrific actors—and wonders why they can't do and be what Tracy and Cagney and Stanwyck did and were. Morris Dickstein analyzes a few of John Wayne's key roles and the integrity that transcended a lot of political incorrectness in his life and career. Peter Rainer takes on *Top Gun* and demonstrates that vacuous stardom often goes hand in hand with incoherent filmmaking. Andrew Sarris discovers Julia Roberts in *Pretty Woman* and exults that, no matter how unworthy the surrounding movie, true stardom will out. With *Body of Evidence* as main exhibit, David Denby explains why Madonna will never be a movie star, or even a credible Dietrich imitator. And Gary Arnold not only finds the neglected *Candyman* a better-than-average horror movie, but argues that C-list actress Virginia Madsen, "the gutsiest leading lady in contemporary movies," has beauty, intelligence, and emotional validity to burn.

ON WHY THE STARS DON'T SHINE AS THEY USED TO

Jay Carr

Despite the presence of Meryl Streep and Robert De Niro, *Falling in Love* is a dull film, an insipid story of nonconsummation, not worth rehashing except for one singular moment that has nothing to do with the storyline. It comes when De Niro, playing one of his many hesitations as a married construction engineer who wants to sleep with Streep but can't allow himself to, makes the brave decision to project character with facial expression and presence alone, by just standing there. With his good-sport smile, his I-can-take-it good humor, and the laugh lines around his eyes, he evokes, for an uncanny moment, the late Spencer Tracy.

It isn't that De Niro is trying to imitate Tracy. He's trying, in his own way, to project the rugged decency Tracy used to project with such consistency and such deceptive simplicity. The moment isn't sustained long—nothing in the film is. But the distance between Tracy's instant authority in the many roles he made his own and De Niro's self-conscious internalizing seems emblematic of the difference between Hollywood stars of today and those of fifty years ago. Today's stars probably have an ethical edge on yesterday's. Many came out of the idealistic sixties when the idea of stardom's ties to the monolithic Hollywood studio system—today more corporate than ever—was repugnant. As today's society is different, today's stars are moved by different imperatives—one being a willingness to disappear in a character.

But today's stars don't—and probably won't—have the same hold upon the public as yesterday's. They aren't impelled to reinvent themselves in terms of yesterday's iconlike mystiques. Yesterday's stars thought it a virtue to change little from film to film while reinforcing the carefully groomed screen personas that define Hollywood stardom. There just aren't many actors we can trust to deliver the same outsize, unique qualities that animated film after Old Hollywood film. Think about it a minute. Imagine yourself a casting director, hired to remake Hollywood's classics. How would you go about finding contemporary equivalents to yesterday's stars? Possibly you could get away with starring Sam Shepard in a remake of Gary Cooper's *High Noon;* both project taciturn, frontier strength. But how would you make the equivalent of a Tracy-Hepburn comedy? Or a Hepburn drama? Streep and Glenn Close have often been compared to Katharine Hepburn, especially Close, who, aside from a superficial physical resemblance, projects some of Hepburn's strength of character. But Streep and Close have little in common with what Hepburn represents. At their best, they project spirituality in working-class people. When Streep goes bowling in *The Deer Hunter,* she makes it seem natural, even incandescent. If Hepburn were to go bowling, she'd carry it off—she always does—but the bowling alley wouldn't seem her natural habitat. She'd seem to be pursuing an eccentricity. Today's actors pursue naturalistic, psychological truth. Yesterday's stars may have seemed to be playing the same character from film to film. But, while seemingly superficial, they actually cut deeper, projecting psychic truths and psychic energies in stylized ways. The best of them compelled assent to the archetypes into which they transformed themselves over the years.

Today's stars are more rational, possibly even more puritanical, in their attitudes toward their work. Yesterday's seemed to know instinctively that movies work best on the level of dreams. They aimed at something more primal. The high gloss of studio artifice on so many of those great old movies is deceptive. Beneath it, they projected gut-level stuff. With all its well-publicized evils, the studio system gave actors the necessary chance to learn how to do this in movie after assembly-line movie. Catering to stars, obnoxious as it may sound in theory, wasn't all bad.

Those rampaging, unashamed egos sometimes generated magic. If you doubt it, compare two film versions of W. Somerset Maugham's novels—*The Razor's Edge* with Bill Murray and the 1934 *Of Human Bondage* with Bette Davis. Murray brings a sweet sixties idealism to *Razor's Edge,* and it goes limp. Leslie Howard, Maugham's thinly veiled portrayal of himself, is passive, too, in *Of Human Bondage.* But while Murray is willing to let things happen, Davis makes them happen as the predatory waitress who makes Howard's life a misery. Davis went for broke, became a star. Will counts for something, but not as much as the belief that stardom is everything, a notion that's suspect today, along with glamour.

Garbo Talks, which wanted to be a sweet little New York Jewish liberal comedy, was an embarrassment because it invoked Garbo's presence and couldn't come anywhere near delivering. There's no contemporary equivalent to Garbo. Who can believe in the kind of panache she unleashes in *Grand Hotel* as she sweeps across the lobby and flamboyantly sighs, "I have never been so tired in my life!" We have no Garbo, nor, I fear, do we have a contemporary equivalent to Cary Grant. Who seems likely to cultivate his kind of febrile brilliance, his ability to impart a dark underside to graceful gaiety? For a while it looked as if we might have a contemporary Jimmy Cagney—at least in the second of his two careers, as hair-trigger tough guy—in Al Pacino, who simmers with nervous energy that seems to leak through the balls of his feet. Pacino seems to be dancing atop a hot griddle. He has the raw material, but after the excess of *Scarface* it's apparent that he has to go back and refine it until he can approach Cagney's economy and precision.

Cagney's extraordinary concentration and fluidity as a dancer have no contemporary Hollywood equivalent. Who can step into a dance routine, as Cagney did in *Footlight Parade,* and instantly transform it with a liquid step and hands scooping space from a crowded stage? Fred Astaire represents an elegance that belongs to a vanished past. Clint Eastwood seems a lesser John Wayne, cut off from the mythic roots Wayne tapped. Paul Newman was probably our best shot at a Clark Gable, but he's eased off into infrequent high-minded efforts. Goldie Hawn may yet approximate Gable's wife, Carole Lombard, the queen of screwball comedy; the jury's still out. Who else? Joan Crawford? Maybe Faye Dunaway, if she gets her act together, but Dunaway lately has seemed to parody prematurely a persona she hasn't yet made her own. And who's going to give us anything as cracklingly complex as Barbara Stanwyck, the fierce moll from the wrong side of the tracks?

The list could go on. Where's our Bogart? Our Jimmy Stewart, with his frontier virtues of laconic toughness and steely will as he backs and stumbles into the limelight? The eighties reissue of the films he made for Alfred Hitchcock in the fifties showed a new generation how unique his stammering charm remains. Stewart made fewer junk films than most, but the whole point was that we didn't mind junk with the right stars. They transformed it, and not just with strength of personality, willing it to life. Those old-timers took stardom seriously. Many were craftspeople.

True, it was easier to seize the public mind in the thirties and forties, before TV, when movies had a virtual monopoly on our shared reservoir of pop imagery. Still, stars worked at being stars. Memoir after memoir will remove any doubt you might have about what experts yesterday's glamour queens were about lighting, camera angles, and what they felt were their prerogatives. Barbra Streisand could, if she got serious, become a funky equivalent to Dietrich and eventually surpass her. She's willing to display a vulnerability Dietrich was incapable of. The two share only one important thing: an unerring instinct for what serves them and the temperament to insist on it. It's a start. Those great old presences were born in huge, determined egos, not egalitarian self-effacement. Where are today's Hollywood icons? You tell me.

Boston Globe, December 2, 1984

ON JOHN WAYNE

■▪■

Morris Dickstein

The flood of articles about the death of John Wayne has already outstripped the drawn-out fascination with the expiring of Hubert Humphrey and may yet overtake the lamentations over Elvis Presley. All the obituaries agree with the U.S. Congress that there was something especially American about John Wayne. The articles quickly turn into nostalgic elegies for an old order of firm masculine virtues and uncomplicated moral solutions. But it takes an intelligent director to crystallize a great screen persona. And Wayne's best directors, John Ford and Howard Hawks, both grasped the ambiguity of the Western myth as Wayne helped them to embody it.

We tend to remember Wayne as a bulky, aging prop of law and order, but when he burst into stardom in 1939 as the Ringo Kid in Ford's *Stagecoach,* he played an escaped convict determined to avenge the death of his father and brother. At the end of the film, his task accomplished, he takes off with a prostitute (Claire Trevor) for his ranch across the border—"saved from the blessings of civilization."

American movies can boast few shots more exhilarating than our first sight of this young outlaw prince standing with his gun and gear in the path of the stagecoach, whose passengers form a microcosm of the social classes. The film deftly exposes its respectable characters as hypocrites, snobs, and even thieves. It endows outcasts Wayne, Trevor, and Thomas Mitchell (as a drunken doctor-"philosopher") with warmth and generous humanity, unstifled by social bias. This is the populist Ford, who was soon to make *The Grapes of Wrath,* with its bleak images of dispossessed community. In *Stagecoach,* the Western hero is not yet obsolete, but an increasingly rigid society has little use for the individual values he represents.

Wayne's next great Western with Ford, *Fort Apache* ('48), the first film of the so-called cavalry trilogy, situates the actor in an even more antiestablishment context amid conflicting social values. Philip French wrote that Wayne "could never figure in a movie that demands much interior complexity in its hero; the complexity, if sought, must come from the film's structure, as in *The Searchers* and

The Man Who Shot Liberty Valance." Ford relied on dual protagonists, coupling Wayne with Henry Fonda in *Fort Apache* and with Jimmy Stewart in *Liberty Valance.*

Fort Apache is surprisingly antimilitary. Wayne understands and sympathizes with the Indians, speaks their language, and tries, above all, to keep peace, but Fonda, as the West Point–educated martinet, chooses disastrously to go by the book. Ford's deepest Irish loyalties are to native wisdom, family, community, and personal honor; in his hands Wayne becomes the vehicle of these supple and tolerant values.

Wayne in *Fort Apache* is Ford's natural man. Yet he is also, like all Western heroes since Owen Wister's Virginian, a gentleman who lives by an intuitive code that makes society's rules seem stiff and arbitrary by comparison. Wayne's courtly treatment of Claire Trevor in *Stagecoach,* his refusal to judge her by her social standing or past mistakes, as well as her help in delivering the child of an army wife (Louise Platt) who had shunned her, expose sanctimonious official morality that takes little account of a person's inner worth.

His first Western with Hawks, *Red River* (filmed '46, released '48), marks a subtle but decisive shift in the actor's screen personality. The unspoiled kid initiated into manhood in *Stagecoach* here becomes an aging but tenacious father figure, set off against the boyish and sensitive Montgomery Clift (in his true film debut), the adopted son he has groomed to inherit his cattle empire. The casual masculinity of the Fordian hero gives way to a brutal toughness obsessed with obedience to authority. Wayne here embodies the blind stubbornness that marks the Fonda character, in addition to his own new hypermasculinity, while Clift becomes the vehicle for Wayne's reasonable tolerance.

Like Ford, Hawks never takes the Western myth at face value; instead he exploits its moral ambiguity. He sees how self-reliance can devolve into paranoid isolation, how the law of the gun can legitimize arbitrary violence, how toughness can degenerate into crass brutality, how emotional restraint can cover emotional deadness, how strong leadership can lead to unbridled power.

Those who criticize the Western myth and say it led to Vietnam don't see how that myth, in the hands of its subtler creators, very early criticized itself. Those who attack John Wayne for his screen persona or his politics don't notice the darker shadings of his best roles, the ones for which he'll ultimately be remembered.

Wayne later speculated that John Ford hadn't realized Wayne could act until he saw *Red River*. Ford very quickly cast him as an older man on his last Indian campaign in *She Wore a Yellow Ribbon* ('49), as a tough, wayward, but inwardly tender husband and father in *Rio Grande* ('50), and most memorably as an ex-soldier with a shady past in *The Searchers* ('56).

In *The Searchers*, Wayne, relentlessly set on avenging the murder of his brother's family, tracks the Indian culprits for years with inhuman ferocity, and nearly kills his own kidnapped niece (Natalie Wood)—the object of his quest—when he finds that she has been turned into an Indian squaw, sexually dishonored. Wayne never played a figure more isolated, more pathologically obsessed, more driven by hatred. Yet the character, Ethan Edwards, still lives within the terms of the Western code. A hero, he's someone who must finally be thwarted and saved from himself, just as Wayne's Thomas Dunson is saved from himself in *Red River*. When this brooding, steel-cold, unapproachable man takes his niece in his arms instead of killing her, it's one of the magical moments of the American cinema, though miles away from the first unspotted apparition of the Ringo Kid in *Stagecoach*. Vengeance and violence have become as problematic as Wayne's personality. Society now administers "justice" and violence more impersonally; the individuality of the Western hero has become both troublesome and irrelevant.

This last chapter of the cowboy's fate is a story told in many late Westerns, but nowhere better than in Ford's last great film, *The Man Who Shot Liberty Valance* ('62). The story begins with preparations for Tom Doniphon's (Wayne's) funeral: the plot is a flashback from a more modern and civilized West in which he no longer has a place. Only a few people remember him from his better days. A gawky Jimmy Stewart plays a transplanted Easterner, Ransom Stoddard, whom Doniphon had protected but whose fortune rose as Doniphon's declined. The territory has become a state; the tenderfoot has won the girl they both loved and become the new state's first senator, though his success derives from the forgotten man's prowess with a gun—it was Wayne, not Stewart, who secretly shot the vicious Liberty Valance (Lee Marvin). By saving Stewart's life and launching his career, by ridding the town of its last lawless men, Wayne, like all Western heroes, initiated his own extinction and prepared the way for the rule of law that made him unnecessary, a nuisance. The Western—and its hero—not only act out their own critique but write their own elegy.

John Wayne was indeed a nuisance in his last years, when he became a willing symbol of the know-nothing right, an American caricature. But he executed the downward curve of his own personal legend with a lumbering but unshakable dignity.

He didn't understand much, but he understood his screen personality well and played out its gruff ambiguities to the hilt. "I played parts men could identify with," he once said. "Although my characters might do cruel or rough things, they were never mean or petty."

Neither was he.

In These Times, June 27, 1979

TOM CRUISE: TOP GUN

■■■

Peter Rainer

Don Simpson and Jerry Bruckheimer, the designer-movie mavens who produced *Flashdance* and *Beverly Hills Cop,* have pitched their penchant for high concept *very* high this time out—into the stratosphere. Their concoction, *Top Gun,* is about world-class jet fighter pilots, and at least one-fourth of it takes place above the clouds. Too bad the entire movie wasn't airborne; whenever the story touches down, it falls apart in the hand like thousand-year-old parchment.

This is the sort of miserably conceived movie, written by Jim Cash and Jack Epps Jr., and directed by Tony Scott, that could have been redeemed only by star power of the highest wattage. Movie stars can sometimes create their own independent drama with a film; their creative tensions, their allure, become the real subject of the movie. But *Top Gun* has Tom Cruise, as "Maverick" Mitchell, the cockpit joy boy who makes it into the Navy's elite Fighter Weapons School at San Diego's Miramar Naval Air Station. Cruise doesn't hold the screen like a movie star, although to a portion of the teen audience he certainly passes for a star. He strikes designer-jeans poses, and his blank, fixated stare and teeth-baring smile make him seem as flat and despiritualized as a Sunset Strip billboard portrait. (A friend suggested the film be retitled *Top Gum.*) Cruise wasn't bad in *Risky Business* ('83); his adolescent gallivanting suited him. But *Top Gun* calls for a mesmeric hell-raiser, someone with a radioactive core of danger. "When I first saw you, you were larger than life," smitten astrophysicist Charlotte "Charlie" Blackwood (Kelly McGillis) tells him late in the movie. How's that again?

Maverick is supposed to be the kind of nonconforming aerialist who both rankles the military and represents its highest hope. He doesn't fly by the rules, he's a menace to his co–top gunners in their joint maneuvers, but he's still the kind of guy you'd want in a pinch when the MiGs start firing at your tail. It's a variation on Gordon Liddy's Watergate poser: "If you were in a sinking ship, would you want me in the boat with you or John Dean?" (How about neither?) Maverick comes from a flying background; his father, shot down over Vietnam in ignominious, still-classified circumstances, was a daredevil, too. So it's in the boy's blood to redeem his father's name and prove he's the best. (*An Officer and a Gentleman,* anyone?)

His chief competition in the Fighter School, "Iceman" (Val Kilmer), derides Maverick's showboating. No matter. This guy "feels the need for speed." The film is full of the kind of pushing-the-edge-of-the-envelope jargon that recalls far happier days aloft in *The Right Stuff.* The characters talk about "pulling Gs" and "yanking and banking," but don't be gulled into mistaking this stuff for authenticity. This is, after all, the kind of movie in which an international incident with the Russians is concocted just so the hero can feel good about himself at the end. (I wouldn't trust its research on nonmilitary matters, either. At one point Maverick, listening to Otis Redding's 1968 recording of "Dock of the Bay," recalls how his parents used to listen to the song when he was a kid. But his father was killed in 1965. Welcome to the Twilight Zone.)

The script for this movie could have been spliced together with taffeta and Krazy Glue. Charlie the astrophysicist comes on like a savvy smart cookie, but might as well be an airheaded hausfrau. The filmmakers have no faith in this woman's brains; she's in the movie to pull some Gs in the romance department, although Maverick seems more interested in beating out Iceman for the top gun best-flyer plaque. That's where the real romantic juices are. The filmmakers seem to know it, too. McGillis doesn't click with Cruise; her passion for him resembles plain old lust, but it's fobbed off as true love. The filmmakers dutifully wedge in a few titillation scenes. Maverick shows up shirtless in the elevator with Charlie, in a scene that looks tacked on after the film was already shot (McGillis' hair doesn't match her hair in the rest of the movie).

Then there's the obligatory bedding-down scene, which appears to have been photographed through turquoise lacquer. (Call it "Night of the Blue Tongues.")

The aerial scenes are where the movie's real coupling takes place. They're kinesthetic in an abstract way, since you're never quite sure who's attacking whom, or from where or why. (It wouldn't have killed the filmmakers to explain what a MiG is—some in the audience thought our boys were firing at "Micks." The IRA is coming!) The confusion in the sky is typical of the movie, which specializes in anything-for-an-effect image clusters thrummed to a rock beat. Even an airmen's volleyball game is edited into a clatter of soaring-ball and beefcake shots. There are a few good moments from Anthony Edwards's "Goose"—Maverick's easygoing radar intercept buddy—and the film's notion that top gunners are spiritual cousins of rock stars is intriguing. But it's also commercially calculating, and the calculation in *Top Gun* is so ruthless and relentless that it's like a slap in the face to the audience.

The Top Gun school was supposedly created in the late sixties because the American fighter pilots' kill ratio—the ratio of enemy to American planes shot down—has been in decline since World War II. The rock-star joy boys in *Top Gun,* loop-de-looping in their $35 million F-14 Tom Cats, are portrayed as America's finest. They're Right Stuff guys. But the movie never gets into how these guys cope with peacetime. Wouldn't they secretly itch for a confrontation with the enemy just to demonstrate their skills in a real-life situation? The movie never digs into the paradox of warriors whose lives are geared for a war that may never come. That's why the filmmakers cook up a MiG fracas at the end; they can't bear to see all that training go to waste. And so we watch enemy planes being incinerated in the air, video game–style, as the audience applauds each kill.

Don Simpson has been quoted as saying that he and his partner "simply love movies, and we want to make the kind of movies that you can see on a Saturday night with a Coke and a box of popcorn." In other words, movie-movies. But even kick-up-your-heels date-night movies have to deliver. Simpson and Bruckheimer are wizards of a small, slickster's domain, where studio market research has been sleeked into an aesthetic style and previous hits are tarted up and recycled. (Simpson was head of production for Paramount when its *Officer and a Gentleman* was in the works.) *Top Gun* doesn't provide the emotional satisfactions of anything as basic as a coherent plot, a good love story, believable characterizations. When, for example, Maverick finds out the truth about his father, the moment is tossed away like a used sparkplug. The film is directed not by dramatic instinct but by boardroom fiat.

Top Gun, by itself, isn't worth blowing a gasket over. But it's symptomatic of the sort of current commercial thinking that believes all you have to give a young audience now to create a hit is a star and a soundtrack album and a checklist of pre-approved elements, like jingoism and snazzy duds. Never mind if they add up to nothing; never mind if this demeans the audience and leaves them with nothing memorable they can take home from the theater. Except, perhaps, the taste of Coke and popcorn.

Los Angeles Herald Examiner, May 16, 1986

JULIA ROBERTS: PRETTY WOMAN

Andrew Sarris

Nobody professes a desire to become a star anymore. The very word has acquired a set of ironic quotes around it to evoke an ego trip from the bygone days of the Hollywood studio system. The common middlebrow wisdom on the subject holds that "stars" were always content to "play themselves" rather than parts that were unlike them. Their "range" was considered narrow. They were mere "personalities." For "real" acting you had to go to Broadway or Piccadilly. The art of acting was thereby confused with the art of disguise.

I am exaggerating for polemical purposes, of course, but not by much. To this day there lingers guilt and shame about a successful movie career, thus inhibiting supposedly serious film critics from analyzing the anatomy of stardom. In recent years revisionist film historians have resorted to the terms "icon" and even "axiom" in order to make the pleasure principle in moviegoing seem profound.

As a revisionist of long standing, I sometimes tire of academic stratagems to conceal the fact that beautiful women and virile men dramatically realized and dynamically visualized provide most of the motivation for moviegoing. They are the stuff our dreams are made of. And so two cheers for the extinct studio system, and a toast to the birth of a new star, namely Julia Roberts in *Pretty Woman,* a Pygmalion–Cinderella–*Born Yesterday* love story that managed to sink *The Hunt for Red October* at the box office before the *Teenage Mutant Ninja Turtles* swept the cinema back to the nursery. I cannot remember the last time a female performance of verve, charm, and subtlety eclipsed a hyped-up, all-male macho romance.

I first noticed Miss Roberts, the kid sister of the eccentric and erratic Eric Roberts, in *Mystic Pizza.* She played the ethnic waitress trying to sleep her way into an Ivy League marriage. The character was set up for the usual humiliation scenes, and Roberts handled them with a toughness that never spilled over into coarseness, and a bravado that never lapsed into bombast. But I was distracted by the mechanical construction of the "Three Coins in the Pizza" plot to the point that I didn't single her out from the rest of the ultracompetent ensemble.

My first epiphany with Roberts occurred at a screening of *Steel Magnolias.* Most of my colleagues in the critical fraternity despised this orgy of female character shtik, as well they should have. But quite by accident I had happened to see the Off-Broadway production, in which the actress who played the doomed, diabetic young wife and mother had a voice that throbbed with premonitory pathos from the minute she walked onstage. By contrast, Roberts treated the same role on the screen as if she were just an ordinarily bouncy-moody bride-to-be until the dramatic machinery ground the joy out of her with a desperate medical dilemma. The ability of Miss Roberts to shift emotional gears from low to high without the slightest trace of screechy hysteria made her for me the supporting actress of the year. I hadn't felt such pride in my fantasy talent-scout expertise since 1962, when I touted Roger Vadim's discovery of Catherine Deneuve in *Tales of Paris.*

Consequently, when people suddenly "discovered" Julia Roberts in *Pretty Woman,* I felt a childish twinge of vindication. She's got "It," whatever It is in the nineties. Richard Gere, on a comeback trail of his own after his modest success in *Internal Affairs,* provides her with a sufficiently charming upscale escort evolving unbelievably from Donald Trump to Henry Higgins as he conducts the hooker played by Roberts from the gutter to the penthouse. Without Roberts, however, *Pretty Woman* would not be worth seeing, and that is about as good an indication as anything that a star has arrived.

To begin with, a hooker as beautiful as she would not have to turn tricks from passing cars on Hollywood Boulevard, particularly since it is established that she has scrupulously refrained from the use of drugs and pimps. She would be more in the position of Jane Fonda's elegant lady of the evening in *Klute* ('71). Movies have gotten so gross and obvious, however, that Roberts has to be costumed and bewigged as if to pass for a transvestite in Times Square. That Roberts survives her gaudy bawd entrance with any dramatic credibility is due more to *her* skills than those of director Garry Marshall and scenarist J. F. Lawton. The very clumsy exposition in which "roommates" played by Roberts and Laura San Giacomo— much more cartoonishly sluttish than she was in *sex, lies & videotape* —try to pretend that they are controlling their own destinies as they practice their sordid profession is acidic fantasizing at its worst.

But once Roberts is let loose on Rodeo Drive, she demonstrates a Chekhovian flair for mingling farce and pathos with force and panache. Her face is too boldly featured to linger enigmatically in repose. It is a jangling symphony of loosened lips, wildly probing eyes, a nose as defiant as her chin, and a potentiality for volcanic amusement. By conventional standards her beauty is flawed to the degree that separates the star from the starlet. When two bitchy salesclerks snub her, she projects pain so deeply and so expressively and yet so discreetly that her measure of vengeful vindication is richly earned, and the audience delights in her social deliverance. When her lover-mentor betrays her for business reasons, she summons a heroic pride without grandstanding for the kids in the balcony.

Marshall and Lawton serve Roberts well in leading her past the potentially buffoonish hazards of social climbing. At crucial points, true gentlemen such as Ralph Bellamy's courtly industrialist and Hector Elizondo's considerate hotelier exemplify Eliza Doolittle's insight in Shaw's *Pygmalion* that what makes a lady is being treated like a lady. The movie still gets its giggles from the gaffes and unladylike exuberance of the "pretty woman," but there is a warm complicity and a rooting rapport in the laughter.

The director and the scenarist are less successful in "reforming" and "humanizing" Gere's corporate vulture into a productive participant in the reindustrialization of America. Of course, it would have been too much to expect that the movie's sentimentality would stop at the door to the boardroom. And it is not exactly original to have Roberts sob at a performance of Verdi's *La*

Traviata after Cher has sobbed at a performance of Puccini's *La Bohème* in *Moonstruck*. Even here I would give Roberts the edge for suggesting more spiritual growth through the experience than Cher's characterization could envisage in its relentlessly lowbrow ethnicity.

I have no idea how far Miss Roberts will go, or how long she will be given opportunities to excel. A career even for the most talented star is much more perilous today than it was in the more work-ethic-oriented past. As of now, this column must content itself with serving as a progress report and a professional love letter. Julia Roberts, you're good. In the Hawksian sense, of course.

New York Observer, April 16, 1990

MADONNA: BODY OF EVIDENCE

David Denby

In *Body of Evidence*, Madonna plays a woman named Rebecca who's on trial for murder. But let's not be silly: Madonna cannot create a character; she cannot yield herself to any fantasy except her own—that she is single-handedly liberating America from its hypocrisies and hangups. The movie, nominally a courtroom drama, is actually just a pretense to exploit the public's fascination with Madonna's sex life, and perhaps the most pathetic thing about it is that the people who made it think they are doing something really dirty. Every time Rebecca reveals some secret, and the prosecuting attorney (Joe Mantegna) says, "You mean you used . . . *handcuffs?*" the extras in the courtroom all murmur *rhubarb kartoffel, rhubarb kartoffel*, or whatever it is that extras are told to murmur in order to create a rumble of consternation. Oooh, shocking! Rhubarb kartoffel!

Onscreen, Madonna is a hot bore, a terrible naked actress. She may pour melted wax on poor Willem Dafoe's privates, but honestly, in *Double Indemnity,* a movie made a half-century ago, the fully dressed Barbara Stanwyck conveyed more dirty lust just by *acting* with her incomparable smoky voice. Since *Body of Evidence* is inept in every way, picking on Madonna may seem unfair,

Madonna contemplates her Muse in *Body of Evidence*. (© 1992 Metro-Goldwyn-Mayer, Inc. All Rights Reserved. Photo courtesy of MGM/UA Home Video, Inc., a subsidiary of Metro-Goldwyn-Mayer, Inc.)

but she obviously wants to be a movie star, and it may be worth saying why she doesn't qualify.

To begin with, her speaking voice is thin and metallic. The director, Uli Edel, is German and may not hear the tin writing in Brad Mirman's screenplay, but surely he can hear the tin in Madonna's voice? Edel doesn't help her there, and his lighting annihilates her. He favors huge swatches of alienating white light, and by the time he and cinematographer Doug Milsome get done illuminating her face, she looks like a gleaming white wafer. There's no depth or range of expression to the face—it's about as sexy as a sundial. In a rock video, she's whirling around and singing, so if you can't see her it doesn't really matter, but in *Body of Evidence* the dramatic effect depends on our "reading" the heroine's ambiguous face (is she telling the truth?), and the harsh lighting reveals only that Madonna cannot hold a closeup. Her face has nothing to say. For a movie actress, that's the point of no return.

Spreading herself out on the floor or climbing atop a car in a parking lot and raising her skirt for Dafoe, she's a coarse, unmysterious object, a seeming escapee from *The Robin Byrd Show*. Madonna plays her self-flattering myth—a naughty girl who's too honest to pretend she's good, a woman so truthful, doing what the rest of us only dream of doing, that she will free us from our lies. But Madonna also makes an attempt to merge her persona with Marlene Dietrich's, wearing a suit and beret at one point, as if she were a dazzling, svelte dish like Dietrich. This is a hapless mistake. Dietrich never relinquished her haughty reserve: the essence of her glamour was the imagined perfection of what she *withheld*. The result was that she was treated as a sex goddess, whereas Madonna, in this movie, is treated as a nasty whore. A pop star can be overexposed, but a movie star cannot. There must be some mystery, or else she doesn't survive onscreen—except in porny flicks.

This movie makes *Basic Instinct* look like a masterpiece. In the cheesy opening sequence, the camera travels up the steps in a stone mansion as lightning flashes through the windows. But all of this menacing atmosphere leads to nothing more powerful than a man sitting in bed looking at a homemade sex video. Is the opening meant to be a parody of gothic thrillers? Where's the punchline? The man is dead the next morning and Rebecca, his lover and the beneficiary of his will, is accused of murdering him. According to the prosecuting attorney, she knew he had a bad heart yet made love to him so wildly that she killed him. The screenplay is so poorly written that one can't tell at first whether this idea is meant as parody either. But no, the filmmakers are serious, and the prosecutor accuses Rebecca of having attempted to screw *other* men to death as well. One of them, a survivor, is played by a shamefaced Frank Langella as a mere shell of a man (too much wax put out his candle).

Though millions of men rape and abuse women every year, the cinema has shown a remarkable interest recently in the murdering sexual *woman*. I suppose there is nothing for us to do but thank Hollywood for bringing this pressing social issue to light.

Dafoe gets to play the victim-sap this time, and he makes me realize how good Michael Douglas is. Dafoe has always had a weighted, overdeliberate method of speaking, as if he were prepping for a job as Charlton Heston's dialogue coach, but here, as Rebecca's hotshot attorney, he is ludicrous. Given that Madonna has only one thing on her mind, his tormented face and dawn-of-consciousness delivery seem more than a little out of it. The audience started giggling at his sexual anguish early in the show and never stopped. As for the other actors, Mantegna looks bored, and Anne Archer, as the dead man's secretary and Madonna's rival, is weepy and creepy. A shadow of crude mediocrity hangs over all of them. Really, I don't get it. Did all these people really want to work with Uli Edel on the basis of his bleak, antagonistic direction of *Last Exit to Brooklyn*? Edel seems ill at ease with human beings, who, unfortunately, are the material a movie director has to work with.

Does *Body of Evidence* make it as a trash classic, a howl for the ages? No. Edel doesn't have enough fantasy and warmth to make enjoyable trash. The only dream here is Madonna's—that men will become so aroused by her they will begin dropping dead all over the place. The movie might, however, be a gift-wrapped package to those academics who make a career of writing analytical papers about the wealthy sex icon. *Body of Evidence* is so denuded of human interest and plausibility that the power relations in it are as clear as the bones of a skeleton. So much to deconstruct! *Body of Evidence* may die in the theaters, but it should keep the academic quarterlies humming.

New York, January 25, 1993

VIRGINIA MADSEN: CANDYMAN

Gary Arnold

Virginia Madsen must be the gutsiest leading lady in contemporary movies. This provocative—but maybe not so enviable—distinction dates back at least as far as the HBO movie *Long Gone* ('87). Miss Madsen confirmed her industrial-strength mantrap credentials in no uncertain terms while impersonating the brazen, carnal schemer who was always a few steps ahead of her chosen loverboy, Don Johnson, in Dennis Hopper's *The Hot Spot* ('90).

Her willingness to boldly go where more discreet and image-conscious actresses would turn back, in perfectly understandable alarm, is reconfirmed by *Candyman,* a horror thriller that operates several astute and imaginative levels above the genre norm. The British writer-director Bernard Rose seems to signal this elevation by commencing with aerial vistas of Chicago. These images culminate in a preview of the demonic threat later unveiled when Tony Todd enters as the title character, a supernatural fiend who haunts the Cabrini Green housing projects and takes a very special, fateful interest in the heroine.

Although Madsen resolved to avoid further nude scenes after *The Hot Spot,* she evidently found it prudent to backslide in order to authenticate a few of the spectacles envisioned by Rose, who transposes a Clive Barker story from Liverpool to Chicago. At once voluptuous and technically skilled, Madsen makes a sounder case for nude exposure than most people. However, *Candyman* takes lurid advantage, asking her to appear simultaneously blood-spattered and naked at one juncture.

Undaunted, she persuades you that she's *still in character* while posed grotesquely. It's a gift, one that's easy to overlook and under-valued. The movie would be in a bind if she couldn't replace a knowing, worldly, intrepid feminine identity with a vulnerable and victimized one when necessary. A virtuoso shock sequence in which she and Todd appear to exchange a soul kiss swarming with bees ought to earn her special cult-film eminence. Talk about Queen of the B's! And how many genuine, camerawise lookers would relish appearing with scalp charred while struggling to rescue a wee babe from an infernal bonfire?

The character who undergoes these (and other) ordeals is named Helen Lyle. The wife of an anthropology professor, Helen is working on a doctoral thesis in collaboration with a friend, Bernadette (Kasi Lemmons). Ambitious and seemingly fearless, she hopes to clarify the legend of "Candyman," rumored to haunt and perhaps rule the housing project, the site of his own victimization back in the nineteenth century. Distinguishing feature: a lethal hook. Incantation: the repetition of his name five times while gazing into a mirror.

Ultimately, the movie resorts to literal-minded and graphically repulsive manifestations of Candyman, elegantly and ferociously embodied by Todd. In the early stages it succeeds in dredging up more sophisticated and pervasive forms of dread and apprehension, especially forms in which racial antagonism and suspicion overlap with sinister aspects of urban living. Helen, for example, reveals her smarts by recognizing that her own upscale highrise is structurally identical to the buildings in the projects. In a deliciously sustained process of sleuthing, she concludes that the entryway for a Candyman—or very real criminals exploiting his myth—can be found in construction shortcuts: she punches out the bathroom cabinet to show Bernadette how easy it is to enter the neighboring apartment.

While nosing around Cabrini in an effort to link a series of unsolved murders with the Candyman legend, Helen discovers more evil than she bargained for. Expanding on the fear of strange motel bathrooms Alfred Hitchcock inculcated in *Psycho,* Bernard Rose takes Virginia Madsen in and out of several squalid and booby-trapped bathrooms. If you weren't phobic on this score before...

For about two acts *Candyman* unfolds in ways that are consistent with realistic apprehension. Rose is especially adept at associating peril with social neglect and decay. However, it wouldn't be a contemporary horror thriller if it didn't inflict fantastic punishment on innocent or unwitting characters, so one is obliged to suffer outrageous gruesomeness as the price of an exceptionally clever and persuasive setup.

Virginia Madsen brings remarkable glamour and emotional validity to horror spectacle. It would be reassuring if one could believe the genre returned the favor, but it probably tarnishes or trivializes more reputations than it enhances. Nevertheless, her Helen will be one to cherish when invoking humanely diabolical characterizations.

Washington Post, October 16, 1992

ACTION

F ifteen years ago this chapter would have been titled "Adventure,"
and it would have surveyed tales of aspiration and derring-do
from *Lives of a Bengal Lancer* ('35) and *Gunga Din* ('39) to *The
Guns of Navarone* ('61) and *The Man Who Would Be King* ('75).
Even ten years ago, the Indiana Jones series and the magnificent
Mad Max films out of Australia might have justified such an
approach. No longer. While it's easy to imagine the great adventure
movies being lifted off the screen and retold as books and stories
(which is what some of them were to begin with), the same cannot
be said of the rush-zap-and-detonate extravaganzas dominating the
market nowadays. In these films—good, bad, and indifferent—story
is mere pretext for sensuous or sensational, hyperkinetic spectacle.
They leap, race, flare, carom, whoosh, roar, and, as frequently and
oleaginously as possible, explode. The definitive review of the new
action movie was filed, time and again, not by any member of the
National Society of Film Critics but by Billy Sol Hurok (John
Candy) and Big Jim McBob (Joe Flaherty) in their "Farm Film
Report" on "SCTV." Big Jim: "It blowed up good!" Billy Sol: "It
blowed up *real* good!"

We decided not to spend pages on the Neanderthal revenge fan-
tasias of Sylvester Stallone's Rambo cycle, the flying kicks and
Adam's-apple crunching of Chuck Norris, Jean-Claude Van

Damme, et al., or even the sleek, impressively machined big gundowns of the Bruce Willis *Die Hards*. (For *Lethal Weapon*ry, see Dave Kehr's essay "On Copping a Plea" in the "Film Noir and Gangster Films" chapter.) Instead, we concentrate on the auteur class acts and deviations from—in the words of Mercury House's Sarah Malarkey—"a beef-eater's view of typically white male hero movies."

David Ansen opens our critical wrecking derby with James Cameron's *Aliens,* the exhilarating and enjoyably exhausting sequel to Ridley Scott's 1979 *Alien* that shifted the emphasis from sci-fi/horror to Action; Cameron is among the few contemporary directors—including George (*Road Warrior*) Miller and, sometimes, Walter Hill—with the personal vision to raise pure action to an art form. Ansen then takes a look at Scott's *Black Rain* and finds that gifted imagist betraying his talent. Andrew Sarris files a minority report in praise of *Blue Steel* and Kathryn Bigelow, the outstanding woman director working this male precinct. Julie Salamon likes the fires in Ron Howard's *Backdraft.* Kevin Thomas harks back to the biker flicks of the late sixties–early seventies and reminds us, via *Angels Hard As They Come,* that the B picture was often a training ground for future big-league talent. At the other budgetary extreme, Kenneth Turan settles in for a good time with the most expensive movie in Hollywood history, *Terminator 2: Judgment Day.* And Armond White praises Walter Hill for the multiracial dynamics of *Trespass.*

ALIENS

David Ansen

The action movie has not been in great shape lately, and if the disappointing turnout for the latest Stallone and Schwarzenegger pictures is any indication, audiences are turning off, too. The genre has gone in two directions—either toward sheer dumb brutality (*Cobra* and *Rambo*) or into self-mocking but equally formulaic send-ups of the old Hollywood conventions (the heirs of *Raiders of the Lost Ark*). But every now and then a director will come along to pump bright red blood into action movies. The flamboyant George Miller did it with his Mad Max trilogy. And James Cameron, having demonstrated his bold kinetic talent in *The Terminator* ('84), unleashes his big guns in *Aliens,* a spectacular sequel to Ridley Scott's 1979 *Alien.*

But, you protest, the first *Alien* was not an action movie. Correct. What Scott fashioned was a terrifying haunted-house movie set in space. Cameron is after something different. Sigourney Weaver is back, and so are those primally yucky creatures (now an entire herd). But the emphasis has shifted to combat: this is a matriarchal science-fiction war movie with Sigourney leading her ever-dwindling troops into battle against the queen alien and her insatiable brood. Motherhood is the movie's unstated theme.

Cameron restores conviction to a debased genre in the simplest way possible—by playing it straight. No arched eyebrows here, no self-conscious old-movie references. Just back-to-basics good storytelling: sturdy characterizations, perilous cliff-hangers, plausible escapes, and a dazzling command of film technique. Cameron plays rough, but he plays fair: you emerge limp from tension, but you don't feel abused.

Fifty-seven years have passed since Ripley (Weaver) survived her first encounter with the aliens. (In hypersleep since then, she hasn't aged at all.) In the meantime, a colony of settlers has set up shop on that forbidding planet; now contact has been lost with them. Against her better judgment, Ripley is coerced into accompanying a troop of Marines to investigate the silence. No one, of course, believes her tales of horror, but *we* know better.

Cameron's script takes its time setting us up for the oncoming nightmare. His motley crew of Marine grunts are an amusing gaggle of B-movie types: a green, in-over-his-head commander (William Hope), a butch Latino woman (Jenette Goldstein), a handsome soldier for just a hint of romance (Michael Biehn). There are also a craven bureaucratic villain (Paul Reiser) and an artificial human (Lance Henriksen) who quips, when sent off on a dangerous mission, "I may be synthetic but I'm not stupid." *Terminator* fans will recognize Cameron's touch in his relish for heavy-metal gadgetry and in the dank, grimy settings (the film is devoid of sunlight). When the troopers finally land, they find only one human alive: a little girl named Newt (Carrie Henn), who becomes Ripley's surrogate daughter—and whom she vows to protect to the death.

What happens next is best left undescribed. Let's just say

Cameron is a master at choreographing ever-more-astonishing catastrophes (his movies never end when you think they're over). For sheer intensity, the final forty-five minutes of *Aliens* is not likely to be matched by any movie soon. But the film is not merely a triumph of bravura action and masterfully slimy monsters. At its core is the ferociously urgent performance of Sigourney Weaver, who hurls herself into her warrior role with muscular grace and a sense of conviction that matches Cameron's step for step. Next to her wonderfully human macho, most recent *male* action heroes look like very thin cardboard.

Newsweek, July 21, 1986

BLACK RAIN

■■■

David Ansen

Remember the quaint *Teahouse of the August Moon* and *Sayonara,* with delicate-as-a-bird Miyoshi Umeki? That was the kind of movie we made about Japan in the 1950s, after we'd nuked them into submission and could afford, from our victor's vantage point, the luxury of benign cultural condescension. Now we make *Black Rain,* a churlish and violent Rambo-era revenge fantasy that suggests, through its furiously overcompensating macho posturing, that we are no longer sure who's Number One. This is not, let's make it clear, an admission this movie makes. But how else to explain, other than a mood of besieged national insecurity, the peculiarly surly and swaggering tone this Ridley Scott movie adopts? Now that the Japanese are beating us at our own industrial games, Hollywood feels free to indulge in a little Asia-bashing again.

So whom do we send to teach the Japanese a lesson in unfettered individualism? Michael Douglas as tough-as-nails New York cop Nick Conklin, and his slightly more affable partner Charlie Vincent (Andy Garcia). Nick and Charlie are supposed to deliver a dangerous young *yakuza* mobster (Yusaku Matsuda) they've arrested in New York to the Osaka police, but they bungle the job and turn him over to the mob instead. This really ticks Nick off and he vows to get his man his own way, not by playing by the Japanese rules of teamwork but in true Rambo fashion. He even says, swear to God, "Sometimes you gotta go for it." He also says things like "Sometimes you gotta choose a side." Somebody should have told the writers, Craig Bolotin and Warren Lewis, that sometimes you gotta write an original line of dialogue.

We are obviously meant to cheer Nick Conklin as a hero for all seasons, but why? Rude, sadistic, charmless, and a corrupt cop to boot, he has one outstanding attribute—the chip on his shoulder. From the minute he lands in Osaka he starts slurring his hosts (they're "Nips" to him, and every epithet is preceded by "little"), making fun of the way they talk and their suspiciously unmanly self-control. When Andy Garcia's character, who at least flashes a smile now and then, gets viciously dispatched early on, your heart sinks: Douglas has to carry the rest of the movie himself. You almost feel sorry for the puffy, miscast actor, glowering strenuously as he tries to convince us he's the next Chuck Norris. For a while, it seems the movie must be setting Conklin up to learn a lesson in humility from the Japanese. On the contrary, it's they who have to learn from us. The lesson: sometimes you have to, yes, go for it.

In movies like *Black Rain,* you know if you see a motorcycle race at the start, you'll get one in the climax. The script is routine formula swill, at best. It's worse when it tries for "significance," dragging in Hiroshima as "motivation" for the *yakuza* chieftain, who, we're told, is producing perfect counterfeit U.S. money as an act of revenge for the Bomb. (The title—which Scott's movie shares with a thoughtful Japanese movie by Shohei Imamura—is a reference to nuclear fallout.)

But the movie certainly doesn't *look* routine: it's got Ridley Scott at the helm. As you would expect from the man who made *Blade Runner* ('82), *Alien* ('79), and more than 2,000 commercials, *Black Rain* is swimming in smoky "style." Having borrowed from urban Japan for *Blade Runner,* he descends on Osaka and turns it into an oppressive, neon-streaked, soul-shrinking industrial landscape. But there's no fun in Scott's flashy, neo-Expressionist filigree this time: it's too cold and alienating a style for the dumb Rambo fantasy he's trying to sell. There's not a moment of honest emotion in the whole movie. Only Ken Takakura, quietly effective as Nick's reluctant Japanese partner, manages to suggest a man with some life behind the eyes. Poor Kate Capshaw is saddled with a thankless role as a bar girl and polished off by an unkind, lopsided haircut.

It's sad to see Scott sinking to this level, but he's not the first talented Brit to fall into the clutches of Stanley Jaffe and Sherry Lansing, the producing team who brought you Adrian Lyne's rancidly successful *Fatal Attraction*. *Black Rain* bears their inimitable touch, cleverly designed to tap into the national neurosis of the day. With their talent for pandering to our worst instincts with slickly packaged products, they ought to be running presidential campaigns, not making movies.

Newsweek, October 2, 1989

BLUE STEEL

■■■

Andrew Sarris

With *Blue Steel* Kathryn Bigelow demonstrates once more that a woman director need not be associated with a kinder and gentler cinema. The adventures and misadventures of Jamie Lee Curtis's Megan Turner, a woman cop stalked by a psychopathic commodities trader (and don't ask if there's any other kind), provide Curtis with the strongest and most controversial female action role since Debra Winger's sexually compromised FBI agent in Costa-Gavras's much underrated *Betrayed* ('88).

Somehow critics and moviegoers, male and female both, are made uneasy by heroines exulting in their expertise with firearms. "What's a nice, pretty girl like you doing in a genre like this?" is a question that might be asked of both Bigelow and Curtis, and both could answer that they had more than a modicum of experience in the darker, bloodier regions of screen narrative. Bigelow's first feature, *The Loveless* ('81), codirected with a fellow neophyte, Monty Montgomery, was a stylishly violent biker-versus-bourgeois collision starring then-unknown Willem Dafoe, while *Near Dark* ('87) was a vampire classic worthy to be included in the same hallowed hall of horror as F. W. Murnau's *Nosferatu*, Carl Dreyer's *Vampyr*, and Tod Browning's *Dracula*. For her part, Curtis made her motion picture debut in 1978 as the virginal survivor in John Carpenter's ultrahomicidal *Halloween* and has seldom found onscreen sanctuaries any more secure since. As the goldfish-bowl offspring of Janet Leigh and Tony Curtis, she has seemed to develop a toughness in her talent that has stood her in good stead during the often soul-destroying process of being typecast for the cheapie circuits. It is not surprising, therefore, that in *Blue Steel* she transcends the trashy stigmata inflicted upon her by the Polo Lounge pundits.

At this point I must confess a minuscule conflict of interest in my reporting on the ongoing career of Kathryn Bigelow. I happen to be a professor in the Film Division of the School of the Arts at Columbia University, the institution at which Bigelow studied with Miloš Forman and from which she graduated in 1978 with a Master of Arts. Earlier, she had been a painter through the painful transition between Abstract Expressionism and post–everything-except-opportunism.

Bigelow's background is not exactly insider-trading privileged information. In fact, my own acquaintance with her led me, at the time of *Near Dark,* to fall into the twin traps of bending over backward to be "objective" and letting familiarity breed condescension. Consequently, I missed the boat on one of the most haunting cinematic creations of the eighties in Bigelow's masterly dialectics of light and darkness on view in that film.

So I may have bent over forward on this occasion not to miss the boat on *Blue Steel.* Again, I must confess that I may be indulging in a certain amount of temperamental overcompensation in plunging into genres with which I am not entirely comfortable. Truth to tell, I feel more affinity with Wimpy than with Popeye. Hence, a little violence on the screen goes a long way, since I am as squeamish as the next graybeard who can still fondly remember an age of comparative reticence and repression.

My own first instinct, therefore, is to warn my readers that *Blue Steel* is the most gut-wrenching exercise in physical and psychological violence since *Fatal Attraction* ('87). Furthermore, Ron Silver's seemingly indestructible serial murderer lacks the almost sympathetic "woman scorned" motivation of the Glenn Close career woman harpy in the Adrian Lyne movie. Silver's blood-soaked marauder is Evil, pure and inexplicable.

If I had my druthers I would rather live in a world of Eric Rohmer epigrams, a civilized enclave of endless conversation. But I happen to be living in New York City in the nineties, and somehow the most violent movies seem increasingly appropriate for the social madness encroaching upon us more each day. Hence, *Blue Steel,* like George A. Romero's brilliantly horrifying *Monkey Shines* in 1988, may indicate that the most interesting cinematic art of the nineties will be in the nature of a lance striking at the festering infection of the body politic in a polluted swamp of anarchic impulses.

When I spoke with the director, she told me that she and her coscenarist Eric Red had done considerable research in police practices and procedures, though they boosted the standard police revolver to near-mythically Eastwoodian proportions. The main point, however, is that badly wounded criminals can behave like wounded lions in their ability to inflict pain and death on their adversaries. In this regard, *Blue Steel* has reminded me of several incidents reported on local newscasts: for example, the megalomania of the Menendez brothers accused of murdering their rich parents; or the eleven, not ten or twelve, but precisely eleven bullets fired by real-life cops in two separate cases. Did the real-life police panic, or did the perpetrators continue charging even after being hit by one or two bullets? Of course, none of the perpetrators was a commodities broker, but the apparent indestructibility of the villain in *Blue Steel* does have some real-life resonance.

The director has hit ten-strikes throughout her career with all her casting, from Dafoe in *The Loveless* to Adrian Pasdar, Jenny Wright, and Tim Thomerson in *Near Dark* to Curtis, Silver, and Clancy Brown as a tough, cynical detective with an inner core of decency and tenderness in the current film. There seems to be an intentional paradox involved in the casting of the small, wiry Silver, who explodes into fragments of lethal aggression, and of the tall, seemingly hard-hearted Brown, who melts slowly into a mound of emotional sensitivity. This instinct for conflict and contrast makes Bigelow's art diametrically opposed to that of most other women directors committed to reconciliation even at the cost of dramatic excitement.

Blue Steel introduces a provocative subplot touching on family violence with stunning performances by Philip Bosco and Louise Fletcher as a policewoman's troubled parents, particularly in a scene of the subtlest horror imaginable. Even here, however, there is a refusal to come up with easy clinical catchwords to explain a drama in which one woman, and perhaps all women, must come to terms and even to grips with the fear and rage lurking around every street corner.

Blue Steel can be appreciated more as mythology than as sociology. The race and class tensions at the root of our urban malaise are conveniently sidestepped here, and drugs are never a factor. Bigelow works in a grand classic tradition, and yet she has found a way to resurrect the romantic purity of Abstract Expressionism in a more mobile medium. What I like most about *Blue Steel*, however, is that the heroine is strengthened and ennobled by her ordeal, and her soul is never sacrificed to the spectacle. Kathryn Bigelow and Jamie Lee Curtis have thus imaginatively collaborated on a work of art of both style and substance.

New York Observer, March 26, 1990

BACKDRAFT

■■■

Julie Salamon

Everything that's good and bad about *Backdraft,* the action picture about fire fighters, is there to see in the picture's opening sequence. A fire fighter takes his young son along to watch a routine tenement fire. The boy gazes adoringly at his dad's fearless climb into the smoking building. The fire fighters rescue a child and all seems fine until his father is sucked back into a violent burst of flames. The boy's happy face turns sad as the musical score swells solemnly.

The opening is both stately and stodgy—and curiously empty of feeling. The only thing that's unpredictable and therefore interesting is the fire itself. The special effects department should really get top billing in this film.

Fire fighting doesn't seem to be the right material for Ron Howard, a deft director of light comedy (*Splash, Parenthood*) and a somewhat less convincing director of science fiction fantasy (*Cocoon, Willow*). He's shot this picture in the style of a science fiction fantasy, which gives the fire fighting scenes a satisfying feel of terror. But the psychological portraits of the fire fighters and the arson mystery that dominate the film are flimsy, like an art student's dutifully crafted reproductions of the great masters. The lines are where they should be and the colors are right, but anyone can tell at a glance that they aren't the real thing.

In fact, *Backdraft* is real—a real Hollywood version of reality (but not topnotch Hollywood, where the fantasy is so good you don't care how farfetched it is). The little boy in the opening shows up twenty years later in the form of William Baldwin, a dreamy-eyed young man with a nice backside (displayed for his teenage fans in a nude shower scene). He's Brian McCaffrey, whose response to his father's tragic death has been to drift—after dropping out at the fire fighter's academy. As the film proper begins, Brian has returned to the academy and completed his training. He's about to start work as a fire fighter. Blocking his way to success and possible fulfillment is his brother Stephen (Kurt Russell), an even more death-defying fire fighter than their father. Screenwriter Gregory Widen maps out the plot of their feud bluntly. They aren't characters so much as representative types: macho vs. sensitive.

The filmmakers demonstrate their admiration for the fire fighters by making them into bloodless icons and the women they're involved with into mannequins. Jennifer Jason Leigh, as the ex-girlfriend of one brother, and Rebecca DeMornay, as the ex-wife of the other, barely move a facial muscle—though each gets to participate in a lovemaking scene in a coldly mechanical way. (The musical score is cold, too, worshipful and deadly. On the few occasions the music lightens up, it's only to have fire fighters rush to a fire to the cheery rock beat of "Heat Wave.")

But the screenwriter is too subtle, or too vague, on important aspects of the movie's other plots, which seem at least as interesting as the predictable feud and reconciliation between the brothers. While the McCaffrey men fight their demons, an investigator (Robert De Niro) suspects that some of the fires they're fighting were set by an arsonist. A sleazy politician (J. T. Walsh) who's been closing down fire stations for political gain is introduced. So is Ronald Bartel (Donald Sutherland), an imprisoned arsonist who likes to play psychological games with his captors.

Ronald comes up with the film's most intriguing idea, the notion of fire as "the animal," a creature you have to love a little to conquer. That's an interesting twist on the notion that cops and criminals are alter egos. But the filmmakers simply remark on the bond between fire fighters and flame, then move on. De Niro and Sutherland aren't wasted, exactly—they give the picture some definition—but their story is so disconnected to the main story of the brothers that both plotlines come off as distractions.

And maybe that's how it should be, since it is the film's fire fighting sequences, not its story, that are undeniably exciting. Cinematographer Mikael Salomon has filmed special effects before, in

Always—Steven Spielberg's fire fighting movie—and *The Abyss*. The uncontrollable bursts of fire that seem to come from nowhere are terrifying—though Salomon has a tendency to diminish the terror by making everything so beautiful.

Wall Street Journal, May 30, 1991

ANGELS HARD AS THEY COME

■■■

Kevin Thomas

Sandwiched between a pair of oldies (but not-so-goodies)—*Naked Angels* and *Angels Die Hard*—on a biker triple-bill is a pretty good newie, *Angels Hard As They Come*. Like so many successful exploitation pictures before it, this New World release delivers the strong action expected, but it also balances that with equally strong characterizations and manages some comment as well. Above all, it shows off a youthful cast to advantage and marks the early filmmaking work of Jonathan Demme and Joe Viola. Demme produces, Viola directs, and they collaborate on the script.

In brief, *Angels Hard As They Come* deals with a brutal encounter between two motorcycle gangs in a ghost town called Lost Cause, inhabited only by a hippie commune. The Angels' leader, Long John (Scott Glenn), is hard-bitten and cynical ("What works is right") but not unintelligent, willing to let well enough alone unless he's hassled. The Dragons' leader, the General (Charles Dierkop), is another matter. Wearing a spiked German World War I helmet, he's a fascist as maniacal as Hitler. Trouble starts to brew when Long John defeats the General in a cycle race, then it boils over.

What Demme and Viola, very much a dynamic duo, achieve so effectively is to play their three main factions against one another to show up the weaknesses of each. The General (who indulges in an insane kangaroo court at one point) is in constant danger of becoming too much even for his slavish followers. On the other hand, Long John finds his don't-get-involved philosophy severely challenged in crisis, while the hippies cruelly learn just how ineffectual gentleness and pacifism are in dealing with a monster like the General. If *Angels Hard As They Come* is pretty violent—though not gratuitously so—it is also thought-provoking.

A flat-nosed banty rooster of a man, Dierkop, the veteran in the cast, is chillingly credible. Glenn comes on like a young Humphrey Bogart, and Gilda Texter radiates genuine sweetness as a hapless hippie. The remainder of the cast is solid.

Los Angeles Times, January 19, 1972

TERMINATOR 2: JUDGMENT DAY

■■■

Kenneth Turan

He has built it. And yes, without a doubt, they will come.

He is the gifted James Cameron, the consensus choice as the action director of his generation. What he's built is *Terminator 2: Judgment Day,* the most eagerly awaited film of summer 1991 and one of the most expensive ever made. More elaborate than the original, but just as shrewdly put together, it cleverly combines the most successful elements of its predecessor with a number of new twists (would you believe a kinder, gentler Terminator?) to produce one hell of a wild ride, a Twilight of the Gods that takes no prisoners and leaves audiences desperate for mercy.

If you don't count *Piranha II*—and Cameron doesn't—the original 1984 *Terminator* was his first job as a director. It remains an exceptional debut, a lean, laconic action classic that benefited not only from the man's enviable skills as an orchestrator of mayhem but also from the tale he came up with: a machine that looks like a human being is sent from the future to the present in order to kill one Sarah Connor, a hapless waitress whose yet-unborn son will, in a distant, post–nuclear holocaust time, lead the forces of humanity in a war against (what else?) power-mad machines.

That assassin is the Terminator, a very tough nut whose modus operandi is described as follows: "It can't be bargained with. It can't be reasoned with. It doesn't feel remorse or pity or fear. And it absolutely will not stop until you are dead." As played by Arnold Schwarzenegger, whose witty *Night of the Living Dead* delivery turned this into the role of a lifetime, the Terminator became a major antihero, the Monster from the Id you couldn't help but admire.

Terminator 2 takes up a decade after the first one ends. Sarah Connor (Linda Hamilton, returning from the original) finds herself in a state mental hospital for insisting that the Terminator was not a figment of her imagination. Her ten-year-old son John (newcomer Edward Furlong), the future hope of the world, is a whiny brat living in the Valley and making life miserable for his foster parents. He thinks his mom is, not to put too fine a point on it, a loser.

Though thwarted in the past, the evil machines of the future refuse to wimp out. They send a new-model Terminator, the T-1000 (Robert Patrick), to finish the job and kill young John. Based on the same computer-generated technology that Cameron first used in *The Abyss* (remember the water magically turning into a face?), the T-1000 is a remarkable piece of special effects sleight of hand, a mercurylike being able not only to change shape at will but also to return to its original form no matter what. Like an old Timex watch, it takes a licking and keeps on ticking.

But Sarah and John are not without resources. A now-outmoded but still canny T-800 model (Schwarzenegger) is reprogrammed to look kindly on humans and sent back to give them a hand. Adding to the T-800's difficulties, however, young John suddenly develops a humanitarian streak and insists that his Terminator not kill anyone when a good maiming will do just as nicely. Watching Schwarzenegger's Terminator cope with these new ethical guidelines is one of the sequel's more delicious conceits.

Despite these new wrinkles, *T2*—as the ads complacently have it—does not so much start slowly (for Cameron likes to let you know whose film you're in as soon as possible) as derivatively. Some of the opening sequences, such as the way the T-800 goes about getting clothes and wheels, feel like more elaborate but not necessarily more involving versions of scenes from the first film. Even in action movies, bigger is not necessarily better.

But *Terminator 2,* like its predecessor, is nothing if not determined, and we are soon won over. For one thing, though Edward Furlong is more irritating as John Connor than he really needs to be, the other principals more than make up for it. Schwarzenegger, for one, reembraces this role like a long-lost relative—no one can say "It must be destroyed" quite the way he can—and Hamilton brings a level of physical intensity to her new-model, pumped-up paranoid Sarah Connor that even devotees of the first film will find pleasantly surprising.

As for the script, Cameron and cowriter William Wisher have done more than make sure that *T2* is well stocked with the kind of wised-up, shoot-from-the-hip wit that characterized the first film. Sensing that a series of Terminator versus Terminator chases would soon become boring no matter how excellent the effects, they sensibly opted to take the middle of the film down a different, more intriguing road, one involving a computer scientist (a very fine appearance by Joe Morton) who is investigating the relics of the first Terminator.

Most of all, what makes *T2* come alive in a major way is Cameron's intuitive understanding of the mechanics and psychology of action films. Unlike many of the wannabes who find themselves in charge of pictures these days, this is one director who really knows how to direct. It's not so much that his virtuoso stunts break an ungodly amount of glass (which they do) as that he packs an astounding ferocity into his sequences. And unlike someone like Paul (*RoboCop*) Verhoeven, he manages to do it without turning our stomachs.

Equally at home in small-scale skirmishes like one-on-one chases down narrow corridors and complex, bravura effects involving tottering helicopters, exploding buildings, and as many as five different special-effects houses, Cameron flamboyantly underlines, for those who may have forgotten, why the pure adrenaline rush of motion is something motion pictures can't live for very long without.

Los Angeles Times, July 3, 1991

TRESPASS

Armond White

Not just another Walter Hill action movie, *Trespass* is a post–Rodney King action movie. Central to its means is the function of a video camera used by one of the story's young black gang members to record a good third of the action that takes place in and around an abandoned church in East St. Louis, Illinois.

Hill dramatizes a standoff between the black gang and a pair of white renegade fire fighters from Fort Smith, Arkansas. The groups converge on the dilapidated site out of symbolic happenstance. The old church is where the gang members congregate and it's the spot the fire fighters go to seek the hidden booty of a historic church vandalism. "We just solved a fifty-year-old crime," Don (William Sadler) says to his fellow fire fighter Vince (Bill Paxton). Their unofficial business overlaps the gang war council between Goose (John Toles-Bey) and King James (Ice-T), whose ruthless posse includes Savon (Ice Cube), Luther (Glenn Plummer), Lucky (De'Voreaux White), Cletus (Tiny Lister), Davis (Tico Wells), and Wickey (Stoney Jackson). Don describes the church with the hidden gold as "like the damn Pyramids, it's gonna outlast all of us." The edifice is more resonant than relevant to these contemporary characters' lives. They're all poised within social history that none of them understands clearly; the gold they eventually fight over is just a maguffin, incidental to the essential antagonism—masculine aggression over turf. The old Catholic church automatically evokes the West and its philosophical means of conquest, but it represents America.

Race is the important, unresolved issue for Hill and his screen-writer-producers, Bob Gale and Robert Zemeckis (the team that also wrote the witty, cynical *Used Cars, Back to the Future,* and *I Wanna Hold Your Hand*). The specter of race war is used to update this genre exercise. That may sound as if Hill and company come to the issue from the wrong direction, but it's really just an aesthetic preference. They have not separated politics from their art; rather, politics is explicit in the way the film is made. The black-white confrontation is matter-of-fact, modern. For Hollywood, this is a radical awareness, implying the depletion of whites-only action cinema. *Trespass* transgresses the racial conservatism of Hollywood action movies that, since film noir in the forties, has pretended to deal with harsh urban reality while ignoring the sociological changes of urban American life and the shifting cast of heroes in America's various existential crises.

Hill, Gale, and Zemeckis are the perfect intellectual bunch to play out this late, inevitable transition. (Stallone, Norris, Seagal, Van Damme, Schwarzenegger, and Willis are personally predisposed against it.) The taboo subject of race has been raised constantly

Ice Cube (left) and Ice-T lead the black gang vying with a passel of rednecks for access to buried treasure in Walter Hill's *Trespass*. (Photo by Sam Emerson. © by Universal City Studios, Inc. Courtesy of MCA Publishing Rights, a Division of MCA Inc. All Rights Reserved.)

throughout Hill's career, from the black child pointing a water pistol at Steve McQueen in Hill's script for Peckinpah's *The Getaway* ('72), to the ethnic plurality and racially explicit dialogues of such films as *The Warriors* ('79), *Southern Comfort* ('81), *Red Heat* ('88), *Johnny Handsome* ('89), and *Another 48HRS.* ('90). Even the Gale-Zemeckis scripts from *1941* ('79) on featured moments of ethnic consciousness and social change (such as the black mayor's little-remarked-upon urban environment in the *Back to the Future* series).

Trespass's moral premise—greed—is not limited to a conventional, white-protagonist plot. The balanced racial view goes a lot further than most post–Reagan-Bush, anti-eighties liberal screeds. Knowledgeably revising *The Treasure of the Sierra Madre*, *Trespass* is charged with the urgent sense of social responsibility and egalitarianism that John Huston's 1948 classic lacked. By showing how greed affects both whites and nonwhites, Hill, Gale, and Zemeckis provide a closer, imaginative scrutiny of the politics that perpetuate racial discord.

This new take on genre fiction became an aesthetic imperative after the 1991 tape of the Rodney King beating: years of academic structuralism and semiotics were outdone as every member of the global village was made to question representation and its related politics. It's a sad irony that after the L.A. riots protesting the acquittal of the white cops who beat King, *Trespass* was pushed back from a summer 1992 release date and had its original title (*The Looters*) changed. Universal Pictures' decision to delay the film's release ignored its makers' conscientious politics. The insulting suggestion that this movie (any movie) would incite social violence by blacks actually showed whites' fear of their own guilt-ridden imagination.

If for no other reason, *Trespass* deserves credit for daring to show black men armed against white men at a time when the guardians of pop culture severely monitor the expression of black discontent in rap records like Sister Souljah's or Paris's "Bush Killer" and even the *Juice* movie poster (Tupac Shakur is not allowed to hold a gun, while Tom Selleck can brandish a baseball bat and Kevin Costner can carry a pistol). *Trespass* exposes how Hollywood's reluctant development of top-grade action movies with black protagonists reflects a white discomfort with black empowerment.

The point here is not the justification of violence but the changing of cultural perception to clarify the use of violence and greed as white privileges, then as folly. The relentless scenes of fighting and shooting in *Trespass* are less intense than the subtextual excitement of colliding myths. Putting *Sierra Madre* in the age of hiphop confounds previous racist notions of white vs. black heroism. Art Evans has the Walter Huston role as the wise, sarcastic Old Man survivor who reveals the other characters to be fools, but there's a significant difference. When the white men offer to buy Evans off, he snaps back: "Forty bucks! What, you gonna give me a mule, too? Fuck you!" The change from acres to dollars is key to the historic resentment that hovers over the film's generic character conflict. It's impossible—foolish—to watch this struggle without thinking of history and politics.

That these updated, hiphop hoodlums are handled as mythic figures is not the same as treating black crooks as stereotypes. With their high-tech videocams, their beepers and mobile phones, a new game is being played. "I ain't no gang member, I'm a businessman!" Ice Cube asserts, following a white capitalist model. He recalls the drug-dealing inmate's rationale in *Red Heat*. And Ice-T, wearing shoulder-length hair and a wide-brimmed hat, evokes the coke-dealing Priest of *Superfly* as another mythological icon of America's New Age greed.

Instead of attempting to explain this phenomenon realistically, Hill confronts the reality through its pop mythological imagery. No, this isn't quite enough to sustain a feature-length drama (although it's as much as one typically gets in an action movie). In fact, Hill and cinematographer Lloyd Ahern and editor Freeman Davies shoot and cut with a casual aplomb that almost seems weary of the action-movie convention. *Trespass* simply isn't as kinetically exciting as *Another 48HRS.* or *The Warriors* or *The Driver* ('78)— that is, until Hill makes sudden shifts to video and the movie's complex mix of politics and fiction ignites.

By switching media, Hill validates the revolution in spectator consciousness that was asserted by the Rodney King video. *Trespass* doesn't offer the nuanced insight into urban reality that comes from a great rap record, but the interplay of film and video imagery, documentary and fiction, is a movie culture milestone. This trope replicates the turntable scratching and sampling of rap DJs; the mix of image textures engenders a different dramatic pulse and perception. (Hill's film manipulates the idea of reality with greater sophistication than the overrated Belgian import, *Man Bites Dog*.) This is not a substitute for psychology, but it is an improvement on the way most genre movies address truth: video realism becomes an active contrast to the cartoonishness of gangsta-rap. Hill's implicit moral criticism is worthy of the way Ice-T and Ice Cube work at their best: through hyperbole, symbolism, sophisticated formal aesthetics.

Anyone who dismisses *Trespass* as irrelevant to the racial antagonism in contemporary America doesn't appreciate how race and class ideology is perpetuated. Hill's emphasis on genre as the site of turmoil cuts to the heart of where the working class (black or white, rappers or not) get their fantasies of empowerment. Like Spielberg in *Indiana Jones and the Last Crusade,* Hill faces the truth of genre as propaganda. *Trespass* is important for its modern realization, and expression, of antiheroics.

Ice-T and Ice Cube, foremost examples of rappers who are movie stars in their own minds, help authenticate Hill's thesis by portraying the big-screen fantasies of themselves as men of action. They are closer to their own truths here than in the blandly moralizing sociological dramas *New Jack City* and *Boyz N the Hood.* (And Bill Paxton is closer to truth here than in the white critics' fave *One False Move.*) The opportunity to fulfill their dreams reveals the necessity for some new fantasies. *Trespass* proves that after the Rodney King tape, Hollywood—and its audience—is obligated to rethink the games men play.

The City Sun (Brooklyn), January 20, 1993

HORROR

During the Depression, they had pretensions to quality: James Whale's and Tod Browning's handsomely art-designed versions of classic horror literature—*Dracula, Frankenstein, The Invisible Man*—and Michael Curtiz's Germanic, two-strip Technicolor shock shows—*Doctor X* and *Mystery of the Wax Museum*. In the forties, the best of them brought a delicate poetry to the genre: producer Val Lewton's series of gracefully muted horror films—*Cat People, I Walked with a Zombie, The Seventh Victim*. In the fifties and sixties, horrorpix were deemed little more than quick-buck exploitation fare; with the qualified exception of some Hammer Films from Britain, the disreputable genre was to be found mainly on drive-in and otherwise déclassé screens.

Then, around the time George A. Romero shot his appalling, brilliant, no-budget *Night of the Living Dead* ('68) somewhere near Pittsburgh, disreputability ceased to be a stigma (life in general having become more horrific) and the horror genre was everywhere—not only thriving at the box office but boasting a new generation of filmmakers with bold new styles and bolder ideas about using the genre for social, political, and even philosophical comment.

Having been made, such a statement immediately needs to be qualified. The popular press—which is to say, the op-ed page as well as the arts and entertainment section—rarely addresses film as anything but a consumer phenomenon, a popcult seismograph of (usually distressing) rumblings in the body politic. The new dominance of the horror film became grist for the sex'n'violence mill that editorial soothsayers love to grind. Yes, a lot of the new horror films were distinctly unsavory in their wanton displays of gore (an entire special-effect subindustry arose to serve this need) and deplorable in their preference for women as objects of atrocity. And a lot of them were just plain bad, dumb, boring movies— mechanical debasings of formulas developed in the few genuinely creative horror films of the time.

But more serious film critics were able to draw the necessary distinctions: to note that Tobe Hooper's *The Texas Chainsaw Massacre* ('74), whose very title was inflammatory enough to make it infamous, and David Cronenberg's *The Brood* ('79) were advisedly grotesque allegories of violence and repression in the nuclear family; that Romero's *Dawn of the Dead* ('79) was a blistering commentary on consumerist culture; that John Carpenter's *Halloween* ('78) was an elegant, magisterially accomplished study of the power of the framed image and of film-watching as an act of voyeurism; that Wes Craven's *A Nightmare on Elm Street* ('85) was a breakthrough work making scary poetry of the slippery resemblances between film and dream imagery. If Romero's zombies were cannibalized by brain-dead shlock merchants who wouldn't know resonance from raspberries, Carpenter's classical manipulations of point of view and his faceless, sex-hating assassin coarsened into the ugly mayhem of the *Friday the 13th* series, and *Elm Street*'s dream-killer Freddy Krueger made into a fond pop icon, the vision and power of the originals remain untainted and worthy of defense.

Our survey here is confined to the past decade. Andy Klein tracks the twisted flight plan of *The Fly*—1986 version—and the disturbing essence of creator David Cronenberg's ideas. Richard Schickel urges that we not overlook the modest, affably screwy *Tremors*. Owen Gleiberman stands in awe of the first horror movie to win the Oscar, Jonathan Demme's *Silence of the Lambs*. In anticipation of Francis Coppola's *Bram Stoker's Dracula,* Dave Kehr stakes out the vampire tradition in cinema, and Richard Corliss meditates on the bravura new film in all its romantic majesty.

THE FLY

Andy Klein

Why is *The Fly* so disturbing? Or, in any case, so disturbing to me? Clearly, David Cronenberg has tapped into something with a pipeline straight to *my* viscera. Whatever that something is, it's *not* the basic story. George Langelaan's original short tale was grotesque but not very challenging, a diverting twenty pages written in a cold and distanced nineteenth-century form. The 1958 film version was fun, but nobody was going to lose any sleep over it.

To summarize the plot may give away a few surprises, but, since *The Fly* doesn't rely primarily on surprise, its effect shouldn't be diminished. Jeff Goldblum plays Seth Brundle, a charming, slightly geeky research scientist who's been working on a teleportation machine that analyzes an object at one end, beams its particles to the other end, and reconstructs the object based on the computerized analysis. He begins an affair with Veronica (Geena Davis), a beautiful science reporter. One night, in a booze- and jealousy-induced moment of colossally poor judgment, he tests the machine on himself.

While the invention itself works, it lacks one crucial ingredient: Black Flag. Alas, a lowly housefly buzzes into the transmitting chamber. The computer combines Brundle and the fly at a molecular level, in a process mimicking the combining of DNA in human conception. The result is a new creature—Brundlefly. At first, Brundle appears normal; he was the larger organism. But as the fly's genetic material starts ordering up new cells, he transforms more and more into a giant fly/human.

Cronenberg takes him through three stages: At first, he is mostly human, but with a fly's strength and impulses. Next, he goes through a painful and gruesome transformation, with human features and appendages dropping off. Finally, the fly's less-than-benevolent impulses become dominant and Brundlefly turns into a traditional Bug-Eyed—well, Bug-Everythinged—Monster. A final bungled attempt to merge himself with Veronica turns him into (if we may) Brundledoor, a hideously grotesque amalgam of flesh and metal with a pathetic iota of humanity lurking somewhere within. (Shades of Thomas Pynchon's mysterious lady/object *V.*: no longer the girl Victoria but the remnants of Victoria combined horribly with the alien, the inanimate.)

Obviously Goldblum's transformation provides plenty of opportunity for nauseating images and blatant shock effects. But these technical exercises in retchismo cannot account for the film's lingering impact. At one point, a minor character has his arm broken so violently that the ragged edge of bone tears through his flesh, accompanied by a hideous CRACK on the soundtrack. It is impossible to refrain from groaning and recoiling, but the scene is nothing more than a shock effect. It has absolutely no reverberation five seconds later.

By contrast, another sequence, far less shocking on the surface, has much deeper impact. Shortly after Goldblum's initial transformation, the camera moves in on him, as he makes love to Veronica. As it gets closer, we notice some odd marks on Goldblum's back; eventually they are revealed as stiff black hairs—the first sign that Goldblum has been combined, intermingled, *polluted* with flyness.

In the abstract, as an isolated image, it's nothing, just some whiskers on a guy's back. In its narrative context, signifying what it does, it's horrifying, disgusting, far worse than a fake bone tearing through fake flesh. The effect of the bone scene disappears if we withdraw from the film and remind ourselves that it's just special effects; the knowledge that (presumably) Jeff Goldblum doesn't *really* have fly parts growing in him in no way diminishes the impact of the other scene. That something has invaded one's body and is taking over, something alien and perhaps even sinister, is a basic fear, long expressed in vampire and werewolf myths, *Dr. Jekyll and Mr. Hyde,* and innumerable sci-fi and horror stories—a feeling experienced by all of us who have ever had our subconscious get the better of us. That a stranger may walk into a bar and snap one's arm in half is *not* a basic fear. At least not in my neighborhood.

Cronenberg has long seemed one of the most studied and intellectual of the younger horror directors. Beneath the surface of gross-out effects, he always invokes a tangle of primal anxieties; still, in the past, only *The Dead Zone* ('83) engaged me emotionally, and not very deeply at that. There was something moving in the sense of doom that seemed to hang about Christopher Walken's shoulders; but Walken lacks Goldblum's easy charm, a characteristic that the director exploits fully. We *like* Goldblum almost instantly. When his first teleportation turns him into a raving megalomaniac, we are not so much angry or irritated as concerned for him.

This time around, Cronenberg has layered the story with so many possible interpretations and resonances that one's head swims. The megalomania followed by deterioration precisely depicts the psychology of the heavy coke abuser—as well as bringing to mind James Mason's terrifying response to cortisone in Nicholas Ray's great 1956 drug film, *Bigger Than Life*. Goldblum's decay also plays on our fears of cancer, cells running amok within, eating us up. As one colleague has suggested, the fear may be even more specifically that of AIDS; Veronica is penalized for having slept with Brundle before his sickness was evident. An innocent act of love may cause her destruction as well. At its broadest, *The Fly* simply presents a condensed version of human mortality. Brundle's burst of energy is cut short by his body's betrayal, in a caricature of the aging process: he weakens, limbs drop off, his senses change, his mind starts to drift into some dreamworld.

If there is a gratuitous element in Cronenberg's scheme, it is the malevolent turn Brundlefly's character takes in the final third. Up to that point, Goldblum's characterization has been poignant. Suddenly, presumably to help provide a punched-up, "dramatic" climax, he becomes no longer an inadvertent threat, but an actual force of evil. Surely Veronica's plight was more interesting when Brundlefly was still fully sympathetic.

The Fly is too good a film to be a blockbuster. Just like Brundlefly, it's a weird mutant crossbreed—Kafkaesque nightmares, taken to the extremes of Grand Guignol and wedded to the moral structure of classic tragedy. Its style is too outré for most adults; its resonances, too genuinely upsetting for a teen audience that tends to prefer horror that's shallow—just a "fun" time. It's great when your date jumps into your lap during *Friday the 13th*; it's quite another matter when she's depressed, nauseated, and recoiling at your touch for the rest of the evening. And you're not likely to want to go out for ice cream after watching Brundlefly's digestive technique—a process charmingly referred to as the "vomit drop."

Los Angeles Reader, August 22, 1986

TREMORS

■■■

Richard Schickel

In winter solstices past, Hollywood has not been as helpful as it might in lifting dulled spirits. Having hyped themselves into exhaustion with their holiday releases, but feeling their annual Oscar anxiety beginning to build, the studios get the January blahs just like the rest of us. In 1990, though, a youthful team of scientists brought out an antidepressant that actually worked for a couple of laughs. Its brand name is *Tremors,* and the curious thing about it is that it's based on an ancient formula—practically a folk remedy. One is almost embarrassed to set it forth: small isolated community is disturbed first by mysterious rumblings; then by alarming disappearances and deaths, after which large, smart, implacable, and previously unimaginable creatures manifest themselves, and desperate defenses are improvised by a cast that is not obviously wiser, braver, or quicker than the average audience.

The featured creatures this time are gigantic earthworms, thirty feet long, capable of comic-alarming subterranean rapid transit (you just see this furrow moving across the desert at Roadrunner speed). When they surface they reveal trifurcated tongues, each extension of which ends in a funny-nasty suction cup. In other words, they are great special effects, informed by the mutant-monster tradition of low-budget fifties horror movies, but satirical of it in a rather delicate way—neither too condescending nor too indulgent.

The town they are terrorizing holds a meeting to name their antagonists, decides "graboids" will do nicely, and starts dithering over defensive strategies. Perfection, Nevada, by this time has a total population of 9, not counting the spunky visiting geologist (Finn Carter), but it has all the social strata a movie needs to make funky, glancing social commentary, rather in the manner of a country-and-western song. The entire upper class is played by a survivalist couple (Michael Gross and Reba McEntire) eager to employ their expensive arsenal against something—anything. The middle class, all four of them, are variously unaware, unconcerned, and unprepared for emergency. Populism being the operative spirit of this genre, it is up to Perfection's two-man lower class, Val and Earl (adorable Kevin Bacon and solid Fred Ward) to get their betters organized. They make their living doing odd jobs, bicker laconically, dream of urban glamour, can't imagine how to obtain it. But staring into a graboid's gaping mouth they're the kind of guys—resourceful, practical, unflappable—you want on your side.

And staring into an empty January evening, this is the kind of good basic movie everyone hopes is lurking out there and rarely is. Shrewdly, unpretentiously written (Brent Maddock and S. S. Wilson), energetically directed (Ron Underwood), and played with high comic conviction, *Tremors* is bound to become a cult classic. But why wait years to rediscover it?

Time, January 22, 1990

THE SILENCE OF THE LAMBS

Owen Gleiberman

Jonathan Demme's sleek and tantalizingly creepy *The Silence of the Lambs* is about an FBI agent-in-training, Clarice Starling (Jodie Foster), and how she struggles to track down a serial killer. But the most exciting presence in the film is Anthony Hopkins as Dr. Hannibal Lecter, the brilliant, incarcerated psychopath who agrees to help her in her search. Lecter lives deep within the bowels of a Baltimore institution for the criminally insane. When Clarice first goes to see him, descending into the darkened, grungy brick corridor reserved for the hospital's most dangerous and deranged patients, she seems to be entering some medieval version of Hell. At the very end of the corridor, behind an impenetrable clear-plastic wall, stands Lucifer himself: Lecter, the psychiatrist who liked to murder people and then eat them, or at least their vital organs. Thus his nickname, "Hannibal the Cannibal."

We in the audience, along with Clarice, are geared to expect a bone-chilling monster, the maniac cutthroat of all time. Instead, the middle-aged man who stands before us is handsome in a soothing, almost fatherly way, his big bright eyes gazing out at the world with exquisite sensitivity. Lecter's dark hair is slicked straight back and his stocky upper body, which is clad in a skintight T-shirt, is calm yet poised, as though he were about to perform gymnastic feats.

There's a touch of androgyny in his ironically serene presence; he's at once virile and soft, like a ballet dancer. And when he begins to talk, the words that come out are seamless, playful, and as thrillingly seductive as a dancer's movements.

Raising his nostrils to the air holes in his transparent wall, he quickly identifies the kind of skin cream Clarice uses, as well as her perfume—even though she hasn't worn it for at least a day. Lecter, you see, is a genius of perception (especially when it comes to his olfactory powers). He's a kind of twisted Sherlock Holmes, able to absorb, with heightened, Zen-like detachment, everything that goes on around him, and to draw visionary inferences from the mass of data his senses take in.

Hopkins, always one of the most dynamic of British actors, gives the performance of his life. He delivers his lines in a rapid-fire hush, but his eyes, in a running counterpoint, are impish, amused, and almost subliminally knowing, as though some pleasurable other-worldly light were passing through them. We can sense that savagery and tenderness coexist in Lecter, that they grow out of the same directness of spirit. What makes the character so prickly and fascinating is that, as the movie presents it, his homicidal impulses are a natural extension of his intelligence, his ability to appreciate people's most intimate qualities. Lecter seeks complete knowledge of everyone he encounters: by killing people and eating them, he literally consumes their identities.

Clarice has been assigned by Jack Crawford (Scott Glenn), of the FBI's Behavioral Science Unit, to submit Lecter to a standardized questionnaire. What Crawford really wants, though, is Lecter's help in apprehending "Buffalo Bill," a sicko who has been murdering women and skinning them. Crawford figures that Clarice, because she's a novice (and extremely attractive), will bring Lecter out in a way that a more experienced agent couldn't. But Clarice turns out to be savvier than Crawford expected. Her girlish ingenuousness *does* get to Lecter, but so does her sharp, intuitive mind, since that's what he values most in a person.

Intrigued and infatuated, Lecter sets a deal in motion. Tell me about yourself, he tells Clarice: reveal your secrets, your fears, your soul, and I'll look over the evidence and help you find Buffalo Bill. *The Silence of the Lambs* jumps among their conversations, Clarice's investigation into the killings, and scenes set inside the small-town lair of Buffalo Bill, aka Jame Gumb (Ted Levine), a would-be transsexual who is keeping his latest prey alive in a dungeonlike hole in the basement.

This is the second screen adaptation of one of Thomas Harris's best-selling serial-killer novels. The first, director Michael Mann's 1986 *Manhunter* (based on Harris's *Red Dragon*—and titled *Red Dragon* till just before release), had a druggy, saturnine intensity; I thought it was the most disturbing and mesmerizing thriller of the eighties. *The Silence of the Lambs* is a far less unsettling movie, in part because Demme and screenwriter Ted Tally have toned down the awfulness of the killer's scheme. In the book, Buffalo Bill's systematic skinning of his victims had a gruesome logic: he literally wanted to wear a woman's torso. Here, his taxidermic ambitions have been made somewhat more vague, and so we aren't hit with the full, shocking horror of what Clarice is up against. I got the feeling that Demme didn't want to spend too many scenes exploring the diseased mind of a misogynist psychopath. Yet artistically speaking, his reticence may have been a mistake. No other pop novelist has gotten as far inside the heads of serial killers as Thomas Harris has. *The Silence of the Lambs* would have been harder to shake off had it been crazier and less "moral"—less of a feminist outcry over the violence perpetrated against women.

For all that, Demme has created a supremely sensuous and hypnotic thriller, one that's likely to become his first major hit. He brings Harris's sensationalistic material an emotional charge virtually unheard of in this genre. Jodie Foster has sometimes projected too much intellectual avidity for the characters she's playing (that was true of both *The Accused* and her overrated teen-hooker turn in *Taxi Driver*). Here, her bright-eyed alertness is just what's called for, and it takes on an almost lyrical quality. Sporting a Southern accent, she gives Clarice a brisk, no-nonsense attitude and, beneath that, a beguiling blend of curiosity and fear. Clarice never seems more accomplished than a freshman overachiever, yet we're also convinced that she's daring enough to lock eyes with a lethal game player like Lecter.

The movie takes its eerie resonance from the bond between these two. The bond works because Lecter, as Hopkins plays him, remains weirdly, perversely likable—despite the fact that he'll tear people's faces off when given the opportunity. It works as well because Clarice's openness with Lecter isn't sentimentalized; it's shown to be part of what makes her a good detective. When she tells him that, as a girl, she once came upon the unendurable sound of lambs being slaughtered, and that the event has haunted her ever since, she's letting down all her defenses. In that moment, Lecter gets to partake of Clarice's identity without killing her. At the same time, he's doing her a favor, offering her a cathartic look in the mirror. What Clarice and Lecter share is a desire for something that few besides born detectives would ever seek: the full, horrifying knowledge of human darkness.

Entertainment Weekly, February 15, 1991

ON VAMPIRES

■■■

Dave Kehr

Vampires are like cars: every year, there are new models.

Early 1992 brought Fran Kuzui's *Buffy the Vampire Slayer,* in which a sunny California girl dispatches a band of mall-haunting Transylvanians, and John Landis's *Innocent Blood,* a curious and ineffective crossbreed of the gangster film and the horror movie, distinguished mainly by the spiffy, glow-in-the-dark contact lenses sported by the cast.

The end of the year brought *Bram Stoker's Dracula,* a star-studded, heftily budgeted effort directed by Francis Ford Coppola that promises to hew closely to the original 1897 novel that first codified the vampire myth.

As Dracula approaches his 100th birthday, one can only wonder at the ability of this crude figure of Victorian pop fiction to adapt and survive, and remain meaningful to each succeeding generation —much like Sherlock Holmes, Dracula's fictional contemporary and his strict, rationalist contradiction.

Intriguingly, Dracula's career runs almost exactly parallel to the birth and development of the movies, a fact that Coppola acknowledges by placing a key scene of his new film at a fairground "cinematograph." Is there a secret affinity between vampires and the cinema, a shadowy, morbid sexuality that links them on some basic level? A French scholar of the fantastic, Jean-Pierre Bouyxou, published a list in 1978 of 6,000 films dealing with vampirism, a figure that, with the videocassette and cable boom, has probably doubled by now.

That sex is the basis of the vampire myth now seems obvious, though according to Dracula historian Leonard Wolf none of the contemporary reviews of Stoker's novel made the connection. For the Victorians, it was necessary to speak in code, to displace sexuality onto bloodletting and death—much as, it should be pointed out, American movies do right now, substituting the forthright sexuality of the sixties and seventies for the graphic, orgasmic violence of the contemporary action film.

There may also have been other factors at work in Dracula's formation. As the nineteenth century drew to a close, it brought with it the completion of a century-long movement toward urbanization and the rise of the middle class. Dracula, the backcountry count visiting the sophisticated, swinging London of the 1890s, may have represented the last gasp of the old ways—of an evil aristocracy playing on the innocence and purity of the bourgeoisie, of primitive superstition and religiosity asserting itself—why will it never go away?—in the midst of a proudly modern, rationalist society.

Where Sherlock Holmes was the agent of the enlightened middle class, driving all mystery and darkness from the world through his powers of ratiocination, Dracula was his ultimate nemesis, spreading mist, chaos, madness—the ghost in the machine. (Curiously, these two enduringly popular, safely public domain characters have never met in a movie as far as I can tell; Christopher Lee, however, has made a career of playing both of them.)

Given the profound appeal of *Dracula,* the only wonder is that it took so long for Stoker's book to reach the screen, and then, in 1922, in an unauthorized version made in Germany. Friedrich Wilhelm Murnau's *Nosferatu* transfers the action from London to Bremen and Dracula into "Count Orlock," a Carpathian aristocrat interested in acquiring some urban real estate.

Orlock, as the real estate agent Thomas Hutter/Jonathan Harker discovers when he visits his castle, is actually one of the "nosferatu" —undead—with plans to devastate the city, beginning with Hutter's beautiful wife Ellen (Mina in Stoker and the export versions).

As closely as Murnau's *Nosferatu* follows Stoker's plotting, it also makes several fascinating alterations. The death ship that brings Nosferatu to Bremen unleashes a plague of rats upon the city, associating the vampire with vermin and disease—an association reinforced by the rodentlike makeup worn by the actor Max

Schreck. With this high, bald head, pointed ears, and clawlike hands, he seems less aristocrat than animal, the manifestation of a hostile, inhuman nature.

Another vampire tradition may also start here. Murnau was a homosexual, and some recent observers have seen in his monster a displacement—filtered through the shame and self-rejection fostered by the times—of his own sexuality. Though strictly heterosexual in the Stoker version, this Dracula drinks the blood of men and women both. If he poses a threat to society at large, it is most directly through his challenge to the stable, heterosexual couple represented by Hutter and Ellen—the building block of Western culture.

In Murnau's version, it is Nosferatu who seduces Harker (there is no intermediary of the three "vampire wives," as in Stoker and most subsequent tellings), but Ellen who seduces Nosferatu, luring the vampire to her bed and keeping him there until dawn—the only sure way of destroying him, as she has learned in *The Book of Vampires.* Sacrificing herself, Ellen destroys the couple in order to preserve it, a nihilistic conclusion that may reflect Murnau's own deep divisions.

Homoeroticism becomes relatively rare in subsequent vampire films, though the more socially acceptable (because of its appeal to male voyeurism) lesbian variant soon took hold (and was probably already present in the three wives of the classic 1931 Bela Lugosi–Tod Browning version).

The competing legend of Elisabeth Bathory, a seventeenth-century Hungarian countess who supposedly bathed in the blood of virgins to preserve her youth, inspired a number of films, including Harry Kumel's enduring Eurotrash classic *Daughters of Darkness* ('71), Stephanie Rothman's stylish, protofeminist *The Velvet Vampire* ('71), and Tony Scott's persistent *The Hunger* ('83), with its witty link of vampirism to the eighties club scene and the addition of sadomasochism.

It isn't necessary to go so far as to identify the vampire with homosexuality to appreciate the figure's function as the eternal outsider, the nocturnal contradiction of all the values daytime society holds dear. Though superficially villainous, the vampire becomes subliminally appealing—a sympathetic scapegoat figure who helps the audience work out its ambiguous feelings and rebellious feelings.

The Hammer horror films that began coming out of England in the late 1950s—beginning with Terence Fisher's *Horror of Dracula* in 1958—rode the first wave of youth culture. Christopher Lee's young and sexy count was a romantic rebel—a beat vampire, out of Marlon Brando and Jack Kerouac—ultimately brought low by the repressive forces of adulthood, represented by Peter Cushing's Professor Van Helsing.

By the time the Hammer series shuddered to an end in 1973, with *Count Dracula and His Vampire Bride,* Lee had aged past Lugosi in the role, leaving the field open for some younger blood. George Romero, the innovative director of *Night of the Living Dead* ('68), stepped into the breach with his 1978 *Martin,* still one of the most creative and provocative entries in the genre. Martin (John Amplas) is either a 900-year-old vampire or a shy teenager with serious sexual problems; the film never resolves the question but merely suggests that both conditions feel about the same and lead to similar consequences. In this era of diminished expectations (the film is set in an economically devastated suburb of Pittsburgh), the supernatural has shrunken, too—no longer the problem of priests, but of social workers.

Also emphatically young are the protagonists of Kathryn Bigelow's 1987 *Near Dark,* which stands as the last major accomplishment in the genre. Adrian Pasdar and Jenny Wright play a young outlaw couple at the center of an extended outlaw family; roving the Southwest (Bigelow suggestively blurs the line between the horror and Western genres), they live in trailers and feed at honky-tonk bars. The European roots of the form have been completely severed, leaving a vision of a violent, self-annihilating America, in which sex, death, and the quest for personal freedom have become permanently fused.

Vampires are not just an Anglo concern. The myth has proved potent enough to survive transplanting in any number of cultures. The early seventies brought the African American variants *Ganja and Hess, Blacula,* and *Scream, Blacula, Scream,* incorporating elements of African religion and ghetto life. Mexican horror star Paul Naschy counted Dracula among his many roles, and MCA Home Video has recently released the Spanish-language version of the 1931 *Dracula,* shot at night on the sets of the Lugosi film with a Latin American cast. The Spanish-version (made for export, before the technique of dubbing was perfected) is longer, more extravagantly acted (by Carlos Villarias as the Count), and considerably steamier. Awakening from a dream about Dracula, this Mina exclaims, "I feel like I've lost my virginity!"

More recently, a whole new genre of vampire films has sprung up in Hong Kong, in the midst of a Chinese culture that contains no native vampire lore. Instead, these films—*Mr. Vampire* is the longest-running series—draw on an elaborate mythology evolved by the movies: these vampires hop instead of fly, find their victims by smell (they can't find you if you hold your breath), can be frozen in place by pinning a prayer strip to their foreheads, and so on.

The challenge for Francis Ford Coppola and his new *Dracula* is to take this highly evolved tradition in a new direction, complete with a sense of fin-de-siècle decadence, of Klimt paintings, symbolist poetry, and absinthe bars. Will Coppola's Dracula, played by British actor Gary Oldman in a series of six different guises, enter the mythology alongside Lugosi and Lee, or will he fall by the wayside, with Frank Langella, Lon Chaney Jr., Jack Palance, and the legions of other unmemorable Draculas?

Chicago Tribune, November 8, 1992

BRAM STOKER'S DRACULA

■■■

Richard Corliss

He is Romeo, whose young wife, believing him dead, kills herself. He is Lucifer, vowing revenge on the God who has betrayed him. He is Don Juan, sucking the innocence out of his conquests. He is the Flying Dutchman, sailing the centuries for an incarnation of the woman he loved. He is Death, transmitting a venereal plague in his blood, in his kiss. He is even Jesus, speaking Jesus' last words as he dies, a martyr whose mission is to redeem womankind. Husband, seducer, widower, murderer, Christ and Antichrist, Dracula contains multitudes. He is every mortal man and every mortality with which man threatens women.

But is he "Bram Stoker's Dracula"? Though the screenplay is more faithful than most vampire movies to the book's plot, its Dracula is light-years from Stoker's. The novel's Count was no demon lover; he was a pestilence, the lord of bats and rats, and his touch was not romantic but rabid. He represented unseductive evil. Bram Stoker's *Dracula* proposed that English innocence could be

Jonathan Harker (Keanu Reeves, left) is having second thoughts about the career opportunity that has sent him to negotiate with a Transylvanian count (Gary Oldman) who wishes to purchase an English abbey. Oldman's hairdo must be tallied among the astounding special effects in *Bram Stoker's Dracula,* the ultra-stylized recasting of the Dracula legend by Francis Coppola. (© 1992. Photo courtesy of Columbia Pictures Industries, Inc. All Rights Reserved.)

sucked dry by European decadence, until English common sense drove a stake through its lurid heart.

Francis Ford Coppola's *Dracula,* to call it by its rightful name, powerfully reimagines this Victorian myth for the age of AIDS. Dracula (Gary Oldman) is a warrior-wooer impaled on the cross of his love; he must track his obsession until he is released from it. His misery gives him mesmeric mastery. The wretched Renfield (Tom Waits—terrific) bays to do Dracula's bidding. Flowers wilt at the Count's passage, and maidens burn at his touch. A young woman's tears turn to pearls in his hand.

So if Dracula is the world's oldest man, he is also the first man of the modern sexual revolution, awakening the erotic impulse in young women like flirtatious Lucy (Sadie Frost) and chaste Mina (Winona Ryder). They have known only puppy love; now they will taste wolf lust. And yet Dr. Van Helsing (Anthony Hopkins), who would purge Dracula's spirit from their bodies, is working his white magic on the wrong subjects. Dracula is the cursed soul in need of exorcism. He has "come across oceans and time" to find it. And only Mina, the avatar of his dead wife, can provide it.

Coppola composes movies as Wagner composed operas, setting primal conflicts to soaring emotional lines. The force of his will is as imposing as the range of his art. He goes for majesty over subtlety and, often as not, finds what he's looking for. Magic-lantern images are everywhere: in the blood pouring from an altar crucifix; in the Castle Dracula chauffeur garbed as Darth Vader; in the endless supertrain of the Count's cape; in the placental gel and rat's-nest cocoons that encase the vampire. But more: in the wonderfully spectral mood that does justice to the romance at *Dracula's* heart.

Everyone knows that Dracula has a heart; Coppola knows that it is more than an organ to drive a stake into. To the director, the Count is a restless spirit who has been condemned for too many years to interment in cruddy movies. This luscious film restores the creature's nobility and gives him peace.

Time, November 23, 1992

SCIENCE FICTION

ike horror, science fiction moved into town and went upscale from the drive-ins in the seventies, a raising of generic profile that began with the success of Stanley Kubrick's ambitious *2001: A Space Odyssey* (initially a reserved-seat Cinerama presentation) in 1968. The computerized seamlessness of *2001*'s special effects seemed a universe away from Georges Méliès's space-bullet in the eye of an angry man-in-the-moon, in the 1902 *Voyage à la lune*. From its opening moment—the mystical alignment of Earth, Moon, and Sun as seen from somewhere out in space—*2001* gave audiences a chance not only to share in an unprecedented visionary experience but, almost literally, to stand where they had never stood before.

In 1977 George Lucas, a young Northern Californian with only two previous features to his credit, completed *Star Wars*, a project most of the studios had turned down. In the movies, epic making is as old as show-biz hyperbole; epoch making is something else again. *Star Wars* became the new all-time box office champion, and a number of finite worlds would never be the same: Hollywood, the sci-fi genre, the art of special effects, the nature of screen spectacle, popular culture at large, and even U.S. geopolitics. A few months later, Steven Spielberg—director of the previous all-time b.o. champ *Jaws,* and sometime partner-to-be of Lucas—certified science fiction's feverish hold on audience enthusiasm with the Christmastime release of *Close Encounters of the Third Kind.*

It tells us something about the nature of screen sci-fi that Lucas stopped directing after *Star Wars,* preferring to exec-produce through his company Lucasfilm and ride herd on his state-of-the-art effects division, Industrial Light and Magic. (See Peter Rainer's essay in the chapter "Movie Adaptations: Sequels and Remakes.") Even the directors shepherding projects—Lucas's or their own—to the screen have to accept that a good deal of their action, atmosphere, even mise-en-scène, will have to be farmed out to the special effects and art departments. This is not the sort of auteurship dear to every filmmaker's (or critic's) heart. But, be this hi-tech heaven or hell, some people still succeed in mastering the medium rather than capitulating to it and get personal work on screen.

That emphatically includes Spielberg; the editor looks at *Close Encounters* as an ode to wonder that, for all the splendors of its 70mm light show, has its feet on terra firma and its heart in classical moviemaking. Michael Sragow praises Philip Kaufman's upscale-urban remake of the classic *Invasion of the Body Snatchers.* Kenneth Turan switches on *Scanners* and proposes that its most special effects are those in writer-director David Cronenberg's imagination. Hard-core effects freaks would find John Carpenter's *They Live* woefully lo-tech, but Henry Sheehan prizes it as a darkly satiric and all-too-relevant work of political science fiction. Peter Keough runs an EKG of *Total Recall,* Paul Verhoeven's 'twixt-*Terminator*s diversion for Arnold Schwarzenegger, and diagnoses crossed wires. Revisiting Ridley Scott's *Blade Runner* via the decade-late "Director's Cut" edition, Joseph Gelmis finds that much of "the future" has already caught up to it.

CLOSE ENCOUNTERS OF THE THIRD KIND

Richard T. Jameson

It's getting harder and harder for a movie to just happen anymore. I'm not talking about the ways movies get made (although, to be sure, that's become an extremely messy business), but the ways movies and audiences get together. In the absence of a vast public that simply "goes to the movies," film-selling has become a matter of creating Events—Events that may or may not live up to the induced expectations but which in any, er, event have an uphill fight to stay alive and spontaneous. *Close Encounters of the Third Kind* is having a harder time than most. It's a twenty-million-dollar film with a lot of investors anxious to recover their money. It's a film in a genre, sci-fi, variously blessed and burdened with an enthusiastic following whose specialized requirements for satisfaction do not necessarily have much to do with a film's being good as a film. It's a film in a genre, moreover, that gave the cinema a Number One Box Office Champ, *Star Wars*, and hence became embattled among critics and commentators deploring the preeminence of "mindless," two-dimensional, feel-good flicks on the top-grossing charts.

The happy facts are that, as with *Star Wars*, you don't have to be hyped on science fiction to dig this movie. Moreover, despite the awesomeness of the premise (We Are Not Alone) and the impressiveness of the major set-pieces, it is immensely satisfying in the basic and magical ways that all good movies are satisfying, regardless of genre. Steven Spielberg is a born moviemaker, and his film owes as much to Frank Capra as to Stanley Kubrick.

The little things matter so much. Not the feasibility of spacecraft design or the correctness of the insignia on some Air Force tunic, but how the night sky looks above a lonely prairie house, the size and clarity of it, the way it seems big and limitless, yet close, friendly, connected to known things: trees, houses and barns, your roof, your bedroom window—the appropriate and available arena for dreams to come true with breathless ease.

This is what has almost always been missing from sci-fi movies, although it's there in abundance in the fiction of Bradbury and Heinlein and the night countries and immense journeys of Loren Eiseley. This is what Spielberg never loses touch with.

It's a gentle, genial vision that informs the whole film. The unknown is awe inspiring but not—unlike the Devil-force in Spielberg's TV movie *Something Evil* ('72), the truck monster in *Duel* ('71), the White Death in *Jaws* ('75)—terrifying. Its first manifestations are disruptive, but, given a chance, Spielberg's favorite characters would rather chase it than pray for it to go away. When power-company employee Roy Neary (Richard Dreyfuss) and nocturnal runaway Barry Guiler (Cary Guffey) and his mother Jillian (Melinda Dillon) "inadvertently" come together on an Indiana hilltop under a suddenly busy sky, they find a family of country people waiting expectantly in a pickup truck. They look pretty lowbrow and just a tad goofy. They're also silently, glowingly happy. They *know.*

There is a moment, about a third of the way into the film, when Roy Neary, last seen in nocturnal depression, blinks himself awake in a soft golden light and listens bewilderedly to the low murmur of a television set. By this time we have got used to the phenomena attending the visitations of whatever-they-are. Among other things, lights and motors that were on have a tendency to go off; conversely, houses that lay still in the night come alive with happy-go-lucky carpet sweepers, mechanical toys, and pulses of moving light. We and Neary assume another visitation is upon us, until Spielberg cuts elsewhere in the room and we see that night has become morning, and Neary's little girl is sneaking a peek at the Saturday morning cartoons. "You aren't going to get mad, are you?" she asks with cautious hopefulness. No, he's not—though, truth to tell, he's a little disappointed.

Those are more of the little things I mean, the way small shocks of information—about power sources, hilltops, offscreen sounds, headlamps glimpsed through a truck's rear window, the soothing, potentially scintillating omnipresence of media—accrete and cross-refer until the movie becomes its own reality system. Which is what, finally, any good movie has to do.

It's obliging of the extraterrestrials to have such a strong directorial instinct. For *Close Encounters*—again, like any good movie—is finally *about* mise-en-scène. From the multitudinous randomness of experience, from all the shapes and sounds available to human sentience, the visitors make selections whose appositeness is not immediately apparent.

"The sun sang to me last night," an old derelict beams, while in the screaming dust storm around him a motley band of scientists and military personnel stand wondering why a flight of Navy planes missing since 1945 should have just set down intact in the Sonora Desert. On a mountain in India, saffron-robed crowds spontaneously repeat a dissonant but regular chant. In Indiana, Barry Guiler plays the same notes on a flute while his painter mother finds herself producing pictures of an odd rock formation—which Roy Neary likewise sees echoed in rumpled pillows and heaps of mashed potatoes.

The evidence piles up. *Evidence?* Mashed potatoes? A child's random piping? Evidence, yes: form that finally compels its own content. Music that becomes light, gesture, mathematical formula, shapes in space. The metamorphosis of reality, the rediscovery of possibility, the translation of ideas into visible action. What movies do. Why movies exist. Small wonder that the foremost pleader of the UFO cause should be played by one François Truffaut.

Spielberg's confidence in his artistry is sufficient that he can sprinkle his film with semididactic inside jokes: early on, Neary mostly ignores C. B. DeMille's once-admired parting of the Red Sea on a background telly, but he pays closer attention to his daughter's cartoon show, which happens to feature Daffy Duck's perplexity in meeting a Martian tar-baby. (In *Sugarland Express*, '74, Spielberg punctuated a respite in the cross-Texas chase with a Roadrunner cartoon, to comic and ultimately disturbing effect.)

Indeed, humor is a crucial ingredient in the director's vision and method. Just as *Jaws* was greatly enhanced in appeal by the low-key elaboration of the Roy Scheider, Richard Dreyfuss, and Robert Shaw characters as men with individualized notions of what's funny, *Close Encounters* relies on its strong but uninsistent comic undertow to persuade us that the human race is vital enough to be *worth* contacting by a superior order of being.

It must be acknowledged, however, that a significant portion of *Jaws's* audience used the character interludes for popcorn and visiting time, returning to their seats only when Bruce's next nosh seemed imminent. Likewise, Spielberg's sharp, affectionate comic indices of human fallibility—a wonderful four-punchline joke about airline reluctance to go official about a UFO sighting, Neary's excited garbling of "aurora borealis," translator Bob Balaban's dogged performance of his job even after the Truffaut character has shifted into English—apparently strike hardcore sci-fi freaks as unnecessary delaying tactics.

Still, it's that human dimension that most appeals to me in the movie, just as the cagey Frank Capra used to validate his most aggressive patriotic or pantheistic aspirations by investing his spokespersons with minutely watchable sets of mannerisms and a strong sense of earthy shrewdness. Spielberg is his own writer this time out and the characterizations wear a little thin; but he has the right hero in the klutzy, hugely sympathetic Dreyfuss, and his direction—or just judicious indulgence—of child actor Cary Guffey is nothing short of inspired.

He also has, in addition to first-cameraman Vilmos Zsigmond

and *2001* special-effects genius Douglas Trumbull, the most distinguished roster of second-unit cinematographers in film history: Douglas Slocombe (*Julia*), William A. Fraker, John Alonzo (*Chinatown*), Laszlo Kovacs. How much more splendid their contributions may look in 70mm, as opposed to the 35mm prints circulating in most venues, remains open to question at this point. But in a slightly perverse way the lack of 70mm projection armament serves to refocus critical attention where it most properly and essentially belongs: on Spielberg's narrative, its rich imagistic and structural cohesion, and on an imaginative sensibility that can adduce the connections among a child's delight with suddenly living toys, a giddy suburbanite's trashing of his tract home to erect a shrine to wonder, and a majestic spacecraft that manages to suggest a cathedral, an opera house, and a movie studio. To turn the film, finally, into a close encounter with Steven Spielberg's machineries of joy.

The Weekly (Seattle), December 14, 1977

POSTSCRIPT: *Close Encounters of the Third Kind* was rereleased several years later in a "Special Edition" that omitted some material from the original version and added 25 minutes' worth of new footage—including, least edifyingly, a scene inside the "Mothership" that arrives for the finale. After years of unavailability, the original *CE3K* can be retrieved on the Criterion laserdisc.

INVASION OF THE BODY SNATCHERS

Michael Sragow

In *Invasion of the Body Snatchers* everything is suspect. That garbage truck near your building—why is it there so late at night, every night? Why is there a pinwheel sticking out of the flower bed—and why is it spinning? And why is everyone quiet . . . too quiet? Director Philip Kaufman's frantic threnody on paranoia of the worst kind—the justified kind—is the most original and exciting film of the year.

It may be a remake, but it isn't slavish. All this film takes from Don

Siegel's 1956 version is its brilliant idea: aliens invade the world not in spaceships but in pods—great string bean–like organisms that turn humans into vegetables, taking over people's identities as they sleep. The only thing missing from the remade humans is emotion. The idea is a liberal nightmare: in the name of progress or civilization, or "passing to a higher form of life," we give up whatever makes us human.

And Kaufman is the filmmaker who can make a sophisticated audience feel this terror in their bones, and probably in their dreams for long nights afterwards. His gifts as an artist go deeper than his political sympathies, down to his primal fears. He has strength where it counts: not only in guts but also in intelligence and humor. He makes you laugh even after fear has knocked you down for the count.

Kaufman has made a career of reversing expectations. Who would have thought that his first big film, *The Great Northfield Minnesota Raid,* would be hiding an anti–law-and-order parable and a revisionist view of the Old West under its archaic title? Or that his next big film, *The White Dawn* (which looks, at first glance, like a shipwreck-adventure story), would be about the destructive vanity of Western white culture at the turn of the century—not only an Eskimo saga, but also the story of a tragic culture clash?

The original *Body Snatchers,* an economical, gripping suspenser, was thought to be a comment on conservatism, with the pod-people as Eisenhower's quietist conformists. But the way Kaufman reworks it, the satiric target is fuzzy-headed seventies enlightenment. Those who talk incessantly about their emotions—even honest, cultivated liberals—may be dissipating them just as much as any uptight conservative. The new vocabulary of est, or transactional analysis, or the other with-it therapies is just another disguise for people who fear their own spontaneity and individuality. It's a new set of clothes for conformity.

Kaufman sets his film not in the small town of the Siegel version but in contemporary San Francisco, "the big city, the real place where paranoia should be dealt with." The nascent pods float through the universe like stingless jellyfish and land in the city like rain. Who would be more likely to welcome the red hybrid flowers that they form than hip San Franciscans, who probably talk to their plants as often as Dr. Doolittle did to the animals? Some of these people are so affected—hung up on psychological jargon or hypnotized by the Forty-Niners—they may be pods already.

The drama's lead figure, a city health inspector (Donald Sutherland), begins to see the zombielike behavior among passersby as a plague. The film acquires not only the cosmic horror of the first film but also the frenzied urban intensity of *Panic in the Streets*.

You may never again identify with thriller heroes as strongly as you do with Kaufman's. They're not mice to be pawed by catlike villains, but intelligent, quirky characters who use and trust their senses. If they're as confused as they are afraid, it's because the cause of their terror is unfathomable. Forget *Interiors* or *The Deer Hunter* or the other movies that have won praise for their pretentious ensemblework: Kaufman's San Francisco quartet is like a rep company at the peak of its cooperation and talent. At first Sutherland is a comic crusader, confronting a restaurateur with a rat dropping passed off as a caper. Then his look clouds over in melancholy. As he fights his own sleepiness and possible transformation, Brooke Adams, his close assistant, supplies a dash of romance. Kaufman releases the warmth and charm Terrence Malick muffled in *Days of Heaven*: Adams is as vivacious as a home-grown Geneviève Bujold. She even gets to jiggle her eyeballs.

Jeff Goldblum as their poet friend—a clown prince of paranoia—uses his tall thin body to cut into other people's company like a knife blade. He whets his wit with aggressive conversation—even when he mumbles to himself. Veronica Cartwright as his wife (who runs the mud baths that support them) is woman enough to put up with him. She's down-to-earth. He's a flake. Yet her feelings, if more rooted, are nearly as close to the skin. She's so spunky that if you boiled down her essence you could turn pods into people. If she and Goldblum can't escape the pods, we feel, no one can.

Leonard Nimoy, as the psychologist whom they approach for help, is the final masterstroke of casting. A saturnine guru, Nimoy exploits his "Star Trek" otherworldliness. He couldn't be a pod, we think. That would be too obvious.

The pods' secrets, obvious to us, are hidden to the San Franciscans. But Kaufman locks us into the humans' hysteria. The film's humor comes from how far he stretches their apprehension, until a newfangled telephone wire slithering into a wall upsets us as much as the squirming pods do.

Kaufman's cinematographer, Michael Chapman, communicates paranoia more effectively than if the theater ushers straitjacketed audiences at the door. He makes the handheld camera seem lighter than air. But he also knows when to stop whirling: a still, early-morning cityscape, with the Transamerica pyramid dead center, has the mystery of quiet before the storm. Since San Francisco is itself off-kilter, when our heroes start to look at it askew we catch their dizziness. Kaufman and Chapman use off-angle shots better than anyone since Carol Reed in *The Third Man*. Even innocent faces on a bus seem infected with this new social disease. The film's shadows have a Rackham-like eerieness. When you get home, brush off your night light.

Unlike Siegel in the earlier film version, Kaufman depicts the humans' death and transfiguration. He builds to it as teasingly as Spielberg playing with the shark's first appearance in *Jaws*. When Goldblum rests side by side with his duplicate, ignorant that the pod-being may invade him while he sleeps, suspense rests on the flicker of his eyelids.

Kaufman's pod-births are as risky as Spielberg's aliens in *Close Encounters*: the concept is so outrageous that some people will snort at it. But the freakiest scenes here are the most terrifying. The pod-people emerge from a throbbing, "bleeding," floral bulb and take shape with obscene unnaturalness—they're adults undergoing fetal births—their infantile gasping is repellent. Even UFO freaks must see that the promised higher form of life is a living death. In a daring Bayside scene, a sleeping girl crumbles in her lover's arms. Her duplicate springs up from nearby rushes, nude, an android Eve in a hellish Eden.

With writer W. D. Richter (best known for the goofy *Slither*), Kaufman plants dramatic metaphors, sight gags, and jokes as fruitful as his visual set-pieces. In this vegetablized context, there's even a comic sizzle when Sutherland slices celery for his wok. Richter and Kaufman have picked the perfect spot for us to see our first closeup pod—the mud baths, where San Franciscans dip into the primal ooze. Kaufman keeps the satire of contemporary hipness flowing with the horror, till you don't know whether to laugh or cry.

Even Denny Zeitlin's music and the hypersensitive soundtrack blend into cacophonous urban horror. When Sutherland thinks he's found an escape hatch, the Royal Scots Dragoon Guards' mooglike rendition of "Amazing Grace" bagpipes up a promise of salvation. But it actually comments on pod-people being born again.

Kaufman must love to wrestle with his fears and pin them to the ground. Only a director fascinated with technology could imbue the mechanical gimmicks with such poetic charge. Only a director with a sincere revulsion toward technology could make blood red garbage trucks a frightening symbol of mechanized death. The plastic garbage pails filled with human remains evoke Vietnam body bags.

Invasion of the Body Snatchers is perhaps the most sophisticated of all sci-fi thrillers. What Brian DePalma achieves in parts of *The Fury*—a hallucinatory tension so heightened we laugh at our own responses—Kaufman seizes on and sustains for an entire movie. Watching this film is catching Kafka's Gregor Samsa in midmetamorphosis, before he realizes he's a bug—and knowing you can't stop his transformation. Kaufman has made a Kafka film for the millions. He's turned a classic B movie into an A-plus.

Los Angeles Herald Examiner, December 22, 1978

SCANNERS

■■■

Kenneth Turan

Doing justice to a chilling, exhilarating film like *Scanners* is chancy. The picture is a genre classic, a masterpiece in its own spooky way, but saying that evokes visions of elitist projects that delicately scrutinize the human condition. *Scanners* is not like that at all. It is a hard-edge, no-nonsense science fiction thriller, an unpretentious gem that knows its own limits and succeeds brilliantly within them.

The force behind *Scanners* is writer-director David Cronenberg, a Canadian whose previous features caused *Halloween's* director, John Carpenter, to say, "Cronenberg is better than all of us combined." Once known for blithely yelling "More blood!" on the set, Cronenberg has toned down his act considerably here. *Scanners* has two scenes of almost indescribable violence, but they are intrinsic to the director's purpose, the creation of a singularly pervasive sense of skin-crawling disorientation.

Scanners turn out to be freaks of nature, people born with a form of telepathy so intense they can totally control the minds and bodies of others. In its raw form scanning is a terrible hindrance, and scanners are so overwhelmed by what one calls "the other voices, the ones without lips" that they can barely function. However, with the help of a drug called Ephemerol, scanning can be controlled, its power concentrated. How potent a force does it become? In one jolting sequence in the film's opening minutes, a scanner literally blows another person's head to little tiny bits.

But the immediate shock value of that splattered head, considerable though it is, is only part of its purpose. The deeper objective is to put the audience firmly and forever off balance, tagging *Scanners* as a film in which knowing what will happen next is impossible. The effect is profoundly disturbing, and once Cronenberg establishes it he never relaxes its grip.

The actual plot of *Scanners* is conventional enough. On one side are the benign scanners, especially our hero, Cameron Vale (Stephen Lack), and his girlfriend (Jennifer O'Neill); on the other, the bad ones, led by the menacing Darryl Revok (Michael Ironside), whose aim in life is to "bring the world of normals to its knees." There is also the usual mysterious scientist, Dr. Paul Ruth (Patrick McGoohan), who knows more than he lets on about the inevitable battle between those forces of good and evil.

What is unusual is the expertness of Cronenberg's direction. He has a natural feel for this kind of material, a sureness while handling it and the great good sense to treat the inflammatory components in as low-key a manner as possible. His central conceit, that the best way to physically show telepathic powers is by having the actors grotesquely contort their faces, is a masterly one, and he also has a fine eye for the small details—a bandaged hole in a man's forehead, a mysterious symbol on a miniature bottle, a melting telephone— that are essential to creating and sustaining believability.

While some of the acting is on the weak side, Cronenberg was fortunate in his choice of a bearded Patrick McGoohan. Once the star of the TV series "Secret Agent" and "The Prisoner," he is ideal as Dr. Ruth, biting off his words in a deep, resonant voice fraught with secret teachings. Better yet is Canadian actor Michael Ironside, who uses his death's-head face and demonic grin to turn Darryl Revok into a blood-chilling personification of sheer, unrelenting evil.

Special effects are crucial to a film like this, and again the choices were wise. Gary Zeller, who worked on *Altered States,* coordinated the various fires, crashes, and explosions, and Dick Smith, Hollywood's preeminent makeup artist (the man who made Dustin Hoffman old in *Little Big Man* and Linda Blair ungodly in *The Exorcist*), created the apocalyptic final scene. That episode, an unrelievedly ghoulish battle between two scanners out to annihilate each other, is as spectacular as it is difficult to sit through without cringing. Like the rest of *Scanners,* though, it is the very best of its kind to appear for a long, long time.

California, February 1981

THEY LIVE

■■■

Henry Sheehan

Politics is generally not invited to the Hollywood party, since it is expected to frighten away too many other guests. However, in John Carpenter's latest, *They Live,* politics is a boisterous gate-crasher, kicking down the front door and sitting at the head of the table. A dead-eyed satire, *They Live*—released on the eve of a Presidential election—is the damnedest American movie of the year, a wonderful concoction of loony crafting, inspired disgust, and visceral pleasure that could only be rigged up by a superb technician like Carpenter going for broke.

Former pro wrestler Roddy Piper stars as John Nada, an unemployed construction worker left penniless and homeless by Reaganomics (although he is too patriotic to put it that way). Arriving in Los Angeles, he manages to land a job but, having to wait a week for his first paycheck, ends up bedding down in a squatters' camp, Justiceville. Once there, he begins to notice queer happenings: a bearded man appears on TV warning people to get away from their sets; people complain that they get severe headaches when they can't watch their favorite shows; a nearby church emits sounds of a choir, but only a few people are inside. John noses around, but just when he is on the verge of discovering what's going on—something to do with mysterious sunglasses hidden in the church—a huge detachment of police, complete with air and armor support, shows up to clear out Justiceville and to arrest and beat a few of the folks who have been hanging around the church.

Carpenter handles these opening sequences with typical aplomb. Although his projects vary in conception, he always executes them in style, making maximum use of the resources at hand. John's

Now you know the truth about those happy talk TV newscasters—they're really extraterrestrial invaders whose camouflage and subliminal mind-warping message have just been revealed in this late scene from John Carpenter's *They Live*. (© by Universal City Studios, Inc. Courtesy of MCA Publishing Rights, a Division of MCA Inc.)

arrival in town, during which he jumps off a freight train in a rusty, graffiti-choked railroad yard, pays obvious *hommage* to Sergio Leone, duplicating in an abbreviated way Charles Bronson's disembarkation at the opening of *Once Upon a Time in the West*. But while the mimicry is knowing and amusing, it is also appropriate. The dramatic entrance pegs John not just as a loner but as a potentially dangerous and somewhat mysterious figure, like a gunfighter. And Carpenter does more than borrow the archetypal image, he modifies it. John carries his tools in a knapsack the way a gunfighter totes his gun in a holster; he is a particular kind of gunslinger, the blue-collar kind.

Building a lowering air of tension and suspense as he follows John through L.A.'s poor downtown streets—streets that look shockingly new because Hollywood's backyard rarely makes it so plainly to the big screen—Carpenter tops off these opening chapters with the police siege. The demolition of the poor people's homes is a superb two-ring circus (the squatters' camp and the church) featuring gradually escalating violence that builds to a blistering climax when a police bulldozer rips the shacks and hovels apart.

Until this point, *They Live* is a notably efficient but thematically unexceptional thriller. But now John dons a pair of those sunglasses and the whole world changes. Not only does color turn to black and white, but subliminal messages also become acutely clear. Billboards that ostensibly feature bikini-clad lasses touting vacations actually contain the message GET MARRIED AND REPRODUCE. Store signs order: CONSUME. Magazine covers blare: OBEY. What's worse, some people don't look like people, but like bulb-eyed humanoid flies. Gradually John realizes that these monsters form part of the upscale shopping crowd—but newscasters and politicians on TV are also plug-uglies.

John has stumbled on a terrible secret: Republican politicians, successful businessmen, and most yuppie types are actually invaders from another planet. Their goal? To turn us into a planet of mindless, will-less consumers. These aliens are after nothing more nor less than galactically expanding markets, and they will crush the spirit of any planetary species in order to ensure brisk sales.

Carpenter manages, to his credit, to maintain the film's sense of threat after John makes his discovery, even though that plot turn is a signal for the movie to embark on a series of wildly comic free-for-alls. For example, the glasses allow the wearer not only to see the truth but to get high as well, and it is not long before John grabs a gun and giddily starts shooting up the town, trading insults all the while with dodging space creatures. ("You look as ugly to us as we do to you." "That's impossible.") He hooks up with an attractive woman, Holly, a minor TV executive (Meg Foster), whom he kidnaps as a hostage. Trouble is, when they start to relax and get to know each other, the woman almost kills him with a couple of expert karate chops.

John thereafter makes his way blindly to the hideout of a human underground out to wage war on the aliens. The aliens' equipment includes a space transporter with all the trappings of a business-commuter airline and a gingerbread function room out of an airport hotel. The action henceforward is laced with parodies of TV commercials, happy-talk news, and, most of all, Republican politics. Carpenter gives us a glimpse of an alien delivering a speech that could have been taken verbatim from either Reagan or Bush on the stump. (*They Live* was filmed in March 1988, so all anyone on the film had to do to check for authenticity was to switch on the tube.)

Carpenter hammers contemporary consumerist politics over and over again, but somehow the point never grows stale, partly because the satire runs deeper than it first appears. When John and his hostage have their run-in, it is not only a funny reversal of their situation but also the physicalization of their social relations. John is a worker, Holly a female executive—in TV yet. So when she bludgeons and nearly kills him, she is only expressing the logical outcome of a corporate feminism in which women are given an equal opportunity to rip off working people.

The film is also kept fresh by Carpenter's resourcefulness. While the director reins in Piper enough to get a coherent performance out of the neophyte actor, he also gives the hammy ex-wrestler a chance to strut his stuff. Besides his moments of crazy braggadocio during the shoot-'em-up scene, Piper get to fight when he tries to make a stubbornly reluctant friend (Keith David) put on the sunglasses and see what's what. Carpenter gets a lot of energy out of what is essentially a send-up, but the notion of found talent—of coming across useful bits of reality or turning apparent limitations to an advantage—also imparts a much-needed dose of authenticity.

Finally, *They Live*'s greatest virtues result from its uncommon bonding of dedicated workmanship and stylistic self-assurance. After a bad experience with the big-budget *Big Trouble in Little China* ('86), Carpenter renounced (at least for a while) mainstream film production and returned to his roots as a low-budget specialist (his late-seventies classic *Halloween* set a record for most profitable independent film to that time). Signing a production agreement with arty Alive for a trio of genre films to be released through Universal, he quickly showed that he was changing more than his budgets. Known for years as Hollywood's most dedicated Hawksian, a champion of sure narrative, invisible editing, and unobtrusive camera placement, Carpenter now shows another side. What clearly matters most to him is his shooting-gallery politics. So, with the assurance of a director who knows all the rules backwards and forwards, he often ignores them, gliding here and there over his story to make his points at will and in whatever tone suits him. And it works.

Carpenter has returned to his own appreciation not of workmanship so much as workers. The heroes in his best films stumble across their adventures in the course of doing their jobs—whether they're intergalactic garbage collectors (*Dark Star*, '74), cops (*Assault on Precinct 13*, '76), babysitters (*Halloween*, '78), or disc jockeys (*The*

Fog, '80). Even in the fantasy of *They Live,* Carpenter's heroes show believable working traits in a dozen different ways. Perhaps because these are the skills that Carpenter himself displays so well, it is no stretch for him to dramatize them. And perhaps—because as a worker in a Wall Street–dominated industry he has had trouble making his voice heard—he knows what it's like for people in a Wall Street–dominated country.

Los Angeles Reader, November 4, 1988

TOTAL RECALL

■■■

Peter Keough

The best science fiction transforms gimmicks and special effects into metaphors. *Total Recall* reverses that process. The project was "inspired" by a story ("We Can Remember It for You Wholesale") by Phillip K. Dick, the late cult favorite who, if not the most visionary of sci-fi writers, was at least the weirdest. It was directed by Paul Verhoeven, whose *RoboCop* ('86) was a winsome and blood-soaked critique of corporate America. And it stars Arnold Schwarzenegger, who blithely embodied the death wish in *The Terminator* ('84). So the project promised to be a new classic of the genre. But add to this formula the biggest budget of the year and the marketing expectations of a blockbuster, and the result is just another summer disappointment. The movie has the bloated cheesiness that only fifty million dollars can buy and just enough inspiration and brilliance to recall the totality of its betrayal.

Before any such brilliance can manifest itself, *Total Recall* has slogged through enough uninspired dialogue and exposition to dim the most optimistic expectations. Schwarzenegger plays Quaid, a twenty-first century construction worker whose placid, lumpen life of labor and domestic bliss with his svelte blonde wife Lori (Sharon Stone) is disrupted by dreams and discontent. A recurrent nightmare involving a beautiful stranger (Rachel Ticotin) and horrible death on the Martian surface makes him wonder about the meaning of it all. "I feel meant for more than this," he says, nuzzling Lori. "I have to be somebody! Let's move to Mars!" Lori points out that

Mars is cold and racked with revolution, adding, "You *are* someone, you're the man I love!" "You're the girl of my dreams!" notes Quaid. "Have a nice day!" coos Lori as Quaid heads for work.

Lines like these would undo Olivier; uttered by Schwarzenegger in his stolid Styrian accent, they establish an immediate, inappropriate tone of camp parody. For the premise of *Total Recall* to have any credibility, the identity of the hero as a blue-collar everyman must be convincing, but Schwarzenegger is absurd as a working stiff regardless of the century. When he climbs aboard the subway and watches a televised ad for Rekall, an agency that implants false memories for recreational purposes, the focus is not on his dewy-eyed temptation but on Verhoeven's cleverly sardonic parody of advertising. No crisis of conscience or identity can be sensed as Quaid broods about the allure of fake adventure compared to the dreariness of his day with a jackhammer and heads at last for the Rekall office.

Quaid orders a memory resembling his recurrent dream, but before the Rekall technicians can implant it in his brain he convulses into a schizoid episode. Another self, a real secret agent from Mars pursued by real enemies, takes over, thrusting Quaid into the middle of an interplanetary chaos involving an insurrection against a despotic Martian mining corporation, ancient alien artifacts in a Martian cave, and a mutant with a baby growing from his belly who spouts a wisdom combining Jean-Paul Sartre and Leo Buscaglia.

Fantasy as a last resort against a tyrannical system provided the thematic backbone of *Brazil* ('85), lending substance to the film's pyrotechnics. *Total Recall*'s subtext is similar, but the perverse possibilities, as well as the coherence of the narrative line, are lost in pretension.

As in *RoboCop* and in all such sagas since *Oedipus,* the hero's only recourse is to discover who he or she really is. For Schwarzenegger and Verhoeven, that entails a lot of madcap gore. But toned down by studio honchos concerned about an X rating, the violence has become even more gratuitous than it would have been otherwise. Instead of providing the tone of diabolic nightmare that edges such earlier Verhoeven works as *The Fourth Man* ('79) into the realm of hysterical allegory, the bloodletting in *Total Recall* merely offers Schwarzenegger a forum for Arnoldisms such as quipping "Screw you" while skewering a squealing adversary with a three-foot drill. The film is filled with gun battles and chases in outlandish settings, from a subway escalator at rush hour to a Martian red-light district known as Venusville. But buried beneath the body count, the discreetly used blood squibs, the snapped necks, impaled skulls, and exploding vehicles, heads, and eyeballs, Quaid's stilted question, "Who am I?", seems not only irrelevant but ridiculous.

Still, Verhoeven works hard to make *Total Recall* meaningful. As in *RoboCop,* his critique of capitalism is archly literal: Cohaagen (Ronny Cox in a histrionic reprise of his role in the earlier film), head of the Martian colony, not only owns the means of production but the air as well, and the proletariat bear the marks of class injustice on their bodies, hideously mutated by exposure to solar radiation. And Quaid's dilemma about what is real and what is dream almost develops into a metaphysical riddle worth solving.

In the end, though, nothing makes any sense and nothing matters; when in doubt, *Total Recall* can always rely on Arnold to do something like stick a probe up his nose and remove a homing device the size of a golf ball. "You're nothing!" Cohaagen screams at him as the movie lurches to the spectacular optical effects of its climax. "You're just a dream!" If only he were that much.

Boston Phoenix, June 1, 1990

BLADE RUNNER

■■■

Joseph Gelmis

The enduring movie image of the imperial skyscraper city of the future was envisioned in 1921, when German Expressionist filmmaker Fritz Lang stood at the rail of an ocean liner steaming into New York harbor and was awestruck by his first sight of the city. Back in Berlin, Lang labored for two full years to create *Metropolis* ('27). Even more than the real city that inspired it, Lang's monumental vision of urban grandeur and squalor, of masters and slaves, became the visual and class-structured starting point for innumerable film fantasies using a metropolis as a melodramatic setting for colossal conflicts.

One of the greatest of these is Ridley Scott's *Blade Runner.* The release of the Director's Cut of that 1982 classic was a major movie event of 1992—the chance to see this visionary masterpiece on a big screen and to lose yourself in the incredibly realistic world of 2019 Los Angeles, which looks like *Metropolis* with add-on mile-high pyramidal megastructures.

Nominally, the news about the rerelease of *Blade Runner* is that Scott has eliminated the voiceover narration and preposterous upbeat ending he added—in hopes of broadening its appeal—at the time of the film's original release. In fact, these changes are less important to the viewer than they are to the director. They restore the integrity of its maker's vision without appreciably improving the film's central flaw: the world in which it immerses us is astonishingly real, but the characters are sushi—cold fish—and we don't really care what happens to them.

Blade Runner is easier to admire than to like. It is bleak, devoid of escapist fun and derring-do. Smiles are sinister. It rains all the time. Several humanoids and humans die hard.

Inspired by a Phillip K. Dick novel, *Do Androids Dream of Electric Sheep?*, *Blade Runner* is about four runaway androids—called replicants in the film—who illegally come to Earth, try to reach their designer to prolong their brief four-year life span, and are pursued by a cop—a blade runner—assigned to destroy them. The artificial humans love life more than the real humans.

Harrison Ford, unsmiling, deglamourized, and fallible, his hair short and his trenchcoat dirty, plays a plodding gumshoe who is regularly mauled by the humanoids and rescued by the script. He's a licensed exterminator disgusted with his job, trying to save his soul as well as his skin.

Each of the characters has a distinctive look. The imperious genius inventor of the Nexus 6 replicants (Joe Turkel) is arrogant, gaunt, Mephistophelian. His prize creation (Sean Young), with whom the detective falls in love, is sleek, with her hair upswept, suit shoulders squared, a blend of 1940 and 1980. The leader of the rogue replicants, hair bleached and flat-topped, a bemused sneer curling the corner of his lips, is played with such convincing menace by Dutch actor Rutger Hauer that he dominates his scenes with the reluctant and scared cop who is trying to kill him.

As an illusion, the movie is a masterpiece. Special effects whiz Douglas Trumbull, collaborating with Richard Yuricich and David Dryer, produces his most dazzling illusions since *2001: A Space Odyssey*. Art director Lawrence G. Paull and "visual futurist" Syd Mead fashion a mind-boggling array of environments and gadgets: realistic flying cars, blimps cruising above the pyramidal skyscrapers, immense outdoor TV screens advertising smokes and pills, teeming street bazaars, derelict neighborhoods, palatial offices, life-sized toys, a police force resembling the Gestapo. The eerie, evocative musical score by Vangelis is a blend of resonating thunder, lingering electronic chords, and tinkly underwater vibrato.

Ultimately, even the human characters' failure to engage our sympathies is part of *Blade Runner*'s vision of a dehumanizing future in which it's hard to tell real people from ersatz humans. The Director's Cut emphasizes this by adding a ten-second daydream and uncanny closeups of Harrison Ford's eyes that subliminally raise questions—never actually answered—about whether he is a man or a replicant.

What the Director's Cut adds is ambiguity. As a romantic, I prefer the preposterous feel-good ending, in which Ford and his android girlfriend, Sean Young, escape into the wilderness, to the Director's Cut, which simply eliminates some footage and ends the film sooner. It's not satisfying. But it fits the new version's mood.

New York Newsday, September 11, 1992

WAR MOVIES

A s J. Hoberman has already observed in his perceptive essay "On How the Western Was Lost," earlier in this book, Hollywood made only one Vietnam War film (John Wayne's *The Green Berets,* '68) during the conflict itself; otherwise, our collective anguish—moral, political, social, emotional—found contemporaneous expression in a variety of other genres, from Western allegories to the "youth movies" of the counterculture. Only after the withdrawal of the last "American advisers" and the fall of Saigon in 1975 did Hollywood gear up for a first and then a second wave of movies portraying the war directly. Interestingly, the least pretentious of them—including one of the best, Ted Post's *Go Tell the Spartans* ('78)—received short shrift at the box office. But some were tailored to be epic Events, and U.S. audiences embraced them with simultaneous trepidation and relief. There was emotional, if not necessarily aesthetic, justice in the inevitability with which a film from each wave was named Best Picture of its year by the Academy of Motion Picture Arts and Sciences: Michael Cimino's *The Deer Hunter* in 1978 and Oliver Stone's *Platoon* in 1986.

Many of the Vietnam movies have been treated at length in our previous Mercury House anthologies. We limit ourselves here to three: *Platoon,* reviewed by Michael Sragow; Stanley Kubrick's *Full Metal Jacket,* discussed by Jay Carr; and Stone's *Born on the Fourth of July,* assessed by Morris Dickstein. But first, we turn to a non-

Vietnam war movie, one of the very best: Roger Ebert talks about *The Big Red One,* an account of America's participation in the European theater of World War II, from the first shot fired to the last, by a guy who was there—Samuel Fuller.

THE BIG RED ONE

Roger Ebert

Sam Fuller's film *The Big Red One* ('80) is a lot of war stories strung together in a row, almost as if the director had filmed it for the thirty-fifth reunion of his old army outfit and didn't want to leave anybody out. That's one of the most interesting things about it—the feeling that the movie's events are included not because they help the plot or make a point, but just because they happened.

Some of them happened to Fuller himself, he tells us, and there's a kid in the movie (Robert Carradine) who's obviously supposed to be young Sam. Other scenes are based on things Fuller heard about. Some of them are brutal and painful, some of them are romantic, a lot of them are corny. The movie takes no position on any of them: this movie is resolutely nonpolitical, is neither pro- nor antiwar, is deliberately just a record of five dogfaces who found themselves in the middle of the action.

The movie's title refers to the U.S. Army's 1st Infantry Division, and the action follows one rifle squad through the entire Second World War. The squad leader is a hard-bitten sergeant, played by Lee Marvin with the kind of gravel-voiced, squint-eyed authority he had more than a decade before in *The Dirty Dozen.* His four squad members are kids in their teens, and his job is to whip them into shape. He does. The squad is so efficient, or competent, or just plain lucky, that it survives to see action in half the major theaters of the war in Europe. At a rough count, they fight in North Africa, Tunis, Sicily, Normandy, Omaha Beach, rural France, Belgium, Czechoslovakia, and Germany. Halfway through this litany we begin to suspect that *The Big Red One* is supposed to be something more than plausible.

The squad fights in so many places, stays together in one piece for so long, experiences so many of the key events of World War II (from the invasion of Europe to the liberation of the Nazi death camps), that of course these characters are meant to be symbols of all the infantrymen in all the battles. But Fuller, who fought in the 1st Division, seems determined to keep his symbols from illustrating a message. They fight. They are frightened. Men kill, other men are killed. What matters is if you're still alive. "I don't cry because that guy over there got hit," Fuller said in an interview, "I cry because I'm gonna get hit next."

This leads to a deliberately anecdotal structure for the film. One battle ends, another begins. A little orphan kid appears out of the smoke, is befriended, braids flowers into the netting of a helmet, is forgotten for the rest of the film. What we have is a series of experiences so overwhelming that the characters can't find sense or pattern in them and so simply try to survive them through craft and experience.

Is this all Fuller got out of the war? He seems to believe it's all anybody really gets, that the vast patterns of war's meaning are really just the creations of novelists, filmmakers, generals, and politicians, and that for the guy under fire there is no pattern, just the desperately sincere desire to get out in one piece.

The Big Red One is Sam Fuller's first film in nearly a decade, and by far the most expensive and ambitious he's ever made. It's like a dream come true, the capstone of a long career. Fuller began as a newspaper reporter in New York, he wrote pulp novels and Hollywood scripts, he fought in the war, he returned to Hollywood and directed a lot of B action pictures that are considered by connoisseurs to be pulp landmarks: *I Shot Jesse James, Pickup on South Street, Hell and High Water, Shock Corridor.* One previous film hardly seen in this country was a 1972 West German production with the marvelous title *Dead Pigeon on Beethoven Street.*

While this is an expensive epic, he hasn't fallen to the temptations of the epic form. He doesn't give us a lot of phony meaning, as if to justify the scope of the production. There aren't a lot of deep, significant speeches. In the ways that count, *The Big Red One* is still a B movie—hard-boiled, filled with action, held together by male camaraderie, directed with a lean economy of action. It's one of the most expensive B pictures ever made, and I think that helps it fit the subject. "A" war movies are about War, but "B" war movies are about soldiers.

Roger Ebert's Video Companion

PLATOON

▬▬▬

Michael Sragow

Platoon is an explosive paradox of a movie. It operates like a single-minded fragmentation bomb. It's the first feature film about Vietnam to be made by a Vietnam vet, writer-director Oliver Stone. But Stone pins his harrowing, firsthand combat saga to a second-hand story about an idealistic recruit, a good sergeant, and a bad sergeant. Stone's images and vignettes are often searing, volatile, upsetting. But the overall arch of his screenplay is nothing more than a banal coming-of-age story, in which a boy reaches manhood by going back and forth between two father figures.

Platoon isn't a case of a filmmaker choosing to Hollywoodize his own experiences by tying together vivid real-life incidents with a prefab plot. The Good and Evil forces in the Americans' ranks are absolutely central to Stone's vision of Vietnam as the place where his hero, Chris Taylor, gets in touch with the eternal mysteries of life and death. Especially the latter.

When we first see him emerge from the maw of a transport plane's tailgate, Taylor (Charlie Sheen) is too insecure and confused to stalk and kill or even move with confidence. The film chronicles how, by going through hell with the 2nd Platoon of Bravo Company, this sheltered college dropout comes closer to real life—the heart of the matter, or maybe I should say the heart of darkness of things. In pseudo-Hemingway fashion, he acts with clearheaded decisiveness only when he finally commits a cold-blooded execution—not of a North Vietnamese, but of a dangerously unbalanced fellow American.

Taylor, who comes to the screen complete with a tendentious first-person voiceover narration, is Stone's spokesman. The movie is just as self-conscious as Taylor is. At one point Taylor refers to the bad sergeant as his platoon's Ahab. At the end he says that the Americans were really fighting themselves—the enemy within. Stone the writer is in love with literary allusions and neat mirror images. Luckily, though, Stone the director is in love with unruly details and outright chaos.

Stone keys the audience to the sheer tumult of battle and the brutal imperative of survival. In the film's best moments, Stone hits on vignettes that have the layered textures of you-are-there reality. When Taylor's platoon plants a night ambush near an imposing Buddha, it's not just for pictorial effect. The lookouts plan to spot the North Vietnamese as they walk the overgrown path leading to the ruined shrine. And when the enemy arrives, Stone isn't afraid to have his surrogate Taylor look foolish. Taylor freezes—and Stone indicates with the sparest means that although his weapons are a few feet from his fingertips, they seem to be a football field away.

Because Stone builds our sympathy for the grunts by focusing first on callow youths and their red badges of courage, he's able to lead us into at least one devastating *emotional* ambush. Probably the most controversial sequence—and surely the most potent one—starts when the platoon investigates an enemy bunker compound. Inside the compound a sprung booby trap strews American limbs. Outside the compound the enemy kills one of the grunts and trusses him to a tree as a taunt to the rest of the platoon. By the time they arrive at a nearby village, they're fighting mad or fighting scared—and they're just as homicidal either way. Stone earns his directorial stripes in this sequence. He evokes the same horrified sympathy for the terrorized villagers as he does for the ignorant, nerve-racked Americans. In this sequence, and in a climactic night battle that reaches truly Homeric proportions, Stone lifts the audience by the short hairs. You're held, but it hurts—just as it should.

Only in a few scenes featuring good Sgt. Elias (Willem Dafoe) does Stone even try to convey military grace and precision. Dafoe imbues Elias with the hip grace of a doper angel. He's an instinctive fighter who's in his element on his own, whether slithering through catacombs or flushing out "spider holes." By contrast, bad Sgt. Barnes (Tom Berenger) acts as the self-starting engine of an infernal machine. Berenger has to wear so much makeup as the heavily scarred Barnes that he appears to have an alligator face. And he acts with a broadness and coarseness to fit Stone's garish conception. Barnes, who turns a search-and-destroy mission into a search-*then*-destroy mission, is a walking defoliant, leaving charred earth in his wake. Stone makes one stab at irony: the resigned, philosophical Elias sees the vengeful Barnes as a true believer in the war—which is how Barnes sees him.

Elias's buddies are the "heads," who refresh themselves with pot and rock music. Barnes's buddies are strictly blood-and-guts types—wholesome, all-American killers. Both sides boast good actors. Notable among the heads is David Keith as King, who has a warming smile, a keen memory for Motown, and most of the good lines. Notable among the blood-and-guts types is Kevin Dillon as Bunny, who rates sex and the Indy 500 about equal, but clearly prefers killing to anything else. Unfortunately, Stone has a trickle-down theory of dramaturgy. In the end, Barnes is a demon, Elias is a saint, and their men are mostly just their pale reflections.

Between the heads and the blood-and-guts types is the brain, Chris Taylor. And *Platoon* is the film someone like Chris Taylor *would* make. It's immediate and distanced simultaneously. Jolting images like a helicopter blowing the tarp off a line of corpses are offset by Samuel Barber's mournfully beautiful "Adagio for Strings," and by the high-flown narration. At the heart-of-darkness conclusion, Stone seems to fall into an *Apocalypse Now* flashback— an impression helped along by Charlie Sheen, who gives the same kind of earnest performance that his father Martin gave in the Coppola movie.

Still, if *Platoon* is easy to overrate, it's also easy to underrate. I recently ran across a 1971 *Esquire* magazine in which editor Harold T. P. Hayes recalled asking classic war novelist James Jones whether Lt. William Calley was guilty of the My Lai massacre. Hayes wrote that Jones began to weep and cried, "My God, doesn't anybody know anything about war?" Oliver Stone may know too much about war fiction for his own good. But he also knows something about war.

San Francisco Examiner, December 30, 1986

FULL METAL JACKET

Jay Carr

Just when you thought the Vietnam War might recede a bit from the national consciousness, that *Platoon* might have purged it, along comes Stanley Kubrick's *Full Metal Jacket.* Nor is that all. John Irving's *Hamburger Hill,* Lionel Chetwynd's *Hanoi Hilton,* and Barry Levinson's *Good Morning, Vietnam,* a black comedy starring Robin Williams as a manic army disc jockey, all follow soon. One of the best Vietnam films, Ted Post's 1978 *Go Tell the Spartans* with Burt

Lancaster ruefully presiding over the initiation of questionable death at America's Thermopylae, is being rereleased after its initial flop despite universal critical praise. It's fitting, when you think about it, that America should look to film for catharsis, as the Greeks looked to theater. So much of our conduct, particularly in foreign affairs, after all, seems to replicate the old movies that never stop flickering in our collective mental attics.

Full Metal Jacket, tracing the life of a handful of young Marines from their arrival in boot camp to their first combat experience, arrives on a tide of anticipation. Kubrick spent five years laboring behind locked doors to make this film. Indeed, the time span involved in making *Full Metal Jacket*—the term for the standard-issue cartridge given to Marines in Vietnam—is one of the things coloring our perception of it. Over the years, Kubrick has become more and more private, with more and more time between films. His last was *The Shining,* in 1980. His last before that was *Barry Lyndon,* in 1975. That followed *A Clockwork Orange* in 1971.

In part, the anticipation of *Full Metal Jacket* is fueled by two earlier Kubrick films, *Dr. Strangelove* ('64) and *Paths of Glory* ('57). The latter was a powerful, but conventional, narrative decrying the institutionalized insanity of military command. *Dr. Strangelove* took on the same subject but upped the ante, thematically and stylistically, skewering nukes and hawks in a surrealistic absurdist style that had begun to blossom audaciously and promisingly in *Lolita* ('62) and reached its apogee here. Critics began to note the increasing depopulation of Kubrick's films, though, starting with the sterile spaceship commandeered by the computer HAL in *2001: A Space Odyssey* ('68).

A Clockwork Orange presented an even bleaker view of humanity, with its English thugs speaking Russian slang. The film seemed as traumatized as Anthony Burgess's novel. Was its humanity as frozen as that of its brutal protagonist and the society poised to lobotomize him? Or was it a cautionary tale, a plea for humanity not to deaden itself? *Barry Lyndon,* although beautifully decorated, played like the dark underside of *Tom Jones,* ending in a scene of Beckettian entropy. *The Shining* took place in a huge hotel, empty except for Jack Nicholson's increasingly crazed writer and his captive wife and son.

The accelerating coldness and alienation of the worlds in Kubrick's films further heightened anticipation of this new one. If anyone seemed poised to tackle the dislocating craziness of Vietnam, it was he. If anything, the fact that ten years had gone by since the war's end is an argument in favor of the film. Great war films are never made while the wars they depict are still going on. Time is needed to digest and assimilate the experience and transmute it into something informed by a deeper, broader insight and humanity. Think of the great World War I films—*Grand Illusion* and *All Quiet on the Western Front*—or the World War II films that stay with us—*From Here to Eternity, Twelve O'Clock High, The Longest Day, The War Lover, Catch-22*. They are the product not of journalism or jingoism, but of something more reflective.

But reflectiveness, while an ingredient in the more illuminating kind of war movie, even a movie about a war that turned into a national exercise in disillusionment, isn't enough, even though *Full Metal Jacket* is consistent with Kubrick's work and viewpoint over a thirty-year period. Its antiwar sentiment is consistent with the director of *Paths of Glory* and *Dr. Strangelove*. But—yes, there's a but—one couldn't help feeling while watching it that Kubrick spent too much time fussing over it, that it ultimately became impossible to sustain over five years the degree of heat a film like *Full Metal Jacket* demands. *Full Metal Jacket* is an honorable work, at times a striking one, at times, although it may seem obscene to say so, even a beautiful one.

But it's powered by craft and dedication, not indignation or the kind of sustained passion *Platoon* gives us. It's almost abstract, dominated by Kubrick's idea about this war. In *Platoon,* Oliver Stone found exactly the right kind of handle on his subject. In a cold fury, he filled his film with a you-are-there quality. Kubrick is more detached, and it costs him in the unfair, but inevitable, comparison to the earlier film. Like *The Deer Hunter* (one of the four significant Vietnam films—*Apocalypse Now* being the other, in addition to *Platoon* and *Go Tell the Spartans*), *Full Metal Jacket* is divided in two. But where the first part of *The Deer Hunter* established the basis of the bonding the film is about and supplied the strong visual metaphor of the western Pennsylvania blast furnace as an analogue to the war, *Full Metal Jacket* spends its first half in Marine boot camp, telling us at length stuff we already know.

The boot camp scenes, animated by Lee Ermey's drill sergeant and Vincent D'Onofrio's increasingly tight-strung scapegoat, are full of a kind of ritualistic mind crunching that plays like an icy-crazy comedic version of Kenneth Brown's celebrated play, *The Brig,* which acted out the pounding of young hearts and minds into robotic obedience machines. Matthew Modine, as the young rebel, is smart enough to simply keep his mouth shut and resist the grinding-down process passively. When he finally gets to Vietnam, he sports a peace button on his flak jacket—not that it helps him when he finds himself under enemy fire. But the boot camp sequences, while brilliant, seem to have yanked the film away from what we feel we should have been a grander design. They seem to have become too much an end in themselves.

The film's momentum is broken in the middle, and must start from ground zero when Modine hits Vietnam as a *Stars & Stripes* journalist. Indeed, Modine's job seems the second in a series of less than optimum choices that hamper *Full Metal Jacket*. It makes him a detached observer twice over, first as a sort of chorus, giving us in voiceovers his views of the irrationality he volunteered for, then as a cynical journalist, taking potshots at the daily absurdity. Soon, though, he finds that the Tet Offensive is bigger than he is. Like everyone else, he's pressed into combat duty. Only then does *Full Metal Jacket* regain its urgency.

It's at its best—and at its best, *Full Metal Jacket* is as powerful as any string of Vietnam War images put on film—when Modine and his outfit are pinned down by sniper fire in a bombed-out section of Hue. The horror of the war is depicted with trenchant specificity as one soldier after another is torn apart by automatic rifle fire as he tries to cross a courtyard. When the war comes down to this particular microcosm of death, *Full Metal Jacket* is second to none in the impact of its sudden bloodletting. It's at this point that the film also brings Modine to the destination it had in mind all the time. It will come as no shock to learn that here, under enemy fire for the first time, he pulls the trigger.

The film ends, however, not on a note of outrage, or heat, but on a note of irony. What should be its shattering conclusion—that what you do, you become—seems not only anticlimactic, but shaky. The fact is that soldiers who kill in combat don't become killers forever, even if they didn't believe in the Vietnam War as World War II veterans believed. Many Americans pulled the trigger in Vietnam and came back home to be solid citizens. A film we waited five years for, which boasts such painterly craftsmanship, should, we feel, have a bigger, grander payoff. Also one more aware of the complexity of human nature.

But *Full Metal Jacket* seems to have lost any compelling overview or architecture it might once have once had, in a concentration on minutiae. Indeed, some of the scenes in blue light, with soldiers advancing through the rubble of Hue into they know not what, seem too posed, too aesthetic. We can't escape the feeling that Kubrick took the easy way out and concentrated on such technical aspects as lighting when he should have grappled more insightfully and rewardingly with the moral ambiguities in his material. Is one climactic killing, for instance, bestial murder, or a mercy killing? In place of its facile and toothless irony, *Full Metal Jacket* sorely needs a more strongly maintained central character and a more penetrating view of the moral questions it tackles. And the immediacy and indignation of *Platoon* or the sense of the sudden chaos of war so unforgettably conveyed in *The Killing Fields* wouldn't hurt, either. Those films, we felt, had fire in their bellies. The fire in *Full Metal Jacket* is pale and cerebral. It's not enough.

Boston Globe, June 28, 1987

BORN ON THE FOURTH OF JULY

■■■

Morris Dickstein

My subject is War, and the pity of War. The Poetry is in the pity.

—Wilfred Owen, 1918

In one of those odd ironies of film distribution, just as peace was breaking out across half the globe in the fall of 1989, a number of impressive war movies were released: Kenneth Branagh's post-Falklands reinterpretation of *Henry V;* Edward Zwick's *Glory,* an account of a black regiment's service in the Civil War; and Oliver Stone's *Born on the Fourth of July.* Each would have been an unlikely project just a few years before; each involved the re-creation of a painful, even grisly subject in strikingly contemporary terms. All showed how the treatment of war has become more frank and daring, more graphic and demanding, especially as the movies come to reflect America's still-troubled conscience about its role in Vietnam.

Only one of these films, *Born on the Fourth of July*—adapted from an angry memoir by a disabled veteran, Ron Kovic—actually dealt with Vietnam, yet none would have been made as they were

Vietnam War vet Ron Kovic (Tom Cruise) gives voice to his protest outside the 1972 Republican National Convention in Oliver Stone's *Born on the Fourth of July*. (Photo by Roland Neveu. © 1989 Universal City Studios, Inc. Courtesy of MCA Publishing Rights, a Division of MCA Inc. All Rights Reserved.)

without our post-Vietnam immersion in the dark, brutal, bitter side of war. They expose audiences to a level of pain and violence unthinkable in earlier war movies, and bring us face to face with the terrible losses and individual sacrifices that mark all serious combat. Though influenced by the *Catch-22* spirit of the Vietnam era, none of them—with the partial exception of Stone's movie—insists that all war is absurd, a mere sham. They allow for patriotism, even for politics, but confront us unforgettably with the high personal cost of victory as well as defeat.

Significantly, not one of these movies deals directly with World War II, the prototype not only of the just war but—as a forties film subject—of the clean war, before Hollywood ever conceived of the bloodcurdling realism of battle that could be achieved by special effects, lighting, and expensive location shooting. Instead, movies of that period aimed at a more official realism available only in cooperation with the armed services, which, as the price for their enormous technical assistance, approved all scripts in advance and blatantly insisted on being shown in a favorable light.

In a sense, then, these were official productions, made with a government seal of approval at a time when few filmmakers would have dreamed of being critical of the American military. From the forties to the sixties—from *The Story of G.I. Joe, Back to Bataan, The Sands of Iwo Jima,* and *Battleground* to *The Great Escape* and *The Dirty Dozen*—the World War II movie is essentially the action movie, but also an effusive tribute to the American soldier and the American way of life. Only a few of these films acknowledge the real harshness of war—Tay Garnett's gloomy, atmospheric *Bataan* ('43), for example, a story of defeat made when the outcome of the war still hung in the balance.

Even without broad appeals to patriotism, these movies are hymns to discipline and collective effort. They show us war almost as a civilizing process: subduing a vicious, unprincipled, almost subhuman enemy, defending a cause worth dying for, and welding an unruly, cacophonous, disparate group of men into a unified fighting force. Just as the great European films like *Grand Illusion* ('37) focus on class or national differences surmounted by the ultimate recognition of a common humanity, American movies—in line with such novels as *The Naked and the Dead*—reflect the regional, ethnic, and religious conflicts of a more plural, more fragmented society. The GIs in most World War II movies were seeing the world—and other kinds of Americans—for the first time but were also learning to subdue their differences toward some larger social goal (working together, achieving justice, winning the war, defending our ideals) that was never seriously to be questioned. Hence, war movies attracted not only the superpatriotic John Waynes but also the sentimental Hollywood liberals—including many who were later blacklisted—who saw the Army as a microcosm of American society, a force for assimilation and mutual tolerance, as well as our bulwark against fascism.

The first half hour of *Born on the Fourth of July,* beginning with the title, is a crude caricature of this traditional ethic of personal sacrifice and national crusade. Stone fills in young Ron Kovic's background with an exceptional heavyhandedness. Instead of realistic details, he gives us the dreamy essence of small-town Americana, from the exhortations of John Kennedy, who brings the message of the World War II generation to the early, hopeful years of the sixties, to the naïve religious patriotism of Ron Kovic's parents, blue-collar ethnics who were especially receptive to Kennedy's call to sacrifice. Kovic gets the same message from boyhood war games, from Fourth of July parades, from his bloodthirsty wrestling coach, and from ramrod Marine recruiters, as if Middle America in the postwar years, beneath its innocent surface, were simply a powder keg of macho violence waiting to be ignited. This is all conveyed by the brutal elisions of Stone's technique, with its choking closeups and wild camera angles, which create an atmosphere of menace and hysteria before anything really happens.

Ron Kovic is yet another vehicle for Oliver Stone's overheated autobiography, his obsession with the problems of a young man growing up in America. In the name of a higher cause Kovic buys into a sickening male fantasy, a power trip, a distorted ideal of manhood, even choosing to make war not love by skipping his high school prom. This foreshadows the way his war injuries will later rob him of his potency until the antiwar movement restores him to a full sense of his own humanity.

If this sounds pat and programmatic, it *is* programmatic. Stone is a preachy but intensely visceral filmmaker, going for the gut of every scene, underlining the obvious, hammering his points home. *Born on the Fourth* is painful to sit through, but Stone's film reaches us even as he works out his own recurrent fixations. *Born on the Fourth of July* really begins not in the stylized home-town sequences or the brief but equally mannered battle scenes, which take us over the same ground as every other Vietnam movie: the tense, jangling atmosphere of an alien terrain, the enormous firepower, the guilt over civilian casualties, the pervasive fear and loss of purpose. The movie takes off after Kovic is injured, flown back to base camp, even given last rites in a sea of writhing, shrieking bodies before the overtaxed doctors have time to operate. This movie is less about Vietnam than about one man's maimed, shattered, almost helpless body, and Tom Cruise, a coldly intense actor, plays it that way, from the outside, as the story of Kovic's anger at a world that has casually deprived him of his body. (For a more subtle, varied, ironically inflected performance, compare Daniel Day Lewis's impersonation of an angry cripple and a handicapped lover in *My Left Foot*.)

Cruise's portrayal works as a *physical* performance more than as a parable of the loss of ideals: it's Tom Cruise of *Top Gun* trapped in a cripple's body, robbed of his athletic grace, robbed of the sex he had barely begun to use. This skews the film toward the personal horror. As David Denby commented, "A boy's loss of potency is put on the same level as a nation's loss of honor." Stone's closeups create a claustrophobic intimacy: they measure the shrinkage of Kovic's world and imprison us in his outlook as he is imprisoned by his injury. Stone and Cruise are remarkably faithful to Kovic's raw, grating personality and to the strident simplicity of his gripping memoir. No war film has ever given us this kind of howling lament of sexual loss and physical debility or shown us these nightmarish details of convalescence in V.A. hospitals, where men lie in their own shit and vomit while well-fed rats nibble along the floor. Earlier rehabilitation movies like *The Best Years of Our Lives, The Men,* and *Coming Home* were made, courageously, in more inhibited times, when the gross physical details were off-limits. Perhaps as a result, they focus more effectively on the psychological dimensions of injury and recovery.

The subjective, claustral world of *Born on the Fourth* has its distinct limits, marked out by Stone's obsessions with masochistic humiliation (as in *Midnight Express*), martyrdom (as in *Talk Radio*), and conversion experiences (as in *Salvador, Platoon,* and *Wall Street*). Never more than in *Born on the Fourth,* Stone is an over-intense, autobiographical filmmaker who projects himself emotionally onto every one of his subjects. He typically sets up his young protagonists between two fathers, or two causes, and makes us a party to their cataclysmic shift of loyalties. These heroes are usually callow innocents (like Charlie Sheen in *Platoon* and *Wall Street*) who learn the rotten ways of the world, or obnoxious troublemakers (like James Woods in *Salvador*) who somehow find a cause they can believe in. The story is really the same though the personalities differ; Ron Kovic is both of these characters, first the innocent, then the troublemaker, and, as always, Stone harnesses a political parable onto a growing-up fable.

Yet it's surprising how much of the Vietnam era Stone works into his movie. The external trappings of the sixties and seventies, such as the antiwar demonstrations, were so crudely stereotyped by television images that they're almost never convincing on film. Stone gets it right, not just the look but the mental atmosphere. Once again, as in *Salvador,* Stone's adrenalin, his emotional extremity, pitches him in the right direction. With the help of Abbie Hoffman in a poignant, funny cameo, this is a chillingly accurate reconstruction of scenes few of us would care to live through again. Yet other moments are starkly surreal, such as the battle of the paraplegics in the Mexican desert, with Willem Dafoe as a ferociously bombed-out vet who stands for what Cruise might yet become. This is a scene out of a Beckett play, or out of the demented climax of Von Stroheim's *Greed,* or the early pages of Ralph Ellison's *Invisible Man,* where the shell-shocked vets gather at the "Golden Day."

Unexpectedly, Stone feels obliged to give us a bit of uplift at the end as Kovic, with his book already published, prepares to address the 1976 Democratic convention, thus ironically fulfilling John Kennedy's call to greatness and his mother's early dreams of fame. Kovic has finally found a cause—and among the antiwar vets, a community—that makes him whole again.

Partisan Review, Fall 1990

THE WOMEN

Most genres are defined formally: film noir by its look and mood; the Western by setting, costume, and ritualistic action; comedy by its main mission of getting laughs; and so forth. Others arise out of the urgency of the time and a continuity of theme and emotional experience that simply demands to be recognized. There's a chapter in this book called "The Women" because, as the random submissions of more than thirty writers passed through the editor's hands, it became clear that there had to be one. *Thelma & Louise,* the most talked-about movie of its year, didn't attract that attention because it was a road movie, a buddy movie, a comedy, an action film, or a modern film noir, though it fulfills certain requirements for all those genres. It became a compulsive conversation piece because, more dynamically and entertainingly than its (shall we say) sisters, it was a milestone in an evolution that seems to be going on everywhere in our cinema and society these days: the redefinition of women—what they can do, how they feel, how much they are trapped by and how forcefully they transcend traditional definitions of who they are and should be.

"The women's picture" was once virtually synonymous with the love story and the weepie. Even then, some stars and some characters had it in them to break out of their assigned niche—up to a point. In a keynote essay, Peter Keough writes their history and measures the price they paid. Kevin Thomas finds more consciousness-raising than you might expect in the women-in-prison B movie *Caged Heat*. Jonathan Rosenbaum takes a reading of both *Fatal Attraction* and its audience. Owen Gleiberman and Stuart Klawans scrutinize two family tales with distinctive heroines, *Men Don't Leave* and *Running on Empty*, respectively. Peter Travers applauds two of 1991's best films, *Thelma & Louise* and then *Rambling Rose* (a breakthrough film for director Martha Coolidge). Gary Arnold sizes up the duel to the death between two women—both curiously admirable—in the sleeper hit *The Hand That Rocks the Cradle* and tells why it works. Two younger women figure in our final entry, *Poison Ivy*, as Peter Travers cheers the intelligence and resourcefulness of underappreciated low-budget filmmaker Katt Shea Ruben.

ON WOMEN, FILMS, AND THE WOMEN'S FILM

Peter Keough

The ending of *Thelma & Louise* didn't leave much room for a sequel; the righteous anger and desire for independence of the two unlikely desperadoes wasn't enough to get them across the great gulf in the heart of America. Nor did the film inspire much in the way of imitation. Subsequent films have exploited the doomed, plucky pair's popularity by caricaturing them, diluting them, or betraying them.

The pissed-off, assertive, and self-reliant woman swells into self-parody in films such as *Terminator 2, Lethal Weapon 3,* or *Batman Returns.* Her rage is demonized and redirected at herself in *The Hand That Rocks the Cradle, Death Becomes Her,* and *Single White Female.* In the rare case in which she's granted independence and a respectable profession, as in *Far and Away* or *Whispers in the Dark,* it's only to treacherously undermine her and restore the uppity woman to her proper place in the home and family.

Geena Davis's most recent role since *Thelma & Louise* epitomizes the image of women that has evolved in Hollywood since that film's abortive breakthrough. In Penny Marshall's treacly *A League of Their Own,* Davis plays a gifted ballplayer given an opportunity to shine briefly in The All-Girls Professional Baseball League, an organization established during World War II to pinch-hit for the men's leagues depleted by military service. Of course, once the boys come marching home the women players do likewise, and this injustice is given only the merest of lip service by Marshall. The film, like the All-Girls League itself, ends up a crude fraud. Pretending to honor women who persist in and excel at nontraditional roles, Marshall's *League* repudiates them, even to the extent of making women who don't fit the stereotype the butt of its cruelest humor.

A League is not just typical of the renewed sexism in recent movies. It's also an ironic reminder that in Hollywood, too, there was a period in which women seemed to have some control of their own images. Not just baseball lost manpower during the war; the studios did as well. And, unlike baseball, the film industry had already developed a powerful female presence and audience ready to fill the gap. The outcome was the same, however, as the postwar period saw a retrenchment of patriarchal values and the reduction of women to housewives, sex objects, victims, or demons.

All these stereotypes, of course, existed from the beginning of cinema. The predatory vamp, the beleaguered waif, the good mother, the perky ingenue, the fallen woman were stock images in the silent era. But the actresses who portrayed them prevailed over the clichés and became icons in their own right, images of womanhood that defied categorization and demanded respect. Not only did women like Mary Astor, Mary Pickford, Gloria Swanson, Louise Brooks, and Greta Garbo have faces then, they had the power to move audiences, and in some cases the power to move studios as well.

The onset of sound released women's voices, and their passions. Marlene Dietrich, Mae West, and Jean Harlow were sexually aggressive without apology; their appetites were healthy, often hilariously articulated, sometimes polymorphous, and generally unpunished. One reason why female sexuality was so frankly depicted when pictures first began to speak was that, often, women were providing the words. As Molly Haskell points out in her classic history of misogyny in cinema, *From Reverence to Rape,* more women worked as screenwriters in the twenties and thirties than in any time before or since. And they also had more women listening: granted suffrage in 1920, "liberated" during the Jazz Age, forced to work in increasing numbers during the Depression, they had seen "a woman's place" expanded to the political arena, the workplace, and the movies.

Inevitably, reaction set in. Instigated by the Catholic Legion of Decency, the Hays Office was established in 1933 to enforce the puritanical strictures of the Production Code. Designed to promote social conformity and expunge all sexuality and other deviancy from the movies, the Code actually encouraged the development of genres—the screwball comedy, the musical—that relied on strong and dexterous women. With sexual dalliance sublimated to banter and dance, women needed to be equal partners or the artifice would fall flat. Colbert and Gable, Astaire and Rogers, Grant and Hepburn were even matches in mating bouts that managed to be delightfully subversive as they waltzed to the inescapable resolutions of marriage and conformity.

Women in Hollywood in the thirties held their own against men in the films of Katharine Hepburn, Barbara Stanwyck, Bette Davis, and Claudette Colbert and stood by each other in films such as *Golddiggers of 1933* and *Stage Door* ('37). By the time Vivien Leigh had dealt with the Civil War, Reconstruction, and Clark Gable in *Gone With the Wind* ('39), the talent, sensibilities, and audience for the so-called women's picture of the late thirties and forties were set.

They were women's pictures because they featured complex and strong female characters confronting issues that leave guys cold—things like mature sexual relationships, the conflict between one's nature and one's social role, the pressures of family, and the specter of mortality. Melodramas for the most part, they were heightened daydreams in which women could ponder and resolve their desires and discontents, identifying themselves with Bette Davis in *Now, Voyager* ('42), Joan Crawford in *Mildred Pierce* ('45), or Olivia de Havilland in *The Heiress* ('49). Invariably, the patriarchal status quo is vindicated, but not before being undermined by a woman's point of view.

But a backlash was brewing as early as 1939 when Crawford, Rosalind Russell, and Norma Shearer tore one another to shreds in *The Women,* and it was well in motion by 1942 with the proto-typical buddy movie *Casablanca,* in which Ingrid Bergman found herself unwelcome in the male-bonding rituals of Rick's Café. Women in films were depicted less as fully developed characters and more as invidious clichés. Film noir instituted the femme fatale as a standard stereotype, an image that would become pro-gressively vitriolic, culminating in Glenn Ford's irrational loathing for Rita Hayworth in *Gilda* ('46) and Jane Greer's cold-blooded ruthlessness in *Out of the Past* ('47). Even the women's picture had been coopted by men in the sublime but reactionary *The Best Years of Our Lives* ('46), as Myrna Loy, Teresa Wright, Virginia Mayo, and Gladys George performed with conviction and skill roles that were essentially the old chestnuts of the dutiful wife, the precocious daughter, the treacherous floozy, and the girl next door.

The boys had marched home for good, and the women who remained behind on the screen found their roles increasingly delimited and dehumanized. The new stars would be Marilyn Monroe, trapped in parts that ranged from bimbo to psycho; or Audrey Hepburn, forever the child bride to codgers such as Fred Astaire, Humphrey Bogart, Gary Cooper, and Cary Grant; or the consummate housewife, Doris Day.

The conservatism of the fifties exploded into the permissiveness of the sixties, but the image of women in film deteriorated even further. The old Production Code dissolved into the ratings system, allowing undreamed-of sex and violence on the screen. The chief victims were women, reduced to sex objects and targets of sadistic and misogynistic rage; their dehumanization was nearly complete.

But it would take another progressive development to finish the job: the women's movement of the late sixties. With women pushing their way themselves into every other aspect of life, the audience, by then mostly male and adolescent, could at least escape them in the movies. Beginning with *Butch Cassidy and the Sundance Kid* ('69), the buddy movie has reigned over Hollywood, confirming what critic Leslie Fiedler has noted about American culture as a whole in his *Love and Death in the American Novel:* "there is no real sexuality in American life and therefore there can't be any in American art." What passes for sexuality is dread and narcissism, reflected in misogyny, violence, and male bonding.

Occasionally, women threaten to make a comeback, only to be quashed swiftly and thoroughly, as they had been after World War II. Such a renaissance seemed to loom in 1991 when *Thelma & Louise, The Silence of the Lambs,* the more modest *Dogfight, Rambling Rose,* and the execrable *Fried Green Tomatoes* proved that women's discontents could mean big box office. The problem was how to make money without making trouble. But crafty Hollywood has compiled over the past fifty years a lexicon of types and motifs by which righteous indignation can be metamorphosed into more palatable misogyny.

The evil twin syndrome of *Single White Female, Poison Ivy,* and

The Hand That Rocks the Cradle can be traced back to Olivia de Havilland's adventures with her bad-girl alter ego in *The Dark Mirror* ('46) or Bette Davis and her shadow Anne Baxter in *All About Eve* ('50). The spectacle of vain and deluded women tearing one another apart is done with class in George Cukor's *The Women*, with camp in Robert Aldrich's *Whatever Happened to Baby Jane?* ('62), and with special effects in *Death Becomes Her*. The beleaguered psychiatrist in *Whispers in the Dark* (Annabella Sciorra) is handled much less crassly and more competently by Ingrid Bergman in Hitchcock's *Spellbound* ('45). And in Orson Welles's masterly *Touch of Evil* ('58), as in 1992's inept *Unlawful Entry*, a woman serves as an unwitting magnet to monsters who are embodiments of the evil at the heart of patriarchal society.

Though in execution the recent films are far inferior to their predecessors, their intent is largely the same—to turn women's anger on the women themselves, to blame their discontent on demonized images of themselves. It is a misogyny based not so much in anger as in fear: once Hollywood recognizes women as human, it will also have to acknowledge the human qualities of understanding, compassion, commitment, and love.

Boston Phoenix, August 21, 1992

CAGED HEAT

■■■

Kevin Thomas

There's scarcely a genre more sleazy than that of the women's prison picture, which today is made mainly in the Philippines and which features women degrading women in the context of sex-and-violence fantasies for the delectation of male audiences. Consequently, *Caged Heat* is especially gratifying. With wit, style, and unflagging verve, writer-director Jonathan Demme sends up the genre while still giving the mindless action fans their money's worth. Demme manages not only to have it both ways but also, in pointing up the absurdity of the genre, points up the absurdity of the often cruel and inhuman conditions of real-life prisons.

Backed by remarkably gifted cinematographer Tak Fujimoto and equally inspired composer John Cale, who ranges easily from the funky to the elegiac, Demme evokes the rich, ironically but compassionately observed atmosphere of a Robert Altman film—and even throws in some well-done Felliniesque dream sequences for good measure.

Juanita Brown, Roberta Collins, Erica Gavin, Ella Reid, and Rainbeaux Smith are inmates at an extremely harsh—and absolutely authentic-looking—women's prison presided over by a sexually twisted and sadistic matron (erstwhile horror picture goddess Barbara Steele, who spoofs her part deliciously). The prisoners are further menaced by a mad resident doctor (Warren Miller), who specializes in hideous behavior modification treatments designed to satisfy his own warped desires.

Demme has such strong control that he manages to make fun of the cliché plot and its conventions while taking the direness of the women's plight seriously, and he shows off his spirited cast to best advantage. Most notably, he treats Erica Gavin, who starred in *Russ Meyer's Vixen,* as an actress rather than a sex object and elicits from her an unexpectedly creditable performance.

In every aspect, *Caged Heat* attests to Demme's virtuosity—and to Fujimoto's and Cale's as well—and thereby demonstrates that all three of them are ready for major projects.

Los Angeles Times, October 31, 1974

FATAL ATTRACTION

■■■

Jonathan Rosenbaum

"A profoundly uninteresting married yuppie lawyer (Michael Douglas) has a weekend affair with a profoundly uninteresting unmarried yuppie book editor (Glenn Close). The latter proves to be insane and makes the former's life a living hell as soon as he ends the relationship, and the plot gradually turns into a sort of upscale remake of *The Exorcist,* with female sexuality (personified by Close) taking over the part of the Devil, and yuppie domesticity (personified by Douglas, wife Anne Archer, and daughter Ellen Hamilton Latzen) assuming the role of innocence. While billed as a romance and a thriller, the movie strictly qualifies as neither. The major emotions appealed to are prurient guilt, hatred, and dread; and with director Adrian Lyne shoving objects like a knife, a boiling pot, and an overflowing bath in the spectator's face to signal that Something Awful's Going to Happen, he can't be expected to display any curiosity about the motivations of the spurned anti-heroine, who eventually becomes, simply, an extraterrestrial robot killer. The perpetrator of the original screenplay is James Dearden, although apparently the minds of producers Stanley R. Jaffe and Sherry Lansing, faced with dissatisfied preview audiences, are responsible for the totally dehumanized finale."

That capsule review of *Fatal Attraction* represents all I wanted to say about the film before it became the top-grossing movie in most major cities across the country. The commercial success hasn't altered my opinion, but it has made me more curious about *Fatal Attraction* and its effect on audiences—curious enough to brave the weekend crowds and see it a second time.

When *The Exorcist* came out in 1973, a good many critics were comparably perturbed about the film's mass appeal, as well as by the peculiar behavior of audiences in relation to it. This was the period of Watergate and gas rationing. Some writers compared the lines at the gas pumps to the lines for the movie, and one of them, Elliott Stein, noted that few spectators seemed to be enjoying the film in any traditional way; he compared their alternately bored and avid responses to those of audiences at porn films, waiting restlessly for "the good parts."

Some of this seems relevant to the odd tension I felt both times I attended *Fatal Attraction.* As was the case with *The Exorcist,* the audience of *Fatal Attraction* seemed to be primed for shocks and jolts, and some sense of guilt and anxiety clearly plays a role in establishing this nervous expectation. But *The Exorcist* had a little girl masturbating with a crucifix, howling obscenities, spewing out green bile, and rotating her head 360 degrees, while *Fatal Attraction* offers nothing much in the way of sex or violence that can't read-ily be found elsewhere. At best there's some slightly steamy sex when the lawyer and book editor make it next to a kitchen sink, and later inside a freight elevator; a little bit of gore when she at-tempts suicide by slashing her wrists, boils his daughter's pet rabbit in a pot, and jabs herself several times with a knife; and perhaps a bit of materialistic outrage when he finds that she's poured acid over his car.

Yet if one can postulate some relationship between the appeal of *The Exorcist* and the feelings of disequilibrium caused by both Watergate and the energy crisis, it seems no less plausible to link the popularity of *Fatal Attraction* to the fear and moral confusion brought about jointly by feminism and the AIDS epidemic. The sense of retribution connected to the hero's weekend fling is so palpably present in the threat posed by his ex-lover that the movie can tap into undercurrents of public hysteria about both subjects without having to allude to them even obliquely, much less deal with them. Apart from the ex-lover's diatribes about the hero's selfishness, and her remarks, after becoming pregnant, about wanting to be a single parent—both of which may be seen as parodies of feminism, as the character's mental illness becomes increasingly apparent—the movie keeps itself squeaky clean as far as AIDS and feminism are concerned. But that doesn't prevent it from milking to the utmost some of the baser emotions aroused by these issues.

To get a better idea of some of the things that *Fatal Attraction* is saying (and doing) to its audience, it may help to recall the last film that coproducers Jaffe and Lansing—both former studio chiefs—worked on together: *Kramer vs. Kramer.* A yuppie film *avant la lettre,* this drama about single parenting placed nearly all its empathy and interest in the father, Dustin Hoffman, while the absent mother, played by Meryl Streep just prior to her stardom, was mainly kept in the wings, emotionally as well as physically. The nuclear family of *Fatal Attraction,* the Gallaghers, is certainly at the dead center of its values, as is amply demonstrated by the film's final shot—a lingering caress of the camera over a framed portrait of father, mother, and daughter. But even though Beth (Archer) and Ellen (Latzen) figure importantly in the plot, the center of identification remains Dan (Douglas) throughout. It is *his* anguish—Douglas clenching and unclenching his jaw muscles with the same masochistic frenzy we associate with his father, Kirk—that guides the storytelling, and the suffering of his family at the hands of his ex-lover mainly functions as a means for escalating his own anger and violence.

And how does Glenn Close's character figure in this structure? Her name, Alex Forrest, provides the beginning of a clue: a man's first name, and a last name suggesting a dense thicket in which a man might lose his way; put them together and you get a precise conflation of the two principal male fears regarding feminism—the phallic woman and female sexuality. It might seem slanted to identify female sexuality exclusively with this character, as I do in the capsule review, and not at all with Beth, a sexy and attractive woman in her own right. But the movie shoves us in that direction early on—while incidentally making an affair for Dan seem justifiable and desirable—by having him return home from walking the dog one night to find Beth in bed with Ellen.

A fuller notion of what the characters represent can be gleaned from the places where they live. When the film opens, the Gallagher family inhabits a comfortable apartment on Manhattan's Upper West Side; before long, they move to a house in a Westchester County suburb, and an entire scene with their friends is devoted to explaining what this means in terms of upward mobility. It is only after Alex invades this latter turf that the film assumes the full dimensions of a horror story, although it comes close when Dan finds that she's poured acid on his car—her first infringement on his precious property.

Alex, on the other hand, lives in a loft downtown in the meatpacking district, and a good deal of Expressionist lighting and smoke is expended to make the most of all that this implies in mythic terms. The dinginess of her building and the infernal yellow lights on the street outside conspire to make her Lucifer even before her madness becomes fully apparent, while the further association of her character with rain doesn't so much douse the hellish fumes as make them more vaporous. Whether Alex qualifies as a yuppie is perhaps open to debate, but if she hadn't come across as one at the publishing party where Dan first meets her, he probably wouldn't have been interested.

Intriguingly enough, the most resounding commercial flop released around the same time as *Fatal Attraction* was a picture that took a reverse position toward Manhattan yuppies, including a lawyer hero. This was Madonna's underrated comedy *Who's That Girl?* (directed by James Foley), which ridiculed most of the same values *Fatal Attraction* treats as sacred. The Rolls-Royce convertible that was gradually trashed over the course of the movie was the occasion for euphoric sight gags, not teeth gnashing and portentous music. Whether the fans of *Fatal Attraction* are all yuppies at heart is another matter; while the ideological thrust of the film is unmistakable, it would be much too facile to assume that the picture's success is predicated on a simple endorsement of what the audience really thinks. People, after all, go to movies for diversion rather than sermons, and it can't be argued that *Fatal Attraction* preaches anything overtly. But all movies are dream scenarios of one kind or another, and part of what appears to be drawing people to this one is the heavy undertow of sexual guilt and anxiety that it exploits. The economic trappings are to some extent merely reflections of what is routinely expected from Hollywood, and they become more blatant here mainly because what the movie chooses to ignore—Alex's mind and background (as opposed to her behavior) —throws them into high relief.

Reportedly, the original ending shot involved Alex committing suicide (a conclusion that would have made the film's allusions to *Madame Butterfly* more functional). The negative response to this in previews convinced the filmmakers to juice things up with some protracted bathroom mayhem, climaxed by Alex's resurrection from the bathtub after being drowned by Dan. (Some critics have objected to this part of the film while praising the rest; speaking for myself, I was so bored and alienated by what preceded it that I was perversely grateful for this ludicrous over-the-top addition.) That this ending makes hash of most of the preceding story doesn't seem to bother spectators much, because the logic of extra-added shocks is so well established by now in horror and sf fare that it seems to have superseded the separate logics of story, character, and genre.

At one point, for example, the film briefly turns into a mystery when Dan sneaks into Alex's loft to search for something he can use against her (such as evidence that another man might be the father of her expected child). The only significant item he uncovers—a newspaper obituary of a man we assume was Alex's father, which contradicts her earlier statement that her father is alive and well— is promptly forgotten by the movie, a red herring whose sole function appears to be its reiteration of the fact that Alex is capable of saying or doing anything. In any case, the abandonment of the mystery plot confirms that the movie's true focus depends on a complete indifference to Alex's psychology; it is only as a grotesque cipher and a supernatural demon that she can contain the full measure of an audience's loathing for the sexuality she represents.

Yet significantly, in line with last summer's hit *Aliens,* it is another woman—Beth rather than Dan—who assumes the key macho role in the film's two showstoppers, which elicited applause and cheers at both showings I attended. The first occurs after Alex kills Ellen's pet rabbit. Dan reveals the weekend fling to Beth in order to explain the tragedy, and, after she recovers from her hysterical response, he dials Alex on the phone to tell her that his wife now knows about their affair. He then hands the receiver over to Beth, who says, "This is Beth Gallagher. If you ever come near my family again, I'll kill you"—a declaration that promptly brings the house down. In the final bloodbath Beth keeps her promise, and that brings on the second wave of cheers. In both cases, the general feeling is that the spirit of John Wayne lives on, in drag, and even if the Duke (or Duchess) couldn't lick the Big C, you can bet that s/he can wipe out the twin menaces of AIDS and pushy women with one effective blast.

The movie's ultimate logic, in other words, depends on external references to other movies rather than internal references to its own characters and plot. There's even a reference to *Psycho* early in the bathroom scene—a lingering shot of water gurgling down the drain—to alert our salivary glands to the mayhem that's on the way. Indeed, it is director Adrian Lyne's penchant for telegraphing his punches well in advance (he pans slowly across a room to a telephone and then pauses, so we can all wait for it to ring) that keeps his audience in tow throughout. It's a technique that he no doubt developed while turning out TV commercials in England (before going on to direct *Foxes, Flashdance,* and *9½ Weeks*), along with his method of turning up the soundtrack's volume and adding bursts of caveman percussion during moments of rage and violence. This is the sort of thing Richard Schickel of *Time* must be talking about when he cites "Adrian Lyne's elegantly unforced direction."

Some other critics have compared this picture to a Hitchcock thriller. But while the Master of Suspense was certainly capable of working with an audience's guilty feelings about illicit sex to generate tension, he always gave this tension a moral weight and a certain amount of moral ambiguity. If he shaped a narrative around a single character's viewpoint, he wouldn't deviate from that viewpoint for trivial reasons, as *Fatal Attraction* often does when it focuses on Alex alone—not to generate any further information about the character or plot, but merely to extend Dan's glib incomprehension and hatred of her by other means, turning this into a universal principle so that it can also be experienced by the filmmakers and audience alike. Thanks to this determined ignorance and hostility, *Fatal Attraction* offers the same kind of fun as a lynching, with the similar satisfaction of a shared group endeavor when it's over.

Chicago Reader, October 2, 1987

MEN DON'T LEAVE

Owen Gleiberman

Men Don't Leave is an exhilarating contradiction: a happy movie about depression. A wonderfully sly and original domestic weeper, it's the first picture Paul Brickman has directed since *Risky Business* ('83), his daringly salacious yet finally glib teen fantasy. Whatever he has been up to in the intervening six years (rejecting scripts, apparently), the break seems to have matured him; he's become a much richer filmmaker. In *Men Don't Leave,* Brickman gazes at his characters with a mixture of compassion and pure delight—even when their hearts are breaking, they tickle him.

The opening scenes with the Macauleys, a boisterous clan living in a verdant suburb of Baltimore, make the very notion of a happy family seem an exotic spectacle (which, of course, it is). As honeyed light pours through the windows, Beth and John Macauley (Jessica Lange and Tom Mason) rise and playfully make love. At the breakfast table they're joined by their two sons—Matt (Charlie Korsmo), who stares expectantly out of large doleful eyes, and Chris (Chris O'Donnell), an exuberant seventeen-year-old who says goodbye to his mother with a quick, affectionate "Later, creator!" After a decade of righteously sarcastic teen flicks, it's a relief—almost a revelation—to encounter a hip yet contented movie family, with parents and kids seen on the same side of the fence.

Then, just as we're drawn into this cozy domestic idyll, the spell is broken. John, a contractor, is summoned to a building site and killed in an explosion. At the hospital Beth wanders the halls in shock, her existence shattered.

In form, *Men Don't Leave* is a conventional therapeutic soaper about how a newly widowed mother and her two kids learn to get on with their lives. The movie's hook is that there's more to the matter than overcoming loss. With Dad, their cornerstone, suddenly gone, Beth and the kids are no longer an emotionally coherent unit. They have to grow into different people to become a family again. Brickman devotes equal time to each of their stories—it's a three-headed coming-of-age film. The sorrow is always there under the surface, yet the movie is also lyrical and rapturously funny, with surprise temptations sprung on the characters like enchanted jokes.

Discovering she's $63,000 in debt, Beth decides to sell the house and move the family into Baltimore. She gets a job as assistant manager of a yuppie grocery store and meets Charles (Arliss Howard), a preternaturally gentle musician who seems to incarnate the term "sensitive male." Yet Beth, still floating in despair, can't quite connect with him. Quietly, defiantly, she takes to her bed. Her depression is presented with a kind of wry detachment, and it will ring true for anyone who's ever spent a weekend hiding under the covers. Before long, Beth's family—the only thing she cares about—begins to drift apart, with both kids finding the spiritual equivalent of alternative families.

Little Matt, who misses his father most, goes through the time-honored prepubescent ritual of befriending a bad kid at school. Meanwhile, Chris finds unexpected hormonal bliss in the arms of the radiology technician downstairs, a weirdly matter-of-fact space cadet (Joan Cusack) who starts turning into his surrogate mom.

In his homegrown American way, Brickman believes in the director as mood spinner. He uses the beautiful, melancholy synth score (by Thomas Newman) for a trancelike emotionalism, and nothing in the film unfolds in quite the way you expect. That's the key to its evanescent charm—it's about a world alive with hidden possibilities. Brickman's style doesn't announce itself. It's there in the dreamy precision of his observational eye—in the impassioned harangues between Beth and Chris, where anger is really the sorrow that won't show itself; in the hilarious moment when Matt's schoolyard chum offers his friendship by slicing a Milk Dud in half with a switchblade; and in the way a simple meet-cute scene between Beth and Charles becomes a shimmering comic epiphany, with Beth dropping the vegetables she's delivering onto the floor as Charles and his ensemble churn out their roiling New Age cacophony.

Wearing flat orange hair, Jessica Lange acts without a trace of the inspirational righteousness that has sometimes marred her portrayal of "ordinary" women. Her Beth is sad yet radiantly sane—a house-wife who loves her life deeply and can't deal with the chasm that's opened up in it. Newcomer Chris O'Donnell may, at first, remind you of half a dozen teen thespians named Corey. But don't be fooled by his Beverly Hills High veneer: there's a smart, vulnerable actor beneath that coiffed brushcut and baby skin.

As Jody, the seductress from Mars, snaggle-toothed Joan Cusack gives a crack deadpan performance. She's a goofy-sexy comedian who steals every scene she's in. And Arliss Howard, with his long hair and slit-eyed, man-in-the-moon face, makes Charles's Zen recessiveness completely winning. The character is a latter-day hippie completely at ease with his own tender nature (he might almost have been beamed in from Northern California), and he's never more attractive than when he's sitting in with a polka band, singing the "ee-eye-ee-eye-o" choruses of the "Café Polka."

Brickman is the rare mainstream filmmaker who's able to empathize with everyone onscreen—even the dislikable characters, such as Beth's abrasive, narcissistic boss (Kathy Bates). That's what keeps the movie's point of view shifting and elusive. Brickman also has a sentimental, poetic streak. Yet even when he resorts to a device like having Beth take a redemptive balloon ride, the moment is so rhythmically right that the scene soars anyway.

Men Don't Leave is rooted in the pain of sudden loss, yet it touches on universal feelings of familial trauma. It could just as well have been a divorce movie as a death-in-the-family movie. The film makes us see that, with Dad gone, the Macauleys had no choice but to break off and pursue private adventures. They had to move beyond one another to reassemble into a family—only now, it's a freer and savvier one, less cocoon than emotional way station. The movie is really about the pleasure and the sadness of growing up; that's why its tears don't feel cheap. The last word goes to Matt, who tells us that he loves and needs his family for primal comfort, to feel "saved." *Men Don't Leave* is a moving tribute to the bonds that shape us all.

Entertainment Weekly, February 16, 1990

RUNNING ON EMPTY

■■■

Stuart Klawans

In 1971, Annie and Arthur Pope bombed a napalm factory, destroying not just some property but the eyesight of a worker who had the bad luck to be passing through an area they had decided would be deserted. The Popes went underground with their infant son, Danny. Pursued by federal agents, they took up a life in a succession of towns under a succession of aliases.

By the late 1980s, they have become much like any other middle-class American family. Now Annie oversees the household and takes pink-collar jobs; Arthur works as a cook and does a little community organizing on the side; Danny tries hard to make the baseball team at his high school. In a society where nuclear families have become the exception rather than the rule, the Popes are, if anything, more normal than their neighbors—except, of course, when the dark sedans start cruising by their home and they once more have to get out of town fast.

One might imagine, from a bare description of this premise, that *Running on Empty* is a political film—at least a film that reflects on political commitments, past and present. If you go to see it with such expectations, you will be disappointed. If you go looking for family melodrama, though, you will most likely feel richly rewarded. As directed by Sidney Lumet from a screenplay by Naomi Foner, *Running on Empty* is a visually messy but emotionally satisfying tearjerker—satisfying, I would say, just because it is a mess.

The muse of melodrama is no doubt the most lackadaisical of immortals, celebrated through the ages as the cheapest date on Parnassus. She works by magnifying the domestic emotions, justifying to us our most common feelings by imagining uncommon motivations for them. Many women feel trapped in their marriages; Annie feels trapped because the FBI is chasing her. Many teenagers have trouble communicating; Danny can't make friends because his whole life is a secret. Many fathers resist letting their sons leave home; Arthur can't let Danny go for fear of never seeing him again. Given her love for such extreme situations, the muse of melodrama —let us call her Luridia—is most alluring when she is allowed to be a bit frumpy. Dressed up, with insistently artful camerawork and editing, she often becomes laughable; the audience knows she's a fake. But in blue jeans, Luridia loses her pushiness. If she has blessed *Running on Empty,* it is partly because Lumet seems not to have cared very much where he placed his camera or what he had in the frame. To a large extent, he gives one the impression of having simply let the scenes happen. The viewer is thus left free to make discoveries about the characters, to understand things that are left unseen.

One understands, for example, what a boon the fugitive life has been for Arthur (Judd Hirsch). He is a good-hearted but weak man, more suited to organizing food co-ops than blowing up napalm factories. The idea for the bombing, we eventually learn, was not his but Annie's. Now, because of the family's situation, Arthur gets to be Daddy. He barks orders, makes pronouncements, drills Danny in the details of his cover story. He even gets to keep Annie.

As played by Christine Lahti, Annie is a woman who takes her marriage as a form of penance. Fairly early in the film, we see that her sexual feelings for Arthur, perhaps never all that strong, have faded. When a comrade in the underground drops by the house to see her after many years, it takes only a minute till she's on her back on the sofa, purring as he gives her a foot massage. Would she have an affair with him? Of course—but Luridia decrees he will have guns in the trunk of his car and be planning a bank robbery. Annie tells him emphatically to get lost, then finds comfort in the arms of the only man she now truly loves—her son Danny.

Bright, handsome, musically talented, Danny (River Phoenix) is forever attracting people and forever refusing their attention. He cannot allow himself to make close friends; so it is a crisis when he begins to fall in love with Lorna (Martha Plimpton), the daughter of his high school music teacher. Something of a deliberate flake, she both enjoys his air of aloofness and is frustrated by it. "You don't transmit too much information," she tells him. Then, breaking his family's most necessary rule, he does.

Given the film's central role, River Phoenix quietly goes about making Danny into a "magnificent" kid, as Arthur proclaims him. There's just enough of a sense of disturbance under the surface to make him seem both plausible and likable. One senses that lying has become automatic to him; he sometimes does it without reason, occasionally slipping into something like willful destructiveness—as much as he can, anyway, given his family's nonstop ethical pulse-taking. It's an admirable performance, fully matched by Christine Lahti's Annie. Lahti has to wait until late in the film to get her big moments; when they arrive, she milks them for everything they're worth. As Arthur, Judd Hirsch is put through the indignity of a drunk scene—one of the film's falsest notes—and puts everyone else through a bit too much TV-actor cuteness. His years in sitcoms have given him a tendency to do things the easy way; here, in what is admittedly the film's most thankless role, he succeeds most of the time in overcoming that occupational hazard.

Which scenes of *Running on Empty* have stayed with me? There are two, which are most notable for what they don't do. They don't advance the plot; they don't have any memorable dialogue; they don't involve dramatic camerawork or showy acting. In one, a scene at the end of Annie's birthday party, the family simply dances around the living room to the radio. In the other, Annie comes into the room in the high school where Danny is practicing the piano, sits next to him, and without a word begins to play the treble part of a simple duet. Without a word, he joins in with the bass. At a time when filmmaking seems to be dominated by theme-park pictures like *Die Hard,* or well-meaning but relentlessly programmed ones such as *Eight Men Out,* it is a blessed relief to come upon scenes such as these two, which respect the audience enough to let them understand and feel on their own. Luridia may have misled the filmmakers occasionally this time; but on the whole, she and her servants deserve our homage.

The Nation, October 31, 1988

THELMA & LOUISE

Peter Travers

Call it a comedy of shocking gravity. *Thelma & Louise* begins like an episode of "I Love Lucy" and ends with the impact of *Easy Rider.* It's a bumpy path between those points, and director Ridley Scott and first-time screenwriter Callie Khouri don't cushion the ride. The film switches moods violently, and sometimes it just jerks your chain. But this is movie dynamite, detonated by award-caliber performances from Geena Davis and Susan Sarandon in the title roles.

Davis plays Thelma, an Arkansas housewife married to a cheating, verbally abusive salesman named Darryl (broadly caricatured by Christopher McDonald) whom she began dating when she was fourteen. "He's an asshole," says Thelma, "but most times I just let it slide." Sarandon plays Thelma's pal Louise, a waitress who is pushing forty and fed up with waiting for her musician boyfriend Jimmy (subtly detailed by Michael Madsen) to stop roving and commit. Louise organizes a weekend fishing trip for herself and

Susan Sarandon and Geena Davis became cultural icons for their performances in *Thelma & Louise,* Ridley Scott's alternately searing, comic, exhilarating 1991 film about two Southern women driven to heroic outlawry on the open road. (Photo courtesy of MGM/UA Home Video, Inc., a subsidiary of Metro-Goldwyn-Mayer Inc.)

Thelma, who doesn't know how to fish. "Neither do I," says Louise, "but Darryl does it—how hard can it be?"

That's the setup: two women putting drudgery and men behind them for a few days of rest and intelligent talk. But before they reach their destination a hungry Thelma asks Louise to stop her '66 T-Bird convertible at a roadhouse, where Thelma knocks back three shots of Wild Turkey and dances with a local Romeo (Timothy Carhart). Louise thinks her friend is just blowing off steam until she catches the guy beating and trying to rape her in the parking lot. Grabbing Darryl's gun (which Thelma has brought along for protection), Louise presses the barrel into the rapist's neck and says, "Just for the future, when a woman's crying like that, she's not having any fun." He hitches up his pants and starts to leave, but not before saying to Louise, "Suck my cock." Louise takes two steps back and fires a bullet into his face. The suddenness of the act—the man is no longer a threat—is shattering. Vividly shot by Adrian Biddle (*Aliens*) and edited by Thom Noble (*Witness*), the scene is made even more potent by Louise's whispered remark to the bloody victim: "You watch your mouth, buddy." In a stunningly poignant performance,

Sarandon shows that the emotionally bruised Louise has been in a similar position before and has finally been pushed past her limit. The dazed women drive off and try to plan their next move. The cops have staked out their homes. When Thelma phones Darryl, detective Hal Slocumbe (Harvey Keitel) urges the pair to stop running. Hal is the film's one sympathetic male character, and he doesn't ring true. Khouri—a Texas-born actress, video producer, and former waitress—doesn't turn her movie into a man-hating tract, but she does show what a lifetime of male sexual threat and domination (disguised as paternalism) can do to women.

As Thelma and Louise—now outlaws—attempt to escape to a new life in Mexico, the movie offers vignettes that are comic, tragic, and surreal, sometimes simultaneously. They pick up J. D., a hitchhiking hunk charmingly played by Brad Pitt. Thelma takes him to bed because she likes his body. "You could park a car in the shadow of Darryl's ass," she tells Louise. For once, Thelma has a sexual experience that isn't "completely disgusting." In bed, J. D.— using a hair dryer as a gun—teaches Thelma the art of armed robbery. Then he robs her. The experience pushes Thelma over the line; she knocks over a convenience store using the J. D. method. "I know it's crazy," she tells Louise, "but I just feel like I've got a knack for this shit." Swilling booze and howling like a dog, Thelma heeds the call of the wild. But Davis, who has never been better, keeps Thelma rooted in reality. Crime has taught her to express herself; she won't go back to a cage.

Surrender doesn't suit Louise, either. She knows the police won't buy the truth because "we just don't live in that kind of world." Besides, she says, "I don't want to end up on the damned 'Geraldo' show." The banter doesn't disguise the terror these women feel, but driving through Utah's Canyonlands—after blowing up the gas tank of a semi whose driver offered to lick them all over—they achieve a kind of serenity.

As the film plunges toward its lacerating climax, some may have conflicting feelings about Thelma and Louise: are they feminist martyrs or bitches from hell? Neither is the case. They're flesh-and-blood women out to expose the blight of sexism. Khouri's script isn't about rage or revenge; it's about waste. Director Scott, whose films (*Alien, Blade Runner, Black Rain*) are noted for their slick surface, cuts to the marrow this time. This wincingly funny, pertinent, and heart-breaking road movie means to get under your skin, and it does.

Rolling Stone, April 18, 1991

RAMBLING ROSE

Peter Travers

Picture Pollyanna as a nymphomaniac and you'll get some idea of what's percolating in this magnolia-scented memory piece about a nineteen-year-old Alabama flower named Rose (Laura Dern) who comes to live with a Georgia family in 1935. The Hillyers are a generous lot, despite the encroachment of the Depression. Mother (Diane Ladd) is a freethinker who's preparing her master's thesis in history while raising three precocious kids—Buddy (Lukas Haas), thirteen; Doll (Lisa Jakub), eleven; and Waski (Evan Lockwood), five. Daddy (Robert Duvall) runs a hotel; his speech runs to effusion. "You will adorn our house," he says, though this nymph errant has hired on to do housework.

Rose is understandably dazzled. The orphaned child of dirt farmers, she's had some hard knocks, including gonorrhea and a brush with prostitution. Daddy knows there are scoundrels out there trying to lead Rose astray. He's confident his home will offer safe haven.

Daddy's in for a few surprises. And so are moviegoers expecting little more from *Rambling Rose* than a ride down the nostalgia trail. Screenwriter Calder Willingham, who adapted his autobiographical novel, sees the story through Buddy, the boy whose life Rose changed forever. The film is bookended by a visit home from the fiftyish Buddy (John Heard), now a writer who reminisces with his father about Rose. The framing device is sappy and unnecessary, but the damage is minimal. The film is richly comic and touching. Willingham (*The Graduate, Paths of Glory*) and director Martha Coolidge (*Valley Girl*, '83) infuse the story with sweetness without sacrificing its spine.

Willingham wrote the novel and the script for *Rambling Rose* in 1972 and watched it languish in movie limbo. In 1990, Dern brought the script to her then boyfriend, director Renny Harlin (*Die Hard 2*), who arranged financing through Carolco and formed his own company to produce it. Suddenly, *Rose* had muscle.

And Dern (*Smooth Talk, Wild at Heart*) knew what to do with it. Her knockout performance ranks her among the best actresses of her generation. From the moment her Rose ambles onto the Hillyers'

Laura Dern shone in the title role and Martha Coolidge (right) moved into the ranks of major American directors with their 1991 *Rambling Rose,* based on the novel by Calder Willingham.

front porch carrying a cardboard suitcase tied with string, Dern wraps up this film in her moonbeam smile and carries it to glory. "Hello, I'm Rose, and I've come to live with you and your family," she tells Buddy. But it's courtly Daddy who sets her aflame. One night, Rose jumps onto his lap—dislodging a perky breast from her dress—as the kids watch through the keyhole. "Wow, he's kissing her," says Buddy in shock. But Daddy comes to his senses. "Replace that tit," he bellows. Duvall is wonderfully funny and human as an Old World gentleman with his dignity under siege. "Wasn't Daddy great!" says Doll to her brothers. "I bet he wanted to kiss her some more and play with her, but he didn't."

In Buddy's room, Rose creeps into his bed to share her heart-break. But Buddy, beautifully played by Haas (the kid from *Witness*), wants more than conversation. While Rose is distracted, he touches her breast over her nightgown. Rose lets him put his hand underneath, but when Buddy's fingers move to her crotch she protests. He continues, pleading natural curiosity. After several minutes, his touch brings Rose to orgasm. Unaware of what he's doing, Buddy is nonetheless in awe as Rose closes her eyes, grits her teeth, and cries out in release. Afterward, Rose is guilt ridden.

"I have robbed a cradle and fallen into Hell," she says, begging Buddy never to tell his parents. It's quite a feat for an actress to keep an audience rooting for her after climbing into bed with a guppy, but Dern's disarming guilelessness does the trick.

Though Rose needs a sexual outlet, she wisely decides to reach outside the Hillyer home. In her clingiest dress she swings into town and soon has the men howling. Daddy has to drive off the polecats with a shotgun. He wants to fire Rose, but his wife objects. "It isn't sex she wants, it's love," says Mother, "and that's the only way she knows how to get it."

Ladd (Dern's real mother) brings welcome feminist bite to her role. It's clear that Coolidge is most engaged when investigating the subtext of sexual prejudice in Willingham's script. As she proved in her first feature, *Not a Pretty Picture* ('75)—the autobiographical story of a high school date rape—Coolidge knows how to observe without moralizing. If there's a villain in the piece, it's Dr. Martinson (Kevin Conway), who diagnoses Rose as a psychoneurotic with "uncontrollable sexual impulses." About to remove an ovarian cyst that Rose and the Hillyers first feared was a pregnancy, the doc suggests removing the other ovary as well to dramatically diminish her sexual drive. Daddy's inclination to go along with Martinson's sadistic plan enrages Mother. "Is there no limit to which you won't go to keep your illusions about yourselves?" she asks. The scene is more satisfying than believable, but it gets at something rare in movies: how males are fascinated and threatened by female sexuality. Men may want to exalt, screw, or spay Rose, but none tries to understand her.

Just as Mother won't let Rose be mutilated, Coolidge won't carve *Rose* into a male fantasy about a fuck bunny tamed by domesticity. The ending is a crock, with the older Buddy and Daddy grieving over Rose's recent death from cancer (the ovary killed her after all). But Coolidge's heart is not in the men's soggy tribute. What electrifies *Rambling Rose* are those moments that disconnect sex from penetration and virtue from repression. Dern's performance lingers like a siren's song. So does the movie. It's a beauty.

Rolling Stone, October 3, 1991

THE HAND THAT ROCKS THE CRADLE

Gary Arnold

The Hand That Rocks the Cradle proves so adept at exploiting the sinister potential in ordinary domestic surroundings that it seems almost certain to become a rabble-rousing hit. This disarming facility, reinforced by superior craftsmanship and performances, results in a more conscientious exercise in suspenseful manipulation than we're accustomed to in contemporary thrillers.

There's a becoming modesty about the means experienced director Curtis Hanson and novice screenwriter Amanda Silver use to terrorize us. For one thing, their villain isn't permitted to go supernatural. The scariest sequences tend to reverse our expectations about normally beneficial objects and peaceful activities: a nursery intercom, an asthma-medication dispenser, and the act of breast-feeding, to mention the most impressively twisted examples.

Ironically, *Cradle* also turns out to be a more faithful revamp of *Cape Fear* than the recent, mad-dog remake perpetrated by Martin Scorsese. Hanson and Silver change the sex of the antagonists, but they've respected the basic sense of popular loyalties in the original *Cape Fear,* where the decent but beleaguered family man played by Gregory Peck was never envisioned as a *deserving* victim of intimidation by Robert Mitchum's cunning psychopath.

Set in the suburbs of Seattle, *Cradle* pits an unwary young wife and mother named Claire Bartel against an insanely vengeful nanny named Peyton. As the imperiled heroine, Annabella Sciorra confirms her appeal as an exceptionally spontaneous and responsive young actress—perhaps the most sympathetic and believable image of an affectionate young woman since Debra Winger was at her peak in *An Officer and a Gentleman* and *Terms of Endearment* a decade ago. Sciorra really is the last actress on earth one would choose to see threatened, from any source. The powerful protective instinct she inspires works like a charm for this particular thriller, which emphasizes Claire's vulnerability in ways that don't rely on threats from a physically intimidating source.

As the demurely demented, insidious, and psychologically threatening Peyton, Rebecca De Mornay appears guaranteed to achieve a belated stardom by provoking audiences into a keenly agitated and gratified lynch mob. She's a schizo to cherish, right up there with Anthony Perkins in *Psycho* and Glenn Close in *Fatal Attraction*. I assume it's no coincidence that her role synthesizes prominent features of those classic lovelorn lunatics: Peyton has a sense of abandonment that echoes Perkins's Norman Bates while possessing the seething self-righteous conviction of Close's Alex Forrest.

The contrasts between good woman and evil woman are very sharply and enjoyably defined throughout *Cradle,* but De Mornay gives Peyton a formidable malicious wit and authority. It's fun watching her try to wreck Claire's life, in part because her vindictive craziness has a grandiose integrity. She emerges as one gorgeous monster by validating Peyton's deranged belief that she's *entitled* to act monstrously.

There's a prologue that explains her delusion on this score, but it would be best to conceal most of its details. Suffice it to say that Claire, while pregnant with the infant boy who later becomes a focus of Peyton's vengeance, is furtively molested by a gynecologist (an excruciating early episode, so be prepared for some clinical shocks at the outset). Persuaded that legal action would be wise, Claire sets off a sequence of events that ultimately brings Peyton to her doorstep, pretending to be a melancholy treasure seeking employment as a live-in babysitter.

The filmmakers need a bit of slack when they insert Peyton in the comfortable, affectionate Bartel household, consisting of Claire, her scientist husband Michael (Matt McCoy), a lively young daughter named Emma (Madeline Zima), and the infant Joe. Claire must be careless about checking references, a point that seems adequately finessed by the fact that she *likes* Peyton and feels touched by her cover tale of woe.

Supposedly, Claire requires the help because she plans to supervise the construction of a greenhouse in the backyard and resume at least a part-time career in botany. There's another employee on the premises, a handyman named Solomon (a potentially mawkish role played with admirable discretion by Ernie Hudson) whose slight mental retardation becomes a weapon in Peyton's campaign to undermine Claire. A boomerang weapon, of course: Solomon is instinctively suspicious of this deceitful newcomer and eventually functions as a crucial defender of the family, like Boo in *To Kill a Mockingbird.*

The objections to Peyton's acceptance by Claire are also covered to some extent by inserting an entertaining minor character who articulates them: Julianne Moore as the heroine's sarcastic realtor friend Marlene. Once the basic elements and significant characters are established and activated, the movie orchestrates ominous and ultimately homicidal events with skill and economy.

The film's fundamental effectiveness resides in its flair for simple and intimate scariness. While observing Peyton scheme to injure and replace Claire, *Cradle* temporarily disrupts our own sense of domestic security and sanctity, exposing vulnerabilities where you need and expect trust. In salutary contrast to the Scorsese *Cape Fear,* Hanson and his colleagues aren't perversely inclined to overrate maliciousness at the expense of innocence. Audiences can rest assured that the film won't violate their sense of loyalty to Claire, but *Cradle* is also astute enough to take abundant advantage of Rebecca De Mornay's aptitude for deceptive malice.

One of the wittiest touches in the script is the selection of a clue that finally opens Claire's eyes to Peyton's enmity. You're set up by Marlene's sleuthing to expect a recognition of one particular detail, but it's something else that clicks with Claire. Pulling this switch is clever in and of itself, but the clue recognized by Claire is also chosen with exceptional wit and logic. It couldn't be more poignant, or more perverse.

Washington Post, January 10, 1992

POISON IVY

■■■

Peter Travers

As the teen fatale of this low-budget, high-style find, leggy Drew Barrymore kicks her *E.T.* image over the rainbow. Now little Gerrie rivals Sharon Stone in indulging basic instincts. She slips the tongue to a tomboy school chum, plays footsie with a man's crotch, fucks on the hood of a Mercedes (in the rain, yet), and kills . . . well, more of that later. *Poison Ivy* sounds like B-movie trash, which sometimes it most deliciously is. This kinky spellbinder also manages to stir thoughts of Nabokov, Joe Orton, Groucho Marx, *All About Eve, Fatal Attraction,* and those dirty videos your cousin Herbie stashes in his locker. *Poison Ivy* moves beyond wickedly

Sara Gilbert (left) and Drew Barrymore form a special, ultimately sinister friendship in Katt Shea Ruben's breakthrough B movie, *Poison Ivy*. (Photo by Kimberly Wright. © 1992 New Line Productions. All Rights Reserved. Photo appears courtesy of New Line Productions.)

erotic fun to become an acutely unsettling psychological thriller. That raises a question: who made this wild thing?

Her name is Katt Shea, an actress turned director who cowrote the *Ivy* script with her former husband, producer Andy Ruben. As protégés of Roger Corman, Ruben and Shea turned out such bimbo-and-slasher cheapies as *Dance of the Damned, Streets,* and *Stripped to Kill I* and *II.* Movie snobs may laugh until they see Shea's gift for transcending pulp. The emotional resonance, visual sophistication, and feminist subtext of Shea's work fuse to create a distinctive style that's worth monitoring.

New York's Museum of Modern Art thinks so; it recently featured a Shea retrospective. Although *Poison Ivy* prompted a few noisy walkouts at the Sundance Film Festival, the *New York Times* acclaimed it as a "commercial art film." B movies give new directors a chance to exercise their subversive talents; look at Jonathan Demme's *Caged Heat* ('74) or Martin Scorsese's *Boxcar Bertha* ('72). Shea follows in that tradition and does it proud.

From the first scene of *Poison Ivy,* Shea shows a remarkable assurance. Sylvie Cooper, superbly played by Sara Gilbert (Darlene the diss queen on TV's "Roseanne"), is sketching a cross entwined with ivy. The model for her drawing is a tattoo on the leg of the new girl at Oakhurst High School, who's gliding dangerously over a ravine on a rope swing. The atmosphere is hypnotically sensual as Phedon Papamichael's camera takes in this mystery creature from her pouty mouth to the peekaboo hole in her boot.

"She's definitely a turnoff—too overt," says Sylvie in a voiceover. "I mean, most girls don't fly through the air with their skirt around their waist." Sylvie, a self-described "politically, environmentally correct, feminist, poetry-reading type," dresses down with a vengeance. Sylvie is fascinated with the other girl's mouth; lips, she's heard, are supposed to be a perfect reflection of another part of a woman's anatomy. "Not that I'm a lesbian," says Sylvie. "Well, maybe I am." As ever, Sylvie is conflicted. She dismisses the sexy stranger as "scangy" and then wishes devoutly that they could be friends.

An accident brings them together. A dog is hit by a car. Sylvie stares helplessly. But the new girl coolly whacks the animal on the head with a pipe and ends its misery. Sylvie is impressed. They share confidences. The girl's a scholarship student; she's been living with her aunt since her cokehead mother died and her father split, even though she tried to hold on to him by dressing like "the chicks in high heels" she found in his *Hustler* collection. Sylvie's a rich kid rattling around in an L.A. mansion; she's impatient with her invalid mother Georgie (edgy Cheryl Ladd), and in deep shit with her reformed-alcoholic father Darryl (a touchingly beleaguered Tom Skerritt) because she called in a bomb threat to the TV station he manages. The two loners form a bond. Sylvie dubs her new friend Ivy, after the tattoo; Ivy's androgynous name for Sylvie also sticks—Coop.

Shea gets the sexual confusion of female adolescence just right. And Barrymore nails every carnal, comic, and vulnerable shading in her role; she's a knockout. Sylvie likes that Ivy makes her parents cringe. But when Ivy moves in with the dysfunctional Coopers (even the maid is uncommunicative) and starts sucking up to them, Sylvie grows more alienated. In a darkly comic scene the girls fight over the affections of Sylvie's mutt, Fred. "The fact that Fred hated every human except me really meant something," says Sylvie.

Things quickly turn sinister. Georgie sees Ivy as a reminder of happier times, when she drove her red Corvette in the rain with the top down. "One day with the top down is better than a lifetime in a box," says Ivy, encouraging suicidal thoughts in Georgie. Darryl, whose sex life ended with his wife's illness, is aroused when Ivy wears Georgie's low-cut dress. One night they find Georgie passed out in bed from Percodan and champagne. Sitting on the edge of the bed while Darryl picks up a broken glass on the floor, Ivy rubs his crotch with her high-heeled foot while Darryl nuzzles between her legs. The only sound is Georgie's tortured breathing.

Shea uses tantalizing eroticism to reveal the film's emotional undercurrents. When Georgie is pushed from her balcony, feelings reach a fever pitch. Though *Poison Ivy* can be read on several levels, it plays most provocatively when seen as Sylvie's guilty nightmare over her mother's death, with Ivy as her imaginary evil twin. As Ivy, Sylvie can express her repressed longings for her father and her hostility toward her mother. As herself, she cannot. Ivy's tattoo, miniskirt, and black fuck-me pumps are the fetishes of a naïve, neurotically insecure girl. The film builds to Sylvie's mature realization that she can't replace Georgie in Darryl's life. That this doesn't come off as dime store moralizing is a tribute to Shea's layered direction and the dynamic Gilbert–Barrymore teamwork. Sylvie's last words about Ivy, "I miss her," become a poignant farewell to childhood.

Shea is examining the differences in how women and men define intimacy and the ways those differences can drive a wedge between families, lovers, and friends when communication stops. These are rare things to do in a thriller, and Shea knows acceptance is hard to come by. Though *Poison Ivy* is more than whoopee, audiences may find the movie easier to get off on than to get into. But why settle for the usual walk around the exploitation block when Shea offers a wild ride with the top down into uncharted territory?

Rolling Stone, May 28, 1992

LITERARY ADAPTATIONS

W hen John Huston made the move from screenwriter to writer-director, he started his new career with an adaptation of Dashiell Hammett's private-eye novel *The Maltese Falcon*. As a first step he had his secretary type out the novel, breaking it down into dialogue sequences and omitting most of the description. Legend has it that a copy of her effort reached studio chief Jack L. Warner, who then congratulated Huston on licking the adaptation and told him to get ready to shoot it. And the fact is, that's pretty much what Huston did.

Translating a novel to the screen is rarely that simple, let alone that successful. There had been two previous Warners films based on Hammett's book—one somewhat faithful, one wildly dissimilar, neither anywhere near the quality of the third version that became a film classic and made *The Maltese Falcon* "John Huston's *The Maltese Falcon*" as well as Dashiell Hammett's. Huston earned that honor by assembling an uncannily right cast to incarnate *Falcon*'s characters and by filming in a hard-surface, fluid, sardonically angled style that perfectly complemented the author's tone.

So the lesson of *The Maltese Falcon* is not "find a novel that's practically a shooting script already and have sense enough to recognize it." Few novels of literary worth would qualify, and even if they did, the filmmaker would still have to find a cinematic voice, a visual vocabulary and rhythm, to translate the verbal music on the page into dialogue, incident, and movement photographed from the correct distance and vantage points. In most cases, of course, the screenplay—that bastard child stranded in the no-man's-land between literature and film—would loom as the first challenge. What to retain from the novel, what to leave out, and what bridges to construct over the gaps? A novelist may have the luxury of fielding a hundred characters over a thousand-page narrative, but a movie's constraints of budget and running time (and viewers' ability to keep track) compel the folding of several minor characters into one or the distilling of an entire transitional section of the book into a single definitive scene—or image. Then, too, dialogue that reads exquisitely in the mind's ear may be precious and unpersuasive if spoken on a soundtrack; writers—or the director and actors—may have to come up with language that *sounds* faithful to the original work yet is actually brand new. And on and on.

The "genre" of Literary Adaptations is as miscellaneous as the variety of works adapted to the screen. We include it here to stimulate reflection on the subtle art of translating literature to film, but also to propose that Literary Adaptations do have something in common—a quality of *expectation* ("Are they going to ruin my favorite novel or make me love it all the more?") that can be more powerful than any generic presuppositions we bring to a new Western, horror film, or film noir. Indeed, it often transpires that, when one has read the book on which a film is based, one ought to see the film at least twice: the first time, to get one's curiosity about the adaptation out of the way; the second time, to see the movie in its own right.

Starting off this chapter, Dave Kehr discusses changes in Hollywood's attitude toward "prestige product" and what they have to do with adaptation. Then Stephen Schiff writes about "the most faithful movie adaptation I know," John Huston's film of Flannery O'Connor's *Wise Blood.* Bruce Williamson diagnoses *The French Lieutenant's Woman* as a victim of "cinematic" overkill. Two novelistic Merchant-Ivory productions, *Mr. and Mrs. Bridge* and *Howards End,* are applauded by Richard Schickel and Peter Travers, respectively. Schickel ventures to suggest that, if anything, Michael Mann's *Last of the Mohicans* improves on James Fenimore Cooper's, and recalls an exhilarating era in Hollywood filmmaking besides. Lastly, Andrew Sarris notes Sally Potter's ambitiousness in even attempting to film so rarified a literary work as Virginia Woolf's *Orlando,* and defines the inevitable limitations of the result.

ON MAKING BOOK

Dave Kehr

Twenty-five years ago, one of the major specialties of the Hollywood studios was the stately, tasteful adaptation of a literary work, drawn from a bestseller (*The Godfather*), from the stage (*The Lion in Winter*), or from the classics reading list (*The Great Gatsby*). It was left to the grungy independent outfits, like American-International, New World, or Crown, to feed the drive-ins with exploitation films, horror movies, and shoot-'em-ups.

Today, that relationship has been almost completely reversed. The majors are turning out the exploitation fare, in films like *Basic Instinct, Lethal Weapon 3,* and *Bram Stoker's Dracula,* while the high-toned, literary properties are left to the independents—Sony Classics with *Howards End,* Miramax with *Enchanted April,* Samuel Goldwyn with *Madame Bovary,* New Line (and its art-house subsidiary, Fine Line) with such elevated European coproductions as *Waterland* and *Damage,* and the domestic theatrical adaptation *Glengarry Glen Ross.*

The irony of this reversal seems most acute at the end of the year, when the majors, as if they just remembered there was such a thing, rush to get their classier pictures into release in time to qualify for Academy Award consideration. Suddenly the screens are flooded with prestige productions—with precisely those literary projects (*A Few Good Men*) and spectacular performances (a Hoffman, a Pacino, a Nicholson or two) that are extremely scarce through the rest of the year.

For the studios, the Oscars have become an embarrassing anachronism, designed to honor exactly the kind of films—worthy, uplifting, slavishly anglophilic—that they are no longer willing to make, either because the audience won't support them in sufficient numbers, or because the industry's executives have long since resigned any real ambition.

"I don't make art," proudly announces Joel Silver, producer of *Lethal Weapon 3* and a noted collector of Frank Lloyd Wright, "I buy it."

Such a statement, however admirably frank, would never have crossed the lips of Louis B. Mayer, Irving Thalberg, David O.

Selznick, or any of the other pioneering producers who founded the Academy essentially to celebrate their own hard-won good taste and certify their contributions to American culture. They may not have made art, either—particularly when they were trying hardest to—but at least the desire was there.

One can only imagine the profound horror Louis Mayer would feel before even the basic idea of *Basic Instinct*. Even a self-styled vulgarian like Columbia's Harry Cohn would have banished a project like *Batman Returns* (the year's highest-grossing film, with revenues of $162,744,850) to the furthest reaches of his B-movie division. In fact, he did—the first *Batman* movie was a Columbia serial produced in 1943.

If Irving Thalberg were to reenter the industry today, he would have trouble getting greenlighted at any of the major studios; a track record that included such dreary seriousness as *The Barretts of Wimpole Street, Romeo and Juliet,* and *The Good Earth* would impress no one, though no body of work was more honored in its time.

By contrast, his chances in public television would be excellent. With Thalberg on staff at PBS, pulling together financing from video companies and exploiting the BBC talent pool, "Masterpiece Theatre" would live its richest era.

Once the staples of exploitation filmmaking, sex and violence, have gone mainstream, the new field of exploitation is good taste—Victorian gardens instead of abandoned motels, rustling crinoline instead of squeaking leather, nosegays and slim volumes of poetry instead of flashing knives and chattering submachine guns. Now that the majors have closed off the low road, the independents must take the high. The way to the tender underbelly of the American audience is no longer through trash, but class.

The advantages of this new configuration of American taste are manifold. For the independent producer, who must operate on a budget, class can be a real cost saver. Spectacular locations can be had for peanuts or the cost of a modest donation to the local historical trust; warehouses full of period costumes, sewn for David Lean movies and since carefully packed away in mothballs, sit waiting in London. Special-effects expenses are minimal, being restricted largely to masking out TV aerials poking through the thatched roofs of quaint English villages. Because most of the authors involved stopped drawing royalties somewhere around the Edwardian age, material—even the very best—can be had cheaply, if not free. Why pay Joe Eszterhas $3 million (for *Basic Instinct*) when Edith Wharton and Gustave Flaubert can be acquired for the cost of a Penguin Classic?

Best of all, Jeremy Irons, Liam Neeson, Miranda Richardson, Emma Thompson, Julian Sands, and the other actorly axioms of the genre can be hired at rates far below those of their American counterparts, though recently Daniel Day Lewis, with all of that Hollywood chest baring in *The Last of the Mohicans,* appears to have priced himself out of the market.

No wonder, then, that *Ethan Frome* has replaced *Slumber Party Massacre* on the lists of independent releases.

The best American movies, of course, have always mixed highbrow and lowbrow inclinations, with lowbrow sources—cheap Westerns, detective novels, Broadway musicals—generally outpointing the classics as promising material for screen adaptation. Though John Ford had his brushes with Eugene O'Neill (*The Long Voyage Home*) and Graham Greene (*The Fugitive*), his most satisfying and artistically complex work had its roots in the drugstore novels of Alan LeMay (*The Searchers*) and Dorothy M. Johnson (*The Man Who Shot Liberty Valance*). The closest Alfred Hitchcock ever came to a literary classic was *Rebecca,* and that was Selznick's idea.

If Ford and Hitchcock's pulp-based projects seem more meaningful and accomplished with every passing year, while the tonier adaptations of Thalberg, Selznick, and Goldwyn Sr. are almost unwatchable today, it's clearly because of the greater leeway nonclassic material allows the director. There is the freedom to associate themes and ideas, bending the material to personal inclinations, and to reinvent visually and psychologically, refitting the material to particular locations and particular actors. When a novel is a known quantity, a film adaptation carries certain expectations that can only be frustrated at great peril. Audiences, and particularly critics, are notoriously unforgiving—remember *Bonfire of the Vanities?*

But lowbrow or high, all material requires the application of a filmmaker's sensibility. Tim Burton's *Batman Returns* is certainly a more personal and cinematic work than Jean-Jacques Annaud's adaptation of Marguerite Duras's *The Lover* or Stephen Gyllenhaal's adaptation of Graham Swift's *Waterland*. It's that sensibility, the willingness to make a project a personal vision, that is missing in so many of the independents' literary films. Too often, the producers of these films hire directors from television or theater who are expected to act as traffic cops, pushing the actors on and off as they say their lines. This isn't an adaptation, it's only a reading.

The new year should bring an interesting test case, in the form of Martin Scorsese's adaptation of the Edith Wharton classic *The Age of Innocence,* starring Daniel Day Lewis and Michelle Pfeiffer. Perhaps this will be the proof, long delayed as it has been, that a good director can make a good movie out of anything. Even a great novel.

Chicago Tribune, December 27, 1992

WISE BLOOD

■■■

Stephen Schiff

We've become accustomed to thinking of the South as a region born again, a land of sunshine and money and prosperous peanut farmers. Within the gleaming skyscrapers of Atlanta, Mobile, and New Orleans, we envision a thousand Larry Hagmans leaping from their swivel chairs to close a deal, a thousand Bert Lances slapping one another's sharkskinned backs, and, in the singles bars, a thousand Hamilton Jordans boogying till the cows come home. The desolate countryside has given way to industry. And tent-show fundamentalism has become an industry too; today's slick Southern preachers minister to the television cameras, and their flocks range from Maine to California.

So it's startling to be plunged into the world of *Wise Blood,* which is a very weird place to inhabit, even for two hours. The movie is set in a sweltering, Jesus-mad backwater that looks very much like the Deep South, the South we've forgotten: the land of street-corner evangelists, toothless con artists, and demented children. But could this South, which combines elements from the last three decades, ever really have existed? Here, faces and cars and roads bend strangely, surfaces seem to rot before our eyes, and people do and say things that people never do or say. Watching this movie is like looking at the world through a piece of ornate glass or through the eyes of a crow—everything is dark and vertiginous and goofy and frightening, all at once. *Wise Blood* is John Huston's thirty-third film, and, though it's often very funny, it's not a warm and likable work, not a work that could ever appeal to a very broad audience. Made independently, on a shoestring, it's the very antithesis of a Hollywood film—it's harsh, literary, and uncompromising. Huston has created an atmosphere of absurdity and dislocation without resorting to creepy music or fish-eye lenses. All he's done is enter the world of Flannery O'Connor, adapting her first novel, a slim volume published in 1952, as faithfully as he knew how. In the end, I think he distorts her peculiar brand of evangelical Catholicism— he's too much a humanist to believe, with her, that we are all clowns of God, dancing toward judgment. But if he's missed O'Connor's theology, he's brought her eerie-ugly-beautiful vision to life, and the result is a portrait of the South as we've never seen it—not the geographical South but the Christian South, the freak- ish landscape of the Southern religious imagination.

For O'Connor, who died of lupus in 1964 at the age of 39, the world is a big, slow whirlpool, with Jesus at the center. Everyone feels His pull, though most people have trouble identifying it as such; and everyone spirals toward Him in his or her own distinctive way: eagerly or blindly, flailing or preaching or splashing against the tide. O'Connor's novellas and short stories are odd theological "proofs," demonstrations that the most outlandish acts we commit are responses to the mysterious attraction of Jesus, to the ineffable mag- netism that some experience as ambition, some as compulsion, some as a sort of fever in the blood. One character calls it "wise blood," and screenwriter Benedict Fitzgerald, who practically grew up on O'Connor's knee, has invented some dialogue explaining it: "It's a gift, like a gift of the prophets . . . where I gotta do some things sometimes; I gotta do some things that I don't even want to do."

As we descend into the maelstrom, our guide is Hazel Motes (Brad Dourif), a staring ostrich of a boy who's just out of the army and headed straight for the city of Taulkingham, Tennessee; he's another young man who says he's out to "do some things." Hazel thinks he's going to be the very model of a modern go-getter, but what he's really trying to do is shake off Jesus, and, to his chagrin, he keeps finding himself drawn back into His thrall. Hoping, per- haps, to look like a city slicker, he buys a dark, narrow suit and a broad-brimmed hat, but the solemn new outfit and his burning eyes have an unfortunate effect: people start mistaking him for a preacher. He wants to wallow in sin, to scream defiance at a faith he can't see or hear or touch, and when he gets to town, he heads

Dueling evangelists Brad Dourif (left) and Harry Dean Stanton face off in John Huston's film of Flannery O'Connor's *Wise Blood*.

straight for the home of a prostitute. "What I mean to have you know is: I'm no goddam preacher," he hisses at the whore, a fat, indolent slattern who spends most of her time clipping her toenails. Whereupon she gives him a sleepy smirk and replies, "That's OK, son. Momma don't mind if you ain't a preacher."

The trouble with Hazel is all that wise blood. Christianity courses through his veins like a drug, and his addiction is congenital —inherited from his grandfather (John Huston), a fire-and-brimstone-preaching evangelist. Wise blood has made him crazy and yet strangely attractive, and people keep gravitating toward him—crazy people. There's Enoch Emery (Dan Shor), a gentle, lonely, moronic boy who follows Hazel around as if he were his acolyte; Asa Hawks (Harry Dean Stanton), a nasty preacher who poses as a blind man, handing out tracts and begging; and Sabbath (Amy Wright), the "blind" preacher's fifteen-year-old daughter, a white-trash temptress. Hazel decides to prove his independence of Jesus by founding his own church, the Church of Truth Without Christ, "where the blind don't see and the lame don't walk and what's dead stays that way." He buys a beat-up jalopy, which he regards as a proud emblem of his apostasy ("Nobody with a good car needs to be justified," he sneers), and, in a series of beautiful scenes that look like something out of a Robert Frank photograph, he stands on the hood of his car, suspended in the night between a traffic light and a neon sign that says JESUS SAVES, bleating out his antigospel. Hazel is no opportunist; he's perfectly sincere. "If Jesus had redeemed you, what difference would it make to you or me?" he yells. "What you need is something to take the place of Jesus, something that would speak plain." No one understands him. A smooth-talking con man (beautifully played by Ned Beatty) even offers to help him set up his phony church. Then the money would really start rolling in.

O'Connor once called the religion of the South a "do-it-yourself religion," and the film is full of down-home heresies and backwoods temptations: Dairy Queens with signs demanding repentance, holy graffiti scrawled on the rocks. Everyone here has an obsession and every obsession is a mad grope toward God. Enoch Emery, the simpleton who becomes Hazel's disciple, answers the call of his blood by worshiping the shrunken corpse of a South American Indian, which he's stolen from a museum. *Wise Blood* is about the conflict between the form of Christianity and its substance. When people see Hazel up there preaching, with his gloomy hat and scorching eyes, they hear Christianity because he looks like Christianity to them—even though Christianity is exactly what he's denouncing. Even when he deliberately runs over a drunken rival with his car, Hazel is mistaken for the Lord's vessel; as he stares down at the highway in astonishment, his bloody victim gurgles out a final confession: "Give my mother a lot of trouble. Never give her no rest . . . Jesus help me." There's no escaping Jesus, and, in the end, Hazel runs head-on into guilt—and slides ineluctably toward his own bleak redemption.

Necessarily, *Wise Blood*'s humor is very dark and even a little cruel. We seem to be chortling at a sideshow, at the holy writhings of grotesques. Part of our discomfort comes from Fitzgerald's too-faithful screenplay. As dramatic as Flannery O'Connor's dialogue looks on paper, it's often too fancy, too plangent for the screen. And this sometimes has the effect of changing a surreal atmosphere into an artificial, theatrical one. The movie is at its worst when it tries to ingratiate itself, to play for laughs. (This is especially true when Alex North's score interrupts its meditations on "The Tennessee Waltz" to kick into a foggy-holler hoot; suddenly you're watching "Hee-Haw.") In order to work, *Wise Blood* must immerse us in the freakishness of its vision without distancing winks and jabs in the ribs. For what O'Connor is after here is something like a parable,

one in which humans are stripped down and made basic and foolish, so that we may watch the workings of the religious mechanism
within them—and then apply the knowledge to our own, more
complex lives. Though they are seldom read that way, O'Connor's
stories are teaching fables. If we can see that we are all whooshing
toward Jesus, she believes, we'll realize that our own strivings and
all the strivings in all the skyscrapers of Atlanta and Mobile are but
varied and sophisticated responses to the tickle of wise blood (I suppose O'Connor puts Jesus where Freud puts sex, at the root of the
human quest). And we'll realize that this variety and sophistication
of response are what we've always called "free will."

With Eric Rohmer's version of Kleist's *The Marquise of O . . . ,*
Wise Blood is the most faithful movie adaptation I know. So it's
strange that it should fail to convey the spiritual substance of
O'Connor's tale. Not that O'Connor herself was particularly adept
at spreading the Holy Word. She is enjoying a revival now, largely
due to the publication of her collected letters in *The Habit of Being*
(edited by Sally Fitzgerald, the mother of *Wise Blood's* screenwriter
and its producers, Michael and Kathy Fitzgerald), but I think
people are drawn to her less by any religious message than by the
eeriness of her stories, by the way they freeze violence and demen-
tia in a placid, crystalline prose. Certainly it's the Southern Gothic
atmosphere that must have attracted so sardonic a director as John
Huston to *Wise Blood,* and it is this which he has best captured.
Filming in the run-down back streets of Macon, Georgia, Huston
has created a drab, dusty South, crumbling and gaudy and hopeless.
You can feel the heat here, but not the light, for cinematographer
Gerald Fisher has flattened the surfaces and perspectives; shadow
and light seem to drain into each other, and everything has a faded,
graying look, the look of old paint. The film abounds in frayed
screen doors, rusty cars, and bad spelling. And the faces in bit parts
and crowd scenes seem to peer out at us from an amber mist of
booze and madness. As we watch, the film takes on the quality of
a hallucination, something brought on by the heat. People laugh at
the wrong times, and say cryptic things and disappear; their emotions seem out of sync with what they're doing. A cop stops Hazel
and runs his car into a lake just because he doesn't like his face, but
this isn't the usual bloated redneck. This cop has deep, kind eyes
and an understanding, almost beatific smile; he's an angel of
vengeance. Amy Wright, who gives a sensational, squirmy performance as Sabbath, changes from a homely child to a purring vamp

in a flash. At every moment, her performance is completely at odds with our expectations. As she lolls seductively in the grass, describing a grotesque suicide as if it were a sunset, we watch her in a sort of trance; if she suddenly told us she were the whore of Babylon, we wouldn't bat an eye. Just as good is Mary Nell Santacroce, as Hazel's aging landlady, who watches the terrible self-mutilations he undergoes in the film's somber final half hour with horror ("It's not normal," she wails. "It's something that people have quit doing—like boiling in oil or being a saint or walling up cats.") and then mysteriously falls in love with him.

Huston keeps pulling the rug out from under us, and yet he takes time to insert a few perfect, realistic details—a cop wondering what color Hazel's faded suit is, for instance, or the landlady remarking that there used to be a fire escape in his room and now there isn't—as if to remind us that we're still on Earth. The "realism" isn't reassuring. Huston toys with the continuity and the connections between scenes, so that everything seems haphazard, out of kilter, fragmented; every rhythm is sprung, every melody is off-key. The only laws that govern *Wise Blood* are the laws of O'Connor's mysterious determinism—the laws of the whirlpool.

Wise Blood is a haunting film, but it's not a moving one. It lacks the one element that would make it great: the spiritualization of the characters to match the spiritualized world that Huston and O'Connor have crafted. We can feel the spooky-holy atmosphere in the storyline and in the way the film looks and moves, but we can't feel it in Hazel Motes, and here, I think, is where O'Connor and Huston diverge. Both book and film evince a noble and warming compassion for even the lowliest characters. But in the novel, it's clear that the compassion comes from O'Connor's respect for the way her figures work toward God; in the movie, it comes from Huston's affection for human lunacy. When Enoch Emery steals a gorilla suit from a movie-promotion truck and jaunts through the town, grabbing people and yelling, "Hi! Shake hands with Gonga!" we feel O'Connor loves him because, in his half-wit way, he's yearning to redeem the people he pounces upon—and to be redeemed in doing so. (O'Connor often refers to the call of Jesus in ape imagery, as if it were an atavistic urge echoing up at us from the evolutionary past.)

But Huston loves Enoch because the kid is plumb crazy. He and Hazel are like all the starry-eyed searchers and hustlers in Huston's movies—like the men who sought the Maltese falcon or the treasure of the Sierra Madre; like the man who would be king. With his scaly, ophidian eyes and his grating voice, Brad Dourif is just right for Hazel Motes, but he doesn't seem to have Jesus in him—only that slyness, the naïveté, and the lust for glory that so many of Huston's characters share. Huston follows Hazel to the threshold of the religious struggle, but he stops at the edge; he never explores the moment in which a person decides to preach or flee or inflict self-punishment. In the pages of the novel, we can feel fate—or, rather, Jesus—grab Hazel by the collar and drag him toward destiny. In Dourif's jumpy, eccentric incarnation, Hazel is but a poor, nutty Southern boy; self-mutilation is just one of his quirks. Paradoxically, it's Huston's humanitarian instinct, not O'Connor's mysticism, that pushes Hazel away from us. And, in the end, when we should be hurting for him, he is hopelessly remote, a mournful figure on the edge of the abyss, spiraling ever downward toward God.

Boston Phoenix, April 8, 1980

THE FRENCH LIEUTENANT'S WOMAN

Bruce Williamson

The peculiar conceits of Harold Pinter's screenplay more or less wreck *The French Lieutenant's Woman,* based on the John Fowles best-seller published in 1969. Fowles is such an accomplished novelist that he can slip in and out of a dark Victorian romance, digressing as the spirit moves him, without missing a stroke. Pinter's terrible idea was to adapt the novel as a movie within a movie, in which Meryl Streep plays the fallen woman who seduces a proper young gentleman (Jeremy Irons), at the same time appearing intermittently as the movie actress who is *making* this movie and having it off, as the English say, with her leading man. That questionable device might be applied to almost any film—with an effect roughly the same as if *Tess,* for example, were interrupted every twenty minutes or so by modern romantic interludes featuring director Roman Polanski and his star, Nastassia Kinski. The movie star couple portrayed by Streep and Irons serve no purpose but to keep

Meryl Streep in the film-within-the-film title role of *The French Lieutenant's Woman*. (Photo courtesy of MGM/UA Home Video, Inc., a subsidiary of Metro-Goldwyn-Mayer, Inc.)

The French Lieutenant's Woman from holding an audience in its spell. Although Irons generates considerable voltage—as intense and ardent as a young Laurence Olivier—the talented Streep seems to me just a shade too sensible and prosaic for the kind of erotic embodiment of a young man's fantasy that the script continually reminds us she is supposed to be. Director Karel Reisz has wrought a very pretty, pallid picture, with Pinter providing a transfusion of bad blood.

Playboy, November 1981

MR. AND MRS. BRIDGE

Richard Schickel

Stolid houses and spacious yards. The whirr of hand-powered lawn mowers in the summer, the scrape of snow shovels in the winter. Romberg on the radio, dinner at the country club once a week, a trip to Paris once in a lifetime. Dad wears vests, Mom wears funny hats, the maid nips at the cooking sherry (must speak to her about that). If their son makes Eagle Scout and one of his sisters pledges Kappa, does it really matter that the other daughter decamps for Greenwich Village and a scattershot involvement with "the arts" which her parents will never understand?

Probably not. For what is really important to Walter and India Bridge (Paul Newman and Joanne Woodward), citizens of suburban Kansas City a half century ago, is that the order of their rounds—diurnal and annual—is preserved. Drama in their lives is like crabgrass on their lawn, something to be rooted out the minute it appears and not dwelt upon thereafter.

Walter can usually wither the untoward with a cold stare through his steel-rimmed spectacles, though sometimes it is necessary to bark a few brusque commands in order to send it scurrying. India, in contrast, has a more coquettish relationship with it: she takes painting classes, flirts momentarily with divorce, psychoanalysis, and the ideas of Thorstein Veblen. But whether the Bridges are confronting a tornado that Walter refuses to let interrupt dinner, their children's romantic and sexual hubbubs, a friend's suicide, or simply the long silences of their own relationship, there is never any question about who is in charge around here.

In the fifties and sixties, when Evan Connell wrote the two quietly stated, delicately crafted novels that are expertly and faithfully conflated in *Mr. and Mrs. Bridge,* we had not yet learned to call marriages of this kind "traditional," putting a slight, sneering spin on the word. Just as it refuses to impose a thrusting dramatic structure on a story that was all incident, this movie refuses to impose anachronistic sociological attitudes toward its people. It retains the novelist's tone—one of ironic compassion—and sustains, as well, the perfect pitch of his voice, never going flat or sharp. That is to say, it neither falls into easy sentiment nor strains for cheap satire. Instead, it grants the Bridges the dignity they—and most of the people of their time, place, and (upper middle) class—worked so hard to achieve, and which is usually denied them in serious film and literature. In the process, it also grants its actors the freedom to explore the humanity of their characters.

They exercise it with delicious subtlety. His children and his friends would be startled if they could overhear Walter bellowing "Stout-Hearted Man" in the privacy of his car. Or see him make a sudden lurching grab for his wife in the privacy of their bedroom one hot summer's day. It does not surprise him. He is entirely aware of his secret life and really quite pleased with it. But that's his business and no one else's. India is less open to herself, but Woodward invests her with sudden flashes of inarticulate understanding, a subtext of surpressed intelligence, that makes her submissiveness all the more poignant. Blythe Danner and Austin Pendleton in supporting roles are touching in much the same way. But then, this memory piece, shy in manner but tough in spirit, has brought out the best in everyone connected to it.

Time, November 26, 1990

HOWARDS END

Peter Travers

Academics usually squeeze the life out of E. M. Forster's classic novel *Howards End* by treating it as an allegory for class war in Edwardian England. Rest assured, there is nothing pedantic about the movie version, which hews closer to Forster's humanism than his symbolism. Incisively witty, provocative, and acted to perfection, this sublime entertainment is a career peak for producer Ismail Merchant, director James Ivory, and screenwriter Ruth Prawer Jhabvala, who also triumphed with Forster's *Room with a View.* Forster's effort to draw meaning and hope from a society divided by money, class, culture, and social responsibility is timelier than ever in the post-*Bonfire* era. The film serves Forster by taking to heart the book's epigraph: "Only connect."

Check the hypnotic opening scene: In the hush of evening, Ruth Wilcox (Vanessa Redgrave)—the mistress of a country manor called Howards End—strolls the grounds, blissfully unconcerned that she's trailing her gown in the sopping grass. Inside the house her businessman husband Henry (Anthony Hopkins) and greedy children busy themselves in separate worlds while her younger son, Paul (Joseph Bennett), flirts with his freethinking houseguest, Helen Schlegel (a radiant Helena Bonham Carter). The scene, deftly shot by Tony Pierce-Roberts, captures the novel's essence in quick strokes. We sense Ruth's love of nature and Henry's abhorrence of it, just as we discern Paul's fear of Helen's emancipation.

Though Helen soon breaks off with Paul, her sharp-witted older sister Margaret (Emma Thompson) befriends his mother. Ruth's spiritual bond to the rural tradition of Howards End strikes a chord in Margaret, who lives with Helen and their student brother, Tibby (Adrian Ross Magenty), in a London Victorian about to be razed for modern flats that Forster called "the architecture of hurry."

Though Redgrave's role is small, she's never given a more delicate or heartfelt performance. Given the actress's leftist politics, the scene in which Ruth chides Margaret for supporting women's suffrage wins unintentional laughs, but Redgrave's hold on her character soon restores the balance. On her deathbed, Ruth scrawls a note leaving Howards End (which belongs to her and not her husband) to Margaret—a note that her family destroys.

A twinge of guilt leads the widowed Henry to pay a call on the Schlegels. He scorns the chaos of their lively London household and their friendship with Leonard Bast (Sam West), a timid married clerk whom the sisters have decided to instruct in the arts and social graces. But Henry is bewitched by Margaret's vitality. His later marriage proposal to her on a staircase is uncommonly funny and touching—he lacks the romantic finesse to do it properly, and she is too filled with ardor to respond in more than monosyllables.

The marriage of Henry and Margaret links the worlds of money and intellect and the strands of the plot. Henry's reluctant efforts to help Bast leave the clerk jobless and nearly homeless, while revelations of adultery and out-of-wedlock pregnancy prompt Henry's older son, Charles (James Wilby), to take precipitous action that results in tragedy.

Hopkins, the thinking Oscar voter's choice for *The Silence of the Lambs,* makes Henry a seductive blend of charm and ruthlessness. And Thompson is thrilling in a performance that ranks her with the best actresses of her generation. Nothing in Thompson's previous film work—the light-comic *The Tall Guy* and *Dead Again*—prepares us for the depth of feeling she brings to Margaret. Growing less verbal and more reflective, she absorbs betrayals, initiates change, and creates the balance necessary for the warring factions around her to achieve a hard-won harmony.

For Forster, the fight over who will inherit Howards End was a symbolic fight over England itself. His acceptance of the melting pot and the blurring of class distinctions didn't stop him from mourning the passing of tradition. Jhabvala's remarkably fluid script cuts to the core of Forster's concerns about the danger of shutting off feeling. In detailing the problems of greed, the film of *Howards End* speaks in fresh, startling ways to a new generation. It's a satisfying irony indeed that a book published in 1910 became the first great movie of 1992.

Rolling Stone, April 2, 1992

THE LAST OF THE MOHICANS

Richard Schickel

"This is the forest primeval. The murmuring pines and the . . ."

Oops. Wrong boring American classic. But Longfellow's lines are appropriate nevertheless to a consideration of Michael Mann's ravishing realization of *The Last of the Mohicans.* From its first images of a deer hunt to its last shots of hero and heroine gazing westward toward mist-shrouded mountains, the film's sensuous evocations of an Arcadian wilderness, of the land that was ours before we were the land's (to borrow from a more pertinent poet), draw us into a remote realm, just as the need to penetrate the majesty and mystery of that landscape draws its characters irresistibly on to fates variously ennobling and tragic.

Perhaps the poignancy of these images derives from our sense that we are looking into a world now almost entirely lost. Perhaps it derives as well from the memories they stir of movie glories past, when sweeping historical spectacle, spread across the screen in a confidently romantic spirit now also largely lost to us, was a cinematic commonplace. Then again, it may simply be the crazy nerve of this project that disarms one's critical faculties: The French and Indian Wars. A protagonist named Hawkeye. A red-coated English army marching in straight stupid lines through the forest. Their wily Indian enemies skittering unseen through the underbrush, a constant menace not just to the soldiery, but to virtuous femininity as well. Anybody around here heard of postmodernism? Or run a survey to find out if anyone under forty has even heard of James Fenimore Cooper's novel, let alone spared a kindly thought for it?

Happily not. Director Mann says his first potent movie memory is of the 1936 adaptation of the book (he gives credit to Philip Dunne's screenplay as a source for the script he wrote with Christopher Crowe). He has gone still further than the older picture did in straightening and strengthening the plot—about a beseiged fort, its commandant's daughters' ill-timed attempt to join him there, and the anarchy that follows its surrender—and in clarifying motives, conflicts, and characterizations. Even Magua, the treacherous Indian villain of the piece—played with deadly relish by Wes Studi—is given a good motive for his dastardliness, the dignity of his otherness, and even a nanosecond of pity for a victim. Above all, Mann has seen to it that something spooky, suspenseful, or just plain action-packed happens every five minutes. In the process, he has eliminated the last traces of Cooper's impenetrable prose and sentiment.

As a result, the novelist's only immortal imaginative achievement, Hawkeye, born Natty Bumppo in a colonial settlement but raised by a Mohican family (his adoptive father and brother are his constant companions), has, at last, a context worthy of his historical importance. For this figure, blending the Old World tradition of gallantry with the New World's belief in the moral supremacy of those who live in close harmony with nature, is our *Ur*-frontiersman, prototype of an archetype on which everyone from William S. Hart to Clint Eastwood has played his variations.

But Daniel Day Lewis plays the character as if he were entirely unaware of the heroic line that derives from Hawkeye. This innocence leaves open an interesting possibility that, not knowing any better, he might implode under pressure instead of exploding into more predictable action. Conversely, Madeleine Stowe, playing the army officer's elder daughter, for whom Hawkeye's admiration has always in the past been more distant, invests her character with a sureness about her needs and a moral courage that is very up-to-date. And Mann rewards them with actual sexual contact, quietly yet fiercely staged, that is a wonderful, even startling, break with tradition.

Whether it was because we were young or the movies were young, or the world was at least youngish, old-fashioned Hollywood history was exhilirating. In retrospect there is something alarming about its simplicities and the enthusiasm with which we bought into them. It's the great virtue of this grandly scaled yet deliriously energetic movie that it reanimates that long-ago feeling

without patronizing it. Or making us think we will wake up some
day once again embarrassed by it.

Time, September 28, 1992

ORLANDO

■■■

Andrew Sarris

Sally Potter's *Orlando,* based on the novel by Virginia Woolf, is liked
enormously by people whose opinions I respect and disliked enormously by other people whose opinions I respect. Unfortunately, I
can see both points of view. As striking as *Orlando* is as spectacle and
as allegory, it is not really a movie in the sense in which I understand the term. There is no narrative or dramatic development.
Things happen after a fashion but with no intimation of an inexorable progression.

It has been argued that one should have read the book beforehand
to appreciate or even enjoy the movie. I would argue instead that to
enjoy the movie, one should be susceptible to Ms. Potter's avant-
garde conceits in the service of her radical feminism. I happen not
to be unconditionally committed to the Peter Greenaway–Derek
Jarman–Sally Potter emotionally emaciated phoenix that has risen
from the ashes of the British commercial film industry. I prefer
instead the humble sparrow mainstream approach of Ken Loach,
Terence Davies, and, now, newcomer Les Blair, whose forthcoming
Bad Behavior enables Sinéad Cusack and Stephen Rea to add a new
chapter to the history of improvisation in the cinema.

But I digress, which is about all I want to do when confronted
with Ms. Potter's Herculean ordeal in bringing her four-million-
dollar production to the screen and, for that matter, obtaining the
four million dollars in the first place for such a nebulous project. As
a longtime lover of Woolf's *Orlando,* I still don't think it can be faithfully adapted to the screen. We are as far from Woolf's Bloomsbury
as we are from the Elizabethans, perhaps even further. Whatever we
may deduce from Woolf's infatuation with Victoria Sackville-West
as the creative impetus for *Orlando,* what remains enduringly
enchanting is Woolf's amusingly discerning and intoxicating love

affair with English literature. Her humor and sweetness and smartness are not entirely absent from Ms. Potter's sensibility, but they are clouded over by the dark mist of a relentless ideology.

The movie is at its best in the Elizabethan sequences, with the marvelously grave Quentin Crisp endowing Queen Elizabeth I with the truly existential urgency of an old woman lusting after the flesh of a young man by ordering it never to decay as she has decayed. In the ritualized movements of the court, Tilda Swinton is dazzling as the androgynous Orlando. A changeling for the ages, Ms. Swinton is less effective in her more activist phases. Indeed, she remains anachronistically androgynous through all the succeeding stages of her transition to self-sufficient womanhood.

Individual sequences sparkle, most notably the Great-Frost-of-1603-when-the-Thames-froze-over episode, photographed by the Russian cameraman Alexei Rodionov with cold-breath atmospherics to spare. What is lacking is Woolf's ability to weave an intricate tapestry of words around even the most grotesque bumblings of social history. Her hilarious demystification of so-called society in the supposedly witty age of Pope, Swift, and Addison is reduced in the movie to a dull diatribe against smug sexism. It is not that Ms. Potter is ever unduly preachy but rather that she is looking at English history from so far outside that the glories of English literature are reduced to their imperialistic and patriarchal subtexts in a series of laborious visual gags. Where Woolf wielded a rapier, Potter pounds down with a broadsword. Ultimately, the book and the movie are not for everyone; though there is an overlap between Woolf's admirers and Ms. Potter's, there is an unbridgeable chasm between the two sensibilities, a chasm as wide as that between literature and cinema at its widest.

New York Observer, June 28, 1993

MOVIE ADAPTATIONS: SEQUELS AND REMAKES

S equels and remakes both derive from previous films, but, whereas sequels aim to trade on their forebears' success, remakes often hope to usurp their ancestors' identity. That is, *Jaws 2* needs you to know and care that there was a *Jaws; D.O.A.* ('88) has a prayer of beguiling an audience only if that audience doesn't know there was another, infinitely superior *D.O.A.* ('49). In either case, ever since movie titles started annexing numerals a couple of decades ago, film critics have tended to regard sequelitis and remake fever as twin plagues—the collective sign of an increasingly desperate film industry and an increasingly undiscriminating film audience.

Yet the practice of remaking proven hits—and readapting books, stories, and plays, especially when the originals are in the public domain—dates back to the silent era. Sequels are a slightly different matter. Up to the seventies, filmmakers rarely attempted to extend a given film story beyond the end title, though they might well recognize the commercial value of allowing a series—recurring stars and/or characters in new stories—to grow out of an original, often unanticipated success (say, the Hope-Crosby *Road* pictures of the forties).

The pattern is not entirely unhealthy. Some sequels—*For a Few Dollars More, Godfather II*—improved on their predecessors. Clark Gable starred in both *Red Dust* and *Mogambo*—each an exemplary MGM version of essentially the same tale. Some classic films are remakes: 1937's *The Awful Truth,* of an undistinguished 1929 comedy; and 1940's *His Girl Friday,* of 1931's *The Front Page*—and also, in bits and pieces, of 1937's *The Awful Truth* . . . but that's another story.

As both audiences and critics usually have no trouble recognizing, quality holds its own. What *did* producer Dino de Laurentiis have in mind when he floated that tagline for his 1976 remake: "There is only ONE *King Kong"?* The Great White shark might as well have done a quick fade to black rather than lend itself to *Jaws 2, Jaws 3,* and *Jaws the Revenge.* And *Psycho* remains *Psycho,* not *Psycho I*—numbers two, three, and four bearing precisely the same relation to Hitchcock's 1960 masterpiece as those latter-day "Sherlock Holmes" novels, written after the Conan Doyle estate's copyright had lapsed, bear to *A Study in Scarlet* et glorious al.

Indeed, in critics' fervor to uphold the integrity of the original film version, quality has even been cultivated in retrospect. To attend the rhetoric when Martin Scorsese's frenzied remake of *Cape Fear* was released in 1991, one might pardonably have assumed that the 1962 J. Lee Thompson version was an august suspense classic. Yet in 1962 the film was mostly deplored for its sweaty manipulativeness—if it got noticed at all. And, aside from Robert Mitchum's brilliant incarnation of monster-from-the-primeval-slime Max Cady (and Bernard Herrmann's music score, which Scorsese had Elmer Bernstein reprise for the remake), it remains at best a competent thriller.

Whatever their individual merits or shortcomings, sequels and remakes are now an established and acknowledged category of film experience. In this chapter, Peter Rainer assesses the trajectory of George Lucas's *Star Wars* series and figures it's time to open the carbonite chamber. Andrew Sarris considers three versions of *The Big Clock*—Kenneth Fearing's 1946 novel, John Farrow's 1948 film version, and Roger Donaldson's 1986 remake, *No Way Out*—and pronounces them all civilized entertainments. Mike Wilmington's review of *Caddyshack II* is funnier than the movie and argues that even mindless comedy has to be minimally smart about itself. Terrence Rafferty discusses how Tim Burton's style and imagination are equal to keeping the *Batman* franchise viable and appealing. And Armond White searches *Cape Fear* for signs of where the career of Martin Scorsese may next lead.

RETURN OF THE JEDI: THE LUCAS MYTH

Peter Rainer

The arrival of *Return of the Jedi,* the third film in the *Star Wars* trilogy, was hailed as more than just an important cinematic event. Even before its official release, it was written about in magazines and discussed on television in terms normally reserved for a major sociopolitical happening—and, in a way, that's appropriate.

George Lucas, the movie's producer and the creator of the series, is a major pop-commercial force in the country—perhaps *the* major force of the late seventies and eighties. Almost every movie he has produced—not only the *Star Wars* series but *American Graffiti* ('73) and *Raiders of the Lost Ark* ('81) as well—has resulted in a magic mountain of fads and spinoffs and merchandising tie-ins. He's influenced the way an entire generation looks at movies, and he's also influenced what that generation expects movies to be. Even his detractors can't deny that fact.

He has produced four of the most popular movies ever made; only his cohort, Steven Spielberg, can claim a similar achievement. It's natural, then, that we should look to *Jedi* for something more than entertainment, although the movie's only goal is to entertain. We look to it as the work of a visionary capitalist—the cinematic equivalent of, say, the Epcot Center.

But as a piece of moviemaking—of mythmaking—there's nothing visionary about *Return of the Jedi.* It delivers the goods all right. It whooshes across misty moons and desert planets with a full cargo of Wookies and Yodas and Jabbas and Vaders and Ewoks. Luke and Han and Leia and Lando are still in tow, and R2D2 and C3PO still perform their squeak-and-squawk duet. We find out the answers to all the questions left hanging in hyperspace in *The Empire Strikes Back* ('80): Will Luke Skywalker finally become a Jedi knight? Will Han Solo be freed from his carbonite sarcophagus? Is Darth Vader really Luke's father? Will the Rebels defeat the Empire at last?

Still, despite all the intergalactic hoopla, it's a surprisingly perfunctory experience. Two and a half years elapsed between *Empire* and *Jedi;* these questions may have stopped burning for you. And as directed by Richard Marquand, *Jedi* doesn't make us burn to find out the answers, either. The movie exists almost solely on a special effects and gadgetry level; emotionally, it's as blank as Darth Vader's visage. This time around, the toys have taken over the toy store.

Perhaps this explains why the actors in the film seem so glum; they know they can't hope to compete with the voluminous blobs and furballs and serpentoids that surround them. For actors, performing in a science-fantasy film must be a special sort of hell—they're almost inevitably upstaged by the hardware. In *Jedi*, when Mark Hamill's Luke confronts Jabba the Hutt, when Carrie Fisher's Princess Leia dallies with a teddy bear–like Ewok, you can see their dismay. Without any strong character to play or any good lines to spout, how can they hope to compete? Even Harrison Ford, normally a rousing presence, seems bummed out.

If there has been almost no human depth to any of the science-fantasy classics, like *2001* and *Forbidden Planet* and *Star Wars,* that's largely because the filmmakers haven't thought in those terms; for them, emotional depth and science fantasy may be mutually exclusive. The one big exception to this rule was *The Empire Strikes Back,* and so it's doubly disappointing that *Jedi* doesn't do justice to *Empire*'s legacy. It's almost as if Lucas and Marquand regarded the riches of that movie as a fluke—an aberration of the genre.

In *Time*'s cover story on *Jedi,* Marquand derides Irvin Kershner, the director of *Empire,* as carelessly straying from the true faith. That's like complaining that Sam Peckinpah didn't turn out "Gunsmoke" instead of *The Wild Bunch.* Kershner, probably the most prodigiously versatile director in America, was, I think, primarily responsible for *Empire*'s greatness. He transformed the pop-comics graphics of *Star Wars* into rich, sinister compositions. It was like opening up the Sunday cartoon pages to Prince Valiant and finding instead the imagery of Bosch or Doré. Luke's rite of passage into Jedihood, his discovery that Darth Vader may be his father, had an emotional resonance unlike any other science-fantasy film. *Empire* was more than an agglomeration of Lucas's storybook fantasies: it was an homage to the whole history of movies—to the marvels that movies can provide.

In *Jedi* the characters run a distant second to the action and the visuals are clean and uninspired—they don't look imagined, they look programmed. The story whizzes by without pause. It seems that the Empire has a new space station under construction that will be even deadlier than its previous base, the Death Star. For Luke to destroy it he must first rescue Han from Jabba the Hutt, a goopy monster who resembles a mating of Sydney Greenstreet and a ton of Jell-O. Then he must reassemble the Rebel starfleet into one vast attack squadron. But the Empire has installed a power plant on the moon of Endor and, unless the shield it generates can be destroyed, the fleet is doomed. Then there's the dark side of the Force to contend with. The Emperor (Ian McDiarmid) forces a showdown between Luke and Darth Vader, hoping that the boy will emerge victorious—and become his newest ally in evil. The story's resolution wraps up the trilogy.

Scrunched inside the 500-plus special effects are some imaginative moments. Jabba and his Huttites are an impressively disgusting array of squish-and-slime creatures—there's something almost Felliniesque about their gloppy grotesquerie. The Ewoks are a cute breed, I suppose, and I'm sure it won't be long before they're elbowing E.T. on toy store shelves around the world. There's an air-bike chase between the Empire's storm troopers and the Rebels that's as exciting as any pursuit ever filmed. It's a kinesthetic whizbang—you feel as if you're zooming through the center of the screen.

But in many ways *Jedi* lacks the spirit of the first two *Star Wars* films and, in this science-fantasy genre, spirit is everything. Nothing is more vacuous than an accumulation of special effects (remember *The Black Hole?*). Yoda and Chewbacca and Obi-Wan Kenobi are hardly given anything to do. Yoda's passing, which should have been a magical moment, barely registers. The lightsaber duel between Luke and Darth Vader is only adequately staged; when Vader is finally unhelmeted, the only surprise is in how unsurprising he looks—he might be Uncle Fester from "The Addams Family." And the Emperor, whose face we *do* see from the start, doesn't carry the requisite almighty malevolence. If the Emperor of the Empire can't make us quake in our spaceboots, who can?

Lucas doesn't have the emotional commitment to this material that he had the first two times out. How else can one explain the short shrift he gives to Luke and Company? Han and Leia hardly bicker at all this time around—did they perhaps attend an intergalactic consciousness-raiser in the intervening years? There's no simplicity in this film, nothing like that great comic moment in *Empire* when Han clonks the short-circuited console of his spaceship and it lights up. The action in *Jedi,* except for that speed-bike chase, isn't something to revel in; there's no exhilaration in the special effects—they come off like diversionary tactics. There are supposed to be six more episodes in the *Star Wars* saga, but I doubt Lucas will want to take it that far. It's time for him to create another storybook epic, in another time and another galaxy, far far away from this one. Better yet, it's time for him to cool out.

In Hollywood, if you produce enough smash hits it's inevitable that you will be regarded as a genius—a seer. Because Lucas is the most commercially successful filmmaker in movie history, he is by now solidly ensconced in the genius category, even though he has made no such claims for himself. (He's as unprepossessing as Francis Coppola is flamboyant.) If Lucas has a genius—and I think he does—it's a genius for knowing where all the pop-cultural loot is buried. With the exception of *The Empire Strikes Back,* all of his big hits have been recycled versions of earlier movies and modes. But the recycling is generally deft enough to give audiences both the reassurance of old pleasures and the glitter of the new.

A movie like *American Graffiti* didn't strike new attitudes; it simply reflected a hankering for the old fifties attitudes of its audience. It was a piece of commercialized nostalgia, but nostalgia without cynicism. Until *Jedi,* it was this lack of cynicism that redeemed Lucas's ardent commercialism. *Jedi* looks as if it had been made to sell toys.

Lucas is one of the rare filmmakers whose private fantasies are in complete sync with popular junk fantasies. (To an extent, the same thing is true for Steven Spielberg, although Spielberg has a gift for transforming junk into poetry.) When he calls *American Graffiti* and *Star Wars* his "personal" films, he really means it. For Lucas, there's no difference between the authentic and the counterfeit. *Star Wars* was both highly entertaining and without a trace of genuine originality. You could pick out the swipes at once—Robby the Robot from *Forbidden Planet,* the little robots from *Silent Running,* the triumphal scene from *Triumph of the Will,* portions of the plotline from Kurosawa's *The Hidden Fortress,* and so on. Everything in that movie had an antecedent. *Raiders of the Lost Ark,* which Lucas conceived and produced and Spielberg directed, was one long cliffhanger—a traffic jam of Saturday afternoon serials. Lucas and Spielberg just kept pinging their B- and Z-movie escapades at us like spitballs. *Raiders,* like *Jedi,* was all escapade and no spirit. There's nothing in Lucas's vastly popular movies to digest because everything has already been predigested. It's the perfect diet for the video game generation.

Unlike such contemporaries as Spielberg, Coppola, Brian

DePalma, and Martin Scorsese, Lucas never worked on low-grade shlock as a way of getting to make the movies that really mattered to him. From the start, with *THX 1138* ('71), he's made only those projects that presumably he cared about. And yet with the exception of *Empire,* he's taken fewer creative chances than any other major filmmaker in his position. He has been quoted as saying, "I know what I liked as a kid and I still like it." That's his credo. But he hasn't brought a child's sensibility to his movies; that is to say, he hasn't brought a child's wonderment to movies. The simplicity of soul that might result in an *E.T.* is not a part of his makeup.

There's no reason why fantasy films can't have as much richness and vigor and depth as any other type of film. (Is Shakespeare's *The Tempest*—the inspiration, by the way, for *Forbidden Planet*—a lesser achievement than, say, *Romeo and Juliet* or *Macbeth?*) It all depends on how it's done. The problem is, fantasy films, to be truly fantastic, require an imaginative range that's beyond the reach of most filmmakers. Lucas has more of a range and a reach than most, but *Return of the Jedi* is his Waterloo. The movie is a demonstration of the limitations of a pop-comic sensibility. There's no imaginative fervor to bind it together for us. It's a myth without a vision.

Los Angeles Herald Examiner, May 22, 1983

THE BIG CLOCK; NO WAY OUT

■■■

Andrew Sarris

If you have not yet seen *No Way Out* and plan to, DO NOT READ BEYOND THIS SENTENCE! Sorry, folks, I intend to commit the most heinous of journalistic felonies by revealing the movie's ending, which just about every other reviewer has condemned without telling you exactly what it is for fear of spoiling the "fun" of your moviegoing. This, alas, will not be my first offense. Mothers still point me out to their toddlers as the meanie who spilled the beans on the Debra Winger character's death in *Terms of Endearment.* For my part, I have always found it strange that the same reviewers who describe in pointillist detail every shot and quote yards of dialogue verbatim suddenly become coy about any climactic twist in the

plot. Woody Allen, for example, would get louder laughs if reviewers didn't pack their notices with his funniest punchlines. Now
that's what I call really spoiling the fun.

The problem is not primarily with critics, who certainly are
entitled to cover their beat as comprehensively as their editors will
permit, but rather with many alleged pleasure seekers who read and
listen to every review and then complain that the chewed-over celluloid is disappointingly déjà vu. Even so, one should not disturb
another's childlike innocence with the movies out of sheer sadism.

In this context, my interest in *No Way Out* is comparatively
benign. I enjoyed the movie enormously and thought it compared
favorably with the 1948 *The Big Clock,* which shares its novelistic
source in Kenneth Fearing's 1946 best-seller of that name. When
two engaging entertainments, forty years apart, employ the same
plot gambit, a rare opportunity arises to compare two different
periods without caricaturing either the past or the present. So-
called remakes are routinely dismissed for a lack of "originality."
But the usual copycat considerations do not apply here since *No
Way Out* is as much a product of the late eighties as *The Big Clock*
was of the late forties. Many current reviewers have casually
assumed that the original version was faithful to the Fearing novel,
and that the remake was radically different. This is not entirely the
case for what amounts to three separate narrative sensibilities.

The sex, for example, is much bawdier and kinkier in the novel
and in *No Way Out* than it is in the censor-inhibited *The Big Clock,*
directed by John Farrow in vintage Paramount light-noirish style.
Hence, the steady erosion of taboos over forty years has enabled an
eighties movie to be as explicit about the facts and fancies of life as
a forties novel. In the transition from the covert to the overt, it can
be argued (though not necessarily by me) that what has been gained
in the frankness of the text has been lost in the subtlety of the subtext. The argument for censorship in these situations is comparable
to the theory that czarist repression was an indispensable condition
for the great Russian literature of the nineteenth century.

In the book the hero, George Stroud, finds himself enmeshed in
a sex-and-murder intrigue with his Luce-like magazine overlord,
Earl Janoth; Earl's doggedly loyal second in command, Steve
Hagen; and Earl's mistress, Pauline Delos. Stroud begins lusting
after the woman in the very first chapter: "I first met Pauline Delos
at one of those substantial parties Earl Janoth liked to give every
two or three months, attended by members of the staff, his personal

friends, private moguls, and public nobodies. It was at his home in the East Sixties. . . . She was tall, ice-blonde, and splendid. The eye saw nothing but innocence, to the instincts she was undiluted sex, the brain said here was a perfect hell."

Stroud is thus poised to plunge headlong into the abyss of carnal temptation, and he takes the dare despite his commitment to his wife, Georgette, and his daughter, Georgia (the conceit of Fearing's bizarre family nomenclature is never explained). Stroud has had affairs before, but this one ends in murder, and as the editor of *Crimeways,* the jewel of the Janoth chain, Stroud is called upon to find a mysterious acquaintance of Pauline, who ostensibly is implicated in her murder. Actually, Janoth killed Pauline himself in a fit of rage when she accused him and Hagen of being attracted to each other. A man whom Janoth perceived only dimly in the shadows happened to observe Janoth entering Pauline's apartment on the night of her murder. Hagen cooks up a scheme to save Janoth by implicating this shadowy figure.

The unknown man is Stroud, and he must somehow stall the magazine's investigation until he can expose Janoth and Hagen. In the midst of all these deadly cross-purposes is the impending financial collapse of the Janoth empire. Just as Stroud is about to be falsely fingered and probably murdered, the Janoth chain passes from its founder's hands and the investigation is aborted. Relieved but unrepentant, Stroud toys with the idea of dallying with a female artist who has materialized as a key witness during his investigation.

Jonathan Latimer's witty, ingenious, but too often facetious screenplay observes the strictures of the Production Code. The Stroud character (Ray Milland), for example, never has any intention of sexually consummating his drunken night on the town with Janoth's mistress (Rita Johnson). Instead, he is awakened by the lady from an innocent nap on the couch in time to slip down the stairs just slightly before Janoth (Charles Laughton) emerges from the elevator. Janoth catches only a glimpse of this "stranger" whom he does not recognize as one of the key members of his staff.

Janoth's homicidal argument with Pauline takes a less deviant tone than in the book. His big line is "At least this one had a clean shirt." In the book Janoth's equivalent insult was "At least, this time it's a man." Hence, Pauline's homosexual parry of Janoth's lesbian thrust. In the movie the insults fly thick and fast over a wide variety of heterosexual involvements by both parties. The bitchiness of the scene is razor sharp, the high point of the movie's sophistication.

Unfortunately, Ray Milland's Stroud is such a dutiful husband that his wearying pose of outraged innocence is never shaded by the noirish guilt of, say, the infinitely more memorable Robert Mitchum character in *Out of the Past*. A more felicitous change in the screen adaptation is the "Big Clock" itself. The book transforms a figure of speech to a piece of movie-made machinery that serves both as a spatial metaphor for Janoth's power and control and an ironically appropriate hiding place for our bedeviled hero. There is also a slight displacement of authority in the casting of Laughton as Janoth and George Macready as Hagen. Laughton tends to ham up his power role so outrageously that Macready's sinister underplaying in the Number Two slot loses some of its focus.

No Way Out replaces Janoth's and Paramount's "Big Clock" with the Pentagon as a maze of mistrust and paranoia feeding on the day before yesterday's headlines. This time it is Gene Hackman's Defense Secretary David Brice who commits the murder out of jealousy, and though the ill-fated Susan (the delectable Sean Young) never taunts Brice about his relationship with his aide (Will Patton), we are eventually informed that the aide is indeed gay. Caught in the middle of the by now familiar not-so-innocent-bystander melodrama is Kevin Costner's Tom O'Farrell, a naval hero who is recruited to put himself on the spot. The location shooting of the eighties as opposed to the controlled studio settings of the forties loosens much of the physical suspense of the Farrow film. Director Roger Donaldson more than compensates by investing his mise-en-scène with an institutional edginess that brings danger hurtling from all directions. Here O'Farrell gets our sympathy and admiration not only for participating in the most delightful sex coupling in recent screen memory (his affair with Susan extends over some months), but also for displaying more enlightened moral attitudes than the bureaucrats around him seem capable of understanding.

But just as we think he has finally escaped from the trap, he turns out to have been a Russian "mole" all along, though possibly a repentant one. The suspected presence of "Yuri" in the Pentagon apparatus has been planted previously as a discredited right-wing fantasy to camouflage the search for the innocent fall guy. The movie's trick ending, thus, does indeed lack genuine foreshadowing. But why is it so unpopular? Could it be that we have a newfound need for completely untarnished heroes without any of the ambiguities and complexities of the real world? Or do some of us suspect that the filmmakers hedged their bets by suggesting that as untrustworthy as the Pentagon and the CIA may be, there still is a Red Menace out there?

It is more likely that Donaldson and screenwriter Robert Garland were too clever by far in seeking to escape the combined gravitational pull of moral equilibrium and old-fashioned conventions of storytelling. Yet the more I think about the ending, the less I mind it. Indeed, I respect *No Way Out* for daring to pull the rug out from under us with a haunting plot riff of unalloyed despair and confusion. And Kevin Costner's portrayal of love's agony under pressure actually gains in stature on second viewing. The first time around, the reticence and nonnarcissism of the Costner character seems merely part of his charm. Once his dark secret is exposed, however, his anguished reactions become richly ambiguous in retrospect. Suspended between fear and despair, confronted at every turn by duplicity and betrayal, he becomes a whole human being by abandoning his double life in a divided world. Can he make it to the high ground? The filmmakers don't say. He is Out There alone with his newly discovered conscience. "Where can he go?" his Soviet sponsor asks rhetorically. The probable doom of Costner's in-between man makes him a fitting hero for our time. There is indeed no way out—for him or for us.

Village Voice, September 29, 1987

CADDYSHACK II

▪▪▪

Michael Wilmington

Remember the early-sixties TV game show "Make Me Laugh"? That awful program pitted a series of sourpuss contestants against three comics of Frankie Fontaine vintage who were given a few minutes to crack the grumps up. If the contestants kept a straight face, they won prizes. The comedians got nothing, except the privilege of working on national TV for people paid not to laugh.

That's what *Caddyshack II* is like: a huge, multimillion-dollar version of "Make Me Laugh"—with no prizes. On and on they come—Chevy Chase, Dan Aykroyd, Jackie Mason, Dyan Cannon, Randy Quaid—all trying to crack us up, all failing miserably. They get desperate. They begin shrieking and babbling, falling all over themselves, thrashing and mugging like clowns possessed. Aykroyd at one point shoots the audience a quarter-moon and, later, in a total frenzy, drives a poisoned arrow into his buttocks. Quaid puts on an ice hockey uniform, crawls over a desk, and hollers until his face turns red. Chevy Chase starts slamming golf balls around a mansion and smirking at his own forearm. Jackie Mason puts on electric-blue polyester, attacks Dina Merrill with a steamroller, and does a tango. The mechanical gopher from the original *Caddyshack* overeats and vomits. And Robert Stack—taking another flyer in farce—dives off his steeplechase horse into a pool of mud and takes a blast of flatulence full in the face.

It's like a nightmare: hell in the Catskills, with Henny Youngman as Mephistopheles. (Take this movie—please!) Has there ever been a worse sequel than this? *Grease II? Jaws 4? Friday the 13th, Part 6?* Even *Rambo III* has more laughs than *Caddyshack II*—and Stallone wasn't even trying. This movie is *soooo* bad (How bad *is* it?) that it makes *Caddyshack I* look like *Godfather II*.

It's hard to figure out what went wrong—beyond the fact that everyone showed up on the set. Perhaps it's casting. Wasn't Jackie Mason's part—boorish vulgarian millionaire mensch battling blue-bloods and divots—originally conceived for *Caddyshack*'s Rodney Dangerfield? Perhaps it's the writers: they get no respect either. Harold Ramis—another *Caddyshack* alumnus, like Chase and the gopher—could have written this stuff in his sleep. Maybe he did. Perhaps it's direction. Allan Arkush directs the whole movie as if he were wearing a lampshade on his head.

Or maybe it's fate. Maybe it's karma. Maybe it's that perfect conjunction of elements where everything comes together and goes wrong. (Occasional exceptions that go right: Chase, Quaid, and Chynna Phillips in their first scenes.) One thing's for sure: If we're lucky—if everyone in this movie is lucky—there won't be a *Caddyshack III*. But if there is, the gopher deserves script approval.

Los Angeles Times, July 26, 1988

BATMAN RETURNS

■■■

Terrence Rafferty

The comic-book hero Batman, who is the costumed alter ego of a lonely millionaire named Bruce Wayne, made his first swoop across the pop-culture landscape in a 1939 issue of *Detective Comics*. The character's appeal, like that of most pop archetypes, seems inevitable only in retrospect. The artists who sweated out a living in the low-rent districts of the entertainment business—churning out comic books, newspaper strips, animated cartoons, B movies, pulp fiction —weren't working with an eye to posterity. They just cranked out material as fast as they could and hoped that they'd get lucky— that something they dreamed up would latch onto the audience's imagination and refuse to let go. Guys like Bob Kane, who created Batman, plied their not entirely reputable trades in the toughest neighborhoods of the cultural metropolis: the law-of-the-jungle areas of the imagination, where speed, alertness, and adaptability are the essential skills. And durable mythic figures like Batman are, in a sense, the survivors of a kind of natural selection that's as piti-less as the evolution of species, and probably even less predictable. Kane brought into being (almost, it seems, by spontaneous genera-tion) a creature that seemed to belong equally to the enchanted realm of fairy tales and to the mean-streets urban battleground of pulp crime fiction. Batman is a hard-boiled crime fighter who operates independently of the police, in the manner of the maver-ick private eyes who were featured in the magazine *Black Mask*. The *Black Mask* heroes—they included, in the twenties and thirties, Hammett's Sam Spade and the Continental Op and Chandler's Philip Marlowe—did not, however, feel a powerful sense of kinship with nocturnal flying animals. (If Marlowe ran into someone named Moose Malloy, the character didn't have antlers.)

When director Tim Burton mounted his big-budget movie version of *Batman* in 1989, he managed to give the material a luxurious masked-ball quality and a sly contemporary wit without violating the myth's low, cheesy origins. The movie respected the arbitrariness, the sheer out-of-the-blue berserkness, of Kane's con-ception. And Burton found a style that seemed to consolidate fifty years' worth of Batman legend, a body of lore which is, in the pop-culture way of things, the end product of countless modifications and embellishments—of constant slapdash tinkering by the writers and artists charged with maintaining the prototype's bizarre allure. Most of these efforts were pretty silly; periodically, the editors at DC Comics (custodian of the Batman franchise) would realize that the stories had become inert and frantically mannered, and an attempt would be made to rediscover the hero's essence, to restore the purity of the character's beginnings. The genius of Burton's approach to Batman was that it reveled in impurity, celebrated the anything-goes recklessness of comic-book art, and made that quality seem as beautiful—as *right,* in its way—as the honed, shapely narrative power of the most affecting fairy tales.

Burton is an artist who isn't fazed by contradictions, who's comfortable with both the higher aspirations and the lower instincts of his nature as an entertainer. (This is, after all, a filmmaker whose first feature was a 1985 vehicle for Pee-Wee Herman, which turned out to be one of the most original and inventive American comedies of the past ten years.) He and Batman are an ideal match. In *Batman Returns,* Burton gives us more of the same good thing he provided in the first picture, introduces a handful of fresh elements, and makes a few adjustments in the formula. He proves that he can keep the series going, and that's not meant to be faint praise. This new Batman story doesn't try to top the previous one, either with splashier special effects or with loftier pretensions to significance; nor does it simply go through the motions, repeating the surefire stuff with a self-satisfied air of professionalism. It's a blend of playful novelty and reassuring familiarity. Getting that mixture right is a difficult trick—perhaps the ultimate test for the pop-culture artist. *Batman Returns* takes care of business reliably but exuberantly; on the evidence of this energetic second installment, there's reason to believe that a series of Batman movies could supply the sort of regular, dependable mindless fun that James Bond's adventures did in the sixties.

In *Batman Returns,* the hero (again Michael Keaton) does battle with a greedy businessman named Max Shreck (Christopher Walken) and the roly-poly archcriminal known as the Penguin (Danny DeVito). Shreck—his name is an allusion to Max Schreck, who played the title role in F. W. Murnau's great silent vampire movie *Nosferatu*—is a relatively conventional villain; his goal in life is simply to suck all the profit he can out of the docile, credulous inhabitants of Gotham City. The Penguin, who made his first appearance in a Batman comic in 1941, is typical of the flamboyant grotesques that Kane and his successors loved to pit their hero against. The movie's Penguin is more alarming than the dapper, dumpy, orotund figure of the comics. (When you read the Penguin's lines in the comics you hear the voice of W. C. Fields.) DeVito gives the character his trademark spitting meanness, and the screenwriter, Daniel Waters, provides him with a background story to motivate all the vile-tempered outbursts: the villain, born Oswald Cobblepot, was abandoned as a baby by his wealthy parents, was raised by penguins in a grotto underneath the zoo, and has resurfaced in order to claim, by any means necessary, what he considers his rightful place in Gotham City society. Shreck tries to exploit the Penguin's bottomless reserves of violence for his own purposes, but the Penguin's personal agenda makes him a rather untrustworthy partner.

These sleazy evildoers are a fine pair of adversaries for Batman: he is kept mighty busy zooming around the city to foil their schemes. The Penguin has a gang of henchmen composed of murderous circus performers, and Batman has to deal with them, too. And whenever the "weird menace to all crime" (as the hero is described in one of the early comics) ventures out on a mission, he runs into a mysterious woman who dresses like a cat and carries a whip. He can't tell whose side the new animal in town is really on. The audience knows, however, that the Catwoman is Selina Kyle (Michelle Pfeiffer), the jittery, put-upon secretary of Max Shreck, who treats her like dirt and then literally pushes her too far. She reinvents herself as a feline feminist avenger, taking to the streets and the rooftops in a skintight black cat suit (which she's stitched from the shiny material of a rain slicker), and gleefully humiliating bad men wherever she finds them—that is, everywhere. At one point she accounts for herself with the tersely eloquent formulation "Life's a bitch; now so am I." She is, of course, the perfect feminine counterpart of the hero, whose costumed forays into the night are also fueled by an obsessive desire for vengeance. In their daytime drag, as Bruce Wayne and Selina Kyle, they seem to recognize something in each other; in their bat and cat getups, the sparks really fly. This hilariously twisted relationship—an apache dance in animal costumes—isn't just an improvement on the hero's romance with the deadly dull Vicki Vale in the first picture; it's the glory of *Batman Returns,* the source of the movie's best gags and most striking visual ideas. There's a lot of high-powered talent in *Batman*

Returns, but Pfeiffer dominates the movie. The cat clothes seem to release something strange and wild in her, as they do in Selina Kyle: this performance is ferociously sexy and uninhibitedly, over-the-top funny.

The design of Gotham City is perhaps a bit less elegant and more whimsical in this picture than it was in the first. (Anton Furst, the brilliant production designer of *Batman,* died last year; this movie's look is the work of Bo Welch, whose previous credits include the Burton films *Beetlejuice,* '87, and *Edward Scissorhands,* '90.) But Burton's narrative technique seems more confident this time around, his rhythms smoother. The story doesn't go flat in the intervals between its showpiece sequences, as *Batman* did. The herky-jerky storytelling of *Batman* made a fascinating contrast to the picture's sleek design; in *Batman Returns,* the pace is even but the settings have a funky, irregular quality. The balance of incongruity comes out about the same, and preferring one kind of contrast to the other is strictly a matter of taste, or mood: a dark bat symbol against a light background, or vice versa.

The menagerie that Burton has assembled in *Batman Returns*—bat, cat, penguin—suggests a possible reason for the unlikely persistence of the pop myth that sprang off the top of Bob Kane's head fifty-three years ago. To survive in the nether regions of the pop-culture world, with its quick-and-dirty aesthetic, you can't let yourself be troubled by reflection or calculation: you have to rely on resourcefulness and reflexes. There's something predatory about the whole endeavor of mass entertainment—an impulse to feed off the audience's imagination. The weird conviction of Kane's early stories may have come from deep in the Batcave of his unconscious, as a disguised acknowledgment of the necessary unscrupulousness of his own artistic kind. And the power of Tim Burton's Batman movies shows that he, too, has looked into himself and found the delightfully unwholesome qualities that make a great popular artist: the knowledge that there are lots of ways to skin a cat, and the willingness to do it over and over again.

The New Yorker, June 29, 1992

CAPE FEAR

▰▰▰

Armond White

Now that Martin Scorsese has been deemed "America's Greatest Director" by publications as resolutely unserious as *Premiere* magazine and *Entertainment Weekly* (who's next, *Cosmopolitan?*), it may be necessary to point out that *Cape Fear,* his latest—and very good—genre revision, is the work of a filmmaker desperate to achieve success in Hollywood terms but long since missing the creative impetus that made him a great director in the first place. That was back in the seventies when the mainstream media either ignored a film like *Mean Streets* ('73) or mostly complained about the violence in *Taxi Driver* ('76).

It was the ethnic-urban experience (particularly the exploration of Catholic morality), connected to a savant's fondness for both film history and pop music, that signaled Scorsese as an original, modern artist. With the release of *Raging Bull* ('80), it was clear that he had exhausted his Italian-American working- and criminal-class subject. The exploration of urban tension that gave *Mean Streets* and *Taxi Driver* their volatile obsessiveness became overblown enough for the media to ignore the film's specific ethnic (Catholic) significance and hail *Raging Bull* for its overwrought stylishness.

Such misjudgment deracinates Scorsese's violent flourishes. By the time of *GoodFellas* last year, Scorsese was being acclaimed as a chef who whipped up gorgeously lurid gangster pictures. The media reveled in the ethnic exoticism—the only thing left after Scorsese abandoned the early, riskily achieved ironic tone and gave in to the corruption and decadence he had been analyzing. Greg Solman's suggestion that *GoodFellas'* conscienceless protagonist was the negative image of the morally burdened Willem Dafoe in *The Last Temptation of Christ* ('88) zeroes in on the conceptual conflict Scorsese faces, one that the media is too shallow to perceive.

As an artist concerned with the morality and politics of form, Scorsese seeks to balance realistic experience with its emotional evocation. But lately his vaunted expressionism has drowned the cultural basis—the subject—of his films. *Cape Fear* is a more successful maneuver but, once again, Scorsese's work is being used for a gross-out, as if both he and his audience misunderstood why he

Max Cady (Robert De Niro, left) is suddenly just about everywhere he wants to be in the life of Sam Bowden (Nick Nolte), the lawyer he holds responsible for his years in prison. Martin Scorsese directed the 1991 remake of the 1962 *Cape Fear*. (© by Universal City Studios, Inc. Courtesy of MCA Publishing Rights, a Division of MCA Inc.)

is an artist. And once again, what is interesting about Scorsese's work are the very things the media won't discuss.

Cape Fear is the first Hollywood remake that literally could be retitled *Return of the Repressed*. Scorsese does his own personal, Catholic, movie-fixated variation on the 1962 *Cape Fear,* which starred Gregory Peck and Robert Mitchum in a good-versus-evil battle as a vicious ex-convict harassed a clean, simple nuclear family. The original, directed by veteran craftsman J. Lee Thompson, was an efficient thriller that nonetheless domesticated its themes of sex and violence. It represented the denial of psychic distress through the narrative expedience with which evil was routed. Scorsese understands that Thompson's *Cape Fear* was an example of Hollywood's twilight—a mainstream attempt to cover up the social wounds of the era. This new version withholds solace, even though Scorsese also provides a full, narrative cycle that closes up the story's dramatic tension.

Anyone who watches Scorsese's film for the simple mechanics of storytelling and dramatic resolution may find it a proficient, if rather delirious, entertainment. The thing is, this delirium is the point. Scorsese means to destabilize a semiclassic by reinvesting the tale with all the moral turbulence that official culture was busy ignoring. This time, the white American nuclear family is rife with guilt and torn by sexual impulses. When the bad guy, Cady (Robert De Niro), circles around the family of District Attorney Sam Bowden (Nick Nolte), he dredges up the neuroses and corruption upon which contemporary society rests.

Cady's vengefulness comes out of class resentment—a particularly unfavorable topic in mainstream work. In *Cape Fear*, this class tension finally pulls equal weight with Scorsese's treatment of sex and religion. The first great confrontation in the movie is Bowden's offer to buy off Cady, which is rejected as a bourgeois insult. When the lawyer platitudinizes to Cady, "You're as good as I am," Cady gives the horrifying response: "Then I can have what you have."

Screenwriter Wesley Strick distills this conflict between good and evil to the civilization-versus-savagery terms of pulp fiction that Scorsese always has favored in post–World War II Hollywood movies. The modernist revision of genre in *Cape Fear* is a deliberate attempt to claim fifties moral themes for their more clear-cut psychology. This film is as full of movie references as anything in the French New Wave, maybe more: *Magnificent Obsession, Night of the Hunter, Bigger Than Life, Rebel Without a Cause, Straw Dogs, Pickup on South Street, Psycho, Lolita, Blow Out, Jaws,* and others are alluded to in this sophisticated pulp allegory.

These movies give Scorsese a bridge to American hypocrisy in general as he addresses the Southern WASP world of the Bowdens. A judge's quotation from Booker T. Washington makes a subliminal connection to the social injustice that powers Cady's attack. We see Bowden's conscious abuse of the criminal justice system (failing his duty as Cady's court-appointed attorney years before) as a form of original sin that leads to the social derangement of the story. It's the way Scorsese lays out social turpitude and shows its roots in sexual and religious fear that makes *Cape Fear* transcend its pulp basis.

Scorsese's delirious social vision is rooted in sexual terror: a rape scene; a conjugal scene in which Bowden's wife (Jessica Lange) shifts her consciousness through Scorsese's brilliant use of a negative image; and Cady's psychological seduction of Bowden's teenage daughter (Juliette Lewis). These scenes are explorations—experiments—rather than definitive studies of family neurosis.

Scorsese uses the psychological thriller for themes usually seen in domestic melodramas (such as *Crooked Hearts,* which also featured talented Juliette Lewis as a troubled teen). He mixes those genres so potently here that he must be getting close to a subject that will inspire him again.

The City Sun (Brooklyn), December 11, 1991

GENRE CLASSICS

Traditionally, something becomes a classic only after it has held its own—or gained in stature—over a generation. That principle has helped us limit the following "Ten Best" lists to something like a baker's dozen each. None of the films featured in this book (they're mostly post-seventies) has been included; their writeups will recommend them, or not. And we have occasionally given pride of place to lesser-known gems rather than textbook classics. The focus is on English-language films only. Order of listing is chronological.

FILM NOIR

Double Indemnity
Woman in the Window
Detour ('45)
The Killers ('46)
Out of the Past
Gun Crazy ('49)

In a Lonely Place
Sunset Boulevard
Pickup on South Street
The Big Combo
Kiss Me Deadly
Touch of Evil

Gangster Films

The Public Enemy
Scarface ('32)
The Roaring Twenties
High Sierra
Key Largo
White Heat

The Asphalt Jungle
The Big Heat
Bonnie and Clyde
The Godfather (I and II)
Mean Streets

Detective Films

The Thin Man
The Hound of the Baskervilles ('39)
The Maltese Falcon ('41)
Laura

Murder My Sweet
The Big Sleep ('46)
The Private Life of Sherlock Holmes
The Late Show

The Colors of Neo-Noir

Gunn
Point Blank
Madigan
The Long Goodbye
The Conversation
Chinatown

Night Moves
Taxi Driver
The Driver
Thief
Blow Out
Cutter and Bone/Cutter's Way

WESTERNS

Law and Order ('32)
Red River
The Naked Spur
The Tall T
Ride the High Country

The Wild Bunch
Once Upon a Time in the West
McCabe and Mrs. Miller
Ulzana's Raid
Pat Garrett & Billy the Kid

John Ford

Straight Shooting
Three Bad Men
Stagecoach
My Darling Clementine
Fort Apache

She Wore a Yellow Ribbon
Wagon Master
Rio Grande
The Searchers
The Man Who Shot Liberty
Valance

COMEDIES

We have limited our list to comedies of the sound era.

Thirties

Trouble in Paradise
Me and My Gal
Footlight Parade
It Happened One Night

Twentieth Century
The Awful Truth
Easy Living
Bringing Up Baby

Forties

His Girl Friday
The Philadelphia Story
The Lady Eve
To Be or Not to Be
The Palm Beach Story

The More the Merrier
The Miracle of Morgan's Creek
Hail the Conquering Hero
Adam's Rib

Fifties–Eighties

Pat and Mike
Beat the Devil
Some Like It Hot
The Pink Panther
Help!
M*A*S*H
Avanti!

Young Frankenstein
Airplane!
Local Hero
Lost in America
Stranger Than Paradise
Off Beat

Star Showcases

Duck Soup
She Done Him Wrong
It's a Gift
A Night at the Opera
Modern Times
The Bank Dick

The Road to Morocco
The Sin of Harold Diddlebock
   /Mad Wednesday
The Nutty Professor
A Shot in the Dark
All of Me

ROMANCE

Sunrise
The Bitter Tea of General Yen
Queen Christina
History Is Made at Night
The Shop Around the Corner
Lady Hamilton/That Hamilton
   Woman
The Major and the Minor
The Clock

I Know Where I'm Going
Letter from an Unknown Woman
The Passionate Friends
Sabrina
Deep End
Robin and Marian
Annie Hall
Chilly Scenes of Winter
Manhattan

MUSICALS

Love Me Tonight
42nd Street
The Merry Widow ('34)
Top Hat
Swing Time
The Harvey Girls
The Red Shoes
On the Town

Singin' in the Rain
A Hard Day's Night
Oliver!
The Ballad of Cable Hogue
Cabaret
Phantom of the Paradise
Nashville
Pennies from Heaven ('83)

Vincent Minnelli

Cabin in the Sky
Meet Me in St. Louis
Yolanda and the Thief
Ziegfeld Follies
The Pirate

An American in Paris
The Band Wagon
Gigi
On a Clear Day You Can See
    Forever

ACTION/ADVENTURE

King Kong
The Lives of a Bengal Lancer
Only Angels Have Wings
Gunga Din
The Four Feathers ('39)
The Treasure of the Sierra Madre

The African Queen
20,000 Leagues Under the Sea
Hatari!
The Great Escape
The Man Who Would Be King
Raiders of the Lost Ark

Swashbucklers

The Scarlet Pimpernel ('34)
Captain Blood (restored version)
The Prisoner of Zenda ('37)
The Adventures of Robin Hood
The Sea Hawk

The Crimson Pirate
Scaramouche
The Duellists
The Road Warrior

Epics

Intolerance
Ben-Hur ('26)
Gone With the Wind

El Cid
Lawrence of Arabia
Zulu

49th Parallel/The Invaders
The Ten Commandments ('56)
Spartacus

The Bible
Hawaii
The Right Stuff

HORROR

The Old Dark House ('32)
The White Zombie
Doctor X
The Bride of Frankenstein
Cat People ('42)
The Seventh Victim
Psycho

Peeping Tom
The Innocents
Carnival of Souls
Rosemary's Baby
Night of the Living Dead ('68)
Carrie
Halloween

SCIENCE FICTION

Things to Come ('36)
The Thing ('51)
The Day the Earth Stood Still
Invasion from Mars ('53)
Forbidden Planet
Invasion of the Body Snatchers ('56)

Village of the Damned
The Time Machine
Five Million Years to Earth
2001: A Space Odyssey
Altered States

FANTASY

The Thief of Baghdad ('24)
Peter Ibbetson
The Ghost Goes West
The Man Who Could
    Work Miracles
The Wizard of Oz
The Thief of Baghdad ('40)

Here Comes Mr. Jordan
Heaven Can Wait ('43)
It Happened Tomorrow
A Matter of Life and Death/
    Stairway to Heaven
It's a Wonderful Life
Portrait of Jennie

WAR

The Birth of a Nation
The Big Parade

A Walk in the Sun
Twelve O'Clock High

All Quiet on the Western
   Front (restored version)
Air Force
Bataan
They Were Expendable

The Steel Helmet
The Red Badge of Courage ('51)
Men in War
Bridge on the River Kwai
The Paths of Glory

BIOPIC

Rembrandt
Young Mr. Lincoln
Citizen Kane
Yankee Doodle Dandy
Gentleman Jim
Lust for Life (compare
   Vincent & Theo)

The Nun's Story
Funny Girl
The Last American Hero
The Buddy Holly Story
Raging Bull
The Elephant Man

SUSPENSE

And Then There Were None
The Spiral Staircase ('46)
Odd Man Out
The Fallen Idol
The Window
Panic in the Streets
The Hitchhiker

The Narrow Margin ('52)
Night of the Hunter
Experiment in Terror
Seconds
Targets
Charley Varrick
Jaws

Intrigue

The Spy in Black
Night Train to Munich
Casablanca
The Ministry of Fear
The Third Man
The State Secret
Five Fingers

The Manchurian Candidate
Charade
Seven Days in May
The Tamarind Seed
The Parallax View
Winter Kills

Alfred Hitchcock

Blackmail
The Man Who Knew Too
  Much ('34)
The 39 Steps
The Lady Vanishes
Rebecca
Suspicion
Shadow of a Doubt

Notorious
Strangers on a Train
Rear Window
The Man Who Knew Too
  Much ('56)
Vertigo
North by Northwest
Psycho

THE WOMEN

Back Street ('32)
Pilgrimage
Alice Adams
Stella Dallas ('37)
Since You Went Away
Mildred Pierce
Black Narcissus
A Letter to Three Wives

All About Eve
Johnny Guitar
There's Always Tomorrow
Imitation of Life ('59)
Klute
Rich and Famous
Ms. 45

THE STAR AS GENRE

Marlene Dietrich:
The Blue Angel
Morocco
Dishonored
The Shanghai Express
Blonde Venus
The Scarlet Empress
The Devil Is a Woman
Greta Garbo:
Camille
Ninotchka
Bette Davis:
Jezebel
The Letter
All About Eve

John Wayne:
Angel and the Badman
Orson Welles:
The Lady from Shanghai
Marlon Brando:
The Wild One
Frank Sinatra:
Man with the Golden Arm
Michael Caine:
Alfie
Steve McQueen:
Bullitt
The Thomas Crown Affair
Jack Nicholson:
The Last Detail

AMERICANA

Judge Priest
Fury
Mr. Smith Goes to Washington
The Magnificent Ambersons
The Human Comedy
Hail the Conquering Hero
The Best Years of Our Lives

Wait Till the Sun Shines, Nellie
Written on the Wind
Rebel Without a Cause
To Kill a Mockingbird
Nashville
Melvin and Howard
Blue Velvet

HOLLYWOOD ON HOLLYWOOD

Show People
What Price Hollywood
The Lost Squadron
Bombshell
A Star Is Born ('37)
Sullivan's Travels
Sunset Boulevard

The Bad and the Beautiful
A Star Is Born ('54)
The Big Knife
Directed by John Ford
Fedora
S.O.B.
Visions of Light

POLITICAL FILMS

Gabriel Over the White House
Mr. Smith Goes to Washington
The Great McGinty
Meet John Doe
Hail the Conquering Hero
All the King's Men

Seven Days in May
The Candidate
All the President's Men
Secret Honor
Henry V ('89)

LITERARY ADAPTATIONS

Little Women ('33)
David Copperfield
Dodsworth
The Long Voyage Home
The Magnificent Ambersons
Great Expectations
Oliver Twist

The Heiress
Intruder in the Dust
An Outcast of the Islands
Lolita
Chimes at Midnight/Falstaff
Women in Love

ABOUT THE CONTRIBUTORS

David Ansen is a movie critic and senior writer at *Newsweek*. He wrote the documentary *The Divine Garbo*, which appeared on TNT in 1990, and *The One and Only . . . Groucho* for HBO in 1991. He has won three Page One awards from the Newspaper Guild of New York. He was formerly the movie critic at *The Real Paper*.

Gary Arnold has been senior movie critic of the *Washington Times* since March 1989. He was the movie critic of the *Washington Post* from April 1969 to September 1984, and he has contributed movie reviews and essays on popular culture to many other publications.

Jay Carr is the *Boston Globe*'s film critic. He was previously the theater and music critic for the *Detroit News*, won the 1971–72 George Jean Nathan Award for Dramatic Criticism, and in 1989 was named Chevalier, Ordre des Arts et Lettres, France.

Richard Corliss is a film critic for *Time* magazine and the author of *Talking Pictures* and *Greta Garbo*.

David Denby is film critic of *New York* magazine and writes the "Rear Window" column for *Premiere*. His articles and reviews have also appeared in the *New Republic*, *The Atlantic*, *The New Yorker*, and the *New York Review of Books*. He is currently working on a nonfiction book for Simon and Schuster on core education.

Morris Dickstein's film criticism has appeared in *American Film*, *Chaplin*, the *Bennington Review*, *In These Times*, *Grand Street*, *The Nation*, and *Partisan Review*, for which he is a contributing editor. He directs the Center for the Humanities at the CUNY Graduate School and is the author of *Gates of Eden* (Penguin). With Leo Braudy, he edited *Great Film Directors: A Critical Anthology*

(Oxford). His latest book is *Double Agent: The Critic and Society* (Oxford).

Roger Ebert is the Pulitzer Prize–winning film critic of the *Chicago Sun-Times,* co-host of "Siskel & Ebert," and author of *Roger Ebert's Video Companion, Two Weeks in the Midday Sun,* a journal of the Cannes film festival, and *Behind the Phantom's Mask.* He is a lecturer on film in the University of Chicago Extension Division.

Joseph Gelmis has reviewed movies for *Newsday* since 1964. His articles on film and filmmakers are syndicated to publications in the United States and Britain by the Los Angeles Times/Washington Post News Wire. He has taught at the State University of New York at Stony Brook, hosted a weekly radio show on WBAI FM, and is the author of *The Film Director as Superstar.*

Owen Gleiberman is the movie critic for *Entertainment Weekly.*

J. Hoberman has reviewed movies for the *Village Voice* since 1978. He is a contributing writer to *Premiere* and has a regular column in *Artforum.* He is coauthor (with Jonathan Rosenbaum) of *Midnight Movies* and the author of *Bridge of Light,* a history of Yiddish-language cinema, and *Vulgar Modernism,* a collection of pieces written in the eighties from the *Village Voice* and elsewhere.

Richard T. Jameson has been the editor of *Film Comment* since 1990. He has written for *Pacific Northwest, The Helix,* and *7 Days,* among other publications, and edited the Seattle Film Society's journal, *Movietone News,* from 1971 to 1981.

Dave Kehr is a movie critic for the *New York Daily News.* From 1975 to 1986, he was the film critic of the *Chicago Reader;* from 1986 to 1993, he was the film critic of the *Chicago Tribune.*

Peter Keough has been the film editor of the *Boston Phoenix* since 1989. He has also written for the *Chicago Reader,* the *Chicago Sun-Times,* and *Sight and Sound.*

Stuart Klawans reviews films for *The Nation* and WBAI radio. His commentaries and fiction have appeared in the *Village Voice, Grand*

Street, the *Threepenny Review, Entertainment Weekly,* and the *Times Literary Supplement.*

Andy Klein has been the film critic for the *Los Angeles Reader* on and off since 1985 and currently also writes for the Hearst/Izvestia publication *We/Mbl.* He was formerly a critic at *Los Angeles* magazine, *Hollywood Reporter, Movieline,* and the *Los Angeles Herald Examiner.* He has also written for *Empire,* the *Chicago Reader,* the *San Francisco Examiner, Film Comment,* and the late, lamented *American Film.*

Terrence Rafferty is film critic for *The New Yorker.* His movie writing has also appeared in *The Nation, Sight and Sound, The Atlantic,* the *Threepenny Review,* and *Film Quarterly.* A collection of his criticism, *The Thing Happens: Ten Years of Writing about the Movies,* was recently published by Grove Press.

Peter Rainer, the chairman of the National Society of Film Critics, writes film criticism and commentary for the *Los Angeles Times.* He is the editor of *Love and Hisses,* the third in the National Society series from Mercury House. From 1981 until its demise in 1989, he was film critic for the *Los Angeles Herald Examiner.* Rainer's writing has also appeared in the *New York Times Magazine, Vogue, GQ, Newsday, Premiere, Connoisseur, American Film,* and *Mademoiselle.* Rainer has appeared as a film commentator on such television shows as "Nightline," "ABC World News Tonight," and "CBS Morning News," and, on radio, for National Public Radio and the Pacifica Network. He has also taught film criticism in the Graduate Division of the University of Southern California Film School.

Carrie Rickey is a film critic for the *Philadelphia Inquirer.* She was previously the film critic for the *Boston Herald* and the *Village Voice,* and her work has appeared in *American Film, Art in America, Artforum, Film Comment,* and *Mademoiselle.*

Jonathan Rosenbaum has written for over fifty periodicals, including *Chicago Reader,* where he has been film critic since 1987. His books include *Moving Places, Midnight Movies* (with J. Hoberman), *Greed, Placing Movies* (forthcoming), and, as editor, *This Is Orson Welles,* by Orson Welles and Peter Bogdanovich.

Julie Salamon is the film critic for the *Wall Street Journal*. She is the author of the novel *White Lies* and the book *The Devil's Candy: The Bonfire of the Vanities Goes to Hollywood*.

Andrew Sarris is film critic for the *New York Observer* and professor of film at the School of the Arts at Columbia University. He is also the author of ten books, including *The American Cinema, Confessions of a Cultist, The John Ford Movie Mystery*, and *Politics and Cinema*. He was a movie reviewer for twenty-nine years at the *Village Voice*. He is currently completing *The American Sound Film, Volume One, 1929–1949*.

Richard Schickel has reviewed movies for *Time* since 1972; before that he was *Life's* film critic. He is the author of many books, most notably *The Disney Version, His Picture in the Papers, D. W. Griffith: An American Life, Intimate Strangers: The Culture of Celebrity, Schickel on Film*, and *Brando: A Life in Our Times*. His monograph on *Double Indemnity* was published last year by the British Film Institute. He is also a writer-producer-director of television documentaries, the latest of which, "Hollywood on Hollywood," appeared in the summer of 1993 on AMC. He has held a Guggenheim fellowship and has won the British Film Institute Book Prize.

Stephen Schiff is critic-at-large of *The New Yorker* and the film critic of National Public Radio's "Fresh Air." A former correspondent on CBS-TV's "West 57th," and a Pulitzer Prize finalist in 1983, he was critic-at-large at *Vanity Fair* from 1983 to 1992 and has written film criticism for *The Atlantic*, the *Boston Phoenix, Film Comment*, the *Washington Post, Glamour*, and *American Film*.

Henry Sheehan is the film critic of the *Orange County Register*. He has written on film and related subjects for *Film Comment, Sight and Sound*, the *Atlantic Monthly, LA Weekly*, the *Los Angeles Reader*, the *Hollywood Reporter*, the *Boston Globe*, the *Boston Phoenix*, the *Chicago Reader, L.A. Style*, and the *New York Times Book Review*.

Michael Sragow was the editor of *Produced and Abandoned: The Best Films You've Never Seen*, the first in this National Society of Film Critics series. He currently reviews movies for the "Goings On about Town" section of *The New Yorker*. He was previously movie critic for the *San Francisco Examiner,* the *Boston Phoenix, Rolling Stone,* and the *Los Angeles Herald Examiner.* His criticism has also appeared in *Harper's Bazaar, Esquire, Mother Jones, The Atlantic, Film Comment,* and *Sight and Sound.*

Kevin Thomas has been a movie critic for the *Los Angeles Times* since 1962. He has served on the juries of the Tokyo, Chicago, Berlin, Montreal, and Tehran film festivals. A fourth-generation California newspaperman and native Angeleno, he was named a chevalier in France's Order of Arts and Letters for his "contributions to French cinema." In 1992 Thomas received a Mayoral Proclamation commemorating his thirty years as a critic for the *Los Angeles Times.*

Peter Travers is the film critic for *Rolling Stone* magazine.

Kenneth Turan is the film critic for the *Los Angeles Times* and "Monitor Radio." He has been a staff writer for the *Washington Post* and *TV Guide* and film critic for *GQ* and National Public Radio's "All Things Considered." He is coauthor of *Call Me Anna: The Autobiography of Patty Duke* and is on the board of directors of the National Yiddish Book Center.

Armond White is the film critic and arts editor of the Brooklyn-based weekly, *The City Sun.* He is the author of the forthcoming Brian De Palma study, *Total Illumination.*

Bruce Williamson has been *Playboy's* movie critic (and a contributing editor) for over twenty-five years. He is also a contributing movie critic for *New Woman* magazine. He was *Time's* movie critic from 1963 to 1967 and a movie-media critic at *Life* for a brief period thereafter, before joining *Playboy.* He appears regularly as a TV critic for "Playboy After Dark" on cable. In addition to membership in the National Society of Film Critics for more than two decades, he is a continuing member and former chairman of the New York Film Critics Circle.

Michael Wilmington is the *Chicago Tribune's* movie critic. From 1984 to 1993, he was a film writer and reviewer for the *Los Angeles Times.* He has contributed to *Film Comment, Sight and Sound,*

Film Quarterly, Movieline, American Film, and *New York Newsday,* and was formerly film editor and lead critic at both *LA Weekly* and *L.A. Style.* He is coauthor with Joseph McBride of *John Ford* (British Film Institute, 1973) and has won five Milwaukee Press Club Awards for arts criticism while working at *Isthmus.*

PERMISSIONS

Every effort has been made to identify the holders of copyright of previously published materials included in this book. The publisher apologizes for any oversights that may have occurred; any errors that may have been made will be corrected in subsequent printing upon notification to the publisher.

Grateful acknowledgment is made to the following for permission to reprint copyrighted material:

Boston Globe: for Jay Carr's articles "On Adult Love Stories" ("Hollywood Rediscovers Adult Love Stories," January 22, 1989), "On Why the Stars Don't Shine as They Used To" ("Why Don't the Stars Shine as They Used To?" December 2, 1984), and his review of *Full Metal Jacket* ("Too Much Mind, Not Enough Gut," June 28, 1987).

Boston Phoenix: for Peter Keough's reviews of *Raising Arizona* (April 10, 1987), *Love at Large* ("Master of Illusion," March 30, 1990), *Total Recall* (June 1, 1990), and his article "On Women, Films, and the Women's Film" ("Skirts of the Demon," August 21, 1992); for Stephen Schiff's reviews of *Body Heat* ("Voluptuous Nightmares," September 22, 1981), *Wise Blood* ("Into the Maelstrom," April 8, 1990), and *The Long Riders* ("The Western Rides Again," May 20, 1980); for Michael Sragow's reviews of *Once Upon a Time in America* ("Making Up for Lost Time," March 5, 1985), *Rear Window* ("Now, Voyeur," October 11, 1983), and *Prizzi's Honor* ("The Discreet Charm of the Mafiosi," June 18, 1985).

Chicago Reader: for Jonathan Rosenbaum's review of *Fatal Attraction* (October 2, 1987).

Chicago Tribune: for Dave Kehr's articles "On Copping a Plea" ("Unlawful," July 12, 1992), "On Anthony Mann" ("Anthony Mann Westerns," July 5, 1992), "On Making Book" ("By the Book," November 8, 1992), "On Vampires" ("Blood Ties," November 8, 1992), and his review of *Unforgiven* (August 2, 1992), © Copyrighted 1992, Chicago Tribune Company, all rights reserved, used with permission.

David Denby: for his review of *Bananas* (August 1971) in *The Atlantic*.

Morris Dickstein: for his review of *Born on the Fourth of July* in *Partisan Review*.

Roger Ebert: for his reviews of *Betrayal* and *The Big Red One* in the *Chicago Sun Times* and *Roger Ebert's Video Companion*.

Film Comment: for Richard T. Jameson's review of *Miller's Crossing* (September 10, 1990); for Stephen Schiff's article "The Repeatable Experience" (March–April 1982).

Owen Gleiberman: for his reviews of *Slacker* ("Shirking-Class Heroes," August 8, 1991), *The Silence of the Lambs* ("Darkness Visible," February 15, 1991), and *Men Don't Leave* (February 16, 1990), in *Entertainment Weekly*.

The Hearst Corporation: for Peter Rainer's reviews of *Top Gun* ("'Top Gun' Aims Squarely for the Pocketbook," May 16, 1986), *Return of the Jedi* ("The Jedi Return with Intergalactic Hoopla," May 22, 1993), *Roxanne* ("'Roxanne' Makes You Glad You're Alive," June 19, 1987), and *Trouble in Mind* ("'Trouble in Mind' Is a Fabulous Fantasia," January 24, 1991), and for Michael Sragow's review of *Invasion of the Body Snatchers* ("Have a Very Scary Christmas," December 22, 1978), in the *Los Angeles Herald Examiner*.

In These Times: for Morris Dickstein's article "On John Wayne" ("Moral Ambiguity in the West," June 27–July 3, 1979).

Isthmus: for Michael Wilmington's review of *GoodFellas* ("The Ultimate Scorsese," September 28, 1990).

Richard T. Jameson: for his reviews of *Against All Odds* (March 7, 1984), *Silverado* (September 1985), *The Shining* (July–August 1980), *Gremlins* and *Ghostbusters* ("Gremlins & Ghostbusters," July–August 1980), and *Close Encounters of the Third Kind* ("Close Encounters," June 1984), in *Film Comment*.

Andy Klein: for his reviews of *The Crying Game* ("Romance: Love or Confusion?" November 27, 1992), and *The Fly* (August 22, 1986), in the *Los Angeles Reader*.

Los Angeles Reader: for Henry Sheehan's reviews of *Defending Your Life* (March 22, 1991), and *They Live* (November 4, 1988).

Los Angeles Times: for Kevin Thomas's reviews of *Angels Hard As They Come* (January 19, 1972), and *Caged Heat* (October 31, 1974).

Los Angeles Times Syndicate: for Peter Rainer's article "On Psychonoir" ("Out of the Past, Darkly," April 8, 1980); for Kenneth Turan's reviews of *Reservoir Dogs* ("City Maul, NY to LA," October 23, 1992), and *Terminator 2: Judgment Day* ("He Said He'd Be Back . . . ," July 3, 1991).

The Nation: for Stuart Klawans's review of *Running on Empty* (October 31, 1988).

Newsday: for Joseph Gelmis's review of *Blade Runner* (September 1, 1992).

Newsweek: for David Ansen's reviews of *Aliens* ("Terminating the Aliens," July 21, 1986), *Another Woman* ("A Serious Step Forward," October 24, 1988), *Black Rain* ("'Rambo' Mike Runs Amok," October 2, 1989), *War of the Roses* and *She-Devil* ("Laughter in the Dark," December 11, 1989). From *Newsweek,* © 1986, 1988, 1989 Newsweek, Inc. All rights reserved. Reprinted by permission.

New York: for David Denby's review of *Body of Evidence* ("Immaterial Girl," January 25, 1993). Copyright © 1993 K-III Magazine Corporation. All rights reserved. Reprinted with permission of *New York* Magazine.

The New Yorker: for Terrence Rafferty's review of *Batman Returns* ("Masked Ball," June 26, 1992).

Philadelphia Inquirer: for Carrie Rickey's article "On Mob Rule" ("Mob Rule," December 23, 1990).

Playboy: for Bruce Williamson's reviews of *The French Lieutenant's Woman* (November 1981) and *A Midsummer Night's Sex Comedy,* November 1982). Reproduced by Special Permission of *Playboy* magazine. Copyright © 1981, 1982 by Playboy.

Rolling Stone: for Peter Travers's reviews of *Thelma and Louise* ("Women on the Verge," April 18, 1991), *Rambling Rose* ("Why She's Gotta Have It," October 3, 1991), *Poison Ivy* ("A Nineties Lolita from Hell," May 28, 1992), and *Howards End* (April 2, 1992). Straight Arrow Publishers, Inc. All Rights Reserved. Reprinted by permission.

Julie Salamon: for her reviews of *The Grifters* ("Stephen Frears's LA Hustlers," January 24, 1991), and *Backdraft* (May 30, 1991), in the *Wall Street Journal.*

San Francisco Examiner: for Michael Sragow's reviews of *The Russia House* ("Melting the Cold War," December 21, 1990), and *Platoon* ("Mysteries of Life and Death in Vietnam," December 30, 1986).

Andrew Sarris: for his reviews of *Groundhog Day* (February 22, 1993), *Pretty Woman* ("Star Roberts: The Stuff Dreams Are Made Of," April 16, 1990), *Blue*

Steel ("Violence of 'Blue Steel' Upstaged by Style," March 26, 1990), *No Way Out* ("Modern Hero," September 29, 1987), and *Orlando* ("'Orlando' Misses Woolf," June 28, 1993), in the *New York Observer.*

Stephen Schiff: for his review of *The Player* (April 1992), in *The New Yorker.*

Time: for Richard Schickel's reviews of *Crimes and Misdemeanors* (October 16, 1989), *Tremors* ("Moving and Quaking," January 22, 1990), *Mr. and Mrs. Bridge* ("The Way We Were," November 26, 1990), and *The Last of the Mohicans* (September 28, 1992); for Richard Corliss's reviews of *Malcolm X* (November 23, 1992), and *Bram Stoker's Dracula* (November 23, 1992). Copyright 1989, 1990, 1992 Time Inc. Reprinted by permission.

Kenneth Turan: for his review of *Scanners* ("Seeing Is Believing," February 2, 1981), in the *Los Angeles Times.*

Village Voice: for J. Hoberman's article "On How the Western Was Lost" ("How the West Was Lost," August 27, 1991), and his reviews of *Spaceballs* ("Farblondjet in Space," June 24, 1987), and *Heathers* ("Geek Squads and Dweebettes," April 4, 1989).

Washington Times: for Gary Arnold's reviews of *Candyman* (October 16, 1992), and *The Hand That Rocks the Cradle* (January 10, 1992).

Armond White for his reviews of *Trespass* ("*Trespass* Makes Race Postmodern," January 20, 1993), and *Cape Fear* ("In *Cape Fear* Scorsese Returns the Repressed," December 11, 1991), in *City Sun.*

Michael Wilmington: for his article "Howard Hawks, Genre Killer" (March 1993), and his reviews of *Dances With Wolves* ("Elegy for the Not-So-New Frontier," December 16, 1990), *The Naked Gun* (December 2, 1988), *The Purple Rose of Cairo* ("Another Bouquet for Allen," March 1, 1985), *The Godfather Part III* ("Coppola's Glorious Disappointment," December 23, 1990), and *Caddyshack II* (July 26, 1988), in the *Los Angeles Times.*

INDEX OF FILMS, DIRECTORS, AND ACTORS

Candy, John, 88, 208
Candyman, 189, 205-207
Cannon, Dyan, 337
Cape Fear, 301, 303, 328, 343-346
Capone, 10
Capra, Frank, 57, 95, 245
Capshaw, Kate, 212
Carhart, Timothy, 296
Carpenter, John, 84, 150, 213, 228, 244,
    252, 254, 255, 256, 257, 258
Carradine, David, 62
Carradine, Keith, 41, 42, 62, 64
Carradine, Robert, 62, 264
Carrie, 102
Carter, Finn, 232
Carter, Helen Bonham, 321
Cartwright, Veronica, 250
Carvey, Dana, 85
Casablanca, 36, 144, 281
Castellano, Richard, 175
Catch-22, 270, 273
Cates, Phoebe, 95
Cat People, 227
Caught, 27
Cazale, John, 173, 174
Ceiling Zero, 142, 147
Chandler, Jeff, 74
Chandler, Raymond, 28
Chaney, Lon, Jr., 240
Chaplin, Charlie, 159, 168, 188
Charles, Jeanette, 86
Chase, Chevy, 84, 85, 178, 337, 338
Chaykin, Maury, 73
Cher, 179, 202
Chetwynd, Lionel, 268
Cheyenne Autumn, 52, 72
Children of Paradise, 13
Chinatown, 33, 42, 248
Choose Me, 40, 120, 121
Ciannelli, Eduardo, 8
Cimarron, 50
Cimino, Michael, 10, 50, 54, 263
Citizen Kane, 1, 173
City Girl, 41
City Lights, 159
City Slickers, 55
Clarke, Mae, 7, 8
Cleese, John, 69
Clift, Montgomery, 194
Clockwork Orange, A, 269
Close, Glenn, 112, 190, 284, 286, 302
Close Encounters of the Third Kind, 88,
    244-248
Cobb, Randall, 92

Cobra, 209
Coburn, James, 179
Cocoon, 164, 216
Coen, Ethan, 3, 20, 23, 90, 91, 92, 93, 94
Coen, Joel, 3, 20, 21, 23, 90, 91, 92, 93,
    94
Cohen, Julie, 15
Colbert, Claudette, 281
Collins, Roberta, 284
Come and Get It, 142, 147
Coming Home, 276
Company of Wolves, The, 126
Connelly, Jennifer, 15
Connery, Sean, 111, 122, 124, 125
Conte, Richard, 9
Conversation, The, 150
Conway, Kevin, 300
Coogan's Bluff, 55, 77, 79
Coolidge, Martha, 279, 298
Cooper, Gary, 59, 77, 143, 190, 282
Coppola, Francis Ford, 9, 150, 169-176,
    228, 236, 241, 242, 268, 332
Corey, Wendell, 151
Corman, Roger, 8, 304
Corsair, 5
Cosell, Howard, 155
Costner, Kevin, 50, 56, 69, 72, 224, 336,
    337
Cotten, Joseph, 123
Count Dracula and His Vampire Bride, 239
Cowboys, The, 54
Cox, Ronny, 260
Cradle Snatchers, The, 143
Craven, Wes, 228
Crawford, Joan, 6, 188, 192, 281
Crenna, Richard, 32
Crimes and Misdemeanors, 44, 130,
    161-163
Criminal Code, The, 142
Crisp, Donald, 59
Crisp, Quentin, 326
Cronenberg, David, 228, 229, 230, 231,
    244, 252, 253, 254
Crooked Hearts, 346
Crosby, Bing, 327
Crossing Delancey, 111
Crothers, Scatman, 138
Crowd Roars, The, 142
Cruise, Tom, 196-199, 275
Cruising, 47
Crying Game, The, 111, 126-129
Cry in the Dark, A, 123
Cukor, George, 283
Culpepper Cattle Company, The, 55

Ermey, Lee, 270
E.T., 95, 164, 303
Ethan Frome, 311
Evans, Art, 225
Exorcist, The, 253, 284, 285, 286
Eyewitness, 35
Falk, Peter, 179
Falling in Love, 189
Fanny and Alexander, 130
Far and Away, 279
Far Country, The, 57, 58, 59
Farewell My Lovely, 42
Farrow, John, 328, 334
Farrow, Mia, 94, 157, 158, 160, 162
Fast Times at Ridgemont High, 99
Fatal Attraction, 178, 213, 214, 278,
   284-289, 302, 303
Fawcett, Farrah, 32
Fazil, 143
Ferrer, José, 157
Few Good Men, A, 309
Fields, W. C., 341
Figgis, Mike, 26, 48
Finney, Albert, 20, 22
Fisher, Carrie, 89, 330
Fisher, Frances, 80
Fisher, Terence, 238
Fistful of Dollars, A, 77
Flaherty, Joe, 208
Flashdance, 196, 289
Flash Gordon, 89
Fletcher, Louise, 179, 215
Fleugel, Darlanne, 14
Fly, The, 228, 229-231
Fog, The, 258
Foley, James, 286
Fonda, Henry, 194
Fonda, Jane, 201
For a Few Dollars More, 77, 327
Forbidden Planet, The, 330, 333
Ford, Glenn, 9, 281
Ford, Harrison, 261, 262, 330
Ford, John, 52, 56, 57, 61, 69, 72, 75, 76,
   78, 90, 92, 147, 148, 193, 194, 311
Foronjy, Richard, 15
Forsythe, William, 14, 92
Fort Apache, 77, 193, 194
48HRS., 75
For Whom the Bell Tolls, 143, 144
Foster, Jodie, 233, 235
Foster, Meg, 256
Fourth Man, The, 259
Fox, James, 124
Foxes, 289

Frankenstein, 227
Frears, Stephen, 43, 44, 45, 113
Freeman, J. E., 21
Freeman, Morgan, 80
French Lieutenant's Woman, The, 308,
   318-319
Freshman, The, 11
Friday the 13th, 228, 231
Friday the 13th, Part 6, 338
Fried Green Tomatoes, 282
Friedkin, William, 47
From Here to Eternity, 270
Front Page, The, 328
Frost, Sadie, 241
Fugitive, The, 311
Fuller, Sam, 9, 264, 265, 266
Full Metal Jacket, 263, 268-272
Furlong, Edward, 220
Fury, The, 252
Gable, Clark, 192, 281, 327
Gallagher, Peter, 179, 180
Galligan, Zach, 95
Gangsters of New York, The, 5
Ganja and Hess, 239
Garbo, Greta, 191, 280
Garbo Talks, 191
Garcia, Andy, 26, 169, 171, 172, 211
Garment Jungle, The, 9
Garnett, Tay, 274
Garr, Teri, 179
Gavin, Erica, 284
Gazzo, Michael, 175
Gentlemen Prefer Blondes, 142, 146
George, Gladys, 8, 282
Gere, Richard, 26, 28, 29, 48, 200, 201
Getaway, The, 62, 224
Ghost, 181, 183
Ghostbusters, 44, 83, 97-99, 159
Gibson, Mel, 45, 47
Gilbert, John, 6
Gilbert, Sara, 304, 306
Gilda, 1, 31, 281
Girl in Every Port, A, 142
Gish, Lillian, 4
Glengarry Glen Ross, 168, 309
Glenn, Scott, 68, 179, 218, 219, 234
Glory, 272
Glover, Danny, 45, 69
G-Men, 7
Godfather, The, 6, 9, 10, 11, 13, 55, 165,
   169, 172, 309
Godfather Part II, The, 10, 169, 171, 174,
   327, 338
Godfather Part III, The, 4, 131, 169-176

Murphy, Eddie, 103
Murray, Bill, 83, 84, 85, 97, 103, 191
Musketeers of Pig Alley, The, 4
My Beautiful Laundrette, 43
My Darling Clementine, 78
Myers, Mike, 85
My Favorite Year, 153
Mystery of the Wax Museum, 227
Mystic Pizza, 200
Naked and the Dead, The, 274
Naked Angels, 218
Naked Gun, The, 83, 86-87
Naked Spur, The, 58
Nashville, 99, 176, 177
Near Dark, 213, 214, 215, 239
Neeson, Liam, 311
Nelson, Barry, 140
Nelson, Ralph, 54
New Jack City, 226
Newman, Paul, 2, 192, 320
Nicholson, Jack, 5, 100, 132, 133, 140, 141, 166, 309
Nicol, Alex, 59
Nielsen, Leslie, 86
Nightmare on Elm Street, A, 228
Night of the Hunter, 345
Night of the Living Dead, 219, 227, 239
Nimoy, Leonard, 250
9½ Weeks, 289
Nolte, Nick, 11, 179, 345
Norris, Chuck, 208, 212, 222
Nosferatu, 340
Not a Pretty Picture, 300
No Way Out, 328, 333-337
Now, Voyager, 281
O'Donnell, Chris, 290
Officer and a Gentleman, A, 39, 197, 198, 301
Of Human Bondage, 191
O. Henry's Full House, 142
Oldman, Gary, 240, 241
Olivier, Laurence, 319
Once Upon a Time in America, 3, 12-16, 17
Once Upon a Time in the West, 12, 76, 255
One False Move, 226
One Froggy Evening, 89
O'Neill, Jennifer, 253
Only Angels Have Wings, 142, 144
On the Waterfront, 9
Orlando, 308, 325-326
Outlaw Josey Wales, The, 75, 80
Out of the Past, 31, 36, 282, 336
Oz, Frank, 84

Pacino, Al, 10, 11, 55, 169, 170, 173, 175, 191, 309
Paid to Love, 143
Palance, Jack, 240
Pale Rider, 50, 56, 73, 80
Panic in the Streets, 250
Parenthood, 216
Parker, Alan, 110, 113
Parrish, Robert, 9
Pascali's Island, 178
Pasdar, Adrian, 215, 239
Pastorelli, Robert, 73
Pat Garrett & Billy the Kid, 54
Paths of Glory, 269, 270, 298
Patrick, Robert, 220
Patton, 184
Patton, Will, 336
Paxton, Bill, 222
Peck, Gregory, 301, 344
Peckinpah, Sam, 16, 18, 52, 53, 54, 62, 64, 65, 75, 78, 224, 330
Pendleton, Austin, 321
Penn, Arthur, 54, 65, 74
Penn, Chris, 24
Pennies from Heaven, 158
Perkins, Anthony, 302
Perkins, Elizabeth, 121
Persona, 130, 160
Pesci, Joe, 17, 18, 19
Petrified Forest, The, 7
Pfeiffer, Michelle, 11, 111, 113, 122, 124, 125, 126, 312, 341
Phillips, Chynna, 338
Phoenix, River, 294
Pickford, Mary, 280
Pickup on South Street, 265, 345
Pinter, Harold, 110
Piper, Roddy, 254
Piranha II, 219
Piscopo, Joe, 11
Pitt, Brad, 297
Plainsman, The, 76
Platoon, 263, 266-268, 270, 272, 276
Platt, Louise, 194
Player, The, 131, 176-184
Plimpton, Martha, 160, 294
Plummer, Glenn, 222
Point Blank, 43
Poison Ivy, 279, 282, 303-306
Poitier, Sydney, 54
Polanski, Roman, 94
Police Academy, 103
Polito, Jon, 20
Pollack, Sydney, 55, 179, 183

About the Editor

Born November 17, 1944, in New Castle, Pennsylvania, and educated at Washington and Jefferson College, Washington, Pennsylvania, Richard T. Jameson has been involved with film one way or another throughout his adult life and then some. In the sixties and seventies he programmed and wrote notes for university and institutional film series, cofounded and operated several film societies, managed and coprogrammed an art theater in the Greater Seattle area (1967–71), and designed and taught cinema courses at the University of Washington (1969–84). His writings on film have appeared in *Film Comment, Film Quarterly, Take One, The Velvet Light Trap, American Film,* and the Seattle Film Society's *Movietone News,* which he edited for most of its history (1971–81). He was film critic of *The Weekly* (Seattle, 1976–78 and 1979–86), *Pacific Northwest* (1986–90), and *7 Days* (1989–90), and has been editor of *Film Comment* magazine since the beginning of 1990. He once enjoyed the distinction of being "the only member of the National Society of Film Critics west of Chicago and north of San Francisco," but then he moved to New York, so forget it. He is married to writer and critic Kathleen Murphy.